Database Design

The Semantic Modeling Approach

Database Design

The Semantic Modeling Approach

Naphtali Rishe

School of Computer Science
Florida International University
Miami, Florida

McGraw-Hill, Inc.

New York St. Louis San Francisco Auckland Bogotá
Caracas Lisbon London Madrid Mexico Milan
Montreal New Delhi Paris San Juan Singapore
Sydney Tokyo Toronto

Library of Congress Cataloging-in-Publication Data

Rishe, Naphtali.
  Database design : the semantic modeling approach / Rishe, Naphtali.
     p.   cm. — (The Database experts' series)
  Includes bibliographical references and index.
   ISBN 0-07-052955-8
   1. Data base design. 2. Relational data bases. I. Title.
  II. Series
  QA76.9.D26R57   1992
  005.75'6—dc20   91-31803
                                                    CIP

 This book is printed on recycled, acid-free paper containing a minimum of 50% recycled de-inked fiber.

   3 4 5 6 7 8 9 0 DOH DOH 9 7 6 5 4 3

ISBN 0-07-052955-8

The sponsoring editor for this book was Neil Levine, the editing supervisor was David E. Fogarty, and the production supervisor was Donald Schmidt.

Printed and bound by R. R. Donnelley & Sons Company.

To Noa Rishe

Contents

Preface

This book is intended for present and future designers of database applications, software engineers, systems analysts, and programmers. It focuses on the fundamental knowledge needed by designers of database applications and on methodologies of structured design. With the exception of an optional chapter on implementational aspects, the book does not go into the system's internals, which are irrelevant to the application designers. The current database technology isolates its users from its internals. Therefore, in-depth understanding of internals will be important only to that small category of system designers who develop new database management systems. In contrast, most software engineers will develop or maintain database applications at one time or another.

The semantic approach

This book presents the field of database design from the perspective of semantic modeling. The focus on semantic modeling serves three purposes:

- The semantic and object-oriented data models are now occupying a significant part of the frontier of the database technology and are expected to become predominant in tomorrow's databases, replacing the current relational database technology. (Although somewhat different in their approach to database modeling, the semantic and object-oriented models are quite similar. Their differences are described in Chapter 10.)

- The semantic modeling approach is used in this book to unify the ideas and terminology of the various database models. Instead of separately introducing the relational database model with its concepts, terminology, and languages, then the network database model with its concepts and terminology, and so on, this book unifies all of the database models into one framework. Most of the concepts and languages are presented in terms of a unifying semantic model. The other models are technically treated as subsets of the semantic model; therefore, the concepts and languages automatically apply to them.

- Most importantly, semantic modeling is presented as a tool of database design in the relational and other database models. Thus, the top-down relational database methodology presented in this book proceeds as follows. First, the user's application is analyzed and specified semantically. This produces a concise, flexible, user-oriented specification of the application's database, unconstrained by computer-oriented concerns. In the second stage, this specification is converted into a relational database schema, with its integrity constraints, data manipulation programs, etc. The semantic description remains a high-level documentation of the database.

Contents

Chapter 1 introduces the fundamental aspects of databases. These aspects are described in terms of a semantic database model, the Semantic Binary Model (SBM). (In later chapters, other database models, such as the relational, network, and hierarchical models, are defined technically as subsets of the semantic model of Chapter 1.) This chapter defines and discusses the concepts of a database, a database management system (DBMS), a database schema, modeling real-world information, categorization of real-world objects, relations between objects, graphic representation of database schemas, integrity constraints, quality of database schemas, sub-schemas, userviews, database languages, services of DBMS, and multimedia databases.

Chapter 2 presents two fundamental database languages, from which most database languages can be derived with some adjustment of syntax. The first language is a fourth-generation data manipulation language. It is shown as a structured extension of Pascal. The second language is a nonprocedural language called Database Predicate Calculus. Chapter 2 defines these languages in terms of the Semantic Binary Model. Later chapters show the use of these languages in other database models.

Chapter 3 defines the Relational Data Model and presents a top-down methodology for the design of relational databases.

Chapter 4 describes relational database languages. Sections 1 and 2 show examples of how the languages of Chapter 2 (the fourth-generation and the logic-based languages) apply to the relational databases. A case study in Section 1 discusses the principles of writing a transaction-processing program for an application. The optional Section 3 defines the Relational Algebra. Section 4 describes SQL, a popular commercial language related to the logic-based language of Section 2. The expressive power and the equivalence of relational languages are discussed in Section 5.

Chapter 5 begins with a case study of the design of an actual database application. Section 2 summarizes the flow of database design. Section 3 compares the methodology of this book to the older methodology of normalization.

Chapter 6 defines the Network (CODASYL) data model and adapts the top-down database design methodology to network databases. Section 3 of this chapter discusses network database languages: application of the generic fourth-generation and logic-based languages and a special navigational language for the Network Model.

Chapter 7 defines the hierarchical data model and adapts the top-down database design methodology to hierarchical databases. Section 3 of this chapter discusses hierarchical database languages: application of the generic fourth-generation and logic-based languages.

Chapter 8 compares the semantic, relational, network, and hierarchical data models with respect to application programming efforts, data independence, and other factors.

Chapter 9 discusses aspects of DBMS implementation. Section 1 describes an efficient algorithm for the implementation of semantic databases. Section 2 addresses questions of transaction handling, including the enforcement of integrity constraints, backup and recovery, and concurrency control. Section 3 addresses issues of data definition languages and data dictionaries.

Chapter 10 addresses object-oriented databases. This chapter discusses the similarities and the minor difference between the semantic and object-oriented databases and augments the Semantic Binary Model with object-oriented features related to modeling database behavior.

Chapter 11 discusses several fifth-generation languages. Sections 1 through 3 address issues of expressive power of logic-based database languages and discuss Prolog-like languages and a logic-based language which attains computational completeness. Section 4 discusses user-friendly interfaces, using the Query-By-Example language as an example.

Chapter 12 is the bibliography. Section 1 gives annotated references to papers on issues of semantic modeling addressed in this book. Section 2 is a listing of recent books on databases.

Chapter 13 contains solutions of problems.

Use of this book as a glossary and a reference handbook

The reader who wants to obtain the definition of a database term can look it up in the index, which provides a pointer to the page on which the term is defined. On that page the user will find the term set in bold face (for easy locating), normally followed by an example. When a term has different uses or aspects in several database models, the index contains several references marked according to their use.

Prerequisites

The reader is expected to be familiar with the fundamentals of the art of programming. Knowledge of structured programming is desirable, preferably in Pascal or a similar language. No knowledge of file organization or data structures is required, except for the optional Chapter 9.

Structure of the book

The book is composed primarily of explanations of concepts and examples. The examples are offset and boxed so that the experienced reader or browser can easily skip them. The examples constitute a continuous case study of an application, for which databases are designed in different models, application programs are written in different languages, etc.

Most sections are followed by problems. Many of the problems are solved in the last chapter of this book. Page-number pointers direct the reader from the problems to their solutions. If after reading a chapter the reader fails to solve a problem marked "Advanced" or "Optional," it does not mean a lack of understanding of the chapter but probably means that the reader has a lack of mathematical knowledge or experience, which is not prerequisite to the reading of this book.

The sections marked with an asterisk (*) contain optional advanced material and may be skipped. Optional advanced material within the regular sections is given in the footnotes.

Acknowledgments

I am grateful to the Florida International University for providing facilities and an environment conducive to writing this book, to the Florida High Technology and Industry Council for their support, and to the following persons for their valuable comments and advice: Michael Alexopoulos, Vanessa Allen, David Barton, David Buker, David Fogarty, Jim Fegen, Randy Goetz, Scott Graham, Ehud Gudes, Carlos Ibarra, Alok Jain, Robert Johnson, Ranjana Kizakkevariath, Neil Levine, Steve Luis, Thomas McElwee, Jai Mokherje, Shamkant Navathe, Jainendra Navlakha, N. Prabhakaran, Timothy Riley, Dan Simovici, Martin Solomon, Wei Sun, Doron Tal, N. Vijaykumar, and Nancy Young.

Naphtali Rishe

School of Computer Science
Florida International University
University Park, Miami, FL 33199, U.S.A.
Telephone: (305) 348-2025, 348-2744
FAX: (305)-348-3549; E-mail: rishen@servax.bitnet, rishen@fiu.edu

CHAPTER 1

SEMANTIC INTRODUCTION TO DATABASES

This chapter defines fundamental concepts of databases. These concepts are described here in terms of the Semantic Binary Model (SBM) of data. A data model is a convention for the specification of the logical structure of real-world information. The cornerstone of the contemporary theory and technology of databases was the development of the Relational Data Model. The recent development of the new generation of data models — the semantic models — offers a simple, natural, implementation-independent, flexible, and nonredundant specification of information. The word *semantic* means that this convention closely captures the meaning of user's information and provides a concise, high-level description of that information.

SBM is one of several existing semantic models. The various semantic models are roughly equivalent and have common principles, even though they somewhat differ in terminology and in the tools they use. SBM is simpler than most other semantic data models: it has a small set of sufficient tools by which all of the semantic descriptors of the other models can be constructed. After mastering SBM, a systems analyst may wish to explore more complex semantic models.

This chapter defines and discusses the concepts of a database, a database management system (DBMS), a database schema, modeling real-world information, categorization of real-world objects, relations between objects, graphic representation of database schemas, integrity constraints, quality of database schemas, subschemas, userviews, database languages, services of DBMS, and multimedia databases.

1.1. Databases, DBMS, Data Models

General-purpose software system — a software system that can serve a variety of needs of numerous dissimilar enterprises.

> *Example:*
>
> A compiler for a programming language.

Application — a software system serving the special needs of an enterprise or a group of similar enterprises.

> *Example:*
>
> The registration of students in a university.

Application's real world — all the information owned by and subject to computerization in an enterprise *or* all such information which is relevant to a self-contained application within the enterprise.

> *Example:*
>
> The examples of this text constitute a case study. Its application world is the educational activities of a university. The information contains:
>
> - A list of the university's departments (including all the full and short names of each department)
> - Personal data of all the students and their major and minor departments
> - Personal data of all the instructors and their work information (including all the departments in which the instructor works and all the courses which the instructor teaches)
> - The list of courses given in the university catalog
> - The history of courses offered by instructors
> - The history of student enrollment in courses and the final grades received

Database — an updatable storage of information of an application's world *and* managing software that conceals from the user the physical aspects of information storage and information representation. The information stored in a database is accessible at a *logical* level without involving the physical concepts of implementation.

> *Example:*
>
> Neither a user nor a user program will try to seek the names of computer science instructors in track 13 of cylinder 5 of a disk or in "logical" record 225 of file XU17.NAMES.VERSION.12.84. Instead, the user will communicate with the database using some *logical* structure of the application's information.

Normally, a database should cover *all* the information of one application; there should not be two databases for one application.

Database management system, DBMS — a general-purpose software system which can manage databases for a very large class of the possible application worlds.

> *Example:*
>
> A DBMS is able to manage our university database and also completely different databases: an Internal Revenue Service database, an FBI *WANTED* database, a UN database on world geographical data, an Amtrak schedule, etc.

Instantaneous database — all the information represented in a database at a given instant. This includes the historic information which is still kept at that time.

The actual information stored in the database changes from day to day. Most changes are additions of information to the database.

> *Example:*
>
> A new student, a new instructor, new events of course offerings.

Fewer changes are deletions of information.

> *Example:*
>
> Historic information past the archival period;
> a course offering which was canceled before it was given.

Some changes are replacements: updates; correction of wrongly recorded information.

> *Example:*
>
> Update of the address of a student;
>
> correction of the student's birth year (previously wrongly recorded).

Hence the life of a database can be seen as a sequence of instantaneous databases. The first one in the sequence is often the empty instantaneous database — it is the state before any information has been entered.

Database model — a convention of specifying the concepts of the real world in a form understandable by a DBMS. (Technically, it is an abstract data structure such that every possible instantaneous database of nearly every application's world can be logically represented by an instance of that data structure.)

The following database models will be studied in this text:

- *Semantic Binary*, in which the information is represented by logical associations (relations) between pairs of objects and by the classification of objects into categories

- *Relational*, in which the information is represented by a collection of printable tables

- *Network*, in which the information is represented by a directed graph of records

- *Hierarchical*, in which the information is represented as a tree of records

The Semantic Binary Model is the most natural of the above models. It is the most convenient for specifying the logical structure of information and for defining the concepts of an application's world. In this text, the other models will be derived from the Semantic Binary Model. The Relational, Network and Hierarchical models are dominant in today's commercial market of database management systems.

1.2. Semantic Modeling

1.2.1. Categorization of objects

Object — any item in the real world. It can be either a concrete object or an abstract object as follows.

Example:

Consider the application world of a university.

I am an object, if I am of interest to the university. My name is an object. The Information Systems Department and its name "Information Systems Department" are two distinct objects.

Value, or **concrete object** — a printable object, such as a number, a character string, or a date. A value can be roughly considered as representing itself in the computer or in any formal system.

> *Example:*
>
> My name and the name "Computer Science Department" are concrete objects. The grade 70 which has been given to a student in a course is also a concrete object.

Abstract object — a nonvalue object in the real world. An abstract object can be, for example, a tangible item (such as a person, a table, a country) or an event (such as an offering of a course by an instructor) or an idea (such as a course). Abstract objects cannot be represented directly in the computer.

This term is also used for a user-transparent representation of such an object in the Semantic Binary Model.

> *Example:*
>
> The Management Science Department, the student of the department whose name is Alex Johnson, and the course named "Chemistry" are three abstract objects.

Category — any concept of the application's real world which is a unary property of objects. At every moment in time such a concept is descriptive of a set of objects which possess the property at that time.

Unlike the mathematical notion of a set, the category itself does not depend on its objects: the objects come and go while the meaning of the category is preserved in time. Conversely, a set *does* depend on its members: the meaning of a set changes with the ebb and flow of its members.

Categories are usually named by *singular* nouns.

> *Example:*
>
> *STUDENT* is a category of abstract objects. The set of all the students relevant to the application today is different from such a set tomorrow, since new students will arrive or will become relevant. However, the concept *STUDENT* will remain unaltered.

An object may belong to several categories at the same time.

Example:

One object may be known as a person and at the same time as an instructor and as a student.

Example:

Some of the categories in the world of our university are: *INSTRUCTOR, PERSON, COURSE, STUDENT, DEPARTMENT.*

Disjoint categories — Two categories are *disjoint* if no object may simultaneously be a member of both categories. This means that at every point in time the sets of objects corresponding to two disjoint categories have an empty intersection.

Example:

The categories *STUDENT* and *COURSE* are disjoint; so are *COURSE* and *DEPARTMENT* (even though there may be two *different* objects, a course and a department, both named "Physics").

    The categories *INSTRUCTOR* and *STUDENT* are not disjoint (Figure 1-1); neither are *INSTRUCTOR* and *PERSON*.

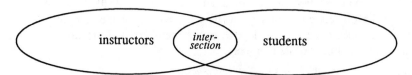

Figure 1-1. Intersecting of categories.

Subcategory — A category is a *subcategory* of another category if at every point in time every object of the former category should also belong to the latter. This means that at every point in time the set of objects corresponding to a category contains the set of objects corresponding to any subcategory of the category.

Example:

The category *STUDENT* is a subcategory of the category *PERSON*. The category *INSTRUCTOR* is another subcategory of the category *PERSON* (Figure 1-2).

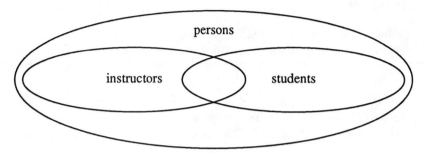

Figure 1-2. Subcategories.

Abstract category — a category whose objects are always abstract.

Concrete category, category of values — a category whose objects are always concrete.

Example:

STUDENT and *COURSE* are abstract categories. *STRING, NUMBER,* and *DIGIT* are concrete categories.

Many concrete categories, such as *NUMBER, STRING,* and *BOOLEAN,* have constant-in-time sets of objects. Thus, those concrete categories are actually indistinguishable from the corresponding sets of all numbers, all strings, and the Boolean values ({TRUE, FALSE}).

Finite category — A category is *finite* if at no point in time an infinite set of objects may correspond to it in the application's world.

Example:

The categories *STUDENT, COURSE,* and *DIGIT* are finite. The category *NUMBER* may be infinite.

Every abstract category is finite.

Example:

The database has a finite size. We cannot have an abstract category *POINT* containing information about every point in a plane.

1.2.2. Binary relations

Binary relation — any concept of the application's real world which is a binary property of objects, that is, the meaning of a relationship or connection between two objects.

Example:

WORKS-IN is a relation relating instructors to departments. *MAJOR-DEPARTMENT* relates students to departments. *NAME* is a relation relating persons to strings. *BIRTH-YEAR* is a relation relating persons to numbers.

At every moment in time, the relation is descriptive of a set of pairs of objects which are related at that time. The meaning of the relation remains unaltered in time, while the sets of pairs of objects corresponding to the relation may differ from time to time, when some pairs of objects cease or begin to be connected by the relation.

Notation: xRy means that object x is related by the relation R to object y.

Example:

To indicate that an instructor i works in a department d, we write:
$$i \; WORKS\text{-}IN \; d$$

1.2.2.1. Types of binary relations: m:m, m:1, 1:m, 1:1

1. A binary relation R is **many-to-one (m:1, functional)** if at no point in time xRy and xRz where $y \neq z$.

Example:

BIRTH-YEAR is an m:1 relation because every person has only one year of birth:

$person_1$	*BIRTH-YEAR*	1970
$person_2$	*BIRTH-YEAR*	1970
$person_3$	*BIRTH-YEAR*	1969
$person_4$	*BIRTH-YEAR*	1965

Example:

MAJOR-DEPARTMENT is also an **m:1** relation, since every student has at most one major department, as in Figure 1-3.

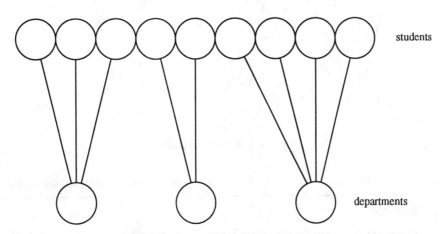

Figure 1-3. A many-to-one relation.

2.   A binary relation R is **one-to-many (1:m)** if at no point in time xRy and zRy where $x \neq z$.

Example:

The relation *MAJOR-DEPARTMENT* is not **1:m**, since a department may have many major students.

If, instead of the relation *MAJOR-DEPARTMENT*, we have the relation *MAJOR-STUDENT* between departments and students, then this relation would be **1:m**, since every student can have at most one major department.

3.   Relations which are of neither of the above types are called **proper many-to-many (m:m)**.

Example:

WORKS-IN is a proper m:m relation because every instructor can work in many departments and every department may employ many instructors, as in Figure 1-4.

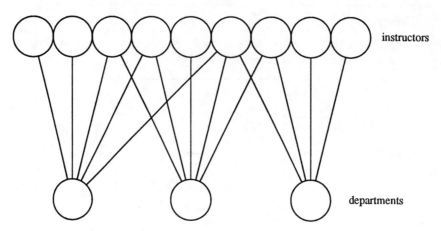

Figure 1-4. A m:m relation

4.   A binary relation which is both *m:1* and *1:m* (always) is called **one-to-one (1:1)**.

Example:

If courses are identified by their names, then the relation *COURSE-NAME* is 1:1, meaning that every course has at most one name, and no character string is the name of two different courses, as in Figure 1-5.

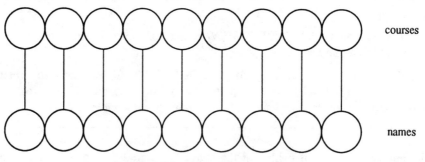

Figure 1-5. A 1:1 relation:
$course_i$ *COURSE−NAME* $name_i$

Example:

Suppose that in the current situation in our real world, the following is true:

(a)   Every registered person has at most one name, and no two persons have the same name.

This does not mean that *NAME* is a 1:1 relation between persons and strings. *NAME* would be a 1:1 relation if condition *a* were true *at all times*: past, present, and future.

The following diagram shows the classification of all relations:

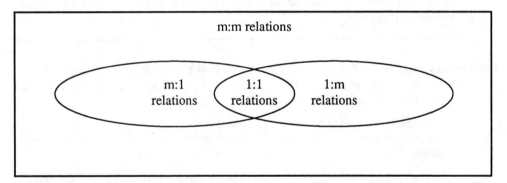

Figure 1-6. Classification of relations.

5.   A binary relation is **proper m:1** if it is m:1 and not 1:1.

6.   A binary relation is **proper 1:m** if it is 1:m and not 1:1.

Example:

All of the types of relations mentioned in the previous example are proper.

Since the *COURSE-NAME* is 1:1, it is also 1:m, m:1, and m:m. Since this relation is *proper* 1:1, it cannot be *proper* 1:m, *proper* m:1, or *proper* m:m.

1.2.2.2. Categories as domains and ranges of relations

Domain and **range** of a binary relation:

Domain of relation R — a category C that satisfies the following two conditions:

a.   Whenever xRy, then x belongs to C (at every point in time for every pair of objects)

b.   No proper subcategory of C satisfies condition a

Range of relation R — a category C that satisfies:

a.   Whenever xRy, then y belongs to C (at every point in time for every pair of objects)

b.   No proper subcategory of C satisfies a

Example:

The domain of *COURSE-NAME* is the category *COURSE* and its range is the category *STRING*. The domain of *WORKS-IN* is *INSTRUCTOR* and the range is *DEPARTMENT*.

Total binary relation — A relation R whose domain is C is *total* if *at all times* for every object x in C there exists an object y such that xRy. (At different times different objects y may be related to a given object x.)

Note: No relation needs to be *total* on its domain.

Example:

Although the domain of the relation *BIRTH-DATE* is the category *PERSON*, the date of birth of some relevant persons is irrelevant or unknown. Thus, the relation *BIRTH-DATE* is not total.

1.2.2.3. Attributes

Some binary relations are often called attributes.

Attribute — A functional relation (i.e., m:1 or 1:1) whose range is a concrete category.

Example:

☐ *first-name* — attribute of *PERSON*, range: *String (m:1)*

☐ *birth-year* — attribute of *PERSON*, range: *1880..1991 (m:1)*

The phrase "*a* is an **attribute of** C" means: a is an attribute, and its domain is the category C.

Example:

Last-name, first-name, and *birth-year* are attributes of *PERSON.*

Problem 1-1.

For each of the following relations determine the type (proper m:m/1:m/m:1/1:1):

☐ *works-in* — relation from *INSTRUCTOR* to *DEPARTMENT* (*?:?*)

☐ *name* — relation from *DEPARTMENT* to *String* (*?:?*) (A department may have several names, but every name is unique.)

☐ *last-name* — attribute of *PERSON*, range: *String* (*?:?*)

☐ *address* — attribute of *PERSON*, range: *String* (*?:?*)

☐ *major* — relation from *STUDENT* to *DEPARTMENT* (*?:?*)

☐ *minor* — relation from *STUDENT* to *DEPARTMENT* (*?:?*)

☐ *year* — attribute of *QUARTER*, range: *1990..2010* (*?:?*)

☐ *season* — attribute of *QUARTER*, range: *String* (*?:?*)

☐ *name* — attribute of *COURSE*, range: *String* (*?:?*)

Solution on page 387.

Problem 1-2.

(*Optional, combinatorics*)

Given:

R is an m:m relation.
A is a category.
The domain of R is A.
The range of R is also A.
Presently, two objects belong to the category A: objects a_1 and a_2.

List the different sets of pairs of objects that may presently correspond to R.

Solution on page 387.

Problem 1-3.

(*Optional, combinatorics*)

Given:

R is a total m:1 relation.
A is a category.
The domain of R is A.
The range of R is also A.
The set of objects that presently corresponds to A is $\{a_1, a_2, a_3, a_4\}$.

How many different sets of pairs of objects may presently correspond to R?

Solution on page 388.

Problem 1-4.

(*Optional, combinatorics*)

Given:

R is an m:1 relation (not total).
A is a category.
The domain of R is A.
The range of R is also A.
The set of objects that presently corresponds to A is {a1, a_2, a_3, a4}.

How many different sets of pairs of objects may presently correspond to R?

Solution on page 388.

1.2.3. Nonbinary relationships

Nonbinary relationships — real-world relationships that bind more than two objects in different roles.

> *Example:*
>
> There is a relationship between an instructor, a course, and a quarter in which the instructor offers the course.

Such complex relationships are regarded in the Semantic Binary Model as groups of several simple relationships.

> *Example:*
>
> The nonbinary relationship of the previous example is represented in the Semantic Binary Model by a fourth object, an offering, and three binary relations between the offering and the instructor, the quarter, and the course, as in Figure 1-7.

In general, the Semantic Binary Model represents any nonbinary relation as:

a. An abstract category of events. Each event symbolizes the existence of a relationship between a group of objects.

b. Functional binary relations, whose domain is category (a). Each of those functional binary relations corresponds to a role played by some objects in the nonbinary relation.

Thus, the fact that objects $x_1, \ldots, x_n$ participate in an n-ary relation R in roles $R_1, \ldots, R_n$ is represented by:

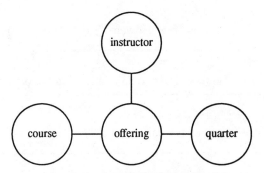

Figure 1-7. A trinary relationship.

a.   An object e in the category R'

b.   Binary relationships $eR_1x_1, \ldots, eR_nx_n$

Example:

The information about a course offered by an instructor during a quarter could be considered a ternary relation between instructors, courses, and quarters. In the Semantic Binary Model, we solve this problem by representing this information as a category *COURSE-OFFERING* and three functional relations from *COURSE-OFFERING*: *THE-INSTRUCTOR, THE-COURSE,* and *THE-QUARTER.*

Instructor i has offered course c in quarter q if and only if there exists a course-offering o, such that:

$$o\ THE\text{-}INSTRUCTOR\ i$$

$$o\ THE\text{-}COURSE\ c$$

$$o\ THE\text{-}QUARTER\ q$$

1.2.4. Instantaneous databases

Formal representation of an instantaneous binary database — as a set of *facts*, unary and binary:

Unary fact — a statement that a certain abstract object belongs to a certain category.

> *Example:*
>
> (The person whose name is "Jane Howards") is a *student*.

Binary fact — a statement that there is a certain relationship between two given objects.

> *Example:*
>
> The *birth-year* of (the person whose name is "Jane Howards") is 1968.

> *Example:*
>
> (The instructor whose name is "John Smith")
works in
(the department whose name is "Information Systems")

> *Example:*
>
> The *final grade* of
>
> (the enrollment of (the student whose name is "Jack Brown") in (the offering of (the course named "Basic Chemistry") by (the instructor named "Veronica Hammer") during (the Fall 1900 quarter)))
>
> is 100.
>
> Although this fact relates to the past, it is still relevant and thus is a part of today's instantaneous database.

Note: In order to be in the current instantaneous database, the fact must have been explicitly or implicitly entered at some time and never canceled since.

1.2.5. Semantic binary schemas

A **semantic binary schema** is a description of the names and the properties of all the categories and the binary relations existing in an application's world.

All the instantaneous databases under the schema should have only those categories and relations listed in the schema. The sets of pairs of objects corresponding, in the instantaneous database, to the categories, and the sets of pairs of objects corresponding to the relations, should satisfy the properties indicated in the schema.

The schema should list the following properties of the categories and relations: the subcategories, the domains and ranges of the relations, and the types of the relations (*proper m:m, proper m:1, proper 1:m, 1:1*).

Semantic Binary Model is a convention of specification of the structure of the real-world information in the form of a semantic binary schema. Technically, the model can be regarded as the set of all the possible binary instantaneous databases.

1.2.6. Schema diagrams

This section shows how schemas can be represented graphically in two dimensions.

1.   In a schema diagram, categories are shown by rectangles.

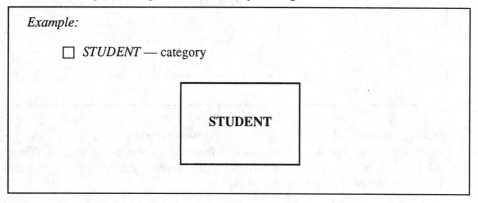

2.   Relations from abstract categories to concrete categories are shown inside the boxes of the domain-categories as follows:

$$relation : range\ type$$

The *range* is specified as a programming language data-type. (We will use the style of *Pascal* here.)

Usually, relations between abstract and concrete categories are *m:1*. This is the *default type of relations whose ranges are concrete categories*, and it need not be explicitly specified in the schema for such relations.

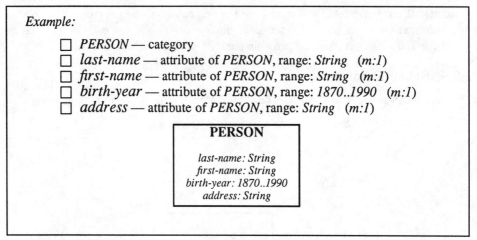

Example:

- [ ] *PERSON* — category
- [ ] *last-name* — attribute of *PERSON*, range: *String* (*m:1*)
- [ ] *first-name* — attribute of *PERSON*, range: *String* (*m:1*)
- [ ] *birth-year* — attribute of *PERSON*, range: *1870..1990* (*m:1*)
- [ ] *address* — attribute of *PERSON*, range: *String* (*m:1*)

> **PERSON**
>
> *last-name: String*
> *first-name: String*
> *birth-year: 1870..1990*
> *address: String*

3. Relations between abstract categories are shown by arrows between the categories' rectangles. (The direction of the arrow is from the domain to the range.) The name and type of the relation are indicated on the arrow. The *default for the type of relations between abstract categories* is *m:m*.

Example:

Figure 1-8 represents:

- [ ] *DEPARTMENT* — category
- [ ] *INSTRUCTOR* — category
- [ ] *works-in* — relation from *INSTRUCTOR* to *DEPARTMENT* (*m:m*)

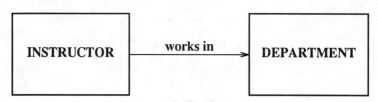

Figure 1-8. A m:m relation.

4.   Subcategories' rectangles are connected to their supercategories' rectangles by arrows with dashes.

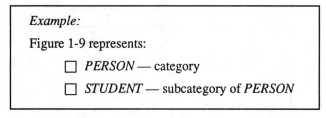

Example:

Figure 1-9 represents:

    ☐ *PERSON* — category

    ☐ *STUDENT* — subcategory of *PERSON*

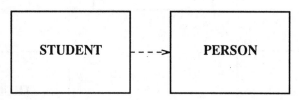

Figure 1-9. Subcategories.

5.   The disjointness of categories is indicated implicitly:

    a.   Two categories which have a subcategory in common are *not* disjoint. (The common subcategory does not have to be their *immediate* subcategory, that is, it may be a subcategory of a subcategory and so on.)

Example:

No two of the categories in Figure 1-10 are disjoint from each other.

Figure 1-10. Intersecting categories.

    b.   Two categories which are subcategories of one category (not necessarily immediate subcategories) are considered *not* disjoint, unless otherwise declared in an appendix to the schema.

Example:

No two of the categories in Figure 1-11 are disjoint from each other.

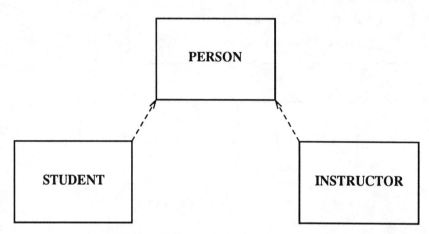

Figure 1-11. Intersecting categories.

c.   The other categories are disjoint from each other, unless otherwise declared in an appendix to the schema.

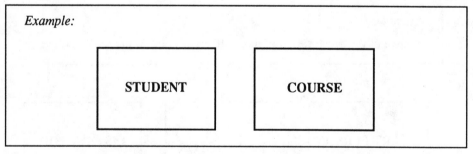

Example:

A semantic schema for a university application is given at the end of this book. This will be the principal reference schema used in the examples throughout the book.

1.2.7. Abstraction of a database storage structure

The physical implementation of a database is a responsibility of the DBMS. The implementation of the database should be completely transparent to the database users, including the database designers and systems analysts.

Nevertheless, it may be helpful to the reader to have a general idea of how the database may be implemented. This section shows a possible idea of database implementation. This is a simplistic implementation. Efficiency is not a concern here. It would be, of course, a concern in any actual implementation.

We can represent the abstract objects as integers. The DBMS will enumerate all the abstract objects. The numbers assigned to the objects will be invisible to the user, as will all the implementational details.

We can represent the instantaneous database as a large table. Every row contains a fact: a unary fact (*object — category*), or a binary fact (*object — relation — object*). This table can be implemented as a file.

Example:

The following is a fragment of a file representing an instantaneous database. The fragment consists of one unary fact and three binary facts.

---

object#	relation or category	object# or value
o21	COURSE-ENROLLMENT	
o21	THE-STUDENT	o18
o21	THE-OFFERING	o17
o21	FINAL-GRADE	100

Example:

The following figure shows an implementation of an instantaneous database for the university application. It specifies the instantaneous database which will be used in examples throughout this book.

category	object#	relation	object# or value
DEPARTMENT	o1	NAME	Computer Science
	o1	NAME	CS
	o2	NAME	Mathematics
	o2	NAME	Math
	o3	NAME	Physics
	o4	NAME	Arts
	o5	NAME	Economics
COURSE	o6	NAME	Databases
	o7	NAME	Gastronomy
	o8	NAME	Football
QUARTER	o9	YEAR	1990
	o9	SEASON	Fall
	o10	YEAR	1990
	o10	SEASON	Winter
	o11	YEAR	1990
	o11	SEASON	Spring
INSTRUCTOR	o12	LAST-NAME	Brown
	o12	FIRST-NAME	George
	o12	BIRTH-YEAR	1956
	o12	ADDRESS	112 Lucky Dr.
	o12	WORKS-IN	o1
	o12	WORKS-IN	o2
	o13	LAST-NAME	Watson
	o13	FIRST-NAME	Mary
	o13	BIRTH-YEAR	1953
	o13	ADDRESS	231 Fortune Dr.
	o13	WORKS-IN	o3
	o14	LAST-NAME	Blue
	o14	FIRST-NAME	John
	o14	BIRTH-YEAR	1950
	o14	ADDRESS	536 Orange Dr.
	o14	WORKS-IN	o2

Figure 1-12. An instantaneous semantic database for the university application.

category	object#	relation	object# or value
COURSE-OFFERING	o15	THE-INSTRUCTOR	o12
	o15	THE-COURSE	o6
	o15	THE-QUARTER	o9
	o16	THE-INSTRUCTOR	o12
	o16	THE-COURSE	o7
	o16	THE-QUARTER	o9
	o17	THE-INSTRUCTOR	o12
	o17	THE-COURSE	o8
	o17	THE-QUARTER	o9
STUDENT	o18	LAST-NAME	Victory
	o18	FIRST-NAME	Elizabeth
	o18	BIRTH-YEAR	1966
	o18	ADDRESS	100 Sun St.
	o18	MAJOR	o1
	o18	MINOR	o5
	o19	LAST-NAME	Howards
	o19	FIRST-NAME	Jane
	o19	BIRTH-YEAR	1965
	o19	ADDRESS	200 Dorms
	o19	MAJOR	o4
	o19	MINOR	o5
	o20	LAST-NAME	Wood
	o20	FIRST-NAME	Michael
	o20	BIRTH-YEAR	1964
	o20	ADDRESS	110 Dorms
	o20	MAJOR	o4
	o20	MINOR	o5
COURSE-ENROLLMENT	o21	THE-STUDENT	o18
	o21	THE-OFFERING	o17
	o21	FINAL-GRADE	100
	o22	THE-STUDENT	o19
	o22	THE-OFFERING	o17
	o22	FINAL-GRADE	70
	o23	THE-STUDENT	o19
	o23	THE-OFFERING	o15
	o23	FINAL-GRADE	80

Figure 1-12. *Continued.*

Problem 1-5.

Design a semantic schema for a wholesaler, covering the following information for each product:

- The name and the address of the manufacturing firm
- For each sale and for each purchase of the product: the date, the quantity of the product, the name and address of the firm selling or buying, and the dollar value of the transaction

Solution on page 388.

Problem 1-6.

Design a semantic schema for a movie studio, covering the following information:

- The title and directors of each film (a film may have several co-directors)
- The names, addresses, and occupations (actor, technician, director, other) of the personnel
- Partitioning of the films into scenes; for each scene, its location, its actors, the props used in it, and the persons assisting in shooting the scene

Solution on page 389.

Problem 1-7.

A *clan* is a group of living and past relatives sharing one last name. The last name can be received from the father at birth or from the husband at marriage. Design a database to store the relations within a clan (by birth and by marriage.)

Solution on page 389.

Problem 1-8.

Design a semantic schema to record sale transactions of items. A *sale* is a transaction of merchandise of a particular *item-type* for a *price* between the *seller* and the *buyer*. The database also contains a bill of material of item-types, that is, the components of each item-type are known.

Solution on page 390.

Problem 1-9.

Design a semantic schema to store information which describes a printed circuit board in terms of the component devices contained thereon and the circuits which connect between the electrical terminals (pins) of the devices. The components of the circuit board are chosen from among a set of component types. Each component has an identifier which distinguishes it from all other components, of like or different type, on the circuit board. Each component has a number of electrically separate terminals (pins) to which wires may be connected. Pins are numbered to distinguish among the pins of a given component. Wires may connect a pin to one or more pins of the same or of other components on the circuit board. A set of such wires which are electrically common (interconnected) is referred to as a circuit. All of the wires of a circuit will be the same color.

Solution on page 391.

1.3. Integrity Constraints

Integrity constraints (synonyms: **integrity law, integrity rules**) — rules attached to a database in order to detect obvious user errors when updating the database.

1. **Static integrity constraints** — rules to detect instantaneous databases which cannot correspond to any probable state of the application's world in the past, present, or future, regardless of the database's update history.

> *Example:*
>
> These are some static integrity constraints in our university:
>
> - No one has two last names
>
> - Every student has at most one major department
>
> - First names of people are composed only of letters
>
> - Students may not participate in a course before they were born or receive a grade in a course before they are 15 years old.

A static integrity law can be regarded as a Boolean function from the set of all the instantaneous databases which are well-formed according to the schema or the database model. This function assigns the value *false* to those instantaneous databases which cannot correspond to any probable state of the application's world.

2. **Dynamic integrity constraints** — as above, but the domain of the function is the set of transitions between instantaneous databases, and *false* is assigned to highly improbable transitions between states of the application's world.

> *Example:*
>
> The following is a dynamic integrity constraint:
>
> > The catalog of courses is unerasable — a course, once entered, may not be removed.

Example:

If we wish to record the sex of persons in our database and we are sure that nobody's sex is ever recorded wrongly (this is usually a dangerous and unreasonable assumption), and we further assume that a woman cannot become a man, then the following would be another dynamic constraint:

Once the sex of x is *female* in an instantaneous database, the sex of x remains *female* in the next instantaneous database.

Note:

(i)   Very often some of the integrity constraints are captured by the schema.

(ii) Integrity constraints should be distinguished from *implementational restrictions*:

Implementational restrictions — the inability of the database to represent some possible situations of the application's world or the inability to represent them in a logical, natural, nonredundant, error-avoiding, flexible way.

Implementational restrictions are caused by considerations such as hardware, software, database model, effort, time, and expenses.

Example:

If for the application world of the university we use a database model less powerful than the Semantic Binary Model, then our implementational considerations may require that every instructor is uniquely identified by social security number. This is not the case in the real world of the university, because sometimes an instructor receives a social security number only several months *after* being hired and becoming of relevance to the university database.

The aforementioned is a static implementational restriction. To cope with it we have either to delay the recording of new instructors or to supply them with some temporary numbers.

If our implementation further requires that the social security number of a person should remain constant in time, then this would constitute a dynamic restriction. Supplying temporary numbers would not help in this case. Also, this dynamic restriction would not allow for correction of a wrongly recorded social security number (due to a data-entry clerk's mistake). In practice, such a correction may be possible but with an extremely high cost in terms of the programming effort and with a chance to inadvertently corrupt the database.

1.4. Schema Quality Criteria

We have defined the term *schema* for the Semantic Binary Model. The following is a more general definition of the term, regardless of the database model.

Schema — a description, in terms of a database model, of the concepts and the information structure of an application's world. It may be the actual data structure of a database. A schema describes all the possible instantaneous databases for one given application's world.

Example:

A schema for our university application should outline the basic relevant concepts of the university, such as *student, instructor*, etc., and the kinds of information to be gathered about them. The schema will not allow the database to contain information about salaries of the instructors or about girl- or boyfriends of students since these are outside the scope of the application's world.

A schema is called **high quality** if it satisfies the following criteria:

1. **Natural**

   The schema describes the concepts of its application's world naturally:

   - The schema describes the objects, categories, and relations as they are in the real world.

   - The users can translate ideas easily in both directions between the concepts of the schema and the natural concepts of the application world.

2. **Nonredundant**

   The schema contains very little or no redundancy. *Redundancy* is the possibility of representing a fact of the application's world more than once in the same instantaneous database (so that if one of the representations is removed from the database, no information is lost; that is, all of the information represented by the instantaneous database remains unaltered).

   The redundancy should be avoided *not* in order to improve the storage efficiency — the storage is not that expensive nowadays. Moreover, the redundancy in the schema is not directly related to the redundancy in the physical storage: a logically nonredundant schema may be physically implemented by a redundant physical structure in order to improve the access-time efficiency.

   The redundancy should be avoided primarily in order to prevent inconsistency of the database and its update anomalies. When two facts in the database represent the same information, and that information is updated, the user may forget to update both facts.

In this case, after the update the two facts would contradict. This contradiction may cause unpredictable behavior of many application programs. The ramifications would be much worse than the local incorrectness of a fact in the database.

When the redundancy is needed for the convenience of the users, it should be introduced into the userviews (to be defined in the next section) but not into the schema.

Example:

The following is a fragment of a redundant *wrong* schema:

> **COURSE**
> **ENROLLMENT**
>
> *final-grade: 0..100*
> *student's-address: String*

Suppose a student s, whose address is a, has two enrollments, e_1 and e_2. Then, the following facts (among others) are logically recorded in the database:

    a.   *s ADDRESS a*

    b. e_1 *THE-STUDENT s*

    c. e_2 *THE-STUDENT s*

    d. e_1 *STUDENT'S-ADDRESS a*

    e. e_2 *STUDENT'S-ADDRESS a*

The facts (d) and (e) can be inferred from the facts (a) through (c). Thus, (d) and (e) can be omitted from the database without altering the information represented by the database. These facts are redundant; the schema should not have allowed their entrance in the first place.

    If the following relation were omitted from the above wrong schema,

        ☐ *address* — attribute of *PERSON*, range: *String* *(m:1)*

then the schema would still remain redundant and wrong, because fact (e) can be inferred from fact (d). (Additionally, it would be a problem to record the address of a student who has no enrollments yet).

In some database models we cannot eliminate the redundancy completely. When we have to have some redundancy, we should at least bind it by integrity constraints. When such constraints are implemented, the user is forced to update all the related facts simultaneously.

> *Example:*
>
> If we cannot avoid having the redundant schema of the previous example, we can at least try to enforce the following integrity constraint:
>
> Whenever
>
> > *s ADDRESS a*   and   *e THE-STUDENT s*
>
> then
>
> > *e STUDENT'S-ADDRESS a*

3. **Nonrestrictive**

The schema does *not impose implementational restrictions;* that is, every situation probable in the real world of the application is fully representable under the schema.

> *Example:*
>
> A schema containing the following relation would prevent very senior citizens from entering our university:
>
> > ☐ *birth-year* — attribute of *PERSON*, range: *1900..2000 (m:1)*
>
> This schema imposes an avoidable implementational restriction, and thus it is *wrong* .

4. **Covering integrity constraints**

The schema covers by itself as many integrity constraints as possible; that is, the class of instantaneous databases formally possible according to the schema is not much larger than the class of all possible situations of the real world.

Constraints that are *not* expressed in the schema cause these problems:

- They are hard to formulate and to specify.

- They are seldom enforced by the DBMS. Thus, they require a substantial application programming effort for their enforcement, are often implemented incorrectly, and usually prevent direct interaction between the user updating the database and the DBMS (the user may not use the standard language for simple updates, which is supplied by most DBMS).

- The users and application programmers often forget or misunderstand such constraints.

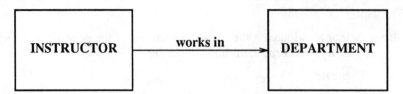

Figure 1-13. A good schema.

Example:

Figure 1-14 shows a fragment of a *poor* schema, with respect to the coverage of the integrity constraints by the schema.

It requires an integrity constraint not expressed in the schema:

> For no instructor are there two events of his or her work in the same department.

A better schema fragment is in Figure 1-13.

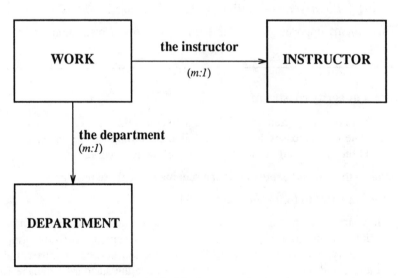

Figure 1-14. A *poor* schema.

5. **Flexible**

The schema is *flexible:* if probable changes in the *concepts* of the application world occur, the schema would not have to undergo drastic changes.

6.   **Conceptually minimal**

The schema is *conceptually minimal:* it does not involve concepts which are irrelevant in the application's real world and limits the accumulation of information which is irrelevant in that world.

Example:

The following would be irrelevant and *wrong* in the schema of our university:

☐ *BEAUTIFUL* — subcategory of *STUDENT*

Example:

The following would be irrelevant and *wrong* in the schema of our university, unless it is unavoidable due to technical problems:

☐ *enrollment-number* — attribute of *ENROLLMENT*, range: *Integer   (m:1)*

The most important issue of the database design is the design of a high-quality schema within the restrictions of the available DBMS and database model. A low-quality schema increases the chances of corruption of the data, makes it very hard to use and maintain the database, and makes it very hard, if not impossible, to adjust the database to the changing concepts of the application's real world.

It is easy to design a high-quality schema in the Semantic Binary Model. The task is much harder in most other models. Moreover, it is usually impossible to describe an application world by a schema in the Relational, Network, or Hierarchical model with the same high quality as with which that application can be described in the Semantic Binary Model.

The following chapters will introduce methodologies to design conceptually adequate schemas in the Relational, Network, and Hierarchical models. Those schemas will be close to the highest quality possible within the restrictions of the respective models. In those methodologies, a semantic binary schema is designed first, and then the schema is translated into the model supported by the DBMS which will service the application.

Problem 1-10.

Design a semantic schema for a simple medical application covering the following information:

1.   A catalog of names of known diseases.

2.   A catalog of descriptions of known symptoms

    a.   Their names

    b.   The units in which the magnitude of their intensity or acuteness is measured

3.   For every disease there is a list of possible symptoms, in which

      for every possible symptom s

         for some magnitudes m of the symptom's acuteness

            there is an estimation of the probability that

               whenever a patient has the disease, he also has the symptom s with acuteness m at least.

4.   A catalog of names of known drugs.

5.   For every disease there are lists of factors which may aggravate, cause, or cure the disease. These factors are drugs, drug combinations, other diseases.

6.   Names, addresses, and dates of birth of patients; names and addresses of physicians. Some physicians are also known as patients. Some persons relevant to the database are neither patients nor physicians. (These other persons can be, for example, parents of patients, paramedical personnel.) For these persons we have only names and addresses.

7.   Physicians' areas of specialization (diseases).

8.   Every patient's medical history, including:

    a.   All his or her present and past illnesses

       — Their duration

       — Their diagnosing physicians

       — Drugs prescribed for them

    b.   All his or her reported symptoms with

       — The duration of the symptom's occurrences

       — An indication of the magnitude of intensity or acuteness of the symptom's occurrence

       — A record of the persons (names and addresses) who reported or measured the symptom's occurrence (a symptom can be reported by the patient, relatives, or medical personnel)

       — Physicians who confirmed the symptom's occurrence

Solution on page 391.

1.5. Subschemas and Userviews

Subschema — a part of the schema, provided this part in itself can constitute a schema for some application world.

> *Example:*
>
> The following figure shows a schema for a very small application world. The only relevant information in that world is the names of the courses.

```
                        ┌─────────────────────────────┐
                        │                             │
                        │          COURSE             │
                        │                             │
                        │         name: String        │
                        │                             │
                        └─────────────────────────────┘

This schema is a subschema of the University Binary Schema of Figure Ref-1.
```

A subschema of a binary schema can be obtained by removing some of the categories and some of the relations (provided, whenever a category is removed, every relation whose domain or range is the category is also removed).

The primary use of the subschemas is to provide subpopulations of the database users with a partial view of the database information. The user of a subschema may regard it as if it were the entire schema and need not be aware of the existence of the information beyond the subschema. The DBMS will conceal from such a user all the information beyond the subschema. This brings the following benefits:

- Users do not have to understand the information concepts which are irrelevant to their activities.

- Users are prevented from accidentally corrupting the information which they had no business to access in the first place but accessed in error instead of the relevant information.

- Malicious users are prevented from accessing information beyond that which they are entitled to access.

- When the database is extended by adding new concepts to the schema, and those new concepts do not affect some existing programs using subschemas, those programs need not be modified.

> *Example:*
>
> The subschema of Figure 1-15 covers the names of the courses and the seasons in which the courses are offered.

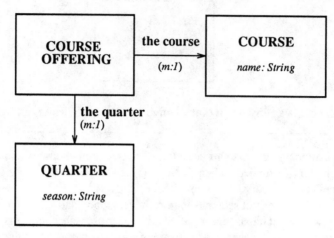

Figure 1-15. Subschema for seasons of courses.

Normally, the schema is partitioned into nondisjoint subschemas according to the needs of the different divisions within the enterprise and the different subapplications.

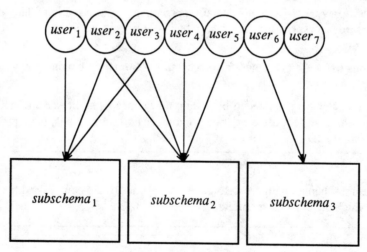

Figure 1-16. The users access the database through subschemas.

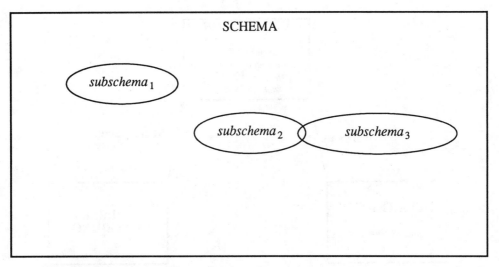

Figure 1-17. The schema is partitioned into subschemas, which need not be disjoint.

Example:

Figure 1-18 shows the subschema used by the Personnel Office.

A generalization of the *subschema* concept, the *userview*, is defined in the remainder of this section.

Inference rules — rules by which new information can be deduced from the information that the users have entered into the database.

Example:

The following are some parts of the information recorded in the university database:

- For every instructor, the classes he or she teaches
- For every student, the classes he or she takes

An inference rule:

- If s takes a class taught by p, then p *TEACHES* s.

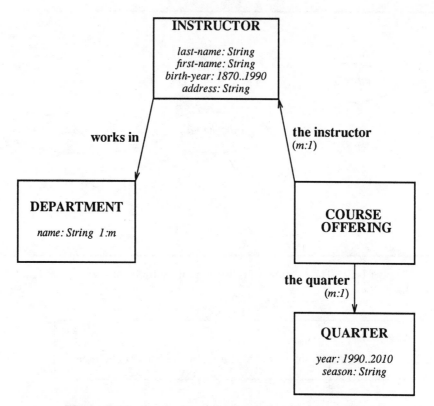

Figure 1-18. A subschema for the University Personnel Office.

Userview — an alternative view on the application world.

A userview is a means of alternative comprehension of a part or all of the application world's information. A userview consists of an alternative schema and inference rules by which every instantaneous database characterized by the original schema implies the (logical) instantaneous database characterized by the alternative schema (Fig. 1-19).

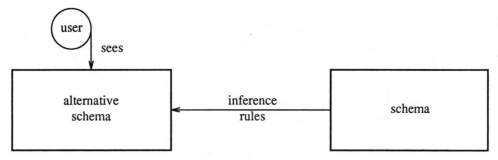

Figure 1-19. A userview.

Example:

Figure 1-20 shows the alternative schema of the userview that covers the names of the courses and the seasons in which the courses are offered. It is more convenient to the user than the subschema of Figure 1-15.

COURSE SEASON

name: String
season: String m:m

Figure 1-20. A userview: seasons of courses.

One userview can be used by a subpopulation of the application world's users. Such a userview would conceal from those users all the information which is irrelevant for them. The remaining information is presented to these users in a form which is most convenient to these particular users.

Example:

The computer science faculty secretary might use a userview containing only the addresses of the faculty. The userview has the alternative schema shown in Figure 1-21.

COMPUTER-SCIENCE-INSTRUCTOR

last-name: String
first-name: String
address: String

Figure 1-21. A userview: computer science instructors.

The inference rule for the category *COMPUTER-SCIENCE-INSTRUCTOR* is:

A computer science instructor is an *INSTRUCTOR* who *WORKS-IN* the *DEPARTMENT* whose *NAME* is "Computer Science."

Example:

A subpopulation of the users is interested only in knowing who taught whom. Their userview has the alternative schema shown in Figure 1-22.

The inference rule for the relation *TAUGHT* has been given on page 35. The other concepts of the alternative schema are copied from the schema.

Some userviews do not omit any information and can be used by all the users. In this case, a userview presents the same information as the schema does, but in a form most suitable for some particular purposes.

All the information which can be deduced from an instantaneous database *idb* by a userview *u* is called the **instantaneous database under userview** *u* corresponding to *idb*.

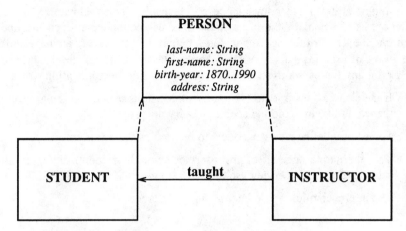

Figure 1-22. A userview: the inferred relation *taught*.

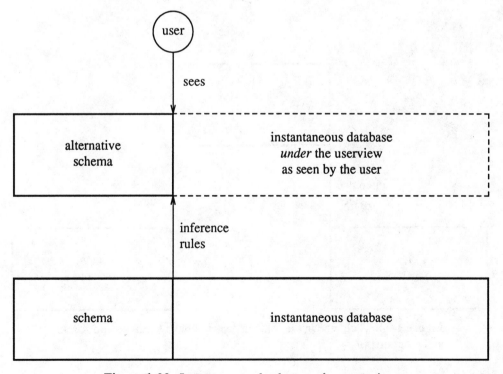

Figure 1-23. Instantaneous database *under* a userview.

Unlike the schema, the alternative schema of a userview may contain redundant information if it adds to the convenience of the users. This redundancy cannot cause inconsistency, as it would in the case of the schema redundancy, since the updates are translated into the terms of the schema updates, before the updates are actually performed.

The usage of userviews also greatly enhances the flexibility of the database. Suppose we have a program that uses a userview, and the concepts of the application world change.

- If the change does not affect the logical decisions of this particular program, then we would like to avoid the need to modify the program.

- So, we will define a new userview to be used by the program.

- The alternative schema of the userview would be identical to the alternative schema of the old userview, so the program would not notice the difference.

- The inference rules would be, of course, different.

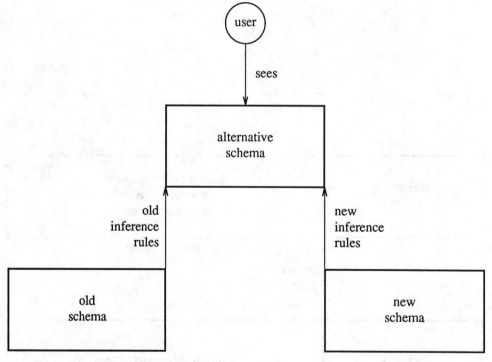

Figure 1-24. A change in the schema does not have to affect some users and programs.

Example:

Suppose we have some programs that use the information of the relation

☐ *works-in* — relation from *INSTRUCTOR* to *DEPARTMENT*
(*m:m*)

Now, the university has become more sophisticated, and for certain future programs it will be important to know the percentage of time that the instructors work for the departments. This new information is irrelevant to most old programs. The new schema will contain the fragment shown in Figure 1-25.

The alternative schema for the unaffected old programs will remain unchanged and will still contain the old relation *WORKS-IN*, but the inference rule of their new userview will be:

If there is a *WORK* whose department is *d* and whose instructor is *i*, then *i WORKS-IN d*.

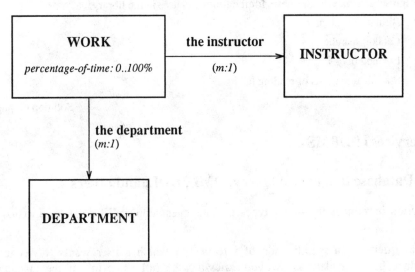

Figure 1-25. A modified schema: a new category *WORK*.

Note :   A *subschema* is a userview whose alternative schema is a part or all of the original schema, and the inference rules are trivial: they copy the information of the alternative schema's concepts.

Problem 1-11.

Use the medical/binary schema (Figure 13-6 on page 395). Define a subschema covering a medical manual. The manual should contain the following information:

1. A catalog of names of known diseases and a catalog of descriptions of known symptoms.

2. For every disease there is a list of its possible symptoms and a probability value is assigned to each such symptom.

Problem 1-12.

1. Design a semantic database schema for a library. The database should cover

    - For every copy of a book: the title, the author, the subject, the publisher, the year of publication, the catalog number of the book, the copy number, and the name, address and phone of the vendor who supplied the book. Additionally, for the books that are currently on loan, the due date and the customer.

    - For every customer: the name, address, phone, and card number.

    - For every employee: the name, address, phone, wage, and social security number.

    - For every late return of a book by a customer: the date and amount of the fine imposed on the customer for the book.

2. Design subschemas or userviews for the following uses in the library:

    a.   Billing of customers

    b.   Catalog searches

    c.   Loaning books

    d.   Statistical analysis of reading habits

Solution on page 396.

1.6. Services of DBMS

1.6.1. Database languages: Query, DML, DDL, and others

This section introduces the major types of languages supported by database management systems.

Retrieval query — a specification of information which a user wants to extract or to deduce from the database without knowing the full extension of the instantaneous database.

> *Example:*
>
> The following is a retrieval query specified in English:
>
> > "What students failed the *Databases* course last year?"
>
> Most DBMSs do not understand English. Thus, a specification in a more

> formal language is needed. Such a formal language need not be a programming language. Most DBMSs support some user-oriented formal language, in which the users can specify queries without writing programs.

Query language — a nonprogramming language in which a user can formulate *retrieval queries* and possibly also update the database. *Nonprogramming* means that the user does not have to specify an algorithm for the problem but only has to define the problem in a formal way.

Some query languages are simple enough to be used by the **end user** — a database user who has no computer knowledge or experience.

Other, more complex, languages are used by computer professionals. Yet, the professional user can save a significant amount of time by using such a nonprogramming language rather than writing a program.

Data manipulation language, DML — a programming language that has a powerful capability of computations, flow of control, input-output, and also has syntactic constructs for database access (the update, retrieval, and dynamic exchange of information between the program and the database). The DML is used by the **application programmer**.

A data manipulation language may be:

1. A **stand-alone DML** — a special-purpose language. In this case, the DBMS provides a compiler or an interpreter for the DML. The disadvantage of the stand-alone language is that it cannot be used for complex programs which perform some database access but also simultaneously perform other tasks, for example, numeric calculation or industrial assembly line monitoring.

2. A **system call interface**. In this case, the user writes a program in a regular programming language. The user performs database access by subroutine calls to the DBMS. In a call, the user provides the system with a description of the user's request, parameters of the request, and output variables in which the system will produce the result of the database access.

Example:

The following is a fragment of a Pascal program with system calls.

```
        ...
    last-name := 'Jefferson'
    dbmscall (
        'Dear DBMS: Please find the instructor whose last name is given in
            the second argument of this call.  Place a reference to that
            instructor into the third argument of this call.  If everything is
            OK, set the fourth argument of this call to 0.  If there are several
            instructors by the given name, set the fourth argument to 1.  If
            there are no such instructors, set it to 2.  If another problem
            occurs, set the fourth argument to a number greater than 2.' (*
            In a real program, of course, a code would be given instead of
            this "short story." *),
        last-name, instructor-reference, return-code);
if (return-code > 0)
    then write (' A DBMS error.')
    else begin
        dbmscall (
            'Dear DBMS: Please relate the instructor, referred to by
                the second argument of this call, by the relation
                BIRTH-YEAR to the number given in the third
                argument.  If everything is OK, set the fourth
                argument of this call to 0.  If a problem occurs, set
                the fourth argument to a number greater than 0.'
                (*Of course, in a real system call, one would
                abbreviate this "short story" by a code*),
            instructor-reference, 1960, return-code);
        if (return-code > 0)
            then write (' A DBMS error.')
    end
```

The system-call interfaces are usually very unfriendly and hard to program in.

The system-calls are interpreted at run-time of the program. One ramification of this is that if a system call contains a syntactically incorrect request, or a request inconsistent with the schema, the user cannot be notified at compile-time but has to wait until the program aborts. Then, the partial effects of the aborted program would have to be undone.

Another ramification is the poor efficiency of the run-time interpretation versus compilation.

3.   **A DML embedded in a host programming language**. This is a database access extension of a general-purpose programming language. In a program, the host language statements are interleaved with DML statements.

Example:

The following is a two-statement fragment of an application program written in an embedded DML language whose host language is Pascal.

    ...

write ('This is a regular Pascal statement which prints this sentence.');

relate: i *WORKS-IN* d (* This is a DML statement *)

The DBMS precompiles the program into a program in the host language without the DML statements. During the precompilation, the DBMS validates the syntax and the compatibility with the schema of the database. The DBMS may also perform optimization of the user's algorithm.

The resulting program is compiled by the host language compiler. When the program runs, it may communicate to the DBMS, but the system calls of this communication are transparent to the user.

Report generator — a language in which the user can specify a query together with requirements on the visual form of the output, such as nicely printed tables with titles, or bottom-of-page summaries.

Data entry language — a language in which the end users can specify database updates online.

Data definition language, **DDL** — a language in which the logical structure of information in the application's world can be defined, together with its pragmatic interpretation for the management of a database, including the schema, integrity constraints, and userviews.

Many DDLs also allow for modification or redefinition of the database structure. This is needed when the concepts of the application world change and when the database designer finds a better description of the existing real-world concepts (particularly during the initial database design process, which is often trial and error).

In many DBMSs, the integrity constraints are specified in languages other than the DDL. In some DBMSs the constraint are incorporated in DML programs.

Many DBMSs do not provide any language at all to express the integrity constraints, other than those expressed in the schema. The other integrity constraints are left as the application programmer's responsibility. In this case, an application programmer should write a DML program which will:

a.   Collect the requests for updates from the users

b.   Check whether these requests would violate the integrity constraints

c.   Reject the requests that would violate the integrity

d.   Submit to the DBMS the remaining good requests

1.6.2. Other services and utilities of DBMS

Most database management systems provide some or all of the following services and utilities.

1.   **Integrity**:

   a.   **Physical integrity** — prevention of a physical corruption of the database, such as placement of incorrect pointers or loss of an index when the power is shut off or the operating system fails.

   b.   **Logical integrity** — enforcement of the integrity constraints.

2.   **Backup** and **recovery**:

   a.   The DBMS keeps backup copies of the database so that when the database is lost, or logically or physically corrupted, it can be restored to a previous state.

   b.   The DBMS keeps a log of the updates it performs in the database so that when the database is restored to an old state, the correct updates kept in the log can be redone to make the new database up to date.

   c.   When an application program is performing a complex update of the database, and the program gets aborted due to a run-time error or violates the integrity of the database or decides that it did not want that update after all, the DBMS can **undo** the update, that is, remove the partial effects of the update.

3.   **Subschemas, userviews, inference rules** — see Section 1.5.

4.   **Security**:

   a.   Prevention of persons who are not authorized database users from accessing the database. (This often involves verification of passwords or a similar procedure.)

   b.   Prevention of persons who are authorized users of a part of the database information from accessing other parts. This control is normally done through subschemas and userviews. A user may be allowed to read and update some information and to only read some other information. More complicated services include the distribution and revocation of information access privileges.

c.   Encryption of the particularly sensitive physical files so that they can not be accessed by bypassing the DBMS.

5.   **Concurrency control**:

Several users and/or programs may access one database simultaneously. Some of the major problems addressed by the concurrency control are:

a.   An incorrect view of the database by one user during a database update being performed by another user.

b.   Inconsistent simultaneous updates being performed by different users.

The logical side (the user's perspective) of these problems is addressed in Section 2.2.2.5.

6.   **Data dictionary**:

The information in the schema can be regarded as a small additional database. This database can be queried by the user.

Example:

A schema query:

What relations have the category *STUDENT* as their domain?

This additional database can also accumulate useful information which is not a proper part of the schema. This may include text explaining the informal meaning of every schema concept.

Example:

A data dictionary explanation entry for the concept 'STUDENT':

STUDENT — "any person who is or was a registered student of the University at any time during the past 15 years, excluding persons who only attended short Extension courses of less than 5 days' duration. 'Registered' means 'paid the minimal registration fee at least once.' Insertion of a new student is initiated by the Office of the Registrar. Removal of a student from the database after the expiration of the 15-year period is performed automatically by the data manipulation program ARCHIVE, which is run every Sunday night. The removal of a student can also be explicitly

> performed by the Office of the Registrar as a correction of an error in inserting that nonstudent."

Some database management systems provide a "data dictionary" which can only assist the DML compiler in validating the program syntax. This is not a proper usage of the term because such a "dictionary" facility is no more than a minimal support of the schema, which is essential in any reasonable database management system.

The update of the data dictionary is normally a responsibility of the **database administrator** — a person who is the technical manager of a database.

7.   **Restructuring**:

When the schema changes, the instantaneous database may become inconsistent with the schema. *Restructuring* is a utility to transfer the old instantaneous database into a new instantaneous database under a new schema.

8.   **Distributed database**:

The database of a large enterprise may be physically partitioned into several subsets which are stored in different geographical sites, such as the branches of the enterprise. In order to avoid the costs and delays of telecommunication, each site physically contains the information which is most frequently used in that site.

Example:

Assume that our University has several campuses. In every campus we would physically store information most frequently used in that campus:

   a.   The departments of that campus

   b.   The instructors who work in those departments

   c.   The students whose majors or minors are among those departments

   d.   The offerings of courses by those instructors

   e.   The enrollments in those offerings

Logically, the users at each site see the whole database (or the fractions thereof which they are authorized to see) regardless of the database's partition. When a user's query or update request necessitates the access to information which is beyond the user's site, the system performs this access in a way transparent to the user.

Example:

Assume that there is a student a at campus c_1 who took some courses offered at another campus, c_2, by instructors of that campus c_2.

Now, an administrator of Campus c_1 submits a query:

'Calculate the grade-point-average of Student s .'

The administrator need not be aware of the physical distribution of the information. During the execution of the query, the DBMS will decide that it needs some information from Campus c_2, contact that campus's computer, and give the user the correct result as if all the data were available locally.

The physical subsets comprising the distributed database do not have to be disjoint.

Example:

a.   The personal information about a student whose major is at one campus and whose minor is at another campus will be stored in both campuses. The enrollments of that student do not have to be duplicated, since enrollments are stored according to the offerings, which, in turn, are stored according to instructors, which are stored by departments.

b.   The information about an instructor who works in Department d_1 of Campus c_1 and also in Department c_2 of Campus c_2 will be stored at both campuses.

c.   The catalog of the names of all the courses can be duplicated at each campus, since it is frequently accessed at each campus.

The possible physical duplication of information introduces one of the major problems of the distributed database management: how to maintain consistency between the copies of information.

One of the other problems is the optimization of the routing of information between the sites during the execution of queries and update requests. Another problem is tolerance for failures: when one site or one communication line goes down, we do not want to shut down the whole system.

Problem 1-13.

A cable TV service needs to gather the following information:

For every cable outlet: the outlet's location (the address and the room); the cable channels which can be viewed at the outlet; the name and the address of the customer.

Additionally, for every customer: the monthly charge.

Design a semantic schema for this application.

Solution on page 398.

Problem 1-14.

1. Design a semantic schema for a bus company. The database should cover the following information:

• The company owns a fleet of buses. For each bus, there is the year the bus was put in service, its license plate number, and the date the next maintenance is due. The buses are classified by their types. Each type has a name and number of seats. (All the buses of one type have the same capacity.)

• The company operates a set of lines. For each line, there is a line-name, line-source, and destination.

• The company schedules on a weekly basis; that is, the schedules of two weeks are identical. In each week, a set of trips is scheduled for each line. The trip goes from the line-source to line-destination. The different scheduled trips of one line differ in their days of the week, their times, their stops, and the types of buses they can use. Each scheduled trip will make several stops at known locations (bus stops) at known times. Thus, the following information is relevant for each scheduled trip:

— The day of the week and time of the departure from the line-source and the day of the week and time of the arrival to the line-destination. No trip can last more than 24 hours, so the arrival day is redundant. (If a trip departs on Monday at 10 a.m. and arrives at 3 p.m., then you know it's same Monday. If it arrives at 8 a.m., then it's Tuesday.)

— The bus types that can be used for the trip.

— The locations and times of the stops. (Note that the list of locations of all the stops served by the company exists independently of particular trips and, thus, should be regarded as a separate abstract category.)

• The company employs drivers and other personnel. For each employee, the name, address, phone, hourly wage, and social security number are relevant. Additionally, for each driver, the expiration date of her or his license, the number of driving violation tickets, and the types of buses he or she is able to drive are recorded.

• The company keeps track of the actual trips performed. The actual trips are instances of the scheduled trips. Since the trips are scheduled on the weekly basis, there are 52 actual trips per year per one scheduled trip. For every actual trip it is known who the driver was and what bus was used.

2. Currently, there is the following instantaneous information. The company owns three buses, maintains four lines, ten stops totally, employs six drivers. (Complete this for a full set of instantaneous information.) Specify (in any formalism you wish) the corresponding binary instantaneous database.

Solution on page 398.

Problem 1-15.

Design a semantic schema for a car dealer. The car dealer is interested in information about the dealership's cars, their makers, models, submodels, specifications (description of all the price-affecting qualities of a car, several cars of the same submodel can share one specification), "extras" (nonstandard equipment appearing in a car specification, such as a stereo system, air-conditioner), colors, prices, deals, customers, selling agents, maker's sales contacts.

Solution on page 400.

Problem 1-16.

Design a semantic schema for the billing matters of a medical clinic.

Solution on page 401.

Problem 1-17.

Design a semantic database schema for a newspaper distribution department, covering the relevant information about customers and deliverers. No financial aspects need to be covered.

We know every customer's:

- Name

- Address

- Deliverer

- Subscription commencing day

- Subscription end day

- Telephone number

Solution on page 402.

Problem 1-18.

Design a semantic schema for an owner of many apartment buildings. The database should contain all of the following information:

- The names of all tenants along with their lease information.

- For each apartment, its size: 1BR, 2BR, and so on.

- Reserved parking information for each tenant. Each apartment building has a small parking lot and spaces are assigned to some apartments.

- Employee information for each building: the manager's name, his or her telephone number, and salary.

You may make reasonable assumptions. The schema should include all graphically representable integrity constraints.

Problem 1-19.

Design a semantic schema for a book store. Your schema should have at least five relations between abstract categories. Specify integrity constraints (not shown in the schema) in English using the terminology of your schema.

Your database should contain for each title ever sold by the store:

- Authors, title, number of pages, bestseller rating
- Price
- Temporary discount price and its end date
- Stock quantity, maximal desirable stock quantity, minimal desirable stock quantity
- Daily sales

(None of the above items *needs* to appear in the schema explicitly, but the information should be derivable.)

Your database should contain additional information that can be used to decide when to change the price of a book.

Problem 1-20.

Design a semantic schema for a department store. Your schema should have at least five relations between abstract categories. Specify integrity constraints (not shown in the schema) in English using the terminology of your schema.

Your database should contain for every product:

> Brand name, manufacturer, supplier, store department, units of size or measure, price, temporary discount price and its end date, stock quantity, maximal desirable stock quantity, minimal desirable stock quantity, employees who have expertise in the product, department manager

Your database should contain additional information that can be used to decide when to change the price of the product.

Problem 1-21.

Design a semantic schema for a kindergarten. Your schema should have at least 10 relations between abstract categories. Specify integrity constraints (not shown in the schema) in English using the terminology of your schema.

Problem 1-22.

Design a semantic schema for a video rental store. The schema should contain 7 to 12 abstract categories (including subcategories), 7 to 12 attributes (relations whose range is a concrete category), and 7 to 15 other relations. Specify as many integrity constraints as are reasonable. Constraints which will not be shown in the schema itself should be specified in English. The schema should contain enough information so that the following query would make sense:

> "For every month, what was the most profitable title?"

1.7. Multimedia Databases

If the DBMS has no implementational restrictions as to the sizes of strings, then the database can store multimedia data as subcategories of the concrete category String. The following are some of such subcategories:

Text — arbitrarily long texts (e.g. the entire text of a book).

Image — digitized color photograph.

Audio — digitized speech or music.

Line-drawing — representation of diagrams, signatures, etc.

Example:

☐ *syllabus* — attribute of *COURSE*, range: *Text* (*m:1*)

☐ *photo* — attribute of *PERSON*, range: *Image* (*m:1*)

☐ *signature* — attribute of *INSTRUCTOR*, range: *Line-drawing* (*m:1*)

☐ *outgoing-message* — attribute of *INSTRUCTOR*, range: *Audio* (*m:1*) (The message to be played by the telephone system when the instructor being called is not available.)

Problem 1-23.

Use the studio/binary schema (Figure 13-2 on page 389). Add the following information to this schema: the scripts, audio, and video of the movies; photographic portraits and voice samples of the actors.

Solution on page 403.

CHAPTER 2

SEMANTIC LANGUAGES

Two abstracted languages, or rather language models for comprehending specific languages, are presented here:

- A fourth-generation structured extension of a structured third-generation programming language (Pascal taken as an example)

- A nonprocedural predicate-calculus language

The languages are defined here for the Semantic Binary Model. Since all the other major database models will be defined as subsets of the Semantic Binary Model, these languages will be used for all the models.

Many languages, similar to one of the two languages studied here, with some syntactic variations, are in use in different database models and different database management systems. The purpose of the presentation here is to delineate the common denominators of the classes of languages, while avoiding the technical details specific to particular systems.

2.1. Notation

The following **syntactic notation** is used in the program fragments and in the definitions of syntactic constructs:

- Language keywords are set in **boldface**.

- The names of the relations and categories from the database are set in *UPPERCASE ITALICS*.

- In syntax description templates, items to be substituted are set in *lowercase italics*.

Example:

- **procedure** — a language keyword

- *LAST-NAME* — a database relation

- *expression* — in a syntax template, substitute for an actual expression, for example, "(7+8*x)"

Gender: the pronoun *he* includes *she* and the pronoun *she* includes *he*.

2.2. Fourth-Generation Programming

2.2.1. Principles

Programming languages which exhibit well-structured flow of control, elaborate typing, and a high degree of machine independence are called **third-generation programming languages**. An example of such a language is *Pascal*. In this section, we shall use the example of Pascal to introduce the principles of *fourth-generation* database manipulation *extensions* of third-generation programming languages.

The essence of the fourth-generation data manipulation languages is the **structured access to the database**. This is contrasted with earlier data manipulation languages, which provided no automatic loops to process bulks of information in the database but only single commands to access one item at a time. As a result, the programmer was left with the responsibility of "navigating" between different data items in the database.

The principal instruction of the language extension to be introduced is the **for** loop, whose body is executed for every object which is present in the instantaneous database (when the program is run) and satisfies conditions given in the **for** statement.

Example:

(* Print the name of every instructor, that is, of every object in the category *INSTRUCTOR*. *)

    for instructor **in** *INSTRUCTOR* **do**

        (* Print the name of the current instructor, that is, of the object referred to by the variable instructor. Separate the current name by a blank ' ' from the name printed in the previous iteration of this loop. *)

write (' ', instructor.*LAST-NAME*)

Example:

(* Print the name of every Computer Science instructor, that is, of every object in the category *INSTRUCTOR* who *WORKS-IN* the department whose name is 'Computer Science'. *)

for department **in** *DEPARTMENT*

where (department *NAME* 'Computer Science')

do

for instructor **in** *INSTRUCTOR*

where (instructor *WORKS-IN* department)

do

(* Print the name of the current instructor, that is, of the object referred to by the variable instructor *)

write (' ', instructor.*LAST-NAME*)

2.2.2. Specification of Extended Pascal

The following is a fourth-generation extension of Pascal for structured access to databases.

2.2.2.1. Data types and parameters

1. **Global parameters** — among the global parameters of a program such as INPUT and OUTPUT, there are the names of the database and of the userview. The database will be accessed through the userview during the execution of the program. The userview will also be accessed during the compilation of the program in order to check for the correct usage of the names of the categories and relations and to correctly interpret the program's commands.

Example:

Let *UNIVERSITY-MASTER-VIEW* be the userview identical to the whole schema. The following may be an Extended Pascal heading for a program using the whole schema of the University database. We assume that the name of the database is *UNIVERSITY-DB*. This name will be used by the DBMS to locate all the files comprising the database.

      program My-program (Input, Output, UNIVERSITY-DB,
                   UNIVERSITY-MASTER-VIEW);

---

2.   **Data type** *ABSTRACT* — a new *basic* data type, in addition to *INTEGER, BOOL, REAL, CHAR*, enumerated types , and *STRING*. (The type *STRING* is not defined in the standard Pascal but is used, sometimes with a different name, in most practical versions of Pascal.)

The variables of type *ABSTRACT* will contain abstract objects. (Practically, these variables will contain logical references to abstract objects. The referencing, however, is transparent to the user.) The variables of this type are called **abstract variables**.

The abstract variables cannot be printed. They cannot receive a value through a *read* instruction. There are no constants of type *ABSTRACT*.

Assignment to the abstract variables can be done from other abstract variables or from the database or by the instruction *create* as discussed later.

In expressions, the only meaningful operation on arguments of type *ABSTRACT* is the test for their equality. The equality test, "=", produces TRUE if the two arguments are one and the same object in the database.

Example:

var jackson: ABSTRACT   (* The abstract variable *jackson* may be used to retrieve from the database a reference to Professor Jackson, that is, to the abstract object of the category *INSTRUCTOR* related by the relation *LAST-NAME* to the string 'Jackson'. *)

2.2.2.2. Extended expressions

There are new operators which can be used in Pascal expressions:

1.   (*expression-of-type-ABSTRACT*   **is a**   *category-from-the-userview*)

This Boolean expression gives TRUE when the left-side subexpression is evaluated into an object which is a member of the category on the right side.

The membership test is done according to the information in the instantaneous database at the run time of the program.

Example:

- (jackson **is a** *STUDENT*)

If the variable *jackson* is uninitialized, then a run-time error results. If this variable contains an abstract object, then the result of the expression is TRUE if that object is a student. If this object is simultaneously a student and an instructor, the result is still TRUE.

---

2.   (*expression   relation-from-the-userview   expression*)

This Boolean expression gives TRUE when the two subexpressions yield objects participating in the relation in the instantaneous database. The types of the subexpressions must be consistent with the relation. For example, if the relation is between abstract objects and real numbers, then the type of the left subexpression must be *ABSTRACT* and the type of the right subexpression must be *REAL*.)

Example:

- (jackson *FIRST-NAME* 'Roberta')
- (jackson *BIRTH-YEAR* 1960)

Instead of one of the subexpressions, the keyword **null** may appear. Then the Boolean expression would give TRUE if the object yielded by the remaining subexpression is related by the relation to *no* object in the instantaneous database.

Example:

- (jackson *WORKS-IN* **null**)

This expression yields TRUE when the person referred to by the variable *jackson* does not work in any department.

> *Example:*
>
> • (jackson *BIRTH-YEAR* **null**)
>
> This expression yields TRUE if, for the person referred to by the variable *jackson*, no birth-year was recorded in the database.

3.   (*expression. functional-relation-from-the-userview*)

Reminder: a functional relation is an m:1 relation. It relates every object of its domain to at most *one* object of its range.

The expression *x.R* produces the object related by the relation R to x; that is, the result is the object y from the instantaneous database such that $(x \; R \; y)$ is TRUE.

If no such object y exists, then a *null* object results, which can cause a subsequent execution-time error.

> *Example:*
>
> • (jackson. BIRTH-YEAR)

> *Example:*
>
> Here is a program fragment to print the age of the person referred to by the variable *jackson*. We assume that the current year is available in the variable *current-year*.
>
>   write (' Professor ', jackson.*FIRST-NAME*, ' ', jackson. *LAST-NAME*, ' is
>   approximately ', (current-year – jackson.*BIRTH-YEAR*), ' years
>   old.')

2.2.2.3. Atomic database manipulation statements

1.   **create new** *abstract-variable* **in** *abstract-category-from-the-userview*

• A new abstract object is *created* in the database

• This object is placed into the specified category (the database is updated to reflect this fact)

• [A reference to] this object is *assigned* to the specified variable

---

Example:

> **var** department: ABSTRACT; ...
>
> **create new** department **in** *DEPARTMENT*

This instruction has two effects:

- A new abstract object is created in the category *DEPARTMENT* in the database.

- A reference to this object is assigned to the variable *department* in the program's memory.

---

2. **categorize**: *expression-of-type-ABSTRACT* **is a** *category*

The expression is evaluated to produce an *existing* instantaneous database object, and this object is inserted into the specified category (in addition to other categories the object may be a member of).

Example:

Let the variable *jackson* refer to an existing instructor Professor Jackson. The following instruction will place Professor Jackson also into the category *STUDENT* (in addition to the category *INSTRUCTOR*).

> **categorize**: jackson **is a** *STUDENT*

This instruction has only one effect: a change in the instantaneous database. It produces no change in the program's working space; that is, it does not change the contents of any variable.

---

3. **decategorize**: *expression-of-type-ABSTRACT* **is no longer a** *category*

The object is removed from the category.

The object is also automatically removed from the subcategories of the category. (Otherwise the database would become inconsistent.)

The object is also automatically removed from the relations whose domains or ranges are categories of which the object is no longer a member. (This automatic removal saves programming effort. This removal is also necessary to maintain the consistency of the database.)

If after the decategorization the object would not belong to any category in the database, then the object is removed from the database.

Example:

decategorize: jackson **is no longer a** *STUDENT*

The person referred to by the variable *jackson* will no longer be a student. She will no longer participate in any relation whose domain or range is the category *STUDENT*. For example, she will be disconnected from her major and minor departments.

Example:

The following instruction removes the object referred to by the variable *jackson* from the database:

decategorize: jackson **is no longer a** *PERSON*

---

4.   **relate**: *expression   relation   expression*

A new fact is added to the database: a relationship between the objects yielded by the two expressions.

Example:

Assuming that the variable *jackson* refers to an instructor whose birth-year was not known until now, the following instruction will set the birth-year:

relate: jackson *BIRTH-YEAR* 1961

Example:

Assuming that the variable *jackson* refers to an instructor who is also a student having a major department, the following instruction will make Jackson *work* in her major department. If she was also working in some other department, she will continue working there too.

relate: jackson *WORKS-IN* jackson.*MAJOR*

---

5.   **unrelate**: *expression   relation   expression*

This has the reverse effect of the instruction **relate**.

Example:

Assuming that the variable *jackson* refers to an instructor whose birth-year has been incorrectly recorded, the following instructions will change the birth-year to 1961:

unrelate: jackson *BIRTH-YEAR* jackson.*BIRTH-YEAR*

(* The expression "jackson.*BIRTH-YEAR*" gives the previously recorded birth-year.*);

relate: jackson *BIRTH-YEAR* 1961

---

6.   *expression.relation* := *expression*

The assignment statement

$$x.R := y$$

means:

- For every z, unrelate $x\ R\ z$
- Then relate $x\ R\ y$.

Example:

Assuming that the variable *jackson* refers to an instructor whose birth-year has not been recorded yet, or has been incorrectly recorded, the following instruction will make the birth-year 1961:

jackson.*BIRTH-YEAR* := 1961

Example:

Assume that the variable *math* refers to the Mathematics department, and the variable *miller* refers to an instructor. What is the effect of the following instruction?

miller.*WORKS-IN* := math

Miller will *only* be working in the Mathematics department.

- If Miller was not working in any department, he will be working in Mathematics.

> - If Miller was working in the Management Science and Physics departments, he is hereby fired from Management Science and Physics, and hired in Mathematics.

2.2.2.4. The for statement

The for statement is the core of fourth-generation programming. This statement creates a structured loop. *Syntax:*

for *variable*   **in** *category*
> **where** *boolean-expression*
> **do** *statement*

Interpretation:

The *statement* after **do**, which may be a compound statement, will be performed once for every object which belongs to the *category* and satisfies the *boolean-expression*.

> *Example:*
>
> Print the last names of all the students born in 1964.
>
> **for** s **in** *STUDENT*
> > **where** s *BIRTH-YEAR* 1964
> > **do** writeln(s.*LAST-NAME*)

> *Example:*
>
> Print the last names of all the students.
>
> > **for** s **in** *STUDENT*
> > > **where true**
> > > **do** writeln(s.*LAST-NAME*)

The **for** statement is *functionally* equivalent to the following algorithm.

> Let *VEC* of length *L* be the vector of all the *category*'s objects in the instantaneous database. The vector is arranged in an arbitrary order, transparent to the user. Then the equivalent algorithm for the **for** statement is:
>
> > **for** i := 1 **to** L **do**
> > > **begin**
> > > *variable* := VEC [i];
> > > **if** *boolean-expression*

> **then** *statement*
> **end**

Abbreviation:

In the **for** statement, the "**in** *category*" part may be omitted. In this case, by default the category is assumed to be a special category *OBJECT*, which is regarded as the union of all the abstract categories in the database. Thus, the body of the loop will be executed for every abstract object (in the instantaneous database) satisfying the condition of the loop. Practically, the condition may explicitly or implicitly restrict the loop to one category.

Example:

Print the last names of all the persons born in 1964.

> **for** s **where** s *BIRTH-YEAR* 1964 **do**
>
> > writeln (s.*LAST-NAME*)

Example:

A larger program fragment:

Who are the persons that taught persons that taught persons that taught persons that taught Mary?

for mary **in** *STUDENT* **where** (mary *FIRST-NAME* 'Mary') **do**

> **for** enrl1 **in** *COURSE-ENROLLMENT* **where** (enrl1 *THE-STUDENT* mary) **do**
>
> > **for** enrl2 **in** *COURSE-ENROLLMENT* **where** (enrl2 *THE-STUDENT* enrl1.*THE-OFFERING.THE-INSTRUCTOR*) **do**
> >
> > > **for** enrl3 **in** *COURSE-ENROLLMENT* **where** (enrl3 *THE-STUDENT* enrl2.*THE-OFFERING.THE-INSTRUCTOR*) **do**
> > >
> > > > **for** enrl4 **in** *COURSE-ENROLLMENT* **where** (enrl4 *THE-STUDENT* enrl3.*THE-OFFERING.THE-INSTRUCTOR*) **do**
> > > >
> > > > > writeln (enrl4.*THE-OFFERING.THE-INSTRUCTOR.LAST-NAME*)

2.2.2.5. Transactions

1.   The **transaction statement**

transaction *compound-statement*

The effects of "**transaction** *S*" are:

a.   While *S* is being executed, the program containing the transaction statement and all the other concurrent programs see the database in its instantaneous state just before *S*.

b.   All the updates are logically performed instantly when *S* is completed, provided the new instantaneous database would not violate the integrity constraints and no error-condition is raised.

Note:

Among the advantages of this statement is the following:

At an intermediate state, the instantaneous information could be incomplete, which could bring failure of an integrity constraint and incorrect comprehension of the database by concurrent programs.

Example:

Assume that the relation *LAST-NAME* is *total*. We wish to create a new person and give her the last name 'Chen'.

The following is a *wrong* program fragment to perform the task:

create new chen in *PERSON*;

chen.*LAST-NAME* := 'Chen'

The above program would violate the integrity of the database when the instruction **create** was performed: there would be a person with no last name, contrary to the totality of the relation *LAST-NAME*. The program would probably be aborted before it reached the assignment statement. To prevent the integrity validation between the two statements, we enclose them in a transaction statement:

transaction begin

create new chen in *PERSON*;

chen.*LAST-NAME* := 'Chen'

end

Also, we would not have to worry that concurrent queries see the database half-updated: a person without a last name.

Example:

The database needs to be changed to pretend that the person referred to by the variable *jackson* is not, nor has ever been, a student. Thus, the object has to be decategorized from *STUDENT*, and all the relevant enrollments have to be erased.

transaction

    begin

        for e **in** *COURSE-ENROLLMENT* **where** (e *THE-STUDENT* jackson) **do**

            decategorize: e **is no longer a** *COURSE-ENROLLMENT*;

        decategorize: jackson **is no longer a** *STUDENT*

    end

A database update statement which is not embedded in a transaction statement is regarded as one transaction.

2. **Error exit**

When the system fails to perform a transaction because of an error, such as a violation of an integrity constraint, it notifies the program by invoking

        procedure Transaction-error-handler (error-description: String)

The body of this procedure can be specified in the program by the user. This allows the programmer to decide what to do in case of error. If the procedure is not defined by the user in the program, then, by default, the system will insert the following specification of the body of this procedure:

    procedure Transaction-error-handler (error-description: String);

        begin

        writeln ('The program was terminated by the default transaction error
            handler when a transaction failed with the following error condition: ',
            error-description);

        stop

        end

Example:

The user can specify the following handler, which prints a message and then allows the program to continue.

> **procedure** Transaction-error-handler (error-description: String);
>
> > **begin**
> >
> > > writeln ('A transaction failed with the following error condition: ', error-description);
> >
> > **end**

2.2.3. A programming example

Example:

The university has decided to expel all the students whose average grade is below 60 (out of 100). To prevent this wrongdoing to computer science students, the department offered a fictitious course, Computer-Pass, by Prof. Good, in which all computer science students are to receive a sufficient grade so as to not to be expelled, if possible.

> The following program fabricates Prof. Good and the Computer-Pass course, enrolls students in this course, grades them accordingly, and prints the names of those computer science students whom this measure cannot help.

program Pass (Input, Output, UNIVERSITY-DB, UNIVERSITY-MASTER-VIEW);

var Computer-Pass-Course, Prof-Good, Good-Offer, comp-science, this-quarter, cs-student, her-enrollment, fictitious-enrollment: *ABSTRACT*;

> desired-grade, number-of-grades, total-of-grades, current-year: *INTEGER*;

begin

(* Get the current year from the standard input file. *)

> read (current-year);

(* Fabricate the course. *)

> **create new** Computer-Pass-Course **in** *COURSE*;
>
> Computer-Pass-Course.*NAME* := 'Computer Pass';

(* Fabricate the instructor. *)

    create new Prof-Good **in** *INSTRUCTOR*;

    Prof-Good.*LAST-NAME* := 'Good';

(* Fabricate the offering. *)

    create new Good-Offer **in** *COURSE-OFFERING*;

    Good-Offer.*THE-COURSE* := Computer-Pass-Course;

    Good-Offer.*THE-INSTRUCTOR* := Prof-Good;

    (* Find the relevant quarter and connect it to the offering Good-Offer. *)

        for this-quarter **in** *QUARTER*

            where (this-quarter.*YEAR* = current-year **and** this-quarter. *SEASON* = 'Winter')

            do Good-Offer.*THE-QUARTER* := this-quarter;

(* The following loop will be performed only once. Inside the body of the loop, the variable *comp-science* will refer to the Computer Science Department. *)

for comp-science **in** *DEPARTMENT*

        where (comp-science *NAME* 'COMPUTER SCIENCE') **do**

begin

(* Make believe that Prof. Good works in Computer Science. *)

    relate: Prof-Good *WORKS-IN* comp-science;

for cs-student **in** *STUDENT*

        where (cs-student *MAJOR* comp-science) **do**

begin (* the current computer science student *)

(* Calculate this student's current statistics: number-of-grades and total-of-grades *)

    number-of-grades := 0;

    total-of-grades := 0;

    for her-enrollment **in** *COURSE-ENROLLMENT*

        where (her-enrollment *THE-STUDENT* cs-student) **do**

        if not (her-enrollment *FINAL-GRADE* **null**) **then**

            begin

number-of-grades := number-of-grades + 1;

total-of-grades := total-of-grades + her-enrollment.*FINAL-GRADE*

end;

(* calculate the minimal desired grade in computer-pass course, by solving the equation $(total + x)/(number + 1) = 60$ *)

desired-grade := 60 * (number-of-grades + 1) — total-of-grades;

if desired-grade > 100 **then**

    (* the student cannot be helped. Print a message *)

        writeln (' The student ', cs-student.*LAST-NAME*, ' cannot be helped. Sorry!')

else if desired-grade ≤ 60 **then**

    (* No need to help. *)

else (* 100 ≥ desired-grade > 60 *)

    transaction begin

        create new fictitious-enrollment **in** *COURSE-ENROLLMENT*;

        fictitious-enrollment.*THE-OFFERING* := Good-Offer;

        fictitious-enrollment.*THE-STUDENT* := cs-student;

        fictitious-enrollment.*FINAL-GRADE* := desired-grade

        end (* transaction *)

    end (* current student *)

  end (* Computer Science Department *)

end.

Problem 2-1.

Use the university/binary reference schema at the end of this book. Write an Extended Pascal program for the following specification. The program reads the standard input file until the end of file. It interprets every line as composed of the last name and first name of a student and a name of the student's proposed major department to be recorded in the database.

If the request cannot be performed, the program prints an error message and proceeds to the next line. The possible errors are: 'student does not exist', 'more than one student exist for the given first and last names', 'department does not exist', 'the student already has a major'.

Problem 2-2.

Use the university/binary reference schema at the end of this book. Write programs or program fragments for the following requirements.

1. Find the first and last names of the persons born in 1967.
2. For every student, list the instructors of the student's major department.
3. What instructors work in every department? (Each relevant instructor shares her time between all the departments.)
4. What instructors taught every student?
5. Who took Prof. Smith's courses?
6. Check whether every student took at least one course.
7. Print a table with two columns, which associates students to their teachers. Only last names have to be printed.
8. Find the number of pairs (instructor, department) where the instructor works in the department.
9. Find the average of grades of student Jane Howard.
10. Print the average of grades for every computer science student (as a table with two columns: the student's name and average).
11. Print the average of all grades given by Prof. Brown.
12. How many students are there in the university?
13. What students have their average grade above 90?
14. When was student Russel born?
15. What courses has Prof. Graham taught?
16. Print the names of the pairs of students who live together.
17. Print the names (last and first), the IDs, the birth-years, the major and minor departments, and the addresses of all computer science students.
18. What is the average grade in the *Databases* course?
19. List the distinct addresses of the students. (Do not list the same address twice.)
20. How many departments have minor students?
21. Find the names of the students who took at least one course.

Problem 2-3.

Use the university/binary reference schema at the end of this book. Write an extended Pascal program to:

1. Remove the student Jack Johnson, born in 1960, from the university database. (Do not forget to remove from the database all the information which will become meaningless when Mr. Johnson is removed.)

2. Print the average number of courses taken last quarter by computer science majors.

Problem 2-4.

Use the university/binary reference schema at the end of this book. Write an Extended Pascal program to normalize the grades of every course offering. (Consistently change the grades so that the average grade would be 75/100.) Computer science majors should be excluded from the normalization. (Their grades will neither be normalized nor will affect normalization of grades of other students.) The students who have not yet received a grade in a course offering should be, of course, excluded from the normalization of that offering.

Problem 2-5.

Use the medical/binary schema (Figure 13-6 on page 395). An illness is *probable* if, when the illness commenced, the patient had all the symptoms he is expected to have with probability of 0.9 at least. Write an extended Pascal program to find out what percentage of the illnesses diagnosed by Dr. Jack Smith are *probable* .

Problem 2-6.

Use the medical/binary schema (Figure 13-6 on page 395). Write an extended Pascal program to remove from the database the patients who have not been sick for the last 30 years.

2.3. Logic as a Nonprocedural Language

2.3.1. Principles

Nonprocedural language — a language in which the user specifies *what* is to be done without specifying *how* it is to be done.

Example:

In a nonprocedural language, the user might say:

　　"Let no student be enrolled twice in the same offering of a course"

The user would probably use a more precise and formal statement, which still would be nonprocedural:

　　"If enrl1 is an enrollment, and enrl2 is an enrollment, and
　　enrl1.*THE-STUDENT* = enrl2.*THE-STUDENT*, and
　　enrl1.*THE-OFFERING* = enrl2.*THE-OFFERING*,
　　then enrl1 = enrl2."

This statement contains no indication as to how the constraint is to be enforced: this is left to the system. The system might enforce the constraint as follows:

Whenever a transaction like

　　transaction begin · · ·

　　　　create new enrl **in** *COURSE-ENROLLMENT*;

　　　　enrl.*THE-STUDENT* := s;

　　　　enrl.*THE-OFFERING* := of;

　　　　· · ·

　　　　end

is being completed, perform automatically the following:

　　(* If there is another enrollment with the same student and offering, then

---

give an error message and stop. *)

for other-enrl **in** *COURSE-ENROLLMENT*

    where (other-enrl.*THE-STUDENT* = s **and** other-enrl.*THE-OFFERING* = of)

do begin

    writeln (' In violation of an integrity constraint, the program has attempted to generate a duplicate enrollment'); **stop**

end

Example:

In a nonprocedural language, the user might request the following information:

    "What instructors give the grade 100 (sometimes)?"

The user would probably use a more precise and formal statement, which still would be nonprocedural:

    "Get instructor.*LAST-NAME* where
    exists enrollment such that
    enrollment.*THE-OFFERING.THE-INSTRUCTOR* = instructor and
    enrollment.*FINAL-GRADE* = 100"

The statement would contain no indication as to *how* this query is to be performed: this is left to the system. The system might use the following algorithm:

for instructor **in** *INSTRUCTOR*

    do begin

        ok := false

        for enrl **in** *COURSE-ENROLLMENT*

            where (enrl.*THE-OFFERING.THE-INSTRUCTOR*
            = instructor **and**

                enrl *FINAL-GRADE* 100)

            do ok := true

        if ok **then** write (' ', instructor.*LAST-NAME*)

    end

Many nonprocedural database languages are based on Predicate Calculus, borrowed from Mathematical Logic. The language of Predicate Calculus will be defined in the following subsection.

Uses: nonprocedural specification of queries, integrity constraints, inference of userviews, and update transactions.

Predicate Calculus is based on Boolean expressions involving variables.

Example:

- instructor.*LAST-NAME* = 'Einstein'
- d *NAME* 'Geology'
- student.*BIRTH-YEAR* > 1970 **or** student.*BIRTH-YEAR* = 1960

Such Boolean expressions can be used to specify queries similarly to the specification of sets in mathematics:

- A set of objects is found which make a Boolean expression to be true.
- These objects or their functions are displayed.

Example:

A query to find the names of the persons born in 1967:

    get person.*LAST-NAME*

        where (person.*BIRTH-YEAR* = 1967)

A query can display several columns of output, in a table form.

Example:

A query to find the first and last names of the persons born in 1967:

    get person.*FIRST-NAME*, person.*LAST-NAME*

        where (person.*BIRTH-YEAR* = 1967)

Several different objects, referred to by different variables, may be used in one row of the output tables.

Example:

For every student, list the instructors of the student's major department.

> **get** student.*FIRST-NAME*, student.*LAST-NAME*, instructor.*FIRST-NAME*,
> instructor.*LAST-NAME*
>
> **where**
>
> > (instructor
> >
> > *WORKS-IN*
> >
> > student.*MAJOR*)

Very powerful constructs of Predicate Calculus are the *quantifiers* **for every** and **exists**. They are used to form nontrivial Boolean expressions.

Example:

What instructors work in every department? (Each relevant instructor shares her time between all the departments.)

get instructor.*LAST-NAME* **where**

> (**for every** d **in** *DEPARTMENT*:
>
> > instructor *WORKS-IN* d)

Example:

What instructors taught every student?

get instructor.*LAST-NAME* **where**

> (**for every** s **in** *STUDENT*:
>
> > **exists** enrl **in** *COURSE-ENROLLMENT*:
> >
> > > ((enrl *THE-STUDENT* s) **and**
> > >
> > > (enrl.*THE-OFFERING. THE-INSTRUCTOR* = instructor)))

2.3.2. First-order predicate calculus expressions

The First-order Predicate Calculus is well-known to those who have studied some Mathematical Logic. This calculus can be applied to databases, if we regard the instantaneous database as a finite structure with binary relations, unary relations (categories), and functions (functional relations). This text, however, does not require a prior knowledge of Predicate Calculus.

Expression — a combination of *constants, variables, operators*, and parentheses. The syntax and semantics are given below.

An expression may depend on some variables. When the variables are interpreted as some fixed objects, the expression can be evaluated with respect to a given instantaneous database and will yield an abstract or concrete object. The following are syntactic forms of expressions:

1. *constant*

     a.   *number*

     b.   *character-string* (in quotes)

     c.   *Boolean value* (TRUE and FALSE)

> *Example:*
>
> 7, 16.5, 'Mary', '87/05/31', TRUE

2. *variable*

A variable is a sequence of letters, digits, and hyphens. The first character must be a letter.

3. (*expression*)

Parentheses in expressions may be omitted when no ambiguity results.

4. (*expression*   *basic-binary-operator*   *expression*)

The basic binary operators are: $+, -, *, /, >, <, \geq, \leq, =, \neq,$ **and, or**.

Each operator may be used only when the expressions yield values of types appropriate for the operator. The only basic binary operators defined for abstract objects are $=$ and $\neq$, which produce TRUE or FALSE as results.

Example:

- $5 + 6 * 7$

- $x \neq y$

- (‘Abc’ > ‘Bcc’) **or** $(1 + 2 > 2)$

---

5. (**if** *expression* **then** *expression*)

Both component expressions must yield Boolean values. When the right expression yields TRUE, the result is TRUE regardless of the left expression. When the left expression yields TRUE and the right expression yields FALSE, the result is FALSE. When the left expression yields FALSE, the result is TRUE regardless of the right expression.

Example:

The following expressions are TRUE:

- **if** 1=1 **then** 2=2

- **if** 1=3 **then** 2=2

- **if** 1=3 **then** 2=4

The following is FALSE:

- **if** 1=1 **then** 2=4

Note:

   if e_1 **then** e_2

is equivalent to

   (**not** e_1) **or** e_2

6. (*expression   relation   expression*)

The *relation* is a relation from the userview. The result is TRUE if the two objects are related by the *relation* in the instantaneous database.

Example:

(x *BIRTH-YEAR* 1960)

The value of this Boolean expression depends on the variable *x*.

---

7.   (*basic-unary-operator   expression*)

The basic unary operators are: –, **not**.

> *Example:*
>
> (**not** (1>1)) = TRUE

8.   (*expression* **is a** *category*)

This Boolean expression yields TRUE when the object is in the *category* in the instantaneous database.

> *Example:*
>
> x **is a** *STUDENT*

9.   (*expression* . *functional-relation*)

x.R is the object related by the relation *R* to *x*; it is the object *y* from the instantaneous database such that (*x R y*) gives *true*. Such an expression is called **dot-application**.

> *Example:*
>
> • x.*BIRTH-YEAR*
>
> • e.*THE-OFFERING.THE-INSTRUCTOR.LAST-NAME*

The dot-application is well-defined only for total functional relations. The case of nontotal functional relations will be discussed later.

10.   (**exists** *variable* **in** *category* : *expression*)

The ':' may be pronounced 'so that the following is true:'.

The contained *expression* must be Boolean.

The result is also Boolean.

It is TRUE when there exists at least one object in the category which satisfies the Boolean *expression*.

The *expression* usually depends on the *variable* but may also depend on additional variables. The resulting expression no longer depends on the *variable*.

Interpretation:

> Let $a_1, a_2, \ldots, a_n$ be all the objects in the *category* in the instantaneous database.

Let $e_1, e_2, \ldots, e_n$ be obtained from the *expression* by substituting each of a_1, $a_2, \ldots, a_n$ for all the occurrences of the *variable* in the *expression*.

Then

      exists variable **in** *category* : *expression*

is equivalent to

      e_1 **or** e_2 **or** $\cdots$ **or** e_n

Example:

(**exists** x **in** *INSTRUCTOR* :

    x.*BIRTH-YEAR* = 1960)

This expression is TRUE if there is at least one instructor who was born in 1960. The whole expression does not depend on the variable x, although its subexpression "x.*BIRTH-YEAR* = 1960" does depend on this variable.

Example:

(**exists** x **in** *INSTRUCTOR* :

    x.*BIRTH-YEAR* = y)

This is TRUE if there is at least one instructor who was born in the year y. The whole expression depends only on the variable y.

The keyword **exists** is often called the **existential quantifier**. It may be abbreviated by the symbol $\exists$.

11. (**for every** *variable* **in** *category* : *expression*)

The ':' is pronounced 'the following is true:'.

The *expression* must be Boolean. The result is also Boolean. It is TRUE when all the objects of the *category* satisfy the Boolean *expression*. The *expression* usually depends on the *variable* and may also depend on additional variables. The resulting expression no longer depends on the *variable*.

Interpretation:

Let $a_1, a_2, \ldots, a_n$ be all the objects in the *category* in the instantaneous database.

Let $e_1, e_2, \ldots, e_n$ be obtained from the *expression* by substituting each of a_1, $a_2, \ldots, a_n$ for all the occurrences of the *variable* in the *expression*.

Then

> **for every** variable **in** *category* : *expression*

is equivalent to

> e_1 **and** e_2 **and** $\cdots$ **and** e_n

Example:

(**for every** x **in** *INSTRUCTOR* :

     x.*BIRTH-YEAR* = 1960)

This expression is TRUE if all the instructors were born in 1960.

Notice that the result is TRUE even if there are no instructors at all in the instantaneous database. (Isn't it true that every *presently living* dinosaur knows Predicate Calculus or that every American monarch is a republican?)

The whole expression does not depend on the variable *x*, although its subexpression "x.*BIRTH-YEAR* = 1960" does depend on this variable.

Example:

(**for every** x **in** *INSTRUCTOR* :

     x.*BIRTH-YEAR* = y)

This is TRUE if all the instructors were born in the year *y*. The whole expression depends only on the variable *y*.

The keyword **for every** is often called the **universal quantifier**. It may be abbreviated by the symbol $\forall$.

Note:

> **for every** *variable* **in** *category* : *expression*

is equivalent to

> **not** (**exists** *variable* **in** *category* : **not** *expression*)

Usage of variables:

The variable after a quantifier in a subexpression should not be used outside that subexpression. Although many versions of Predicate Calculus do not have this requirement, it does not decrease the power of the calculus but improves readability, prevents some typical errors in query specification, and simplifies the semantics.

> *Example:*
>
> WRONG:
>
>> (**exists x in** *PERSON*: x **is a** *STUDENT*) **and** (x *BIRTH-YEAR* 1970)
>
> Here, *x* appears in the quantifier of the left subexpression but also appears in the right subexpression. Logically, these are two distinct variables, and they should not be called by the same name x.

To use the expressions correctly, we shall need to know what variables are *quantified* in an expression and on what variables an expression depends.

Quantified variable — variable *v* is quantified in expression *e* if *v* has an appearance in *e* immediately after a quantifier.

> *Example:*
>
> The variable *v* is quantified in:
>
>> ((z > 0) **or** (**exists v in** *STUDENT*: v **is an** *INSTRUCTOR*))

Expression *e* **depends on** variable *v* if *v* appears in *e* and is not quantified.

> *Example:*
>
> The following expression depends on *z* and *x* but not on *y*.
>
>> ((z > 0) **or** (**exists y in** *STUDENT*: x = y.*BIRTH-YEAR*))

Notation: When an expression *e* depending on variables $x_1, x_2, \ldots, x_k$ is referred to (not in the actual syntax of the language), it may be denoted as

$$e(x_1, x_2, \ldots, x_k)$$

> *Example:*
>
> The expression of the previous example may be referred to as *e(z,x)*.

(In many texts, a variable on which an expression depends is called a **free variable** in that expression. An expression which depends on no variables is called a **closed expression**.)

Condition on variables $x_1, x_2, \ldots, x_k$ — a Boolean expression which depends on $x_1, x_2, \ldots, x_k$.

> *Example:*
>
> (x+y>3) is a condition on x and y.

Assertion — a Boolean expression which does not depend on any variable; that is, every variable is restricted by a quantifier.

Interpretation: For a given instantaneous database, the assertion produces TRUE or FALSE.

> *Example:*
>
> Assertion that every student took at least one course in 1990:
>
> **for every** st **in** *STUDENT*:
>   **exists** enrl **in** *COURSE-ENROLLMENT*:
>   ((enrl *THE-STUDENT* st) **and**
>   (enrl.*THE-OFFERING. THE-QUARTER. THE-YEAR*=1990))

Dot-application of nontotal functional relations

If f is not total, then $e.f$ may be ambiguous. The concerned user might wish to avoid such expressions. However, a smart DBMS may be able to follow the user's intuition in using such expressions. This is discussed further in Section 2.3.6.

2.3.3. Queries

Specification of a query to retrieve a table, that is, a set of rows of values:

   get *expression, . . . ,* expression

   where

      (*condition-on-the-variables-on-which-the-expressions-depend*)

Interpretation of the query   **get** $e_1, . . . , e_n$ **where** $(\phi(x_1, . . . , x_k))$

- The variables $x_1, . . . , x_k$ are assigned all the possible tuples of objects which objects are in the current instantaneous database and which make the assertion $\phi(x_1, . . . , x_n)$ evaluate to TRUE.

- The expressions $e_1, . . . , e_n$ are evaluated for the above selected tuples and the corresponding results are output. (The output is not printable if any of the expressions produces an abstract object.)

Example:

Who took Prof. Smith's courses?

get student.*LAST-NAME* **where**
  exists enrl **in** *COURSE-ENROLLMENT*:
    (enrl.*THE-STUDENT*=student **and**
    enrl.*THE-OFFERING. THE-INSTRUCTOR. LAST-NAME*='Smith')

Abbreviation:

The following abbreviation is used in some literature for the query syntax. It is akin to the mathematical notation for sets.

$$\{e_1, \ldots, e_n \,|\, \phi(x_1, \ldots, x_k)\}$$

Abbreviation:

Queries which output only one value may be specified without the "**where** *condition*" part, as:

$$\textbf{get } \textit{expression}$$

(provided the *expression* depends on no variables).

Example:

The following is a yes-or-no query which displays TRUE if every student took at least one course.

get

   (**for every** s **in** *STUDENT*:

      exists enrl **in** *COURSE-ENROLLMENT*:

         s=enrl.*THE-STUDENT*)

Headings of output columns:

The columns in a table which is an output of *get* can be labeled:

   get *heading*$_1$: e_1, . . . , *heading*$_n$: e_n **where** *condition*

Example:

Print a table with two columns, which associates students with their teachers. Only last names are printed.

> **get** Teacher: instructor.*LAST-NAME*, Student-taught: student.*LAST-NAME* **where**
>
> **exists** enrl **in** *COURSE-ENROLLMENT*:
>
> > enrl.*THE-STUDENT* = student **and**
> >
> > enrl.*THE-OFFER. THE-INSTRUCTOR* = instructor

When no heading for e_i is specified, then, by default, the following heading is assumed:

- If e_i ends in ".*relation*", then the heading is the *relation*.
- Otherwise the heading is the number i.

Example:

The query

> **get** x.*LAST-NAME*, x.*BIRTH-YEAR*
>
> **where** x **is a** *STUDENT*

produces a table with two columns, whose headings are:

> *LAST-NAME, BIRTH-YEAR*

2.3.4. Integrity constraints in Logic

Specification of static integrity constraints — by assertions.

Example:

No student may be enrolled twice in the very same offering of a course.

for every enrl **in** *COURSE-ENROLLMENT*:

> **for every** enrl2 **in** *COURSE-ENROLLMENT*:
>
> > **if** enrl.*THE-STUDENT*=enrl2.*THE-STUDENT* **and**

> enrl.*THE-OFFERING*=enrl2.*THE-OFFERING*
>
> **then** enrl=enrl2

Specification of dynamic integrity constraints:

A *dynamic* integrity constraint is syntaxed as a static integrity constraint, but categories and relations may be suffixed with *-old* to denote the concepts of the previous state of the database.

> *Example:*
>
> The Student Council has secured that from 1991 once a grade has been reported (and thus, probably has been made known to the student) it may not be retroactively decreased.
>
> **for every** enrl **in** *COURSE-ENROLLMENT*:
> **if** enrl.*FINAL-GRADE-old*>enrl.*FINAL-GRADE* **then**
> enrl.*THE-OFFERING.THE-QUARTER.THE-YEAR*<1991

Dynamic integrity constraints are rarely dictated by the logic of a user's world, since their existence may cause irreversibility of some users' errors.

> *Example:*
>
> In the previous example, a data-entry clerk who erroneously enters the grade of 80 instead of the correct grade of 70 may not be able to correct the typo.

2.3.5. *Extensions of Logic: aggregates, userviews, transactions, query forms

This is an advanced section.

2.3.5.1. *Aggregate operations: sum, count, average

Defined here is a second-order extension to enable set operations, such as summation, counting, etc. This is done by extending the syntax of *expression* with the **summation quantifier**:

$$\sum_{\substack{variables \\ \textbf{where} \\ condition}} expression_1$$

Example:

The sum of the birth-years of all students =

$$\sum_{s} s.BIRTH\text{-}YEAR$$
$$\textbf{where}$$
$$s \textbf{ is a } STUDENT$$

Example:

The number of pairs (instructor, department) where the instructor works in the department.

$$\sum_{instructor, department} 1$$
$$\textbf{where}$$
$$instructor\ WORKS\text{-}IN\ department$$

(In the above formula, 1 is a constant function. Thus, for example, $\sum_{i=1}^{5} 1$ equals 5. Adding up the constant 1 is thus the same as counting the object pairs satisfying the condition under the sum.)

The *variables* under Σ are quantified by the summation symbol. In addition to these *variables*, the *condition* and/or the *expression*$_1$ may depend on other variables.

Example:

The sum of the grades of student s. The sum depends on the variable s, meaning s remains free in the sum.

$$\sum_{enrl} enrl.FINAL\text{-}GRADE$$
$$\textbf{where}$$
$$enrl \textbf{ is a } COURSE\text{-}ENROLLMENT \textbf{ and}$$
$$\textbf{not } (enrl\ FINAL\text{-}GRADE \textbf{ null}) \textbf{ and}$$
$$enrl\ THE\text{-}STUDENT\ s$$

Interpretation:

Let e be an expression, and let $\phi(x_1, \ldots, x_n, y_1, \ldots, y_k)$ be a condition. Then the following is also an expression (it depends on the variables $y_1, \ldots, y_k$):

$$\sum_{x_1, \ldots, x_n} (\quad e(x_1, \ldots, x_n, y_1, \ldots, y_k))$$
$$\textbf{where}$$
$$\phi(x_1, \ldots, x_n, y_1, \ldots, y_k)$$

When all the parameter-variables $y_1, \ldots, y_k$ are interpreted as some fixed objects, the **sum** yields a number. This number is the result of summation of the values of e computed for every tuple of objects $x_1, \ldots, x_n$ satisfying $\phi(x_1, \ldots, x_n, y_1, \ldots, y_k)$.

The Σ acts like a quantifier for $x_1, \ldots, x_n$. Therefore, although the subexpression e does depend on $x_1, \ldots, x_n$, the whole Σ expression does not. The variables $y_1, \ldots, y_n$ remain unquantified.

Alternative (linear) notation (we would not use the two-dimensional notation of Σ in a real computer language):

$$\textbf{sum } e$$
$$\textbf{for } x_1, \ldots, x_n$$
$$\textbf{where } \phi(x_1, \ldots, x_n, y_1, \ldots, y_k)$$

Abbreviation:

When $x_1, \ldots, x_n$ are exactly the variables on which the expression e depends (that is, all x_i and none of y_i appear free in the expression e), the **for** clause may be omitted:

$$\textbf{sum } e \textbf{ where } \phi(x_1, \ldots, x_n, y_1, \ldots, y_k)$$

Example:

For every information systems student, print his last name and the sum of his grades.

> **get**
>
> > student.*LAST-NAME*,
> >
> > (**sum** enrollment.*FINAL-GRADE*
> >
> > > **where** enrollment *THE-STUDENT* student)
>
> **where**
>
> > student **is a** *STUDENT* **and**
> >
> > (student.*MAJOR DEPARTMENT-NAME* 'Information
> > Systems')

Example:

Print the sum of all the grades given by Prof. Smith. This query outputs only one value (the sum). There is no "**where** *condition*" for the "**get**" of the query.

get (**sum** enrollment.*FINAL-GRADE*
     where
        'Smith'=enrollment.*THE-OFFERING.*
            THE-INSTRUCTOR.LAST-NAME)

Abbreviation for **count**:

$$\text{count } x_1, \ldots, x_n \text{ where } \phi(x_1, \ldots, x_n, y_1, \ldots, y_k)$$

stands for:

$$\textbf{sum } 1 \textbf{ for } x_1, \ldots, x_n \textbf{ where } \phi(x_1, \ldots, x_n, y_1, \ldots, y_k).$$

Example:

How many students are there in the university?
  get (**count** std **where** std **is a** *STUDENT*)

Abbreviation for **average**:

$$\textbf{average } e \ldots$$

stands for:

$$(\textbf{sum } e \ldots) / (\textbf{count } e \ldots)$$

Example:

What students have their average grade below 60?

    get std.*LAST-NAME*
      where std **is a** *STUDENT* **and**
           60 > (**average** enrl.*FINAL-GRADE*
                  where enrl *THE-STUDENT* std)

Note: this query could *not* be formulated as follows, since only the distinct grades would be then taken into account:

    get std.*LAST-NAME*
      where 60 >
        average fgrade
          where

> **exists** enrl **in** *ENROLLMENT*:
>   (enrl *FINAL-GRADE* fgrade **and**
>   enrl *THE-STUDENT* std)
>
> If a student has three enrollments with grades 100, 50, and 100, then the average calculated in the first version would be 250/3=83 (correct), and in the second version 150/2=75 (incorrect).

2.3.5.2. *Shorthand notation for n-ary relationships

> *Example:*
>
> Often we need to specify a condition like:
>
>   The instructor i offered course c in quarter q.
>
> In calculus this can be stated as:
>
>   **exists** offer **in** *COURSE-OFFERING*:
>
>   offer *THE-INSTRUCTOR* i **and**
>
>   offer *THE-COURSE* c **and**
>
>   offer *THE-QUARTER* q
>
> The above statement can be written in a shorthand notation as:
>
>   *COURSE-OFFERING*
>
>   (*THE-INSTRUCTOR*: i,
>
>   *THE-COURSE*: c,
>
>   *THE-QUARTER*: q)

Abbreviation:

   $category\ (relation_1\colon expression_1\, ,\ldots,\ relation_k\colon expression_k)$

stands for

   exists x **in** *category*:
   (x *relation*$_1$ *expression*$_1$ **and** $\cdots$ **and** x *relation*$_k$ *expression*$_k$)

Example:

Print the names of the courses taught by Prof. McFarland.

get c.*NAME*

where

    exists i in *INSTRUCTOR*:
            i *LAST-NAME* 'McFarland' **and**

        COURSE-OFFERING (*THE-INSTRUCTOR*: i, *THE-COURSE*: c)

2.3.5.3. *Inference rules of userviews

Reminder:

A userview consists of an alternative schema and inference rules. The inference rules specify the categories and relations of the alternative schema in terms of the categories and relations of the original schema.

Specification of an inferred relation

      userview relation: *expression*$_1$ *new-relation* *expression*$_2$
      where *condition*

Example:

The following is a specification of an inferred relation *TAUGHT* (between instructors and students) in terms of the relations existing in the schema.

    userview relation: instructor *TAUGHT* student

    where

      exists enrl **in** *COURSE-ENROLLMENT*:

        enrl.*THE-STUDENT* = student **and**

        enrl.*THE-OFFER. THE-INSTRUCTOR* = instructor

Example:

The following is a specification of an inferred relation

    □ *average-grade* — attribute of *STUDENT*, range: *0..100* (*m:1*)

userview relation: student *AVERAGE-GRADE*

      (**average** e.*FINAL-GRADE*

> **where**
>
> > e **is a** *COURSE-ENROLLMENT* **and**
> >
> > e *THE-STUDENT* student)
>
> **where** student is a *STUDENT*

Specification of an inferred abstract category

Usually, but not always, an inferred abstract category is a new subcategory of an existing category. Its purpose is usually to restrict the userview user to a subset of objects which are relevant to that user's task. An inferred category can be specified as a set of objects which is derived from the categories and relations of the database. The specification is:

> **userview subcategory**: *expression* **is a** *new-subcategory*
> **where** *condition*

> *Example:*
>
> **userview subcategory**: s **is a** *COMPUTER-SCIENCE-MAJOR*
>
> > **where**
> >
> > > s **is a** *STUDENT* **and**
> > >
> > > s.*MAJOR   NAME*   'Computer Science'

Specification of representation of relationships by a category

The definition is preceded by an example.

> *Example:*
>
> We wish to have (in the userview) a category of events of work of instructors in departments:
>
> > ☐ *WORK* — category
> >
> > ☐ *the-department* — relation from *WORK* to *DEPARTMENT*   (*m:1*)
> >
> > ☐ *the-instructor* — relation from *WORK* to *INSTRUCTOR*   (*m:1*)
>
> The user of the user-view will perceive the category *WORK* as containing objects (events) which are distinct from any other objects in the database. These new objects will be perceived only through the userview, without actually existing in the database. Thus, they are *virtual* objects.

This is done by specifying a category of virtual objects with relationships to existing objects. The syntax is:

> **userview category**:
> *new-category* (*relation*$_1$: *expression*$_1$, . . . , *relation*$_k$: *expression*$_k$)
> **where** *condition*

Let $x_1, . . . ,x_n$ be the variables on which the *condition* and the *expressions* depend. (They must depend on the same variables.) For every tuple of values of variables satisfying the *condition*, one new virtual object is created. That object is related by the new relations *relation*$_1$, . . . , *relation*$_k$ to the values of the expressions *expression*$_1$, . . . , *expression*$_k$.

Example:

The following is a specification of an inferred category *WORK* and two inferred relations, *THE-DEPARTMENT* and *THE-INSTRUCTOR*, whose domain is *WORK*. The specification is in terms of the the relations existing in the schema.

userview category:

WORK (*THE-DEPARTMENT*: department, *THE-INSTRUCTOR*:
   instructor)

where instructor *WORKS-IN* department

2.3.5.4. *Transactions

This section extends Predicate Calculus to allow specification of transactions — creation of sets of objects, categorization and decategorization of objects, relating and unrelating objects, and so on.

The operations in Calculus are usually not atomic but work on sets of objects. One single operation can create a *set* of new objects, place them in categories, and relate them to different existing objects by *several* relations.

Creation of new abstract objects and relating them to existing or concrete objects:

> **insert into** *category*
> (*relation*$_1$: *expression*$_1$, . . . , *relation*$_k$: *expression*$_k$)
> **where** *condition*

- If no *where* clause is specified, then only one new abstract object is created. This object is put into the *category* and related by the relations to the values of the expressions.

> *Example:*
>
> Create a new department named 'Computer Engineering'
>
> **insert into** *DEPARTMENT* (*NAME*: 'Computer Engineering')

- Some of the names of the relations may be identical. This allows one object to be related to several objects by one relation (m:m or 1:m).

> *Example:*
>
> Create a new department named 'Computer Engineering' and 'CE'.
>
> **insert into** *DEPARTMENT* (*NAME*: 'Computer Engineering', *NAME*: 'CE')

- If a *where* clause is specified with a *condition* on variables $x_1, \ldots, x_n$, then for every tuple of values of the variables satisfying the *condition*, one new object is created and related accordingly.

> *Example:*
>
> Enroll the computer science student Jack Johnson into the *Databases* course given by Prof. Smith in Fall 1990.
>
> **insert into** *COURSE-ENROLLMENT* (*THE-STUDENT*: *s*, *THE-OFFERING*: offer) **where**
>
>   *s.MAJOR NAME* 'Computer Science' **and**
>
>   *s.LAST-NAME*='Johnson' **and**
>
>   *s.FIRST-NAME*='Jack' **and**
>
>   offer.*THE-QUARTER.YEAR*=1990 **and**
>
>   offer.*THE-QUARTER.SEASON*='Fall' **and**
>
>   offer.*THE-COURSE.NAME*='Databases' **and**
>
>   offer.*THE-INSTRUCTOR.LAST-NAME*='Smith'

- The variables on which the *condition* depends must be those on which the *expressions* depend.

> *Example:*
>
> Enroll all computer science students into the *Databases* course given by Prof. Smith in Fall 1990.
>
> **insert into** *COURSE-ENROLLMENT (THE-STUDENT: s, THE-OFFERING:* offer)
>
> **where**
>
>   s.*MAJOR NAME* 'Computer Science' **and**
>
>   offer.*THE-QUARTER.YEAR*=1990 **and**
>
>   offer.*THE-QUARTER.SEASON*='Fall' **and**
>
>   offer.*THE-COURSE.NAME*='Databases' **and**
>
>   offer.*THE-INSTRUCTOR.LAST-NAME*='Smith'

- When the *insert* statement calls for an insertion of a new object while there is already an object having the same relationships as those of the new object, the new object is not inserted.

> *Example:*
>
> If the department named 'Management' already exists, then the following command produces no effect:
>
>   **insert into** *DEPARTMENT (NAME*: 'Management')

Connection between existing abstract objects, between existing abstract objects and concrete objects, between existing abstract objects and categories:

$$\textbf{connect } fact_1, \dots, fact_k \ [\textbf{where } condition \ ]$$

Each *fact$_i$* is either

$$expression_i \ \ category_i$$

or

$$expression_i \ \ relation_i \ \ expression'_i$$

Interpretation:

- If no *where* clause is specified, the values of the expressions are related by the *relations* and/or categorized by the categories.

- If a *where* clause is specified with a condition ϕ on variables $x_1, \dots, x_n$, then for every tuple of values of the variables satisfying ϕ the values of the expressions are related and categorized as above.

- The variables on which the condition ϕ depends must be those on which the expressions depend.

Example:

Let 'CS' be an alternative name for the department named 'Computer Science'.

    connect dept *NAME* 'CS'

    where

        dept **is a** *DEPARTMENT* **and**

        dept *NAME* 'Computer Science'

Example:

Give the grade 100 to the computer science student Jack Johnson enrolled in the *Databases* course given by Prof. Smith in Fall 1990.

    connect enrl *FINAL-GRADE* 100

    where

        enrl.*THE-STUDENT.MAJOR NAME* 'Computer Science' **and**

        enrl.*THE-STUDENT.LAST-NAME*='Johnson' **and**

        enrl.*THE-STUDENT.FIRST-NAME*='Jack' **and**

        enrl.*THE-OFFERING.THE-QUARTER.YEAR*=1990 **and**

        enrl.*THE-OFFERING.THE-QUARTER.SEASON*='Fall' **and**

        enrl.*THE-OFFERING.THE-COURSE.NAME*='Databases' **and**

        enrl.*THE-OFFERING.THE-INSTRUCTOR.LAST-NAME*='Smith'

Example:

Give the grade 100 to all computer science students enrolled in the *Databases* course given by Prof. Smith in Fall 1990.

> **connect** enrl *FINAL-GRADE* 100
>
> **where**
>
> > enrl.*THE-STUDENT.MAJOR NAME* 'Computer Science' **and**
> >
> > enrl.*THE-OFFERING.THE-QUARTER.YEAR*=1990 **and**
> >
> > enrl.*THE-OFFERING.THE-QUARTER.SEASON*='Fall' **and**
> >
> > enrl.*THE-OFFERING.THE-COURSE.NAME*='Databases' **and**
> >
> > enrl.*THE-OFFERING.THE-INSTRUCTOR.LAST-NAME*='Smith'

Removal of connections and **removal of objects**:

$$\textbf{disconnect } fact_1, \ldots, fact_k \ [\textbf{where } condition]$$

Interpretation:

- If no *where* clause is specified, the values of the expressions are unrelated and/or decategorized. Objects that are removed from all their categories are removed from the database.

- If a *where* clause is specified with a condition ϕ on variables $x_1, \ldots, x_n$, then for every tuple of values of the variables satisfying ϕ the values of the expressions are unrelated and decategorized as above.

- The variables on which the *condition* depends must be those on which the expressions of the *facts* depend.

Example:

Let 'CS' no longer be an alternative name of a department.

> **disconnect** dept *NAME* 'CS'
>
> **where**
>
> > dept **is a** *DEPARTMENT* **and** dept *NAME* 'CS'

Example:

The computer science student Jack Johnson has dropped the *Databases* course given by Prof. Smith in Fall 1990.

> **disconnect** enrl *ENROLLMENT*
>
> **where**
>> enrl.*THE-STUDENT.MAJOR NAME* 'Computer Science' **and**
>>
>> enrl.*THE-STUDENT.LAST-NAME*='Johnson' **and**
>>
>> enrl.*THE-STUDENT.FIRST-NAME*='Jack' **and**
>>
>> enrl.*THE-OFFERING.THE-QUARTER.YEAR*=1990 **and**
>>
>> enrl.*THE-OFFERING.THE-QUARTER.SEASON*='Fall' **and**
>>
>> enrl.*THE-OFFERING.THE-COURSE.NAME*='Databases' **and**
>>
>> enrl.*THE-OFFERING.THE-INSTRUCTOR.LAST-NAME*='Smith'

Example:

Void all the grades in the *Databases* course given by Prof. Smith in Fall 1990.

> **disconnect** enrl *FINAL-GRADE enrl.FINAL-GRADE*
>
> **where**
>> enrl.*THE-OFFERING.THE-QUARTER.YEAR*=1990 **and**
>>
>> enrl.*THE-OFFERING.THE-QUARTER.SEASON*='Fall' **and**
>>
>> enrl.*THE-OFFERING.THE-COURSE.NAME*='Databases' **and**
>>
>> enrl.*THE-OFFERING.THE-INSTRUCTOR.LAST-NAME*='Smith'

Correction of facts:

$$\textbf{update } fact_1, \ldots, fact_k \textbf{ [where } condition\textbf{]}$$

This is a combination of *disconnect* and *connect*. Before a connection *aRb* is made, the relationships *aRx* are removed for every *x*. Before a connection *aC′* is made, the facts *aC* are removed for every *C*.

Example:

Let 'CS' be the new name instead of 'Computer Science'.

update dept *NAME* 'CS'

where

    dept **is a** *DEPARTMENT* **and**

    dept *NAME* 'Computer Science'

Example:

Give the grade 100 to the computer science student Jack Johnson enrolled in the *Databases* course given by Prof. Smith in Fall 1990. If a grade has been previously given, replace it by the new grade.

    update enrl *FINAL-GRADE* 100

    where

        enrl.*THE-STUDENT.MAJOR NAME* 'Computer Science' **and**

        enrl.*THE-STUDENT.LAST-NAME*='Johnson' **and**

        enrl.*THE-STUDENT.FIRST-NAME*='Jack' **and**

        enrl.*THE-OFFERING.THE-QUARTER.YEAR*=1990 **and**

        enrl.*THE-OFFERING.THE-QUARTER.SEASON*='Fall' **and**

        enrl.*THE-OFFERING.THE-COURSE.NAME*='Databases' **and**

        enrl.*THE-OFFERING.THE-INSTRUCTOR.LAST-NAME*='Smith'

Example:

Increase by 10 percent the grades of all computer science students enrolled in the *Databases* course given by Prof. Smith in Fall 1990.

    update enrl *FINAL-GRADE* 1.1×enrl.*FINAL-GRADE*

    where

        enrl.*THE-STUDENT.MAJOR NAME* 'Computer Science' **and**

        enrl.*THE-OFFERING.THE-QUARTER.YEAR*=1990 **and**

        enrl.*THE-OFFERING.THE-QUARTER.SEASON*='Fall' **and**

> enrl.*THE-OFFERING.THE-COURSE.NAME*='Databases' **and**
>
> enrl.*THE-OFFERING.THE-INSTRUCTOR.LAST-NAME*='Smith'

2.3.5.5. *Parametric query forms

Often the users ask similar queries which differ only in the values of some parameters.

> *Example:*
>
> 1.   What are the grades of the student whose name is 'Jackson'?
> 2.   What are the grades of the student whose name is 'Smith'?

It is desirable that such queries are predefined in parametric form, and the users would supply only the values of the parameters.

> *Example:*
>
> What are the grades of the student whose name is x, where x is supplied by the end user when the query runs?

Such a predefinition is called a **query in parametric form** or **query form**. It saves time on specification of similar queries and allows the less-sophisticated end users to use queries which can be specified only by more sophisticated users, such as programmers and analysts.

In calculus, query forms are specified by the following syntax:

depending on *parameters*

get *expressions*

where *condition*

The condition and the expressions may depend on the parameters.

Example:

What are the grades of the student whose name is *x*, where *x* is supplied by the end user when the query runs?

> **depending on** x
>
> **get** e.*THE-OFFERING.THE-COURSE.NAME*, e.*FINAL-GRADE*
>
> **where**
>
>> e **is an** *ENROLLMENT* **and**
>>
>> e.*THE-STUDENT.LAST-NAME* = x

2.3.6. *Nontotal functional relations: interpretation of the dot-application

If *f* is not total, then *e.f* may be ambiguous. However, a smart DBMS may be able to follow the user's intuition in using such expressions. In order to provide a meaningful result, the dot-application *e.f* of a nontotal functional relation *f* to an expression *e* is interpreted by the smart DBMS by analyzing the whole condition or assertion containing the dot-application.

Example:

Consider the following assertion which contains a dot-application of the nontotal relation *BIRTH-YEAR*.

> **for every** y **in** *STUDENT*:
>
>> y.*BIRTH-YEAR* > 1980

This assertion will be interpreted by a smart DBMS as

> **for every** y **in** *STUDENT*:
>
>> **exists** x **in** *Integer*:
>>
>>> y *BIRTH-YEAR* x **and** x > 1980

This interpretation of the dot-application of nontotal functional relations can be defined formally as follows.

An expression *e.f*, where *e* is an expression and *f* is a database functional relation, is regarded as a syntactic abbreviation. Let $x_1, \ldots, x_k$ be the variables on which the expression *e* depends. For the above example, the only such variable is *y*.

Let ϕ be the largest subexpression (within the whole assertion or condition) containing *e.f* and still depending on all the variables $x_1, \ldots, x_k$; that is, none of these variables is quantified in the subformula ϕ. (ϕ may depend also on additional variables.) For the above example,

$$\phi = (y.BIRTH\text{-}YEAR > 1980)$$

Let C be the range of f.

Let $\psi = \phi|_{e.f}^{x}$. (That is, ψ is obtained from ϕ by substitution of a
new variable x for all the occurrences of $(e.f)$ in ψ.) For the above example,

$$\psi = (x > 1980)$$

Then ϕ stands for:

$$(\textbf{exists} \ x \ \textbf{in} \ C : ((e \ f \ x) \ \textbf{and} \ \psi))$$

Problem 2-7.

Use the medical/binary schema (Figure 13-6 on page 395). A patient's illness is *improbable* if
when the illness commenced the patient did not have a symptom he would be expected to have with
a probability of 0.9 at least. Write a calculus query to print the names of the patients and the names
of the diseases for all those improbable cases.

   You may assume that the userview you are using contains the whole schema and, additionally,
the inverses of all the schema relations. For example, in addition to

   ☐ *occurred* — relation from *DISEASE* to *SICKNESS*   (*1:m*)

there is the inverse relation

   ☐ *the-disease* — relation from *SICKNESS* to *DISEASE*   (*m:1*)

Solution on page 405.

Problem 2-8.

Use the medical/binary schema (Figure 13-6 on page 395). Specify the following integrity
constraints in calculus:

*   A patient could not have suffered from any disease or suffered any symptom before he was
    born.
*   In the catalog of symptoms for each disease, a symptom can have at most one probability
    value for that disease.
*   Any other integrity constraint involving at least two abstract categories.

Problem 2-9.

1.   Design a binary database schema for a theater ticket reservation office. The following
     information must be covered (or be deducible from your database):

     *   Telephone number and name of the customer, her credit card information, her charge, her
         seats, and the performance
     *   Seats available for different performances and their prices

You may explicitly make reasonable assumptions.

2.   Write a calculus expression to find the customers each of which reserved all the seats for an entire performance ("bought the performance").

Problem 2-10.

Use the university/binary reference schema at the end of this book. Write query to print the names of the students who took course(s) with instructor(s) not working in the student's major or minor department.

> For example,
> > if Jack Benson took a course offered by Prof. King, where
> > > Benson's major and minor are CS and Mathematics,
> > > > but King works only in the departments of History and Music,
> > then 'Benson' will appear in the output.

Write this query in

1.   Calculus

2.   Extended Pascal

CHAPTER 3

FROM THE SEMANTIC TO THE RELATIONAL MODEL

Chapter 3 defines the Relational Data Model and presents a top-down methodology for design of relational databases. The theoretical foundations of the relational model were introduced by E. Codd in 1970. By late 1980s this model had become the state of the art in commercial database management.

3.1. Time Invariant Attributes and Keys

Time-invariant attribute — An attribute A is *time-invariant* if once an object x becomes related by A to a value y, the object x will forever be related by A to y, as long as x exists.

There are no time-invariant attributes in the natural user world. Even if the laws of physics or society do not allow for an attribute to change in time, the attribute may change in the perceived real world due to discoveries of errors in earlier perception. For example, a social security number could be wrongly reported and then corrected. Thus, *time-invariance* is defined only in implementational restrictions. Such restrictions are unavoidable in the relational database design. The methodology of relational schema design that is presented below has among its goals the minimization of the negative effect of such implementational restrictions.

Example:

None of the attributes given in the previous examples is truly time-invariant. The following attributes are the next closest thing: they change only when an error is discovered.

> *birth-year* of *PERSON*;
> *year* and *season* of *QUARTER*.

The following attributes may sometimes change in time "in the real world." Thus, declaring them as time-invariant would be a stronger implementational restriction.

> *last-name* and *first-name* of *PERSON*;
> *name* of *COURSE*.

The following attributes have a high probability of change in time; no reasonable database design would restrict them as time-invariant.

> *address* of *PERSON*;
> *final-grade* of *ENROLLMENT*.

Keys

1. **Single-attribute key**

A time-invariant attribute of a category is called its *key* if it is *1:1* and *total*. That means that the values of the attribute can be used to identify the objects of the category.

Example:

If we assume that the attribute *name* of *COURSE* is time-invariant, then it is probably also a key since:

a.   It is *total*, provided we do not want our database to contain courses without names

b.   It is 1:1, that is, no two courses have the same name, and no course has two names.

Due to the *time-invariance* requirement, no attribute is really a key in the natural user's world. Thus, the property of a *key* is defined only in implementational restrictions, which are unavoidable in the relational database design. Also, the requirement of *totality* is very rarely an integrity constraint imposed by the logic of the user world but rather is an implementational restriction.

Example:

Would the attribute *social-security-number* of the category *PERSON* be its key? Let us assume that we have already imposed an implementational restriction of *time-invariance* on this attribute (thus making it very hard and dangerous for our users to correct errors).

To be a key, this attribute must be *one-to-one* and *total*. It is indeed one-to-one. But in the real world it is not really total: there are some persons who do not have social security numbers before they are reported to our database. The totality can be imposed as an implementational restriction with one of the following practical provisions:

a. Persons who do not have social security numbers would be assigned the dummy default number 0, which would be called a "social security number" for the purposes of the database. But then this attribute would no longer be *one-to-one* since two persons may have the same number 0.

b. For persons who do not have real social security numbers, generate dummy temporary numbers in such a way that all these numbers are different and not in the range of possible real social security numbers. For example, if the real s.s. numbers may never begin with the digit 9, then begin all the dummy numbers with this digit.

Apart from the unnaturalness and "cheating" which are bound to result in misinterpretation of the computer's reports, there is a serious technical problem: What if a person did not have a real s.s. number at first, but later received one, and this new number is a valuable piece of information which the user wants to keep in the database? If we allow replacement of the old dummy number by the new real one, then the *time-invariance* requirement is violated.

c. Yet another possibility is to disallow recording of information about persons who do not have s.s. numbers. I am afraid that our client might be unhappy with such a restriction.

Example:

We can generate a new artificial attribute to serve as a key. Let *id#* be a new artificial attribute of the category *PERSON*, generated in such a way that when new persons enter the database, they are assigned arbitrary meaningless numbers which have not been used before. (When a person is deleted from the database, the number is not reused.) This attribute would be a key.

Convention: In this text, we shall name the attributes constrained to be keys with the suffix *-key*.

Example:

name-key of COURSE

The name of the attribute *name-key* implicitly defines a constraint or implementational restriction "This attribute is a key of its domain, the category *COURSE*."

---

2.   Multiattribute key

The following definition extends the concept *key* to a collection of attributes.

Key of a category — a *collection* of total time-invariant attributes $f_1, f_2, \ldots, f_n$ whose domain is that category and which satisfy two requrements:

(i)   For any collection of values, $x_1, \ldots, x_n$ there is no more than one object y of the category s.t.

$$x_1 = y.f_1 \text{ and } x_2 = y.f_2 \text{ and } \cdots \text{ and } x_n = y.f_n$$

(ii)   No proper subcollection of these attributes *always* satisfies (i).

Practically, requirement (i) means that the collection of attributes is sufficient to identify every object of the category. Requirement (ii) means that the collection is minimal: if one of the attributes is not known then the remaining attributes might not provide sufficient information to identify every object of the category.

Example:

(*the-year, the-season*) is the only key of the category *QUARTER*.

Either attribute alone does not identify each object. Together they do.

Convention: In this text, when a category is constrained to have exactly one key, and the key is composed of several attributes, we shall name these attributes with the suffix *-in-key*.

Example:

the-year-in-key and *the-season-in-key* of *QUARTER*

Note:

(i) In the real world a category usually has *no* key. Thus, the existence of a key is usually not an integrity constraint but rather an implementational restriction. This restriction will be imposed when unavoidable due to limitations of a DBMS or a database model, especially the relational model.

(ii) Existence of a key makes every object of the category identifiable with the values of the key and eliminates the necessity to refer to abstract objects.

Example:

Courses can be identified with strings *name-key*. Quarters can be identified with pairs *(the-year-in-key, the-season-in-key)*.

(iii) A category which has no key may still have all its objects completely identifiable (using different relations and their combinations for different objects), but the identification would not be uniform.

Example:

The category *DEPARTMENT* does not have a key (it does not have any attribute at all; the relation *NAME* is not an attribute because it is 1:m). However, if the relation *department-name* is total, then, being 1:m, it distinguishes between every two departments according to their names.

If the relation *department-name* is not total, then we might have a problem distinguishing between two departments that have no names at all. In that case, it is possible that the "anonymous" departments can be distinguished by their relationships of *works-in* with instructors.

Example:

We have not defined any key for the category INSTRUCTOR. However, most instructors have unique names and can be identified by their names. Few instructors have common names, and their identification requires names of their departments in addition to their first and last names. Some of the instructors have nonunique names but do not work for any department at all. These rare persons can be identifiable by their names in conjunction with their birth years or with courses they teach or with their addresses (whichever of this information is available and sufficient for identification).

This identification is nonuniform because different instructors are identified by different relations.

The nonuniform identification is quite common and satisfactory in the real world and in the Binary Model, but the implementational restrictions of the Relational Model will necessitate a *uniform* identification of the objects of a category.

(iv) When a key is composed of several attributes it is still *one* key.

(v) A category may theoretically have several keys. However, since categories in the real world rarely have even one key, the existence of more than one key would be an unnecessarily strong implementational restriction, which is not required by database management systems. Thus, the possibility of multiple keys will be ignored in this text.

3.2. Relational Schemas Defined

A binary schema is called **table-oriented** or a **relational schema** if:

(i)   All the abstract categories of the schema have keys.

(ii)   All the abstract categories are pairwise disjoint.

(iii) The only relations are attributes.

Thus, all the information in a relational schema is represented by attributes of categories.

Example:

Figure Ref-2 (on the last page of this book) could be a relational schema for the university application, provided:

- All the categories are restricted to having keys as shown.

- There are no persons but students and instructors.

- The categories *INSTRUCTOR* and *STUDENT* are disjoint.

We shall see later that this schema can be used even without imposing the severe restriction of disjointness.

Example:

Consider the category *COURSE-ENROLLMENT*. In the relational schema it has no relations to the categories *STUDENT* and *COURSE-OFFERING*. Instead, it has attributes giving essentially the same information. Thus, instead:

☐ *the-student* — relation from *COURSE-ENROLLMENT* to *STUDENT* (*m:1*) the category has the attribute:

☐ *student-id-in-key* — attribute of *COURSE-ENROLLMENT*, range: *Integer* (*m:1*)

Table-declaration, relation-declaration — any subschema of a relational schema having only one abstract category with all of its attributes and their ranges. The *name* of the *table* is the name of that category.

> *Example:*
>
> Here is the table-declaration *QUARTER*.
>
> **QUARTER**
>
> *year-in-key: 1990..2010*
> *season-in-key: String*

Instantaneous table, instantaneous relation — an instantaneous database viewed under a table-declaration. This means that an instantaneous table is a part of an instantaneous relational database containing all the objects of one table and all their relationships (attributes).

Representation of an instantaneous table — a printable table whose title is the name of the category, the names of the columns are the attributes, and for every object in the category there is a row (called a **tuple**) composed of the values of the attributes of that object.

> *Example:*
>
> The following is an instantaneous table of *STUDENT*. (Of course, in this example the instantaneous table is unrealistically small. It would contain thousands of tuples for a normal university.)

STUDENT

id-key	last-name	first-name	birth-year	address	major-dept-main-name	minor-dept-main-name
12345	Victory	Elizabeth	1966	100 Sun St.	Computer Science	Economics
12348	Howards	Jane	1965	200 Dorms	Arts	Economics
43532	Wood	Michael	1964	110 Dorms	Arts	Economics

Figure 3-1. An instantaneous table.

Note:

(i)   There cannot be two identical rows in an instantaneous table because this would imply that there are two objects with the same values of the key.

(ii) The order of tuples (rows) is immaterial; the order of columns is immaterial.

> *Example:*
>
> The following figure represents the very same instantaneous table as the previous example.

STUDENT

birth-year	address	major-dept-main-name	id-key	last-name	first-name	minor-dept-main-name
1964	110 Dorms	Arts	43532	Wood	Michael	Economics
1965	200 Dorms	Arts	12348	Howards	Jane	Economics
1966	100 Sun St.	Computer Science	12345	Victory	Elizabeth	Economics

Figure 3-2. Some columns and rows have been moved in the representation without changing the instantaneous table.

Representation of an instantaneous relational database — a collection of instantaneous tables.

Example:

The following figure is a representation of an instantaneous database for the schema of Figure Ref-2. This instantaneous database represents the same state of the application's real world as the binary instantaneous database of Figure 1-12 on page 22.

STUDENT

id-key	last-name	first-name	birth-year	address	major-dept-main-name	minor-dept-main-name
12345	Victory	Elizabeth	1966	100 Sun St.	Computer Science	Economics
12348	Howards	Jane	1965	200 Dorms	Arts	Economics
43532	Wood	Michael	1964	110 Dorms	Arts	Economics

INSTRUCTOR

id-key	last-name	first-name	birth-year	address
11332	Brown	George	1956	112 Lucky Dr.
14352	Whatson	Mary	1953	231 Fortune Dr.
24453	Blue	John	1950	536 Orange Dr.

DEPARTMENT

main-name-key
Computer Science
Mathematics
Physics
Arts
Economics

DEPARTMENT NAMING

name-key	main name
CS	Computer Science
Math	Mathematics
Physics	Physics
Mathematics	Mathematics
Computer Science	Computer Science
Arts	Arts
Economics	Economics

Figure 3-3. An instantaneous database for the relational schema of the university application.

(The figure is continued on the next page.)

WORK

instructor-id-in-key	department-main-name-in-key
11332	Computer Science
11332	Mathematics
14352	Physics
24453	Mathematics

COURSE

name-key
Databases
Football
Gastronomy

QUARTER

year-in-key	season-in-key
1990	Fall
1990	Winter
1990	Spring

COURSE OFFERING

instructor-id-in-key	course-name-in-key	year-in-key	season-in-key
11332	Databases	1990	Fall
11332	Football	1990	Fall
11332	Gastronomy	1990	Fall

COURSE ENROLLMENT

instructor-id-in-key	course-name-in-key	year-in-key	season-in-key	student-id-in-key	final-grade
11332	Gastronomy	1990	Fall	12345	100
11332	Gastronomy	1990	Fall	12348	70
11332	Databases	1990	Fall	12348	80

Figure 3-3. *Continued.*

An alternative **representation of relational schemas (linear, nongraphic):**

$$table\ name\ [\ attribute : range, \ldots, attribute : range\ ]$$

$$\cdots$$

$$table\ name\ [\ attribute : range, \ldots, attribute : range\ ]$$

Example:

Here is a linear representation of the schema of Figure Ref-2:

DEPARTMENT [main-name-key: String]

DEPARTMENT-NAMING [name-key: String, main-name: String]

STUDENT [id-key: Integer, last-name: String, first-name: String, birth-year: 1870..1990, address: String, major-department-main-name: String, minor-department-main-name: String]

INSTRUCTOR [id-key: Integer, last-name: String, first-name: String, birth-year: 1870..1990, address: String]

WORK [instructor-id-in-key: Integer, department-main-name-in-key: String]

QUARTER [year-in-key: 1990..2010, season-in-key: String]

COURSE [name-key: String]

COURSE-OFFERING [instructor-id-in-key: Integer, course-name-in-key: String, year-in-key: 1990..2010, season-in-key: String]

COURSE-ENROLLMENT [instructor-id-in-key: Integer, course-name-in-key: String, year-in-key: 1990..2010, season-in-key: String, student-id-in-key: Integer, final-grade: 0..100]

Problem 3-1.

A small enterprise is described by the following binary schema:

- ☐ *EMPLOYEE* — category
- ☐ *name* — relation from *EMPLOYEE* to *Text*   (*m:1*)
- ☐ *the-boss* — relation from *EMPLOYEE* to *EMPLOYEE*   (*m:1*)
- ☐ *PROJECT* — category
- ☐ *proj-name* — relation from *PROJECT* to *Text*   (*1:1,total*)
- ☐ *is-a-part-of* — relation from *PROJECT* to *PROJECT*   (*m:m*)
- ☐ *works-for* — relation from *EMPLOYEE* to *PROJECT*   (*m:m*)

Design a relational schema for the enterprise.

Solution on page 406.

Problem 3-2.

Design a relational schema for a post office, covering the following information:

- The zip code of every house in the United States. (When a state, a city, a street, and a street number are known, the zip code can be found.)

- The names and addresses of the postmen employed by *this* post office.

- For every address in the post office's service area, the postmen serving the address.

Note: There are too many houses in the United States. You cannot allot a row in a table for every house in the United States if the data is to be kept at a local post office.

3.3. Implementational Restrictions: Pros and Cons

Consequences of implementational restrictions in the Relational Model:

- The schemas often deviate from the real world.

- The schemas are often unnatural, inflexible, and redundant.

- The integrity constraints are often underrepresented in the schemas.

- The queries are usually harder to specify.

Example:

Instead of

$$(i \ WORKS\text{-}IN \ d)$$

we have to say:

    (**exists** w **in** *WORK*:

        i.*ID-key* = w.*INSTRUCTOR-ID-in-key* **and**

        d.*MAIN-NAME-key* = w.*DEPARTMENT-MAIN-NAME-in-key*)

Purposes of implementational restrictions in the Relational Model:

- **Exclusion of nonattribute relations,
  exclusion of intersecting categories,
  exclusion of sub- and supercategories** — allow for readable and simple representation of the instantaneous database as everyday tables.

- **Totality and uniqueness of keys** — allow:

  — A standard printable representation for every object

  — Readable reference to objects of one table from objects of another table

  — Unambiguous definition of simple updates

- **Time-invariance of keys** — prevents inconsistent update of keys.

  If the values of the key of an object are updated, then all the references to this object throughout the instantaneous database become wrong. The human user cannot be relied upon to find and update all the references. The database management system is normally unaware of these references and thus cannot update them automatically, unless it is a very advanced system having a high-level support for the so-called **referential integrity**.

Many database management systems do not explicitly require the time-invariance but do not provide a high-level support for the referential integrity either. This does not mean that those systems do not need the time-invariance. Rather, this means that they do not check for the time-invariance, and, without warning to the user, they corrupt the database when the user modifies a value of a key.

Note: It is hard to say whether the severe implementational restrictions can really be justified by the benefits of the model.

Totality of nonkey attributes

Many relational database management systems require a further implementational restriction: they require that all the attributes be total.

Relational DBMS that do not require the totality of attributes allow **null values of attributes**.

The restriction of the totality of the nonkey attributes pragmatically requires a modification of the meaning of an attribute which is nontotal in the real world. A special value is identified which can never be a value of the attribute in the real world. This value is assigned to the objects that do not have any real value of the attribute.

Example:

We can assign the dummy grade "–1" to the enrollments which do not have any real grade. Thus we convert:

☐ *final-grade* — attribute of *COURSE-ENROLLMENT*, range: *0..100   (m:1)*

into:

☐ *new-final-grade* — attribute of *COURSE-ENROLLMENT*, range: *-1..100   (m:1)*

so that:

x.*NEW-FINAL-GRADE* = -1 **iff**

x *FINAL-GRADE* **null**

Such "cheating" will, however, cause inconvenience and misinterpretation of queries of naive users.

Example:

The query

> **get** enrl.*STUDENT-ID* **where**
>
> > enrl **is a** COURSE-ENROLLMENT **and**
> >
> > enrl.*new-FINAL-GRADE* < 60

will also retrieve the students who have no grades at all. The system will also believe that two students who really have no grades have identical grades, and thus will mislead the user.

Some relational database management systems allow the analyst to define **default values of attributes**. These would be the values for the objects when the user has entered no value. The definition of default values enhances the convenience of updates, but it does not solve the problem of the misinterpretation of queries. A default value is still a regular value as far as the system is concerned.

Example:

We can define "-1" to be the default grade. This will be the grade of all the enrollments for which the user has not provided a grade.

In many cases the default value is defined as 0 or the empty string.

Example:

We should not define 0 as the default for the grade if our intention is to use the default value as a substitute for *null*. This is because 0 might be a real grade of a poor student.

We can use the empty string '' as the default for *last-name*.

3.4. Relational Database Design

The purpose of this section is to show how a high-quality relational database can be designed once we have a semantic binary schema for the application.

3.4.1. Design principles

Schema-conversion — replacement of a schema by another schema having the same information content. This means that each of the two schemas can be regarded as a userview of the other.

Schema-conversion is a means of database design: a schema is first designed in a higher-level database model and then translated into a lower-level model which is supported by the available DBMS (when a DBMS for a higher-level model is unavailable or inadequate).

Note :

(i)   Schema conversion is usually done in order to impose implementation restrictions needed because of the database model or the database management system. Thus, the latter schema is usually of lesser quality than the former.

> *Example:*
>
> We shall see in this section how the semantic schema of the university application can be converted into the relational schema of Figure Ref-2.

(ii)   Although only the latter schema (or its descendants after more conversions) will be used by the DBMS software, after conversion the former schema *must* be kept and maintained as a documentation of the application's real world.

(iii)   After conversion, the former schema is called the **conceptual semantic schema** of the latter *physical* schema or its descendents.

(iv)   When the concepts of the real world change, the conceptual semantic schema must be changed *first,* and only then is the physical schema *regenerated* from the conceptual semantic binary schema by conversion.

This section presents a conversion algorithm of a semantic schema into a relational schema whose quality is among the highest possible for the Relational Model, provided the original semantic schema is of high quality.

This algorithm can be performed manually by the database designer. Alternatively, an automatic tool can be used to perform all the busywork, while prompting the database designer for intelligent decisions (and using defaults when the designer fails to provide such a guidance). One such tool has been developed at the Florida International University and the University of California by the author and his students.

3.4.2. Composition and split of relations

Two auxiliary definitions of terminology that will be used in the conversion algorithm follow.

Composition of relations

Let the range of Relation R_1 be the domain of Relation R_2.

Relation R is the composition of R_1 on R_2 if

$$xRy \text{ iff exists } z \text{ such that } xR_1z \text{ and } zR_2y.$$

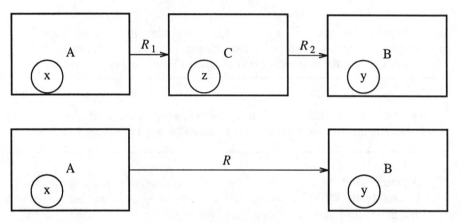

Figure 3-4. Relation R is the composition of two relations, R_1 and R_2: xRy is whenever xR_1z and zR_2y.

Example:

Consider two relations:

- ☐ *the-course* — relation from *COURSE-OFFERING* to *COURSE* (*m:1*)

- ☐ *name* — relation from *COURSE* to *String* (*1:1*)

The composition of *THE-COURSE* on *NAME* is:

- ☐ *the-name-of-the-course* — attribute of *COURSE-OFFERING*, range: *String* (*m:1*)

Relation-split — conversion of a schema having a relation R into another schema having, instead of R, a new abstract category C and two total functional relations R_1, R_2, whose domain is C, such that:

There is a fact xRy

if and only if

there exists an object z in C for which zR_1x and zR_2y.

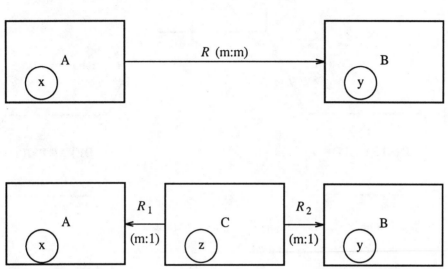

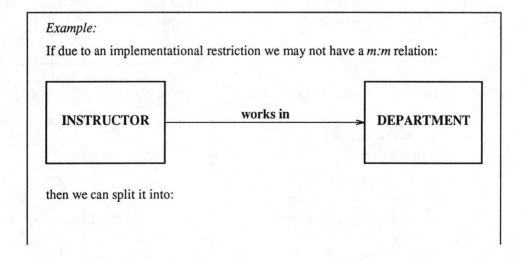

Figure 3-5. Relation R is split into a category C and two relations, R_1 and R_2. Every relationship $x-y$ is broken into $x-z$ and $z-y$.

Example:

If due to an implementational restriction we may not have a *m:m* relation:

then we can split it into:

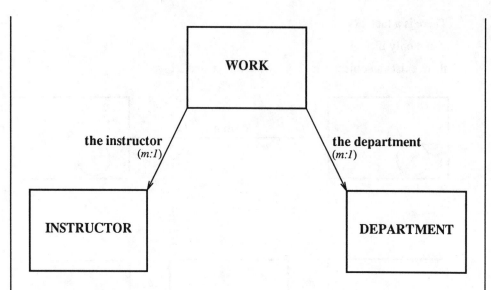

This split necessitates additional integrity constraints:

- Both new relations are total.

- For any combination of an instructor and a department there is at most one object in work.

  The latter constraint is more rigorously formulated in calculus, as follows.

for every w **in** *WORK*:

    for every v **in** *WORK*:

        if w.*the-instructor* = v.*the-instructor* **and**
            w.*the-department* = v.*the-department*

        then *w=v*.

The composition of relations and relation-split can be regarded as userviews.*

---

* The following is a formal definition of the *composition* in Predicate Calculus for the inference rules of userviews. Here, the category C is the range of R_1.

userview relation: $x R y$

    where exists z **in** C:

        $(x R_1 z$ **and** $z R_2 y)$

The following is a formal definition of the *relation-spilt* in Predicate Calculus for the inference rules of userviews.

    userview category C $(R_1: x, R_2: y)$ **where** $x R y$

The following subsections present the conversion algorithm

3.4.3. Determination of keys

Step 1. Choose a key for every abstract category, excluding subcategories of other categories, as follows.

    a.   **(single-attribute key)**

        if the category has an attribute which is *1:1*, time-invariant, and total, *then* let that attribute be the key;

    b.   **(''forced'' single-attribute key)**

        else if the category has an attribute which can be implementationally restricted to be *1:1*, time-invariant, and total, without very harmful alteration of the real world, *then* make that attribute into a key (declare the implementational restriction);

> *Example:*
>
>

name-key of *COURSE*

>
> It is not a very far reaching alteration of the real world to make this implementation restriction: "Every course has exactly one name, and this name may never be changed."

    c.   **(multiattribute key)**

        else if the category has a collection of attributes which are time-invariant and total, and jointly identify all the objects in the category, *then* let a minimal such collection be the key;

> *Example:*
>
> (*season-in-key, year-in-key*) of *QUARTER*

    d.   **(''forced'' multiattribute key)**

        else if the category has a collection of attributes which can be implementationally restricted to be time-invariant and total, and to jointly identify all the objects of the category, without very harmful alteration of the real world, *then* make a minimal such collection of attributes into a key;

    e.   **(inferred key)**

        else if a collection of attributes can be inferred from the information existing in the schema and from keys of other categories, so that

- these attributes can be implementationally restricted, without very harmful alteration of the real world,

    (i)   to be time-invariant and total, and

    (ii) to jointly identify all the objects of the category,

then

  (i)   choose a minimal such collection of inferable attributes;

  (ii)   add to the schema those attributes from the collection which are not already in the schema;

  (iii) make this collection of attributes into a key (declare the implementational restrictions);

  (iv)   convert the inference rule of these attributes into constraints. (Since these will now be new attributes, their values will be updated by the users with possible inconsistency relative to the information from which these attributes are inferable.)

Example:

To obtain a key for *DEPARTMENT* we alter the real world slightly: we require every department to have at least one name; we shall call the first name ever given to a department the *main-name*, and we require that the *main-name* of a department may never be changed. We add the new attribute

☐ *main-name-key* — attribute of *DEPARTMENT*, range: *String* (*m:1*)

and the constraint

for every d **in** *DEPARTMENT:*

d *NAME* d.*MAIN-NAME-key*

Note: In conjunction with the implicit constraint -*key*, the above constraint means that the main-name is the first name ever given to the department, and that it will remain the department's name forever.

Example:

More characteristic examples of inferred keys are for the categories *COURSE-OFFERING* and *COURSE-ENROLLMENT*. These will be given and generalized after we have a key for *PERSON*.

f.   **(enumerator ID key)**

else create a new external enumeration for the objects in the category (thus altering the real world) and add it as an attribute, which will be the chosen key.

Example:

The key of *PERSON* will be a new attribute *id-key.*

Pragmatically, a program should be written to generate new values of an *enumerator id key.* These numbers will be assigned by the user to the new objects of the category. The numbers may not be reused when an object is removed. The numbers themselves should bear no correlation to the other information in the database, since the other information may change in time, while the key is time-invariant.

It is also advisable not to assign the numbers sequentially but rather in an arbitrary sequence. Otherwise, the irrelevant information on the "seniority" of objects will be hidden in the ID. Any hidden information will be abused by the application programmers. Since it is not always possible to update such hidden information correctly, the programs will not produce the expected results in some special cases.

Note: The step of finding keys is performed simultaneously for all the categories, since we might need to know the key of one category in order to find a key of a related category.

Example:

An *inferred key* of *COURSE-OFFERING* can be obtained when keys for *QUARTER*, *COURSE*, and *PERSON* have been chosen. The inferred key of *COURSE-OFFERING* will be

> {the name of the course, the year of the quarter, the season of the quarter, ID of the instructor}

Hence, we add four new attributes to *COURSE-OFFERING*. The *inferred* key of *COURSE-ENROLLMENT* will be five new attributes

> {ID of the student, the key of the offering}.

(The "key of the offering" consists of four attributes. Thus, there is a total of five attributes in the key of *COURSE-ENROLLMENT*.)

Example:

The category *COURSE-OFFERING* is now:

> **COURSE**
> **OFFERING**
>
> *instructor-id-in-key: Integer*
> *course-name-in-key: String*
> *year-in-key: 1990..2010*
> *season-in-key: String*

The above is an example of the prevalent case of an *inferred key*. The following is a generalization of this example.

Assume that a category C is the domain of total functional relations $f_1, \ldots, f_n$ which jointly identify all the objects of the category.

Example:

Every course offering is uniquely identified by its instructor, course, and quarter. Thus, the total functional relations

   THE-INSTRUCTOR, THE-COURSE, THE-QUARTER

jointly identify all the objects of their domain, the category *COURSE-OFFERING*.

The above assumption means that there is an integrity constraint

  for every x **in** C:

    for every y **in** C:

      if $x.f_1 = y.f_1$ **and** $\cdots$ **and** $x.f_n = y.f_n$

      then x = y

Example:

for every x **in** *COURSE-OFFERING*:

  for every y **in** *COURSE-OFFERING*:

    if

      x.*THE-INSTRUCTOR*=y.*THE-INSTRUCTOR* **and**

> x.*THE-COURSE*=y.*THE-COURSE* **and**
>
> x.*THE-QUARTER*=y.*THE-QUARTER*
>
> **then** x=y

In this case, once the keys of the ranges of the functional relations $f_1, \ldots, f_n$ are known, a key of C can be inferred from them. Let the keys of the ranges be $k_1, \ldots, k_n$. Let k_i-of-f_i be the set of inferred attributes obtained by the composition of the attributes comprising the key k_i and the relation f_i.

Example:

There are three such sets of inferred attributes for the category *COURSE-OFFERING*:

- id-of-the-instructor
- the-name-of-the-course
- the-year-of-the-quarter, the-season-of-the-quarter

The key of C is contained in the union of compositions of the relations f_i onto the keys of their ranges, that is,

$$\{(k_1 \text{ of } f_1), \ldots, (k_n \text{ of } f_n)\}$$

Notice that the key of C is *contained* in the above union of compositions. Usually the key of C is equal to that union of compositions but sometimes it is *properly* contained.

Example:

Let us change the meaning of *COURSE-OFFERING*. Now, it does not have to occur in one particular quarter but can last several quarters, as long as the quarters are within one academic year (Figure 3-6). There are two relations between offerings and quarters:

☐ *beginning-quarter* — relation from *COURSE-OFFERING* to *QUARTER* (*m:1,total*)

☐ *ending-quarter* — relation from *COURSE-OFFERING* to *QUARTER* (*m:1,total*)

The key of *COURSE-OFFERING* is properly contained in

> {the name of the course;
> the year and season of the beginning quarter;
> the year and season of the ending quarter;
> ID of the instructor}

The attribute *THE-YEAR-OF-THE-ENDING-QUARTER* is not a part of the key, since this attribute is not needed for identification of the offerings. For a given beginning quarter and the season of the ending quarter, we can deduce the year of the ending quarter, since we know that the offering is within one academic year.

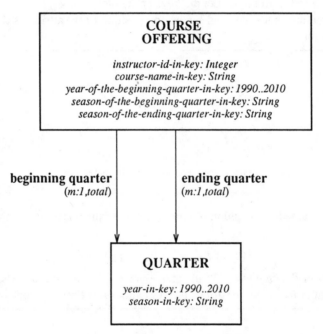

Figure 3-6. The case of multiquarter course offerings limited to one academic year. The key is shown.

Example:

The semantic schema of the university application has been converted so far into the schema on the following page.

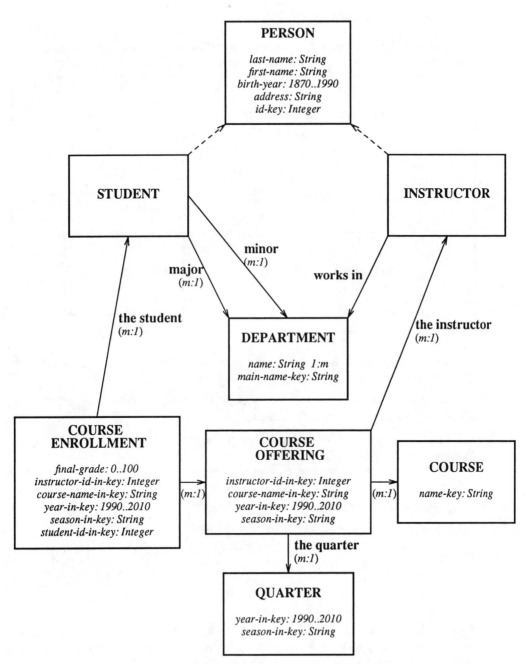

Figure 3-7. The university schema with keys.

3.4.4. Disjointness of categories

Step 2. Convert the intersecting abstract categories into disjoint categories by the following procedure for every group of intersecting categories.

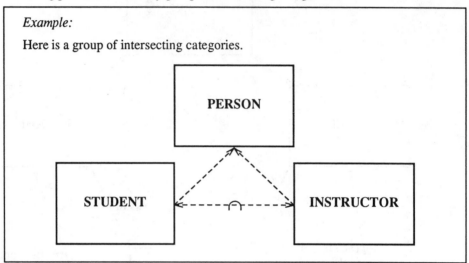

Example:

Here is a group of intersecting categories.

A. Consider a **complete group of categories** so that every category outside the group is disjoint from every category in the group.

Let C denote the union of all the categories in the group. If such a category C does not already exist in the schema, then add it.

Let $S_1, S_2, \ldots, S_n$ be the other categories in the group. (All of them are direct or indirect subcategories of C.)

Example:

$C = PERSON$, $S_1 = INSTRUCTOR$, $S_2 = STUDENT$.

Let

$$S_0 = C - \bigcup_{i=1}^{n} S_i$$

S_0 is the hypothetical category consisting of the objects of C which do not belong to any of the subcategories. The category S_0 is considered in order to ensure that no information is lost during the conversion. It is not added to the schema at this time. It may or may not be added to the schema at a later step, depending on decisions made at that step.

Example:

If there may be other persons in addition to instructors and students, then
$$S_0 = OTHER\text{-}PERSON$$

Otherwise, $S_0 = \varnothing$, and it would not have to be added to the schema at any step.

In the continuation of this case study in the examples we will assume the latter case: no "other persons."

B.   Estimate the **intersection factors** π and ρ.

In order to chose the best way of conversion, we shall need to estimate the following quantities.

Example:

For the above group of intersecting categories, the choice of the method to eliminate the intersection of the categories will depend on the correlation of two parameters:

- The percentage of people who are both students and instructors, π

- The percentage of relations specific to students or instructors among all the relations which can be relevant to persons, ρ

$$\rho = \frac{number\ of\ relations\ whose\ domain\ or\ range\ is\ S_1\ or\ \cdots\ or\ S_n}{number\ of\ relations\ whose\ domain\ or\ range\ is\ C\ or\ S_1\ or\ \cdots\ or\ S_n}$$

Example:

For the group of the previous examples, $\rho = 5/10$.

$$\pi = \frac{expected\ total\ number\ of\ objects\ in\ the\ intersections}{expected\ total\ number\ of\ objects\ in\ C}$$

The above formula is rather informal.[*]

---

[*] More formally:

$$\pi = \frac{expected\ cardinality\ of\ \bigcup_{i \neq j} (S_i \cap S_j)}{expected\ cardinality\ of\ C}$$

Example:

To estimate π, we have to predict the future of our database. It is reasonable to assume that about 5 percent of all persons would be simultaneously students and instructors, so $\pi = 0.05$.

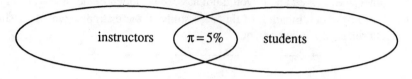

Example:

If we had several intersecting categories, we would count all the intersections:

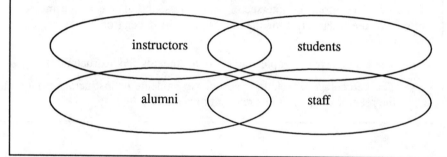

C. Select the best conversion into disjoint categories.

Example:

Consider the nondisjoint categories *INSTRUCTOR* and *STUDENT*, which are subcategories of the category *PERSON=INSTRUCTOR* $\cup$ *STUDENT*. The following are several possibilities of conversion. We will later select the best of the possibilities, depending on the circumstances.

a. *Conversion into one category (**Union**)*

Example:

Substitute the whole group of categories by their union, the category *PERSON*. This category will serve as the domain or the range for all the relations whose domain or range was one of the original categories. In addition, this category will have two Boolean attributes, *IS-AN-INSTRUCTOR* and *IS-A-STUDENT*, associating the value TRUE with objects representing instructors and students respectively.

> **PERSON**
>
> *id-key: Integer*
> *last-name: String*
> *first-name: String*
> *birth-year: 1870..1990*
> *address: String*
> *is-a-student: Boolean*
> *is-an-instructor: Boolean*

☐ *major* — relation from *PERSON* to *DEPARTMENT* (*m:1*)

☐ *minor* — relation from *PERSON* to *DEPARTMENT* (*m:1*)

☐ *the-instructor* — relation from *COURSE-OFFERING* to *PERSON* (*m:1*)

☐ *the-student* — relation from *COURSE-ENROLLMENT* to *PERSON* (*m:1*)

☐ *works-in* — relation from *PERSON* to *DEPARTMENT* (*m:m*)

b.   Conversion into artificially disjoint categories of Events

Example:

Substitute these categories by two disjoint categories of events: *Event-of-being-a-STUDENT* and *Event-of-being-an-INSTRUCTOR* (usually abbreviated just *STUDENT* and *INSTRUCTOR*, but the meaning of the full names is intended).

An instructor who is also a student will be represented by two distinct objects of the aforementioned categories.

The objects of the new categories are not persons but rather their "hats" — a person may have two "hats": one as an instructor and one as a student. The two categories of "hats" are disjoint.

The relations whose domain or range is the category *PERSON*, for example, the relation *ADDRESS*, will be replaced by two relations having the new categories as their domains or ranges, such as the relations *STUDENT'S-ADDRESS* and *INSTRUCTOR'S-ADDRESS*.

STUDENT *id-key: Integer* *last-name: String* *first-name: String* *birth-year: 1870..1990* *address: String*	**INSTRUCTOR** *id-key: Integer* *last-name: String* *first-name: String* *birth-year: 1870..1990* *address: String*

It may appear that by introducing the categories of "hats" we have succeeded in fooling the system. Actually, we have fooled ourselves. Without understanding the relationship between two hats of one person, the system will not be able to correctly interpret some queries of naive users and may cause inconsistency in the stored information and other problems:

- When the address of a person is updated, it may get updated in one category but not in the other. The database will become inconsistent.

- A naive query like "How many people are there?" will involve double count of persons who are instructors and students simultaneously.

*c.   Conversion into **Union+Events***

Example:

As Figure 3-8 shows, we can retain the category *PERSON* with all its relationships and define two categories of events which will inherit all the relationships of *STUDENT* and *INSTRUCTOR*, and additionally will have keys and special 1:1 relationships with the category *PERSON*:

- ☐ *PERSON* — category   (retains its relations from the binary schema)

- ☐ *Event-of-being-a-STUDENT* — category   (inherits all the relations of *STUDENT*)

- ☐ *Event-of-being-an-INSTRUCTOR* — category   (inherits all the relations of *INSTRUCTOR*)

- ☐ *student-person* — relation from *Event-of-being-a-STUDENT* to *PERSON*   (*1:1,total*)

□ *instructor-person* — relation from *Event-of-being-an-INSTRUCTOR* to *PERSON*   (*1:1,total*)

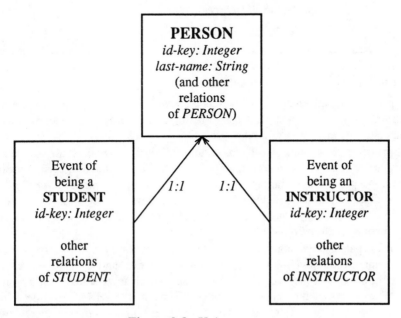

Figure 3-8. *Union +events*

Example:

To further explore the differences between the three approaches, consider the formulation of the query "Print the names of all the students."

Events :

    get s.*LAST-NAME*

        where s **is a** *STUDENT*

Union :

    get s.*LAST-NAME*

        where

            s **is a** *PERSON* **and**

            s.*IS-A-STUDENT*

Union+Events :

> **get** p.*LAST-NAME*
>
> > **where**
> >
> > > p **is a** *PERSON* **and**
> > >
> > > **exists** s **in** *STUDENT*:
> > >
> > > > s.*ID-key* = p.*ID-key*

Relative disadvantages of each approach

The principal disadvantage of **Events** is the *redundancy*. For example, the birth-year of an instructor who is also a student has to be logically represented twice in the database, which can cause inconsistency and other problems.

The principal disadvantages of **Union** are the *unnaturalness* of the schema and the *under-coverage of integrity constraints*. For example, an additional integrity constraint has to be defined to prevent association of a nonstudent instructor with *a major department of studies*. Another important deficiency is the *null-values*, causing significant problems in formulation of queries. (We say that "*p.MAJOR* is **null**" if the person p is not related to any department by the relation *MAJOR*.)

The principal disadvantages of **Union+Events** are the *unnaturalness* of the schema and significant difficulties in the formulation of queries and other operations. These difficulties, however, can be overcome by the use of userviews which would conveniently redefine the concepts of the schema. This requires that the DBMS provide a high-level support for userviews, including the capability to specify updates through userviews. Most relational DBMS, however, do not provide sufficient support of userviews.

Conclusion

Unless the DBMS provides sufficient support for userviews as discussed above, we have to exclude the **Union+Events** approach.

Both other approaches, **Union** and **Events**, would result in low-quality schemas, but the relational database designer has to choose the better of the two.

> *Example:*
>
> The choice should usually depend on the correlation of two parameters: the percentage of people who are both students and instructors, π, and the percentage of relations specific to students or instructors among all the relations which can be relevant to persons, ρ.

The relative redundancy in **Events** increases when π increases and when ρ decreases. The unnaturalness and the undercoverage of constraints in **Union** increase when π decreases and when ρ increases.

The following provides a decision criteria for an arbitrary group of categories. The decision is made according to the π:ρ ratio. A comparison quotient of 0.6 is suggested, which is quite often reasonable, as has been shown by analysis of a class of databases. If $π/ρ > 0.6$ then the **Union** approach would usually be preferable. In some special cases, however, the database designer should consider a different comparison quotient. The number 0.6 is only a "rule of thumb."

When there is chain of sub-sub-categories, the approach **Events** becomes too complicated and is not recommended. It is, however, the most natural approach in the majority of situations, because in the majority of cases π is small, the subcategory hierarchy is rather flat (no sub-sub-categories), and the DBMS does not provide a sufficient support for userviews.

D.   Convert the group of categories into disjoint categories.

    a.   *if* the DBMS provides a high level support for userviews, including specification of updates, *then* (*Union+Events*):

        (i)   Substitute every direct or indirect subcategory S of C in the schema being converted by the category **Event-of-being-a[n]-**S. Each object in this new category is an event of membership in the category S; that is, if x is an S then "x is an S" is one element in Event-of-being-an-S. (The categories of events are disjoint. For simplicity, the former names S may be kept but the new meaning is assumed.)

Example:

    ☐ *[Event-of-being-a-]STUDENT* — category
    ☐ *[Event-of-being-an-]INSTRUCTOR* — category

Example:

If we also had

    ☐ *TENURED-FACULTY* — subcategory of *INSTRUCTOR*

then we would convert it into

    ☐ *Event-of-being-TENURED-FACULTY* — category

    (ii)   Retain the category C.

Example:

☐ *PERSON* — category

(iii) Connect every new category of events S to each immediate supercategory of S by a new relation. Specify integrity constraints that these new relations are one-to-one and total.

Example:

☐ *student-person* — relation from *Event-of-being-a-STUDENT* to *PERSON* (*1:1,total*)

(iv) Let every new category of events S have all the relations that the former category S had.

Example:

☐ *major* — relation from *Event-of-being-a-STUDENT* to *DEPARTMENT* (*m:1*)

(v) Specify and add a key for every category of events S. The simplest way to do this is to inherit the key of C.

Example:

☐ *id-key* — attribute of *Event-of-being-a-STUDENT*, range: *Integer* (*1:1,total*)

---

b. **else if $\pi/\rho > 0.6$ *or*** there is a chain of sub-sub-categories **then** (**Union**):

(i) Replace the whole group of categories by one category C.

Example:

☐ *PERSON* — category

(ii) Bring all the relations exiting or entering the former subcategories to C.

Example:

□ *the-student* — relation from *COURSE-ENROLLMENT* to *PERSON*   *(m:1)*

(iii) Add to *C* total Boolean attributes named **is-a[n]-***S* for every direct and indirect subcategory *S* of *C* in the schema being converted.

Example:

□ *is-a-student* — attribute of *PERSON*, range: *Boolean*   *(m:1,total)*

□ *is-an-instructor* — attribute of *PERSON*, range: *Boolean* *(m:1,total)*

(iv) Add an integrity constraint stating that any object of *C* may participate in a former *S*'s corresponding relation only if the respective function is-an-*S* gives TRUE.

Example:

for every p **in** *PERSON*:

  if   exists d **in** *DEPARTMENT*:   p *WORKS-IN* d

then p.*IS-AN-INSTRUCTOR*

Example:

for every p **in** *PERSON*:

  if not (p *MAJOR* **null**)

  then p.*IS-A-STUDENT*

(v) Whenever there are attributes is-an-S_1 and is-an-S_2, where S_1 is a subcategory of S_2 in the original schema, add a constraint enforcing that in terms of the new attributes.

> *Example:*
>
> If we had:
>
> ☐ *UNDERGRADUATE* — subcategory of *STUDENT*
>
> then we would add a constraint:
>
> **for every** s **in** *PERSON*:
>
> **if** s.*IS-AN-UNDERGRADUATE*
>
> **then** s.*IS-A-STUDENT*

(vi) Whenever there are attributes is-an-S_1 and is-an-S_2, where S_1 and S_2 are disjoint in the original schema, add a constraint enforcing that in terms of the new attributes.

> *Example:*
>
> If the category *UNDERGRADUATE* was disjoint from the category *INSTRUCTOR*, then we would add a constraint:
>
> **for every** s **in** *PERSON*:
>
> **if** s.*IS-AN-UNDERGRADUATE*
>
> **then not** (s.*IS-AN-INSTRUCTOR*)

c. ***else*** (***Events***):

(i) Substitute the categories $S_1, \ldots, S_n$ by the corresponding n categories **Event-of-being-a-S_1**, ..., **Event-of-being-a-S_n** of the events of membership in categories; that is, if x is an S_i then "x is an S_i" is one element in the category Event-of-being-an-S_i. (The categories S_i are disjoint. For simplicity, former names S_i may be kept but the new meaning is assumed.)

> *Example:*
>
> ☐ *Event-of-being-a-STUDENT* — category
>
> disjoint from
>
> ☐ *Event-of-being-an-Instructor* — category

(ii) If there are, or *may* be in the future, objects in C that do not belong to any of the subcategories $S_1, \ldots, S_n$, then add a new category S_0 to the schema.

This will be the category of the objects that do not belong to any of the subcategories. This category is usually called **other-C**.

Example:

    □ *OTHER-PERSON* — category

  (iii) Replace every relation R whose domain or range is C, by new relations of the same name as R but having the categories S_i as their domains or ranges. (The relation R is partitioned into several relations according to the restricted domains or ranges S_i.)

Example:

    □ *birth-year* — attribute of *Event-of-being-a-STUDENT*, range: *1870..1990   (m:1)*

  (iv) Eliminate the category C.

  (v) Specify integrity constraints to prevent inconsistency of the redundant information:

> "If an object x of the category Event-of-being-an-S_i has the same key values as an object y of the category Event-of-being-an-S_j, then the other relations of C (inherited by the categories of events) must be equal for x and y."

Example:

We choose this alternative (**Events**) for the intersecting group of the subcategories of *PERSON* in the case-study database.

    The schema now has redundancy, which should be controlled by an integrity constraint, if possible. The integrity constraint is

for every s **in** *Event-of-being-a-STUDENT*:

for every i **in** *Event-of-being-an-INSTRUCTOR*:

    if

        (s.*ADDRESS* ≠ i.*ADDRESS* **or**

        s.*LAST-NAME* ≠ i.*LAST-NAME* **or**

        s.*FIRST-NAME* ≠ i.*FIRST-NAME* **or**

        s.*BIRTH-YEAR* ≠ i.*BIRTH-YEAR*)

    then s.*ID-key* ≠ i.*ID-key*

(Note: The constraint could have been written without negations, "in a positive spirit," but then the meaning of the absent values could be misinterpreted.)

Example:

The semantic schema of the university application has been converted so far (by **Events**) into the schema on the following page.

3.4.5. Removal of relations

Step 3. **Convert** every proper **1:m** or **m:m** relation whose **range is a concrete category** into a new abstract category with its two functional relations through a relation-split.

Example:

Instead of the relation

      ☐ *name* — relation from *DEPARTMENT* to *String*   (*1:m*)

we shall have

      ☐ *DEPARTMENT-NAMING* — category

      ☐ *the-department* — relation from *DEPARTMENT-NAMING* to *DEPARTMENT*   (*m:1,total*)

      ☐ *the-name* — relation from *DEPARTMENT-NAMING* to *String* (*1:1,total*)

Step 4. **Convert** every **1:m** relation into an m:1 relation by changing its direction and its name.

Example:

We do not have such relations in the university schema. If we assume we have the relation

      ☐ *provides* — relation from *DEPARTMENT* to *COURSE*   (*1:m*)

then we would change it into

      ☐ *the-department-providing-the-course* — relation from *COURSE* to *DEPARTMENT*   (*m:1*)

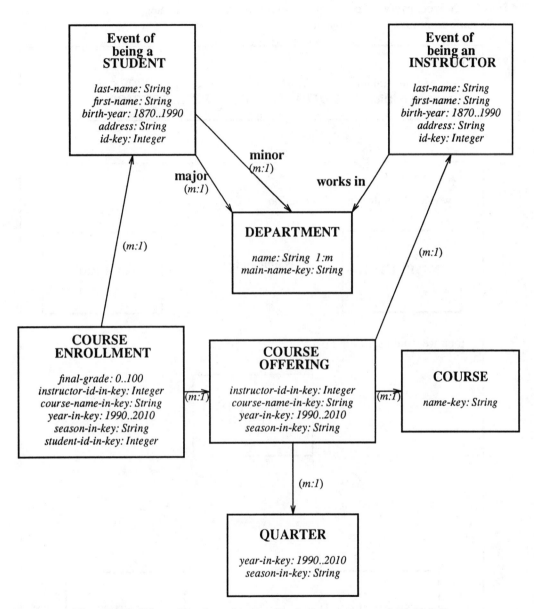

Figure 3-9. The university schema with the categories made artificially disjoint.

Step 5. Convert every proper **many-to-many** relation into a category and two functional relations through a relation-split.

Example:

We split the relation *WORKS-IN* into a new category *WORK* and its two functional relations *THE-DEPARTMENT* and *THE-INSTRUCTOR*.

Example:

If we had the following m:m relation

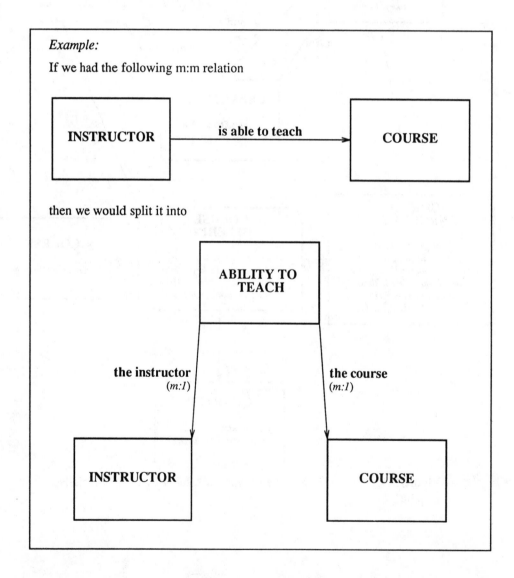

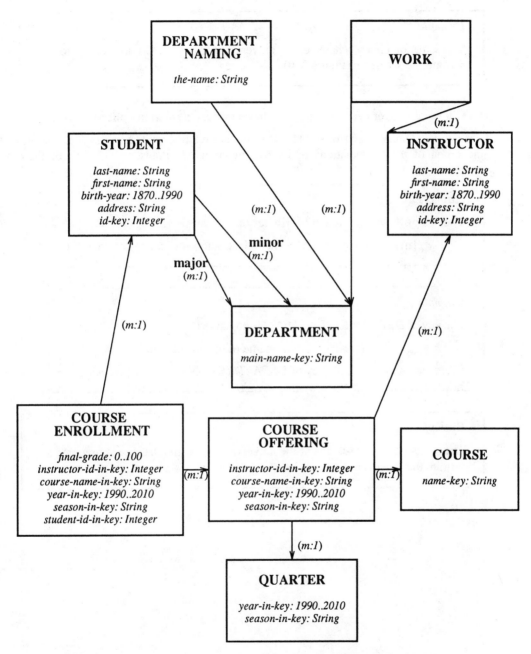

Figure 3-10. The university schema after all the relation splits have been performed.

> *Example:*
>
> The semantic binary schema of the university application has been converted so far into the schema in Figure 3-10.

Step 6. Choose a key for every category produced through a **relation-split** as follows.

For every category which was obtained through a relation-split, a key is contained in the union of the compositions of its two functional relations on the keys of their ranges.

> *Example:*
>
> The key of *WORK* is two new attributes of this category:
>
> > {main-name of the department, instructor-id of the instructor}

> *Example:*
>
> The key of *DEPARTMENT-NAMING* is contained in
>
> > {the-name, main-name of the department}
>
> Since *the-name* is 1:1, the key of *DEPARTMENT-NAMING* is *{the-name}*.

> *Example:*
>
> The semantic binary schema of the university application has been converted so far into the schema in Figure 3-11.

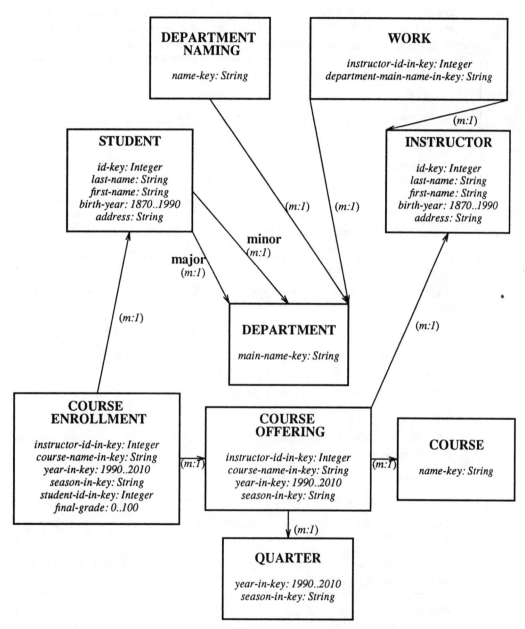

Figure 3-11. The university schema after the relation splits have been performed and keys have been chosen for every category.

Step 7. Replace every **m:1 relation** f whose **range is an abstract category** by the composition of f on the chosen key of its range, that is, by attributes $b_1, \ldots, b_n$, where $x.b_i = (x.f).a_i$, and $a_1, \ldots, a_n$ is the chosen key of f's range.

Example:

Instead of

      ☐ *major* — relation from *STUDENT* to *DEPARTMENT*   (*m:1*)

we shall have

      ☐ *major-dept-main-name* — attribute of *STUDENT*, range: *String* (*m:1*)

Step 8. Remove redundant nonkey attributes.

From every category **remove attributes** which are not in the key but are **inferable** from other attributes of the same category.

These attributes would usually have resulted from a "blind" application of this algorithm, particularly

a.   A nonkey attribute which is always equal to an attribute in the key.

    Note: It is possible that step (7) brought to a category C an attribute b which is always equal to an attribute in the key of C.

b.   A redundant Boolean attribute brought in step (1):

    Suppose:

- We were converting intersecting categories C, $S_1, \ldots, S_n$ into disjoint categories.

- We replaced them by one ***Union*** category C.

- one of the categories S_i was disjoint from all of the rest S_j's.

Then the new attribute is-an-S_i is inferable from the rest of the attributes is-an-S_j.

This attribute should be removed from the schema. (It may be present in a userview, where it would be an inferred attribute.)

Example:

If we had

      ☐ *ILLITERATE* — subcategory of *PERSON*   (disjoint from INSTRUCTOR and from STUDENT) and furthermore, there were no other persons but students, instructors, and illiterate persons, then the attribute *is-illiterate* would be derivable:

for every p in PERSON:

p.*IS-ILLITERATE* =

(not p.*IS-A-STUDENT* and not p. *IS-AN-INSTRUCTOR*)

> *Note:* The removal of several attributes should *not* be performed simultaneously. Otherwise, two attributes mutually inferable, but not inferable from the rest, might be removed.

3.4.6. Integrity constraints

Step 9. Translate the integrity constraints into the terms of the new schema:

a.   The constraints of the original schema.

b.   The additional constraints accumulated during the conversion process.

> *Example:*
>
> The semantic schema of the university application has been converted into the relational schema of Figure Ref-2.

Problem 3-3.

Use the university/relational reference schema at the end of this book. Specify in calculus all the integrity constraints which are not covered by this relational schema but are covered by the binary schema, that is, the constraints generated during the conversion from the binary schema.

Problem 3-4.

Use the university/binary reference schema at the end of this book. Convert this schema into a relational schema, assuming

- 50 percent of the instructors are students and 40 percent of students are instructors.
- An instructor can give the same course several times during one quarter.
- Every name of a department is subject to change.
- The DBMS does not support userviews.

Specify the integrity constraints which are not covered by your relational schema but are covered by the binary schema.

Problem 3-5.

Use the university/binary reference schema at the end of this book. Solve the previous problem replacing the *userviews* assumption:

- The DBMS provides excellent support for userviews, including userview updates.

In the following problems, design a relational schema equivalent to the appropriate binary schema. Specify the integrity constraints incident to the conversion from the binary schema to the relational schema.

Problem 3-6.

Use the clan/binary schema (Figure 13-3 on page 390).

Solution on page 407.

Problem 3-7.

Use the wholesaler/binary schema (Figure 13-1 on page 388).

Solution on page 408.

Problem 3-8.

Use the studio/binary schema (Figure 13-2 on page 389). Design a relational schema for the Studio application. Specify in English the integrity constraints (besides the keys) which should accompany the above relational schema but are implied by the binary schema.

Solution on page 410.

Problem 3-9.

Use the circuit/binary schema (Figure 13-5 on page 391).

Solution on page 411.

Problem 3-10.

Use the sales/binary schema (Figure 13-4 on page 390).

Solution on page 412.

Problem 3-11.

Use the medical/binary schema (Figure 13-6 on page 395).

1. Design a relational schema for the medical world. Your database should be equivalent in the information content to the binary database described by the above binary schema.

2. Specify in calculus all the integrity constraints that have to be added to the schema during conversion.

3. Whenever the conversion algorithm allows a selection between alternatives, discuss the alternatives, show briefly every alternative way, and justify your selection.

Solution on page 413.

Problem 3-12.
Use the busstop/binary schema (Figure 13-11 on page 399).

Solution on page 416.

Problem 3-13.
Use the carsale/binary schema (Figure 13-12 on page 400).

Solution on page 417.

Problem 3-14.
Use the newspaper/binary schema (Figure 13-28 on page 419).

Solution on page 419.

Problem 3-15.
Use the clinic/binary schema (Figure 13-13 on page 401).

Solution on page 420.

Problem 3-16.
Use the library/binary schema (Figure 13-7 on page 396).

Solution on page 421.

CHAPTER 4

RELATIONAL DATABASE LANGUAGES

This chapter describes relational database languages. Sections 1 and 2 show examples of how the languages of Chapter 2 (the fourth-generation and the logic-based languages) apply to the relational databases. The principal example of Section 1 discusses the principles of writing a transaction-processing program for an application. The optional Section 3 defines the Relational Algebra. Section 4 describes SQL, a popular commercial language related to the Relational Predicate Calculus of Section 2. The expressive power and equivalence of relational languages is discussed in Section 5.

4.1. Fourth-generation Programming

The structured extension of Pascal for relational databases is the same as the extension of Pascal for semantic databases but is used for the relational schema. (Every relational schema is a binary schema. Thus, every language used for the Binary Model can be used for the Relational Model.)

Example:

The university has decided to expel all the students whose average grade is below 60 (out of 100). To prevent this wrong-doing to computer science students, the department offered a fictitious course, Computer-Pass, by Prof. Good, in which all computer science students are to receive a sufficient grade so as to not to be expelled, if possible.

The following program fabricates Prof. Good and the Computer-Pass course, enrolls students in this course, grades them accordingly, and prints the names of those computer science students whom this measure cannot help.

---

program Pass (Input, Output, UNIVERSITY-DB, UNIVERSITY-MASTER-VIEW);

var Computer-Pass-Course, Prof-Good, Good-Offer, computer-science-name, comp-science, cs-student, her-enrollment, fictitious-enrollment: *ABSTRACT*;

   the-grade, desired-grade, number-of-grades, total-of-grades, current-year: *INTEGER*;

begin

(* Get the current year from the standard input file. *)

   read (current-year);

transaction begin

   (* Fabricate the course. *)

      create new Computer-Pass-Course **in** *COURSE*;

      Computer-Pass-Course.*NAME-key* := 'Computer Pass';

   (* Fabricate the Prof. Good. *)

      create new Prof-Good **in** *INSTRUCTOR*;

      Prof-Good.*LAST-NAME* := 'Good';

      Prof-Good.*ID-key* := 1234; (* Let's hope that this fabricated ID number does not already belong to a legitimate instructor. Otherwise, an error will result. *)

   (* Fabricate the offering. *)

      create new Good-Offer **in** *COURSE-OFFERING*;

      Good-Offer.*COURSE-NAME-in-key* := 'Computer Pass';

      Good-Offer.*INSTRUCTOR-ID-in-key* := 1234;

      Good-Offer.*YEAR* := current-year;

Good-Offer.*SEASON* := 'Winter'

end;

(* The following two nested loops will be performed only once. Inside the body of the second loop, the variable *comp-science* will refer to the Computer Science Department. *)

for computer-science-name **in** *DEPARTMENT-NAMING*

where (computer-science-name.*NAME-key* = 'COMPUTER SCIENCE') **do**

for comp-science **in** *DEPARTMENT*

where (comp-science.*MAIN-NAME-key* = comp-science-name.*MAIN-NAME*) **do begin**

(* Make believe that Prof. Good works in Computer Science. *)

(* In terms of the binary schema, **relate**: Prof-Good *WORKS-IN* comp-science *)

transaction begin

create new work **in** *WORK*;

work.*INSTRUCTOR-ID-in-key* := 1234;

work.*DEPARTMENT-MAIN-NAME-in-key* := comp-science.*MAIN-NAME-key*

end;

for cs-student **in** *STUDENT*

where (cs-student.*MAJOR-DEPARTMENT-MAIN-NAME* = comp-science.*MAIN-NAME-key*) **do**

begin (* the current computer science student *)

(* calculate this student's current statistics: number-of-grades and total-of-grades *)

number-of-grades := 0;

total-of-grades := 0;

for her-enrollment **in** *COURSE-ENROLLMENT* **where** (her-enrollment.*STUDENT-ID-in-key* = cs-student.*ID-key* **and not** her-enrollment *FINAL-GRADE* **null**) **do begin**

the-grade := her-enrollment.*FINAL-GRADE*;

number-of-grades := number-of-grades + 1;

total-of-grades := total-of-grades + the-grade

end;

(* calculate the minimal desired grade in computer-pass course, solving the equation

$(total+x)/(number+1)=60$ *)

desired-grade := 60 * (number-of-grades + 1) — total-of-grades;

if desired-grade > 100 **then**

(* the student cannot be helped. Print a message *)

writeln (' The student ', cs-student.*LAST-NAME*, ' cannot be helped. Sorry!')

else if desired-grade > 60 **then**

transaction begin

create new fictitious-enrollment **in** *COURSE-ENROLLMENT*;

fictitious-enrollment.*STUDENT-ID-in-key* := cs-student.*ID-key*;

fictitious-enrollment.*COURSE-NAME-in-key* := 'Computer Pass';

fictitious-enrollment.*INSTRUCTOR-ID-in-key* := 1234;

fictitious-enrollment.*YEAR* := 1990;

fictitious-enrollment.*SEASON* := 'Winter';

fictitious-enrollment.*FINAL-GRADE* := desired-grade

end (* transaction *)

end (* current student *)

end (* computer science department *)

end.

4.1.1. Transaction processing

Many application programs process a continuous sequence of end-user requests for transactions. In each cycle, such a program accepts a request from an end-user, translates it from the data-entry form into the terms of the database, determines the validity of the request, and performs it.

Most relational DBMS are unable to automatically enforce the integrity constraints, particularly *referential integrity*. In this case, the busy-work of **manual integrity validation** must be performed by the application programs processing the user transactions.

Example:

The following program reads from the standard input a series of requests for enrolling students in classes. For every request, the program checks its integrity against the database. If the request is integral, the program performs the update. Otherwise, an error message is printed.

It is assumed that the DBMS is unable to automatically enforce the referential integrity.

```
program Enroll (Input, Output, University-database, University-master-userview);
var
    student-id, instructor-id, year: Integer;
    course-name, season: String;
    student, instructor, course, quarter, offering, enrollment: ABSTRACT;
    student-ok, instructor-ok, course-ok, quarter-ok, offering-ok, enrollment-ok: Boolean;
procedure Erroneous-transaction (explanation: String);
    (* This procedure is called

        •   from Transaction-error-handler, when an error is detected by the DBMS

        •   from the program, when an error is detected by the program.  *)

begin
    writeln ('The enrollment request listed in the following line could not be granted for
        the reason: ', explanation);

    writeln (student-id, instructor-id, course-name, year, season)

end
procedure Transaction-error-handler (error-description: String);
    begin
    Erroneous-transaction (concatenate('System error: ', error-description);

    end
begin
while not eof(Input) do
transaction begin
    (* Get a request for the next enrollment transaction  *)
```

readln (student-id, instructor-id, course-name, year, season)

(* Check student ID *)

student-ok := false;

for student **in** *STUDENT*

    where (student.*ID-key* = student-id)

    do student-ok := true;

if not student-ok **then**

    Erroneous-transaction ('No student known by the student-id submitted in
the first field of the enrollment request');

(* Check instructor ID *)

instructor-ok := false;

for instructor **in** *INSTRUCTOR*

    where (instructor.*ID-key* = instructor-id)

    do instructor-ok := true;

if not instructor-ok **then**

    Erroneous-transaction ('No instructor known by the instructor-id submitted
in the second field of the enrollment request');

(* Check course name *)

course-ok := false;

for course **in** *COURSE*

    where (course.*NAME-key* = course-name)

    do course-ok := true;

if not course-ok **then**

    Erroneous-transaction ('No course known by the course-name submitted in
the third field of the enrollment request');

(* Check quarter *)

quarter-ok := false;

for quarter **in** *QUARTER*

    where (quarter.*YEAR-in-key* = year **and** quarter.*SEASON-in-key* = season)

    do quarter-ok := true;

if not quarter-ok **then**

Erroneous-transaction ('No quarter known by the year and season submitted in the fourth and fifth fields of the enrollment request');

(* Check the offering *)

offering-ok := false;

for offering **in** *COURSE-OFFERING*

where (offering. INSTRUCTOR-ID-in-key = instructor-id **and** offering.-*COURSE-NAME-in-key* = course-name **and** offering.*YEAR-in-key* = year **and** offering.*SEASON-in-key* = season)

do offering-ok := true;

if instructor-ok **and** course-ok **and** quarter-ok **and not** offering-ok **then**

Erroneous-transaction ('No offering known by the instructor-id, course, year and season submitted in the second through fifth fields of the enrollment request');

(* The following check of nonduplicate enrollment is not strictly necessary, since it can be performed automatically by the DBMS, which knows to enforce the uniqueness of the keys. Thus, the only practical reason for this test is to produce a better message than what would be produced by the system by default. *)

(* Check that student is not already enrolled in the offering *)

enrollment-ok := true;

for enrollment **in** *COURSE-ENROLLMENT*

where (enrollment.*STUDENT-ID-in-key* = student-id **and** enrollment.-*INSTRUCTOR-ID-in-key* = instructor-id **and** enrollment.*COURSE-NAME-in-key* = course-name **and** enrollment.*YEAR-in-key* = year **and** enrollment.*SEASON-in-key* = season)

do enrollment-ok := false;

if not enrollment-ok **then**

Erroneous-transaction ('The requested enrollment of the student already exists')

if student-ok **and** instructor-ok **and** course-ok **and** quarter-ok **and** offering-ok **and** enrollment-ok

then

(* Insert the new enrollment *)

begin

create new enrollment **in** *COURSE-ENROLLMENT*;

            enrollment.*STUDENT-ID-in-key* := student-id;

            enrollment.*INSTRUCTOR-ID-in-key* := instructor-id;

            enrollment.*COURSE-NAME-in-key* := course-name;

            enrollment.*YEAR-in-key* := year;

            enrollment.*SEASON-in-key* := season

            end

       end (* transaction *)

end.

Problem 4-1.

Use the studio/relational schema (Figure 13-21 on page 410). Write a relational data manipulation program in the structured extension of Pascal for the following task:

> Create a new film "Memories of Actress Jane Smith." For every scene that Jane Smith has played, this film should contain a scene to be shot at Jane's home.

Solution on page 424.

Problem 4-2.

Use the projects/relational schema (Figure 13-16 on page 406). Write a program in Extended Pascal for the following task:

> Let employee whose ID is 555 work for all the projects for which his or her immediate subordinates work. You may assume that the employee is already known in the data base.

Solution on page 425.

4.2. Logic for Relational Databases

Relational Calculus — Predicate Calculus, when used for the relational schema. (Since every relational schema is a binary schema, we already know Relational Calculus.)

> *Example:*
>
> What are the last names of all the students?
>
> **get** s.*LAST-NAME*
>
>   **where** s **is a** STUDENT

Example:

What are the distinct last names of the students? (No name may be printed twice.)

get n

  where

  exists s **in** *STUDENT*:

  n = s.*LAST-NAME*

Tuple-oriented Relational Calculus — Relational calculus with the following restriction: the quantification is done only on abstract categories (i.e., tables).

Among the languages of the Relational Model, more languages are based on the tuple-oriented Predicate Calculus than on the more general form of Predicate Calculus.

Example:

The previous example was not in the tuple-oriented form because the variable *n* was implicitly quantified over the concrete category *String*.

The following examples *are* in tuple-oriented form.

Example:

Has every student enrolled in at least one course in 1990?

  for every st **in** *STUDENT*:

  exists enrl **in** *COURSE-ENROLLMENT*:

  ((enrl.*STUDENT-ID-in-key* = st.*ID-key*) **and** (enrl.-*YEAR*=1990))

Example:

Who took Prof. Smith's courses?

get student.*LAST-NAME* **where**

    (student **is a** *STUDENT* **and**

    exists enrl **in** *COURSE-ENROLLMENT*:

        (enrl.*STUDENT-ID-in-key*=student.*ID-key* **and**

        exists inst **in** *INSTRUCTOR*:

            (inst.*LAST-NAME* = 'Smith' **and**

            enrl.*INSTRUCTOR-ID-in-key*=inst.*ID-key*)))

Example:

Print the average grade of every computer science student.

    get student.*LAST-NAME*,

        (**average** enrollment.*FINAL-GRADE*

            where

                enrollment.*STUDENT-ID-in-key* = student.*ID-key*)

    where

        student **is a** *STUDENT* and

        (student.*MAJOR-DEPT-MAIN-NAME* = 'Computer Science')

Example:

How many students are there in the university?

    get (**count** std **where** std **is a** *STUDENT*)

> *Example:*
>
> What students have their average grade below 60?
>
> > **get** std.*LAST-NAME*
> >
> > **where** std **is a** *STUDENT* **and**
> >
> > > 60 >
> > >
> > > > **average** enrl.*FINAL-GRADE*
> > > >
> > > > **where**
> > > >
> > > > > enrl **is a** *COURSE-ENROLLMENT* **and**
> > > > >
> > > > > enrl.*STUDENT-ID-in-key* = std.*ID-key*

Problem 4-3.

Use the studio/relational schema (Figure 13-21 on page 410). Write a query in Calculus to find the following information from the above relational database:

> The names of the actors who assisted in or directed the same *film* in which they acted.

Solution on page 426.

Problem 4-4.

Use the projects/relational schema (Figure 13-16 on page 406). Write a query in Relational Predicate Calculus to find the following information from the database:

> The names of the employees who do not work for any project but do supervise somebody.

Solution on page 426.

Problem 4-5.

Use the projects/relational schema (Figure 13-16 on page 406). Specify in English a meaningful integrity constraint (not necessarily one of the above) which cannot be specified in the Relational Calculus even if aggregate functions are used.

Problem 4-6.

An attribute A of table T is said to be **functionally dependent** on a set of attributes $\{B_1, \ldots, B_k\}$ of T if for no tuple of values $(b_1, \ldots, b_k)$ of these attributes there may be two different values of A in the table at the same time.

Let T be a table with four attributes A, B, C, and D. Specify in Relational Calculus the constraint:

> "D is functionally dependent on $\{A, B\}$"

Solution on page 426.

4.3. *Relational Algebra

Relational Algebra is an algebraic language in which new tables are defined by applying operators to other tables.

This is a language of expressions. In it, a new table is defined as an expression involving original tables and operators.

The most important operators are:

- **Projection operator** creates a new table containing some of the columns of another table.

- **Join operator** combines the rows of the first table with "related" rows of the second table.

- **Selection operator** extracts some rows from a table according to a given condition on the values of the row.

Example:

{The last names of the students born in 1975} =

(*project*-the-column-*LAST-NAME*

    (*select*-the-rows-where-the-*BIRTH-YEAR*-is-1975

        (the table *STUDENT*)))

In this section, the operators of Relational Algebra are defined by inference laws in Predicate Calculus.

Consider two tables:

    table T, whose attributes are $A_1, \ldots, A_n$

    table T', whose attributes are $A'_1, \ldots, A'_{n'}$

1.   The **projection operator** (. . .[attributes]) creates a new table containing some of the columns of another table.

    Let $F_1, \ldots, F_k$ be some of the attributes (columns) of table T. Then

$$T [F_1, \ldots, F_k] =$$

    get $F_1: v_1, \ldots, F_k: v_k$

        where exists x **in** T:

            $x.F_1 = v_1$ **and** $\cdots$ **and** $x.F_k = v_k$

Note: When several tuples of T have the same values in the columns being projected, only one row will appear in the result. Thus, the resulting table may have fewer tuples than T.

Example:

A list of the distinct last names of the students =

STUDENT [LAST -NAME]=

get *LAST-NAME*: name

where

exists x **in** *STUDENT*:

x.*LAST-NAME* = name

Example:

Last names and majors of all the students =

STUDENT [LAST-NAME, MAJOR-DEPARTMENT-MAIN-NAME] =

get *LAST-NAME*: name, *MAJOR-DEPARTMENT-MAIN-NAME* : major

where

exists x **in** *STUDENT*:

x.*LAST-NAME* = name **and**

x.*MAJOR-DEPARTMENT-MAIN-NAME* = major

Example:

We can define an inferred table *STUDENT-BASIC* containing all the information from the table *STUDENT* except the departments:

STUDENT-BASIC = STUDENT [ID-key, LAST-NAME, FIRST-NAME, BIRTH-YEAR, ADDRESS]

2.   The **renaming operator** (. . .[attribute/new-name]) changes the name of a column in a table.

$T[A_i \, / \, \overline{A}_i] =$

(* Copy the attributes $A_1, \ldots, A_{i-1}, A_{i+1}, \ldots, A_n$; rename the attribute A_i. *)

get A_1: x.$A_1, \ldots,$ A_{i-1}: x.A_{i-1}, $\overline{A}_i$: x.A_i, A_{i+1}: x.$A_{i+1}, \ldots,$ A_n: x.A_n

where x **is a** *T*

Example:

A table just like *STUDENT*, with 'FAMILY-NAME' column title instead of 'LAST-NAME':

$$STUDENT\ [LAST\text{-}NAME/FAMILY\text{-}NAME]$$

---

3. The **cartesian product operator** $\times$

For every row of the first operand and for every row of the second operand, the product operator produces the concatenation of the two rows.

The number of rows in the result =

(the number of rows in the first operand $\times$

the number of rows in the second operand)

The number of columns in the result =

(the number of columns in the first operand +

the number of columns in the second operand)

This operation is syntactically erroneous when the two tables have a common attribute.

Cartesian product =

$T \times T' =$

  get $A_1{:}x.A_1, \ldots, A_n{:}x.A_n, A'_1{:}y.A'_1, \ldots, A_{n'}{:}y.A_{n'}$

  where x **is a** T **and** y **is a** T'

4. **Set operators**

The following operators are defined only when the two tables have the same attributes.

a. **Union of tables** produces all the rows of the first table and all the rows of the second table.

 $T \cup T' =$

  get $A_1{:}v_1, \ldots, A_n{:}v_n$

   where

    exists x **in** T :

     $x.A_1{=}v_1$ **and** $\cdots$ **and** $x.A_n{=}v_n$

or exists x **in** T':

$$x.A_1 = v_1 \text{ and } \cdots \text{ and } x.A_n = v_n$$

Example:

All the persons =

STUDENT-BASIC $\cup$ INSTRUCTOR =

    get *ID-key* : id, . . . , *ADDRESS* : addr

        where

            exists x **in** *STUDENT-BASIC*:

                x.*ID-key* = id **and** $\cdots$ **and** x.*ADDRESS* = addr

            or exists x **in** *INSTRUCTOR* :

                x.*ID-key* = id **and** $\cdots$ **and** x.*ADDRESS* = addr

---

b.   **Intersection of tables** produces the rows which appear in both tables.

$T \cap T' =$

    get $A_1{:}v_1, \ldots, A_n{:}v_n$

        where

            exists x **in** T :

                $x.A_1 = v_1$ **and** $\cdots$ **and** $x.A_n = v_n$

            and exists x **in** T':

                $x.A_1 = v_1$ **and** $\cdots$ **and** $x.A_n = v_n$

Example:

Instructors who are students =

    INSTRUCTOR $\cap$ STUDENT-BASIC

---

c.   The **difference of tables operator** (−) produces the rows of the first table which do not appear in the second table.

$T - T' =$

    get $A_1{:}v_1, \ldots, A_n{:}v_n$

        where

exists x **in** T:

$x.A_1 = v_1$ **and** $\cdots$ **and** $x.A_n = v_n$

and not exists x **in** T':

$x.A_1 = v_1$ **and** $\cdots$ **and** $x.A_n = v_n$

Example:

Instructors who are not students =

INSTRUCTOR – STUDENT-BASIC

---

5.   The **selection operator (...[condition])** extracts some rows from a table according to a given condition for the values of the row.

Let $F_1, \ldots, F_k$ be some of the attributes of T.

Let *boolexp* $(v_1, \ldots, v_k)$ be a Boolean expression with k variables.

Then

$T\ [boolexp\ (F_1, \ldots, F_k)]$ =

   get $x.A_1, \ldots, x.A_n$

      where

         x **is a** T **and**

            boolexp $(x.F_1, \ldots, x.F_k)$

Example:

The student whose first name is Mary =

STUDENT [*FIRST-NAME*='Mary']

Example:

The instructor whose name is Chung and who is not a student (as distinguished from another Chung who is both an instructor and a student.)

All the instructors whose name is 'Chung' =

INSTRUCTOR [*LAST-NAME*='Chung']

The nonstudent instructor(s) whose name is 'Chung' =

INSTRUCTOR [LAST-NAME='Chung'] – STUDENT-BASIC

Example:

Names of the instructors teaching databases.

All the combinations of instructors and offerings (including the unrelated ones) =

(INSTRUCTOR × COURSE-OFFERING)

(*product*)

All combinations of instructors and their offerings =

(INSTRUCTOR × COURSE-OFFERING)
[ID-key=INSTRUCTOR-ID-in-key]

(*selection*)

All combinations of instructors and their offerings of *Databases* =

(INSTRUCTOR × COURSE-OFFERING)
[ID-key=INSTRUCTOR-ID-in-key]
[COURSE-NAME-in-key='Databases']

(*selection*)

The last names of the instructors offering *Databases* =

(INSTRUCTOR × COURSE-OFFERING)
[ID-key=INSTRUCTOR-ID-in-key]
[COURSE-NAME-in-key='Databases']
[LAST-NAME]

(*projection*)

---

6.   The **join operator** combines the rows of the first table with "related" rows of the second table. It is equivalent to a selection from the cartesian product.

T [boolexp (attributes)]T´ =

(T × T´)[boolexp (attributes)]

Example:

Names of instructors teaching databases.

All combinations of instructors and their offerings =

(*INSTRUCTOR* [*ID-key=INSTRUCTOR-ID-in-key*] *COURSE-OFFERING*)

(**join**)

The last names of the instructors offering databases =

(*INSTRUCTOR* [*ID-key=INSTRUCTOR-ID-in-key*] *COURSE-OFFERING*)
[*COURSE-NAME-in-key*='Databases']
[*LAST-NAME*]

---

7.   The **natural join operator** $\square$ combines two tables according to the equal values of the common attributes (column names) of the two tables.

Let the table T have k attributes with names identical to the names of k attributes of the table T', that is:

- the attributes of T are: $A_1, \ldots, A_k, A_{k+1}, \ldots, A_n$
- the attributes of T' are: $A_1, \ldots, A_k, A'_{k+1}, \ldots, A'_{n'}$

Then

   $T\square T' =$

   get $A_1{:}v_1, \ldots, A_n{:}v_n, A'_{k+1}{:}w_{k+1}, \ldots, A'_{n'}{:}w_{n'}$

   where

   exists x **in** T:

   x.$A_1{=}v_1$ **and** $\cdots$ **and** x.$A_n{=}v_n$

   and exists x **in** T':

   x.$A_1{=}v_1$ **and** $\cdots$ **and** x.$A_k{=}v_k$ **and** x.$A'_{k+1}{=}v_{k+1}$ **and** $\cdots$
   and x.$A'_{n'}{=}w_{n'}$

Example:

Names of instructors teaching databases.

The table *INSTRUCTOR* with the column *ID-key* renamed in order to be naturally joinable with the table *COURSE-OFFERING* =

(*INSTRUCTOR* [*ID-key/INSTRUCTOR-ID-in-key*]

(*rename*)

All combinations of instructors and their offerings =

(*INSTRUCTOR* [*ID-key/INSTRUCTOR-ID-in-key*] ☐
    COURSE-OFFERING)

(*natural join*)

The last names of the instructors offering databases =

(*INSTRUCTOR* [*ID-key/INSTRUCTOR-ID-in-key*] ☐
    COURSE-OFFERING)
    [*COURSE-NAME-in-key*='Databases']
    [*LAST-NAME*]

Uses of the Relational Algebra:

1. Specification of userviews (inference rules).

2. Specification of queries. Albeit, the language is not friendly enough to be used for specification of complex queries.

3. An intermediate language, because it is easy to implement Relational Algebra. Other, more friendly languages, can be translated into Relational Algebra.

4. A tool to evaluate and compare different languages. We can estimate the expressive power of an arbitrary language by checking whether it is

    a.   Able to specify every query expressible in Relational Algebra.

    b.   Able to specify every query expressible in Relational Algebra and more.

    c.   Able to specify a subset of the queries expressible in Relational Algebra, where the subset is defined by weakening the Algebra through eliminating some of its operators. The list of the eliminated operators shows the weakness of the language. The list of the remaining operators shows the power of the language:

        •   Many simple query languages can express *projection* and *selection* but not *join* or *difference*.

        •   More powerful languages can express *join*.

        •   Languages which are even more powerful can also express *difference*.

Problem 4-7.

Use the studio/relational schema (Figure 13-21 on page 410). Write a Relational Algebra expression to find the names of the directors of the films showing helicopters as props.

Solution on page 426.

Problem 4-8.

Use the projects/relational schema (Figure 13-16 on page 406). Write a relational algebra expression to find the names of the projects beginning with the letter Z in which Smith works.

Solution on page 427.

4.4. SQL

4.4.1. Preview

SQL has become a very popular language of commercial relational database management systems.

The acronym *SQL* stands for Structured Query Language.

A basic query in SQL   **select**s the values of some attributes

from some rows of a table or tables

where the rows satisfy a condition

Example:

When was student Russel born?

    select *BIRTH-YEAR*

    from *STUDENT*

    where *LAST-NAME*='Russel'

Example:

List the names of all students.

    select *FIRST-NAME, LAST-NAME*

    from *STUDENT*

    where true

Example:

What courses has Prof. Graham taught?

    select *COURSE-NAME*

    from *COURSE-OFFERING, INSTRUCTOR*

> **where** *INSTRUCTOR.NAME* = 'Graham' **and** *INSTRUCTOR.ID* =
> *COURSE-OFFERING. INSTRUCTOR-ID*

4.4.2. Basic queries

Syntax:

> **select** *expression*$_1$, . . . , *expression*$_n$
>
> **from** *table*$_1$ *var*$_1$, . . . , *table*$_n$ *var*$_n$
>
> **where** *condition*

The *condition* is a Boolean expression without quantifiers. It may depend on the variables $var_1, \ldots, var_n$.

Meaning:

> **get** *expression*$_1$, . . . , *expression*$_n$
>
> **where**
>
> > *var*$_1$ **is a** *table*$_1$ **and** $\cdots$ *var*$_n$ **is a** *table*$_n$ **and**
> >
> > *condition*

Example:

Print the names of the pairs of students who live together.

> **select** *s*$_1$.*LAST-NAME*, *s*$_2$.*LAST-NAME*
>
> **from** *STUDENT s*$_1$, *STUDENT s*$_2$
>
> **where** *s*$_1$.*ADDRESS* = *s*$_2$.*ADDRESS*

Abbreviation:

> If a table *T*$_i$ appears exactly once in the *from* list, then it does not have to be explicitly accompanied by a variable. Implicitly, the name of the variable is identical to the name of the table.
>
> > **select** *expression*$_1$, . . . , *expression*$_n$
> >
> > **from** *table*$_1$, . . . , *table*$_n$
> >
> > **where** *condition*

Example:

Print the names of the pairs of a student and an instructor who live together. (This includes an instructor who is also a student and lives with alone.)

select *STUDENT.LAST-NAME, INSTRUCTOR.LAST-NAME*

from *STUDENT, INSTRUCTOR*

where *STUDENT.ADDRESS = INSTRUCTOR.ADDRESS*

Abbreviation: When there is only one table in the *from* list, then whenever *T.attribute* appears in the query, it may be shortened to *attribute* without the prefix *T*.

Example:

Print the names and the addresses of all computer science students.

select *LAST-NAME, ADDRESS*

from *STUDENT*

where *MAJOR-DEPARTMENT-MAIN-NAME* = 'Computer Science'

Abbreviation: When the *select* list consists of all the attributes of the *from* tables, the select list may be abbreviated by "**select ∗**".

Example:

Print the names (last and first), the IDs, the birth-years, the major and minor departments, and the addresses of all computer science students.

select ∗

from *STUDENT*

where *MAJOR-DEPARTMENT-MAIN-NAME* = 'Computer Science'

Note:

- The output of a query is a partial instantaneous binary database. It can be printed as a table (in the common sense of the word *table*).

- Often, but not always, the output of a query is an instantaneous table in the sense of the Relational Model. This is not always true since the output of a query may contain identical rows, while a relational instantaneous table may not contain identical rows.

4.4.3. Basic aggregates

Basic aggregates are predefined functions which are applied to the whole output of a query. Syntactically, the functions are applied to the expression(s) in the *select* list.

1. **count** — when this function is applied to the *select* list, it replaces the output of the query by the number of rows in the output.

> *Example:*
>
> How many computer science students are there?
>
> > **select count**(∗)
> >
> > **from** *STUDENT*
> >
> > **where** *MAJOR-DEPARTMENT-MAIN-NAME* = 'Computer Science'

2. **avg** — when the *select* list consists of only one expression, and the expression produces numerical values, the function **avg** replaces the output by the average of the values in the output.

> *Example:*
>
> What is the average grade in the *Databases* course?
>
> > **select avg**(*FINAL-GRADE*)
> >
> > **from** *COURSE-ENROLLMENT*
> >
> > **where** *COURSE-NAME-IN-KEY* = 'Databases'

3. **sum** — when the *select* list consists of only one expression, and the expression produces numerical values, the function **sum** replaces the output by the sum of the values in the output.

4. **max** — when the *select* list consists of only one expression, and the expression produces numerical values, the function **max** replaces the output by the maximum of the values in the output.

5. **min** — when the *select* list consists of only one expression, and the expression produces numerical values, the function **min** replaces the output by the minimum of the values in the output.

6. **distinct** — eliminates duplicate rows in the output. This function must be applied to the whole *select* list. (In many implementations, this function is called "**unique**.")

Example:

List the distinct addresses of the students. (Do not list the same address twice.)

> **select distinct**(*ADDRESS*)
>
> **from** *STUDENT*
>
> **where** TRUE

---

7.   The function **distinct** can be combined with any other aggregate function. The function **distinct** is applied first, and then another function is applied to the result.

Example:

How many departments have minor students?

> **select count** (**distinct** *MINOR-DEPARTMENT-MAIN-NAME*)
>
> **from** *STUDENT*
>
> **where** TRUE

4.4.4. Nested queries

Query forms are represented in SQL by allowing some expressions to contain variables which are not defined (either explicitly or implicitly) in the *from* list. A query form would become a query if the expressions with undefined variables were replaced by constants. Query forms are used in SQL primarily in order to construct nested queries.

Example:

The following is not a query because it contains an undefined variable s. It is a query form, which would become a query if the expression s.*ID-KEY* were replaced by a constant, such as 345466.

> **select** ✳
>
> **from** *COURSE-ENROLLMENT*
>
> **where** s.*ID-KEY = COURSE-ENROLLMENT.STUDENT-ID-IN-KEY*

The nested queries are obtained in SQL by extending the syntax of the **where** *condition* by allowing the following subconditions within the *condition*:

1. **exists**   *query-form*

    This subcondition gives TRUE when the result of the query form is not empty —
    when it contains at least one row. (This subcondition is evaluated when all the
    variables on which the query form depends are interpreted.)

    Example:

    Find the names of the students who never took a course.

    > **select** *LAST-NAME*
    >
    > **from** *STUDENT*
    >
    > **where**
    >
    > > **not exists**
    > >
    > > > (**select** ∗
    > > >
    > > > **from** *COURSE-ENROLLMENT*
    > > >
    > > > **where** *STUDENT.ID-KEY = COURSE-*
    > > > *ENROLLMENT.STUDENT-ID-IN-KEY*)

    Example:

    List the instructor IDs and course names such that the instructor is the
    exclusive teacher of the course (i.e. no other instructors have offered the
    course).

    > **select** *INSTRUCTOR-ID-in-key, COURSE-NAME-in-key*
    >
    > **from** *COURSE-OFFERING* co
    >
    > **where not exists**
    >
    > > **select** *INSTRUCTOR-ID-in-key*
    > >
    > > **from** *COURSE-OFFERING* co1
    > >
    > > **where** co.*COURSE-NAME-in-key*=co1.*COURSE-NAME-in-key* **and**
    > > **not** co.*INSTRUCTOR-ID-in-key*=co1.*INSTRUCTOR-ID-in-key*

    ---

2. *expression*   **in**   *query-form-producing-only-one-value-per-row*

    This subcondition gives TRUE when the value of the *expression* constitutes a row in
    the output of the *query-form*

Example:

Find the names of the students who took at least one course.

> **select** *LAST-NAME*
>
> **from** *STUDENT*
>
> **where**
>
> > (*ID-KEY* **in**
> >
> > > **select** *STUDENT-ID-IN-KEY*
> > >
> > > **from** *COURSE-ENROLLMENT*
> > >
> > > **where** TRUE)

3.   *expression*   **not in**   *query-form-producing-only-one-value-per-row*

This subcondition gives TRUE when the value of the *expression* does not constitute a row in the output of the *query-form*

Example:

Find the names of the students who never took a course.

> **select** *LAST-NAME*
>
> **from** *STUDENT*
>
> **where**
>
> > (*ID-KEY* **not in**
> >
> > > **select** *STUDENT-ID-IN-KEY*
> > >
> > > **from** *COURSE-ENROLLMENT*
> > >
> > > **where** TRUE)

4.   *<expressions>*   **in**   *query-form*

This subcondition gives TRUE when the values of the *expressions* constitute a row in the output of the *query-form*

Example:

Find the names of the students who may be spouses of instructors — those who have the same last name and address as an instructor.

> **select** *LAST-NAME, FIRST-NAME*

> **from** *STUDENT*
> **where**
>> *<LAST-NAME, ADDRESS>* **in**
>>> **select** *LAST-NAME, ADDRESS*
>>> **from** *INSTRUCTOR*
>>> **where** TRUE

5.   *<expressions>*   **not in**   *query-form*

This subcondition gives TRUE when the values of the *expressions* do not constitute a row in the output of the *query-form*

> *Example:*
>
> Find the names of some students who are certainly not spouses of instructors.
>
>> **select** *LAST-NAME, FIRST-NAME*
>> **from** *STUDENT*
>> **where**
>>> *<LAST-NAME, ADDRESS>* **not in**
>>>> **select** *LAST-NAME, ADDRESS*
>>>> **from** *INSTRUCTOR*
>>>> **where** TRUE

6.   *query-form*   **contains**   *query-form*

This subcondition gives TRUE when every row produced by the right query form is also produced by the left query form.

Example:

Find the names of the students who took all the courses.

> **select** *LAST-NAME, FIRST-NAME*
>
> **from** *STUDENT*
>
> **where**
>
>> **select** COURSE-NAME-IN-KEY
>>
>> **from** *COURSE-ENROLLMENT*
>>
>> **where** *STUDENT.ID-KEY = COURSE-ENROLLMENT.STUDENT-ID-IN-KEY*
>
>> **contains**
>>
>>> **select** *NAME-KEY*
>>>
>>> **from** *COURSE*
>>>
>>> **where** TRUE

7. *expression   comparison   query-form-producing-only-one-value*

The allowed comparisons are: =, <, >, >=, <=, <>.

Example:

Find the names of the students who took more than 1000 course offerings.

> **select** *LAST-NAME, FIRST-NAME*
>
> **from** *STUDENT*
>
> **where**
>
>> 1000 <
>>
>>> **select count** (∗)
>>>
>>> **from** *COURSE-ENROLLMENT*
>>>
>>> **where** *STUDENT.ID-KEY = COURSE-ENROLLMENT.STUDENT-ID-IN-KEY*

8. *expression   comparison   **any**   query-form*

This subcondition is TRUE if the comparison with at least one row of the query-form's output is TRUE.

Example:

Find the names of the students who studied something in the first 20 calendar years of their life.

> **select** *LAST-NAME, FIRST-NAME*
>
> **from** *STUDENT*
>
> **where**
>
> > *BIRTH-YEAR* + 20 > **any**
> >
> > > **select** *YEAR*
> > >
> > > **from** *COURSE-ENROLLMENT*
> > >
> > > **where** *STUDENT.ID-KEY = COURSE-ENROLLMENT.STUDENT-ID-IN-KEY*

---

9. *expression   comparison*   **all**   *query-form*

This subcondition is TRUE if the comparison with every one of the query-form's output rows is TRUE.

Example:

Find the names of the students who studied nothing (as far as the database knows) in the first 20 calendar years of their life.

> **select** *LAST-NAME, FIRST-NAME*
>
> **from** *STUDENT*
>
> **where**
>
> > *BIRTH-YEAR* + 20 <= **all**
> >
> > > **select** *YEAR*
> > >
> > > **from** *COURSE-ENROLLMENT*
> > >
> > > **where** *STUDENT.ID-KEY = COURSE-ENROLLMENT.STUDENT-ID-IN-KEY*

Example:

List the instructor IDs and course names such that the instructor is the exclusive teacher of the course (i.e. no other instructors have offered the course).

> **select** *INSTRUCTOR-ID-in-key*, *COURSE-NAME-in-key*
>
> **from** *COURSE-OFFERING* co
>
> **where** *INSTRUCTOR-ID-in-key* = **all**
>
> > **select** *INSTRUCTOR-ID-in-key*
> >
> > **from** *COURSE-OFFERING* co1
> >
> > **where** co.*COURSE-NAME-in-key*=co1.*COURSE-NAME-in-key*

Example:

An alternative code for the above query:

> **select** *INSTRUCTOR-ID-in-key*, *COURSE-NAME-in-key*
>
> **from** *COURSE-OFFERING* co
>
> **where** 1 =
>
> > **select count** (**distinct** *INSTRUCTOR-ID-in-key*)
> >
> > **from** *COURSE-OFFERING* co1
> >
> > **where** co.*COURSE-NAME-in-key*=co1.*COURSE-NAME-in-key*

4.4.5. Grouping of rows

The aggregate functions can by applied to subsets of rows produced by *select*. For this purpose, the rows resulting from *select* can be partitioned into groups according to the values of some attributes.

Syntax:

> **select** *expression*$_1$, . . . , *expression*$_n$
>
> **from** *table*$_1$ *var*$_1$, . . . , *table*$_n$ *var*$_n$
>
> **where** *condition*
>
> **group by** *attribute*$_1$, . . . , *attribute*$_k$

Each *attribute$_i$* has the form

$$variable \ .attribute\text{-}name$$

When no ambiguity arises, the table-name can be used instead of the variable:

$$table\text{-}name.attribute\text{-}name$$

When no ambiguity further arises, the table-name can be omitted:

$$attribute\text{-}name$$

Meaning:

The rows satisfying the *condition* are combined into groups so that in each group the attributes of the grouping have constant values; that is, two rows r_1 and r_2 are in the same group if and only if

$$r_1.attribute_1 = r_2.attribute_1 \text{ and}$$
$$r_1.attribute_2 = r_2.attribute_2 \text{ and} \cdots$$
$$r_1.attribute_k = r_2.attribute_k$$

For every group, only one cumulative row is produced in the result. The resulting cumulative row is obtained by evaluation of the *expressions* of the **select** clause. The aggregates in those expressions are interpreted as applying not to the whole output but only to the rows comprising one group.

Example:

For every department, list the number of instructors it employs.

> **select** *DEPARTMENT-MAIN-NAME-in-key*, **count**(*INSTRUCTOR-ID-in-key*)
>
> **from** *WORK*
>
> **group by** *DEPARTMENT-MAIN-NAME-in-key*

Example:

For every student who took classes in a summer, for every instructor who gave grades to the student in a summer, print the average of the summer grades given by the instructor to the student.

> **select** *STUDENT-ID-in-key, INSTRUCTOR-ID-in-key,* **avg**(*FINAL-GRADE*)
>
> **from** *COURSE-ENROLLMENT*
>
> **where** *SEASON* = 'Summer'
>
> **group by** *STUDENT-ID-in-key, INSTRUCTOR-ID-in-key*

Some of the groups produced by **group by** can be screened out according to the values of aggregate functions applied to the group. A group screening condition can be specified in a **having** clause as follows.

select *expressions*

from *tables*

where *condition-on-the-source-rows-of-the-tables*

group by *attributes*

having *condition-on-the-groups*

The *condition-on-the-groups* is a Boolean expression. The aggregate functions appearing in this condition apply to the rows comprising one group.

Example:

What departments employ more than 100 instructors each?

> **select** *DEPARTMENT-MAIN-NAME-in-key*
>
> **from** *WORK*
>
> **where** true
>
> **group by** *DEPARTMENT-MAIN-NAME-in-key*
>
> **having count**(**distinct** *INSTRUCTOR-ID-in-key*) > 100

Example:

For every student who took classes in a summer, for every instructor who gave grades to the student in a summer, so that the average of the summer grades given by the instructor to the student is greater than 60, print the average of the summer grades given by the instructor to the student.

> **select** *STUDENT-ID-in-key, INSTRUCTOR-ID-in-key*, **avg**(*FINAL-GRADE*)
>
> **from** *COURSE-ENROLLMENT*
>
> **where** *SEASON* = 'Summer'
>
> **group by** *STUDENT-ID-in-key, INSTRUCTOR-ID-in-key*
>
> **having avg**(*FINAL-GRADE*) > 60

Example:

What students have taken classes with every instructor?

> **select** *STUDENT-ID-in-key*
>
> **from** *COURSE-ENROLLMENT*
>
> **group by** *STUDENT-ID-in-key*
>
> **having count**(∗) =
>
> > (**select count**(∗) **from** *INSTRUCTOR*)

4.4.6. Sorting

The output of an SQL query can be sorted for the purpose of printing in any desired order or for delivery to an application program in a desired order. This is accomplished by an **order by** clause specifying one or more attributes to sort by:

> *query*
>
> **order by** *attributes*

When more than one sorting attribute is given, the output's primary order is according to the first attribute, then according to the second, and so on.

> *Example:*
>
> List all computer science majoring students sorted by their minors.
>
> > **select** *
> >
> > **from** *STUDENT*
> >
> > **where** *MAJOR-DEPARTMENT-MAIN-NAME* = 'Computer Science'
> >
> > **order by** *MINOR-DEPARTMENT-MAIN-NAME*

4.4.7. Update transactions

Update transactions can be specified in SQL.

1. Deleting a set of rows from a table.

    > **delete from** *table*
    >
    > **where** *condition-on-rows-to-be-deleted*

    > *Example:*
    >
    > Delete the student whose ID is 11111.
    >
    > > **delete from** *STUDENT*
    > >
    > > **where** *ID-key = 11111*

    > *Example:*
    >
    > Delete all music majors.
    >
    > > **delete from** *STUDENT*
    > >
    > > **where** *MAJOR-DEPARTMENT-MAIN-NAME = 'Music'*

2. Inserting a row into a table.

    > **insert into** *table*
    >
    > $$attribute_1, \ldots, attribute_n$$
    >
    > **values**
    >
    > $$value_1, \ldots, value_n$$

The attributes of the table which are not specified in the *insert* command are set to *null* values for the row being inserted.

Example:

Let the instructor whose ID is 22222 work in the department whose main name is *Arts*.

> **insert into** *WORK*
>
> > INSTRUCTOR-ID-in-key, DEPARTMENT-MAIN-NAME-in-key
>
> **values**
>
> > 22222, 'Arts'

---

3. Inserting a set of rows into a table. A set of rows to be inserted can be defined as the result of a query.

> **insert into** *table*
>
> $$attribute_1, \ldots, attribute_n$$
>
> *query*

Example:

Let all physics instructors work also in *Arts*.

> **insert into** *WORK*
>
> > INSTRUCTOR-ID-in-key, DEPARTMENT-MAIN-NAME-in-key
> >
> > **select** *INSTRUCTOR-ID-in-key, 'Arts'*
> >
> > **from** *WORK*
> >
> > **where** *DEPARTMENT-MAIN-NAME-in-key = 'Physics'*

---

4. Modifying the values of some attributes in a set of rows of a table. The set of rows can be specified by a **where** condition. The new values can be specified as constants or as expressions using the old values of the row being updated.

> **update** *table*
>
> **set**
>
> > $$attribute_1 = expression_1, \ldots, attribute_n = expression_n$$
>
> **where** *condition*

> *Example:*
>
> Decrease by 10 percent all grades above 90.
>
> > **update** *COURSE-ENROLLMENT*
> >
> > > **set** *FINAL-GRADE = FINAL-GRADE*0.9*
> > >
> > > **where** *FINAL-GRADE > 90*

4.4.8. DDL

SQL has a data definition capability.

Specification of a table

> **create table** *table-name*
>
> *attribute*$_1$ *data-type*$_1$, ..., *attribute*$_n$ *data-type*$_n$
>
> > *Example:*
> >
> > **create table** *QUARTER*
> >
> > | *YEAR-in-key* | Integer |
> > |---|---|
> > | *SEASON-in-key* | String |

Specification of a userview table

> **create view** *new-table-name*
>
> *attribute*$_1$, ..., *attribute*$_n$
>
> **as** *select-command*
>
> > *Example:*
> >
> > **create view** *TAUGHT*
> >
> > *STUDENT-ID HIS-TEACHER-ID*
> >
> > **as**   **select** *STUDENT-ID-in-key, INSTRUCTOR-ID-in-key*
> >
> > > **from** *COURSE-ENROLLMENT*

4.4.9. SQL extension of Pascal

SQL can be used not only interactively but also as a DML extension of a programming language. This section shows how SQL can be embedded in Pascal. The embedding in other programming languages is similar.

Host variables in SQL statements

Wherever a constant can appear in SQL, a host program variable can appear instead. Before the SQL statement is performed, the variable is evaluated to give a value. To distinguish between host program variables and SQL variables, the host variables are preceded by a colon (:).

Example:

Create a new course whose name is in the Pascal variable *course-name*.

insert into *COURSE*

$$NAME\text{-}key$$

values :course-name

Example:

For each standard input line create a new course whose name is the string appearing in that line.

var course-name: String;

begin

while not eof(Input) **do begin**

   readln (course-name);

   insert into *COURSE*

      NAME-key **values** :course-name

   end

end.

Retrieving a row of values from the database

If we anticipate that a select command will retrieve exactly one row of data, we can have this data placed into variables of the host program by the following command.

select-command **into** *host-variables*

Example:

(* Get the total number students born in 1980 into the variable *myvar*. *)

    select count ($*$)

    from *STUDENT*

    where *BIRTH-YEAR* = 1980

    into :myvar

Processing of multirow output of a query

The program can retrieve a set of rows of data from the database.

- Such a set of rows can be defined as the output of a *select* command. The program would then process the retrieved rows, one row at a time.

Example:

select *BIRTH-YEAR*

from *STUDENT*

where *MAJOR-DEPARTMENT-MAIN-NAME* = 'Management';

- To scan such rows in a program, SQL defines a **cursor**, a logical pointer to the current row. The declaration of a cursor defines a query.

Example:

declare current-student **cursor for**

    select *BIRTH-YEAR*

    from *STUDENT*

    where *MAJOR-DEPARTMENT-MAIN-NAME* = 'Management';

- The opening of the cursor performs the query.

Example:

open current-student;

- The **fetch** command then brings to the program one row each time and advances the cursor to point to the next row.

> *Example:*
>
> **fetch** current-student **into** :birth-year;

- When a *fetch* is attempted beyond the last row in the output of a query, the special variable *sqlstatus* is set to the value of the special constant **not-found**.

> *Example:*
>
> (* Print the logarithm of the birth year of every management student (major) *)
>
> > **declare** current-student **cursor for**
> >
> > > **select** *BIRTH-YEAR*
> > >
> > > **from** *STUDENT*
> > >
> > > **where** *MAJOR-DEPARTMENT-MAIN-NAME* =
> > > 'Management';
> >
> > **open** current-student;
> >
> > **repeat**
> >
> > > **fetch** current-student **into** :birth-year;
> > >
> > > **if** sqlstatus ≠ not-found **then** writeln(log(birth-year))
> >
> > **until** sqlstatus = not-found

The relevant commands are:

a. **declare** *cursor-name* **cursor for** *select-command*

b. **open** *cursor-name*

c. **fetch** *cursor-name* **into** *host-variables*

Update and delete of fetched rows

After a row has been *fetch*ed, it can be updated or deleted provided the row belongs to one table of the schema (and not to a join of tables).

a. **update** *table-name*

  set

$$attribute_1 = expression_1 , \ldots , attribute_n = expression_n$$

where current of *cursor-name*

Example:

(* Replace the birth year of every management student (major) by the logarithm of the birth year. *)

    declare current-student **cursor for**

        select *BIRTH-YEAR*

        from *STUDENT*

        where *MAJOR-DEPARTMENT-MAIN-NAME =*
          'Management';

    open current-student;

    repeat

        fetch current-student **into** :birth-year;

        birth-year := log (birth-year);

        if sqlstatus ≠ not-found **then**

          update *STUDENT*

            set *BIRTH-YEAR* = :birth-year

            where current of current-student

    until sqlstatus = not-found

---

b.   **delete from** *table-name*

    where current of *cursor-name*

Example:

(* Display the name of every student; prompt the user whether the student should be deleted; if the user replies 'yes' — delete the student. *)

    declare current-student **cursor for**

        select *LAST-NAME, FIRST-NAME*

        from *STUDENT*

    open current-student;

    repeat

        fetch current-student **into** :last-name, :first-name;

        if sqlstatus ≠ not-found **then begin**

> writeln (' Would you like to delete ', last-name, ' ', first-name,
> '?');
>
> readln (answer);
>
> **if** answer='yes' **then**
>
> **delete from** *STUDENT*
>
> **where current of** current-student
>
> **end**
>
> **until** sqlstatus = not-found

Problem 4-9.

Use the studio/relational schema (Figure 13-21 on page 410). Write an SQL query to find the titles of Fellini's films.

Solution on page 427.

Problem 4-10.

Use the projects/relational schema (Figure 13-16 on page 406). Write in SQL a query to find the names of the projects which have subprojects.

Solution on page 427.

In the following problems, translate the English specification into SQL.

Problem 4-11.

Use the sales/relational schema (Figure 13-23 on page 412).
What are the ID numbers of all persons whose name is *Johnson*?

Solution on page 427.

Problem 4-12.

Use the sales/relational schema (Figure 13-23 on page 412).
What items has Johnson bought?

Solution on page 427.

Problem 4-13.

Use the sales/relational schema (Figure 13-23 on page 412).
What are the names of the persons who bought something from Rothschild?

Solution on page 428.

Problem 4-14.

Use the sales/relational schema (Figure 13-23 on page 412).
For what prices were nails sold?

Problem 4-15.

Use the sales/relational schema (Figure 13-23 on page 412).
For all sale transactions above $100, list the sale-id, price, the item type, and the IDs of the seller and the buyer.

Solution on page 428.

Problem 4-16.

Use the sales/relational schema (Figure 13-23 on page 412).
Who sold an item for a lower price than he himself paid for the same (or identical) item?

Solution on page 428.

Problem 4-17.

Use the sales/relational schema (Figure 13-23 on page 412).
How many sale transactions were there for the price of $1?

Solution on page 428.

Problem 4-18.

Use the sales/relational schema (Figure 13-23 on page 412).
What is the average price of one nail?

Solution on page 428.

Problem 4-19.

Use the sales/relational schema (Figure 13-23 on page 412).
What are the *different* items that Tsai bought?

Solution on page 429.

Problem 4-20.

Use the sales/relational schema (Figure 13-23 on page 412).
How many *different* items has Tsai bought?

Solution on page 429.

Problem 4-21.

Use the sales/relational schema (Figure 13-23 on page 412).
For every item type, list its average price.

Solution on page 429.

Problem 4-22.

Use the sales/relational schema (Figure 13-23 on page 412).
What items cost more than $1000 on the average?

Solution on page 429.

Problem 4-23.

Use the sales/relational schema (Figure 13-23 on page 412).
What items cost more than $1000 on the average, ignoring the nominal transactions for a token price of $10 and less?

Solution on page 429.

Problem 4-24.

Use the sales/relational schema (Figure 13-23 on page 412).
List all persons sorted by their names.

Solution on page 430.

Problem 4-25.

Use the sales/relational schema (Figure 13-23 on page 412).
Delete the person whose ID is 555.

Solution on page 430.

Problem 4-26.

Use the sales/relational schema (Figure 13-23 on page 412).
Delete all car sale transactions.

Solution on page 430.

Problem 4-27.

Use the sales/relational schema (Figure 13-23 on page 412).
Insert a new person whose ID is 333 and whose name is Vasudha.

Solution on page 430.

Problem 4-28.

Use the sales/relational schema (Figure 13-23 on page 412).
For every hammer transaction, let there be a nail transaction between the same persons. The price of the nail will be 1 percent of the price of the hammer. The ID of the nail transaction will be 100000 + the ID of the hammer transaction.

Solution on page 430.

Problem 4-29.

Use the sales/relational schema (Figure 13-23 on page 412).
Decrease by 10 percent all prices above $90.

Solution on page 431.

Problem 4-30.

Use the sales/relational schema (Figure 13-23 on page 412).
Define the table *PERSON*.

Solution on page 431.

Problem 4-31.

Use the sales/relational schema (Figure 13-23 on page 412).
Define a userview table which contains IDs of persons and descriptions of the items they bought.

Solution on page 431.

Problem 4-32.

Use the sales/relational schema (Figure 13-23 on page 412). Write an SQL/Pascal program fragment
(* Create a new item-type whose description is in the Pascal variable *item.* *)

Solution on page 431.

Problem 4-33.

Use the sales/relational schema (Figure 13-23 on page 412). Write an SQL/Pascal program
(* For each standard input line create a new item type whose description is the string appearing in that line. *)

Solution on page 431.

Problem 4-34.

Use the sales/relational schema (Figure 13-23 on page 412). Write an SQL/Pascal program fragment
(* Get the total number of sale transactions below $10 into the variable *total.* *)

Solution on page 432.

Problem 4-35.

Use the sales/relational schema (Figure 13-23 on page 412). Write an SQL/Pascal program fragment
(* Print the item of every $20 transaction. *)

Solution on page 432.

Problem 4-36.

Use the sales/relational schema (Figure 13-23 on page 412). Write an SQL/Pascal program fragment
(* Modify the price of every sale transaction by applying to it the Pascal function *modify* (defined elsewhere in the program). *)

Solution on page 432.

Problem 4-37.

Use the sales/relational schema (Figure 13-23 on page 412). Write an SQL/Pascal program fragment
(* Display the description of every item type; prompt the user whether the item type should be deleted; if the user replies yes — delete the item type. *)

Solution on page 433.

Problem 4-38.

Use the circuitboard/relational schema (Figure 13-22 on page 411). Write the following query in SQL.

For circuit name = databit01, list the function of each component to which the circuit is connected.

Solution on page 433.

Problem 4-39.

Use the circuitboard/relational schema (Figure 13-22 on page 411). Write the following query in SQL.

For each circuit name list the components and the pins sorted by circuit name, then by component ID, then by pin number.

Solution on page 434.

Problem 4-40.

Use the circuitboard/relational schema (Figure 13-22 on page 411). Write the following query in SQL.

List the circuits that contain only one pin (this would be a design error).

Solution on page 434.

Problem 4-41.

Use the circuitboard/relational schema (Figure 13-22 on page 411). Write the following query in SQL.

List the distinct component type names of the components whose pin 14 is connected to a red-colored circuit.

Solution on page 434.

Problem 4-42.

Use the circuitboard/relational schema (Figure 13-22 on page 411). Write the following query in SQL.

Generate a list of types and functions of all the components.

Solution on page 434.

Problem 4-43.

Use the circuitboard/relational schema (Figure 13-22 on page 411). Write the following transaction in SQL.

Change the circuit name from *databit01* to *databit02*.

Solution on page 434.

4.5.　Expressive Power of Relational Query Languages

Ignoring minor differences in expressiveness, such as the output of identical rows, the following languages have approximately equal power. A query that can be expressed in one language can also be expressed in the others:

- Tuple-oriented Relational Calculus without aggregate functions
- Relational Algebra
- SQL without aggregate functions

The aggregate extension of the Predicate Calculus and SQL with aggregate functions have a higher power.

The structured extension of Pascal, being a general-purpose programming language, has a much higher power of expressiveness.

Problems to compare the different relational languages

For each of the following tasks write an appropriate statement or program in each of the following languages (excluding those languages in which the particular task cannot be specified).

- Relational Calculus
- Extended Pascal
- Relational Algebra
- SQL

Use the university/relational reference schema.

Problem 4-44.

Find the names of the persons born in 1967.

Solution on page 435.

Problem 4-45.

For every student, list the instructors of the student's major department.

Solution on page 436.

Problem 4-46.

What instructors work in every department? (Each relevant instructor shares her time between all the departments.)

Solution on page 437.

Problem 4-47.

What instructors taught every student?

Problem 4-48.

Who took Prof. Smith's courses?

Solution on page 441.

Problem 4-49.

Display 'TRUE' if every student took at least one course.

Solution on page 443.

Problem 4-50.

Print a table with two columns, which associates students with their teachers. Only last names are printed.

Solution on page 444.

Problem 4-51.

Find the average birth year of the students.

Solution on page 446.

Problem 4-52.

Find the number of pairs (*INSTRUCTOR, DEPARTMENT*) where the instructor works in the department.

Solution on page 446.

Problem 4-53.

Find the average of grades of student Jane Howard.

Solution on page 447.

Problem 4-54.

Print the average of all grades given by Prof. Brown.

Solution on page 448.

Problem 4-55.

How many students are there in the university?

Solution on page 449.

Problem 4-56.

What students have their average grade above 90?

Solution on page 450.

Problem 4-57.

What are the last names of all the students?

Solution on page 451.

Problem 4-58.

When was student Russel born?

Solution on page 451.

Problem 4-59.

What courses has Prof. Graham taught?

Solution on page 452.

Problem 4-60.

Print the names of the pairs of students who live together.

Solution on page 453.

Problem 4-61.

Print the names and the addresses of all computer science students.

Solution on page 453.

Problem 4-62.

How many computer science students are there in the database?

Solution on page 454.

Problem 4-63.

What is the average grade in the *Databases* course?

Solution on page 454.

Problem 4-64.

List the distinct addresses of the students. (Do not list the same address twice.)

Solution on page 455.

Problem 4-65.

Find the names of the students who never took a course.

Solution on page 455.

CHAPTER 5

MORE ON DATABASE DESIGN METHODOLOGY

This chapter begins with a case study of a design of an actual database application. Section 2 summarizes the flow of database design. Section 3 compares the methodology of this book to the older methodology of normalization.

5.1. A Case Study of an Application

The university database studied in the examples of the other chapters of this book is a small "toy" application. The objective of this chapter is to show a real application. This chapter describes a database that has been developed for the Hydrology Division of the Everglades National Park. (Actually this application is a self-contained subapplication of a larger database covering various activities of the Park and consisting of more than 1000 categories, relations, and attributes.)

The first part of this chapter presents the semantic analysis of the relevant subschemas. It contains information based on our interviews with the Client's representatives. We have translated this analysis into formal concepts. The specification of every concept herein consists of:

- The **concept's name**, which should be clear and meaningful to the database users

- **Technical characteristics** of the concept

- A **comment** defining the meaning of the concept

A correct definition in the comment is important. Its purposes are to:

- Verify that the systems analysts correctly understand the meanings of the application's concepts

- Concisely convey the meanings of the application to the programming personnel who will work on the application in the future

- Provide online comments on all database entities to the future users of the database on the Client's side

- Provide an information reference manual for use by the Client's personnel and for training of new employees, whether they will be using the database or not

- Facilitate decision making at the Client's managerial and executive levels by providing a graphic overview and a comprehensive directory of the information owned by the Client (as a supplement to the other decision support resources: a directory of the personnel employed, a directory of financial and tangible assets owned, and the database itself)

- Specify informally integrity constraints beyond those shown in the graphical schema

For every numeric attribute, a range of its possible values is given. For example, 23.5..100.7 means that the values may not be less than 23.5 or greater than 100.7 and that the precision is one digit after the decimal point. It is desirable that a range be as narrow as possible while still allowing for all the possible values that may be meaningful in the database at any time in the future. The range specification is used to check the input in order to eliminate data entry typos.

The schema is partitioned into several subschemas each of which is small enough to be displayed on one page. The interconnections between the subschemas are shown by having some categories appear in more than one subschema. For every category, one subschema is the **home subschema** of that category and contains all of its attributes. If that category appears also in other subschemas, it has no attributes there, but, instead, a reference to its home subschema. The category appears in subschemas other than its home subschema in order to show relations with other categories of those subschemas.

Example:

The Equipment History subschema covers information relevant to all the equipment of the Park. It is the home subschema of the category *EQUIPMENT*. The Hydrology Stations Equipment subschema has additional information about the equipment installed at hydrological stations. The category *EQUIPMENT* appears in Figure 5-1 as a pointer to the Equipment History subschema.

```
┌─────────────────────────┐
│                         │
│      EQUIPMENT          │
│                         │
│   ⇒: equipment-history  │
│                         │
└─────────────────────────┘
```

Figure 5-1. Interschema reference.

5.1.1. Semantic analysis

The semantic categories of this section and the corresponding relational tables are listed in the Index of this book. This facilitates cross-referencing between them.

5.1.1.1. Hydrology stations (includes marine rainfall stations)

Principal interviewer: Michael Alexopoulos. Client representatives interviewed: De Witt Smith, David Sikema. Revised by Naphtali Rishe 03/19/91.

- ☐ *HYDROLOGY-STATION* — category (A catalog of hydrology stations which reside within the Everglades National Park.)

- ☐ *FIXED-STATION* — subcategory of *HYDROLOGY-STATION* (A hydrology station which is housed in a permanent structure.)

- ☐ *TEMPORARY-STATION* — subcategory of *HYDROLOGY-STATION* (A hydrology station which only exists for a period of time and it is not housed in a permanent structure.)

- ☐ *CONTINUOUS-STATION* — subcategory of *FIXED-STATION* (A fixed hydrology station which collects data continuously.)

- ☐ *DISCONTINUOUS-STATION* — subcategory of *FIXED-STATION* (A fixed hydrology station which collects data only for specific intervals of time.)

- ☐ *STATION-CONTINUITY-PERIOD* — category (A catalog of periods during which a discontinuous station is active and various data is collected.)

Every object of the category *HYDROLOGY-STATION* must also belong to its subcategory. The following subcategories are disjoint: FIXED-STATION TEMPORARY-STATION.

Every object of the category *FIXED-STATION* must also belong to its subcategory. The following subcategories are disjoint: CONTINUOUS-STATION DISCONTINUOUS-STATION.

- ☐ *the-discontinuous-station* — relation from *STATION-CONTINUITY-PERIOD* to *DISCONTINUOUS-STATION* (*m:1,total*) (The discontinuous station which was active for periods of time collecting data.)

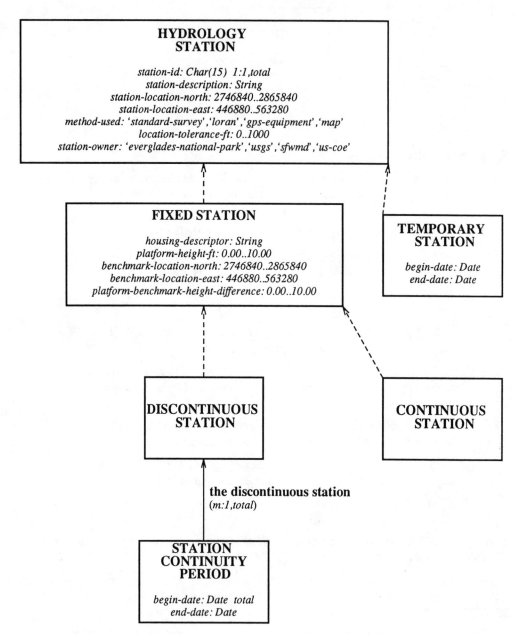

Figure 5-2. Semantic subschema for Hydrology Stations.

The objects of the category *HYDROLOGY-STATION* are identified by: station-id.

The objects of the category *STATION-CONTINUITY-PERIOD* are identified by: begin-date the-discontinuous-station.

- ☐ *station-id* — attribute of *HYDROLOGY-STATION*, range: *Char(15)* *(1:1,total)* (Identification.)

- ☐ *station-description* — attribute of *HYDROLOGY-STATION*, range: *String* *(m:1)* (English name or designation of the station.)

- ☐ *station-location-north* — attribute of *HYDROLOGY-STATION*, range: *2746840..2865840* *(m:1)* (UTM north coordinate of a hydrology station.)

- ☐ *station-location-east* — attribute of *HYDROLOGY-STATION*, range: *446880..563280* *(m:1)* (UTM east coordinate of a hydrology station.)

- ☐ *method-used* — attribute of *HYDROLOGY-STATION*, range: *'standard-survey'*,*'loran'*,*'gps-equipment'*,*'map'* *(m:1)* (The method used to derive the location coordinates of a station.)

- ☐ *location-tolerance-ft* — attribute of *HYDROLOGY-STATION*, range: *0..1000* *(m:1)* (Tolerance of the location of a station, in feet. A value *x* assigned to this attribute means that the tolerance is +/-*x* feet.)

- ☐ *station-owner* — attribute of *HYDROLOGY-STATION*, range: *'everglades-national-park'*,*'usgs'*,*'sfwmd'*,*'us-coe'* *(m:1)* (The agency which owns the station.)

- ☐ *housing-descriptor* — attribute of *FIXED-STATION*, range: *String* *(m:1)* (Description of the housing of a fixed station.)

- ☐ *platform-height-ft* — attribute of *FIXED-STATION*, range: *0.00..10.00* *(m:1)* (The height of the station platform from the water surface, in feet.)

- ☐ *benchmark-location-north* — attribute of *FIXED-STATION*, range: *2746840..2865840* *(m:1)* (UTM north coordinate of the benchmark which corresponds to a fixed station.)

- ☐ *benchmark-location-east* — attribute of *FIXED-STATION*, range: *446880..563280* *(m:1)* (UTM east coordinate of the benchmark which corresponds to a fixed station.)

- ☐ *platform-benchmark-height-difference* — attribute of *FIXED-STATION*, range: *0.00..10.00* *(m:1)* (The difference between the height of the station platform and the height of its corresponding benchmark, in feet.)

- ☐ *begin-date* — attribute of *STATION-CONTINUITY-PERIOD*, range: *Date* *(m:1,total)* (The date during which a discontinuous station was activated and started the generation of data for some parameters.)

☐ *end-date* — attribute of *STATION-CONTINUITY-PERIOD*, range: *Date* (*m:1*) (The date during which a period of activation for some discontinuous station ended.)

☐ *begin-date* — attribute of *TEMPORARY-STATION*, range: *Date* (*m:1*) (The starting date of the life of a temporary station.)

☐ *end-date* — attribute of *TEMPORARY-STATION*, range: *Date* (*m:1*) (The ending date of the life of a temporary station.)

5.1.1.2. Equipment

Principal interviewer: Michael Alexopoulos. Client representatives interviewed: De Witt Smith, David Sikema. Revised by Naphtali Rishe 03/19/91.

☐ *EQUIPMENT* — category (A general catalog of equipment owned by the Everglades National Park.)

☐ *REPAIR-PERIOD* — category (A list of periods during which various repairs were made to equipment.)

☐ *BATTERY-CHANGE* — category (A list of dates during which a battery change was done to equipment.)

☐ *CALIBRATION* — category (A list of calibrations done to equipment.)

☐ *CALIBRATION-USING-EQUIPMENT* — subcategory of *CALIBRATION* (Calibration of equipment while using other equipment.)

☐ *CALIBRATION-USING-OTHER-TECHNIQUE* — subcategory of *CALIBRATION* (Calibration using a technique which is documented here. However this technique does not use instruments which are recorded in the database, i.e., this category is disjoint from CALIBRATION-USING-EQUIPMENT.)

Every object of the category *CALIBRATION* must also belong to its subcategory. The following subcategories are disjoint: CALIBRATION-USING-EQUIPMENT CALIBRATION-USING-OTHER-TECHNIQUE.

☐ *the-equipment-repaired* — relation from *REPAIR-PERIOD* to *EQUIPMENT* (*m:1,total*) (The equipment repaired.)

☐ *in-equipment* — relation from *BATTERY-CHANGE* to *EQUIPMENT* (*m:1,total*) (The equipment for which the battery was changed.)

☐ *the-equipment-calibrated* — relation from *CALIBRATION* to *EQUIPMENT* (*m:1,total*) (The equipment which was calibrated.)

☐ *has-used* — relation from *CALIBRATION-USING-EQUIPMENT* to *EQUIPMENT* (*m:m*) (The equipment used to calibrate some other equipment.)

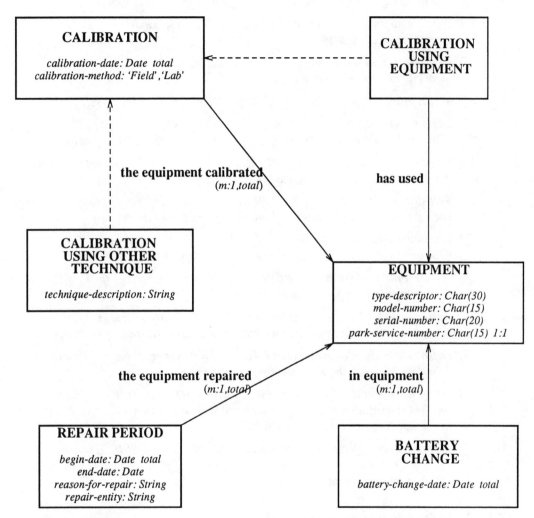

Figure 5-3. Semantic subschema for Equipment and Equipment History.

The objects of the category *CALIBRATION* are identified by: calibration-date the-equipment-calibrated.

The objects of the category *REPAIR-PERIOD* are identified by: begin-date the-equipment-repaired.

The objects of the category *BATTERY-CHANGE* are identified by: battery-change-date in-equipment.

The objects of the category *EQUIPMENT* are identified by: park-service-number.

☐ *type-descriptor* — attribute of *EQUIPMENT*, range: *Char(30)* *(m:1)* (The type of the equipment.)

☐ *model-number* — attribute of *EQUIPMENT*, range: *Char(15)* *(m:1)* (The model number of the equipment.)

☐ *serial-number* — attribute of *EQUIPMENT*, range: *Char(20)* *(m:1)*

☐ *park-service-number* — attribute of *EQUIPMENT*, range: *Char(15)* *(1:1)* (The number assigned to the equipment by the Everglades Park authorities.)

☐ *begin-date* — attribute of *REPAIR-PERIOD*, range: *Date* *(m:1,total)* (The date on which the equipment was taken for repairs.)

☐ *end-date* — attribute of *REPAIR-PERIOD*, range: *Date* *(m:1)* (The first date during which the equipment was functioning again after the repair.)

☐ *reason-for-repair* — attribute of *REPAIR-PERIOD*, range: *String* *(m:1)* (The reason for which the equipment was not functioning.)

☐ *repair-entity* — attribute of *REPAIR-PERIOD*, range: *String* *(m:1)* (The legal entity which repaired the equipment.)

☐ *battery-change-date* — attribute of *BATTERY-CHANGE*, range: *Date* *(m:1,total)* (The date on which the battery of some equipment was changed.)

☐ *calibration-date* — attribute of *CALIBRATION*, range: *Date* *(m:1,total)* (The date on which the equipment was calibrated.)

☐ *calibration-method* — attribute of *CALIBRATION*, range: *'Field'*, *'Lab'* *(m:1)* (The equipment was either removed from the station and was calibrated in the lab, or it was calibrated in the field.)

☐ *technique-description* — attribute of *CALIBRATION-USING-OTHER-TECHNIQUE*, range: *String* *(m:1)* (A description of the technique used to calibrate the equipment.)

5.1.1.3. Daily hydrology observations

Principal interviewer: Michael Alexopoulos. Client representative interviewed: David Sikema. Revised by Naphtali Rishe 03/19/91.

☐ *DAILY-HYDROLOGY-OBSERVATION* — category (A catalog of daily hydrology observations which originate from stations within the Everglades National Park.)

☐ *DAILY-STAGE* — subcategory of *DAILY-HYDROLOGY-OBSERVATION* (Daily mean stage measurements.)

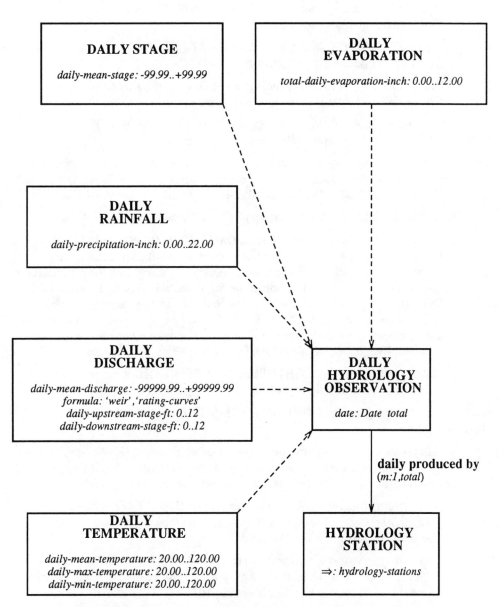

Figure 5-4. Semantic subschema for daily stage, rainfall, discharge, evaporation, and temperature observations.

☐ *DAILY-RAINFALL* — subcategory of *DAILY-HYDROLOGY-OBSERVATION* (Daily total rainfall measurements.)

☐ *DAILY-DISCHARGE* — subcategory of *DAILY-HYDROLOGY-OBSERVATION* (Daily mean discharge measurements.)

☐ *DAILY-TEMPERATURE* — subcategory of *DAILY-HYDROLOGY-OBSERVATION* (Daily temperature measurements.)

☐ *DAILY-EVAPORATION* — subcategory of *DAILY-HYDROLOGY-OBSERVATION* (Daily total evaporation measurements.)

Every object of the category *DAILY-HYDROLOGY-OBSERVATION* must also belong to its subcategory. The following subcategories are disjoint: DAILY-EVAPORATION DAILY-TEMPERATURE DAILY-DISCHARGE DAILY-RAINFALL DAILY-STAGE.

☐ *HYDROLOGY-STATION* — category (See subschema hydrology-stations.)

☐ *daily-produced-by* — relation from *DAILY-HYDROLOGY-OBSERVATION* to *HYDROLOGY-STATION* (*m:1,total*) (The station which generates daily measurements. Daily stage and rainfall measurements can only be generated by continuous stations owned by one of the following agencies: U.S. Army COE, SFWMD, USGS. Daily discharge measurements can only be generated by one of the following agencies: USGS, SFWMD. Daily evaporation and temperature measurements can only be generated by stations owned by one of the following agencies: Everglades RC, SFWMD, U.S. Army COE.)

☐ *date* — attribute of *DAILY-HYDROLOGY-OBSERVATION*, range: *Date* (*m:1,total*) (The date during which a hydrology observation was made.)

The objects of the category *DAILY-HYDROLOGY-OBSERVATION* are identified by: date daily-produced-by.

☐ *daily-mean-stage* — attribute of *DAILY-STAGE*, range: *-99.99..+99.99* (*m:1*) (The daily mean stage quantity measured in ft/100. That is the value 1.23 means 0.0123 feet. This field is left blank when data is not available.)

☐ *daily-precipitation-inch* — attribute of *DAILY-RAINFALL*, range: *0.00..22.00* (*m:1*) (The daily total precipitation quantity measured in inches. This field is left blank when data is not available.)

☐ *total-daily-evaporation-inch* — attribute of *DAILY-EVAPORATION*, range: *0.00..12.00* (*m:1*) (The total water evaporation for the day, measured in inches. This field is left blank when data is not available.)

☐ *daily-mean-discharge* — attribute of *DAILY-DISCHARGE*, range: *-99999.99..+99999.99* (*m:1*) (The mean discharge quantity for the day, measured in cubic feet per second. This field is left blank when data is not available.)

☐ *formula* — attribute of *DAILY-DISCHARGE*, range: *'weir'*, *'rating-curves'* (*m:1*) (The formula used to compute the mean discharge value.)

☐ *daily-upstream-stage-ft* — attribute of *DAILY-DISCHARGE*, range: *0..12* (*m:1*) (Upstream stage level for the day, measured in feet.)

☐ *daily-downstream-stage-ft* — attribute of *DAILY-DISCHARGE*, range: *0..12* (*m:1*) (Downstream stage level for the day, measured in feet.)

☐ *daily-mean-temperature* — attribute of *DAILY-TEMPERATURE*, range: *20.00..120.00* (*m:1*) (The mean temperature for the day, in degrees Fahrenheit. This field is left blank when data is not available.)

☐ *daily-max-temperature* — attribute of *DAILY-TEMPERATURE*, range: *20.00..120.00* (*m:1*) (The maximum temperature for the day, in degrees Fahrenheit. This field is left blank when data is not available.)

☐ *daily-min-temperature* — attribute of *DAILY-TEMPERATURE*, range: *20.00..120.00* (*m:1*) (The minimum temperature for the day, in degrees Fahrenheit. This field is left blank when data is not available.)

5.1.1.4. Hourly hydrology observations

Principal interviewer: Michael Alexopoulos. Client representative interviewed: David Sikema. Revised by Naphtali Rishe 03/19/91.

☐ *HOURLY-HYDROLOGY-OBSERVATION* — category (A catalog of hourly hydrology observations which originate from stations within the Everglades National Park.)

☐ *HOURLY-STAGE* — subcategory of *HOURLY-HYDROLOGY-OBSERVATION* (Hourly mean stage measurements.)

☐ *HOURLY-RAINFALL* — subcategory of *HOURLY-HYDROLOGY-OBSERVATION* (Hourly total rainfall measurements.)

☐ *HOURLY-WIND* — subcategory of *HOURLY-HYDROLOGY-OBSERVATION* (Hourly wind speed and wind direction measurements.)

Every object of the category *HOURLY-HYDROLOGY-OBSERVATION* must also belong to its subcategory. The following subcategories are disjoint: HOURLY-WIND HOURLY-RAINFALL HOURLY-STAGE.

☐ *HYDROLOGY-STATION* — category (See subschema hydrology-stations.)

☐ *hourly-produced-by* — relation from *HOURLY-HYDROLOGY-OBSERVATION* to *HYDROLOGY-STATION* (*m:1,total*) (The station which generates hourly either stage or rainfall or wind speed and direction measurements. Hourly stage and rainfall measurements can only be generated by continuous stations owned by the Everglades Research Center. Hourly wind

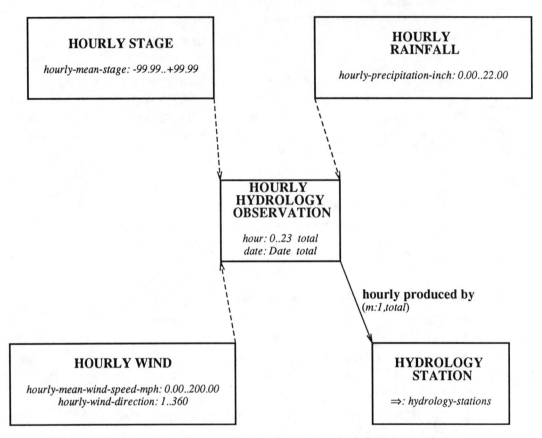

Figure 5-5. Semantic subschema for hourly stage and rainfall observations.

speed and direction measurements can only be generated by stations owned by
any of the following agencies: Everglades Research Center, SFWMD, U.S.
Army Corps of Engineers, NOAA.)

☐ *hour* — attribute of *HOURLY-HYDROLOGY-OBSERVATION*, range: *0..23*
(*m:1,total*)   (The hour during which the hydrology observation was made.)

☐ *date* — attribute of *HOURLY-HYDROLOGY-OBSERVATION*, range: *Date*
(*m:1,total*)   (The date on which the hourly hydrology observation was made.)

The objects of the category *HOURLY-HYDROLOGY-OBSERVATION* are identified by:
hour date hourly-produced-by.

☐ *hourly-mean-stage* — attribute of *HOURLY-STAGE*, range: *-99.99..+99.99*
(*m:1*)   (The hourly mean stage quantity measured in ft/100. That is, the value
1.23 means 0.0123 feet. This field is left blank when data is not available.)

□ *hourly-precipitation-inch* — attribute of *HOURLY-RAINFALL*, range: *0.00..22.00* *(m:1)* (The hourly total precipitation quantity measured in inches. This field is left blank when data is not available.)

□ *hourly-mean-wind-speed-mph* — attribute of *HOURLY-WIND*, range: *0.00..200.00* *(m:1)* (The mean wind speed for the hour, measured in miles per hour. This field is left blank when data is not available.)

□ *hourly-wind-direction* — attribute of *HOURLY-WIND*, range: *1..360* *(m:1)* (The wind direction for the hour, measured in degrees. This field is left blank when data is not available.)

5.1.1.5. Monthly hydrology observations

Principal interviewer: Michael Alexopoulos. Client representative interviewed: David Sikema. Revised by Naphtali Rishe 03/19/91.

□ *MONTHLY-HYDROLOGY-OBSERVATION* — category (A catalog of monthly hydrology observations which originate from stations within the Everglades National Park.)

□ *MONTHLY-STAGE* — subcategory of *MONTHLY-HYDROLOGY-OBSERVATION* (Monthly mean stage measurements.)

□ *MONTHLY-RAINFALL* — subcategory of *MONTHLY-HYDROLOGY-OBSERVATION* (Monthly total rainfall measurements.)

□ *HYDROLOGY-STATION* — category (See subschema hydrology-stations.)

Every object of the category *MONTHLY-HYDROLOGY-OBSERVATION* must also belong to its subcategory. The following subcategories are disjoint: MONTHLY-STAGE MONTHLY-RAINFALL.

□ *monthly-produced-by* — relation from *MONTHLY-HYDROLOGY-OBSERVATION* to *HYDROLOGY-STATION* *(m:1,total)* (The station which generates monthly stage and/or rainfall measurements. Monthly stage and rainfall measurements can only be generated by discontinuous stations owned by the Everglades Research Center.)

□ *month* — attribute of *MONTHLY-HYDROLOGY-OBSERVATION*, range: *1..12* *(m:1,total)* (The month during which a hydrology observation was made.)

□ *year* — attribute of *MONTHLY-HYDROLOGY-OBSERVATION*, range: *1940..2040* *(m:1,total)* (The year during which a monthly hydrology observation was made.)

The objects of the category *MONTHLY-HYDROLOGY-OBSERVATION* are identified by: month year monthly-produced-by.

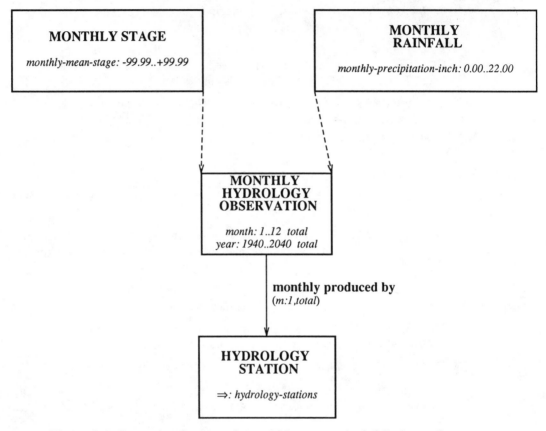

Figure 5-6. Semantic subschema for monthly stage and rainfall observations.

☐ *monthly-mean-stage* — attribute of *MONTHLY-STAGE*, range: *-99.99..+99.99* (*m:1*) (The monthly mean stage quantity measured in ft/100. That is the value 1.23 means 0.0123 feet. This field is left blank when data is not available.)

☐ *monthly-precipitation-inch* — attribute of *MONTHLY-RAINFALL*, range: *0.00..22.00* (*m:1*) (The monthly total precipitation quantity measured in inches. This field is left blank when data is not available.)

5.1.1.6. Hydrology stations equipment

Principal interviewer: Michael Alexopoulos. Client representatives interviewed: De Witt Smith, David Sikema. Revised by Naphtali Rishe 03/19/91.

☐ *HYDROLOGY-STATION* — category (See subschema hydrology-stations.)

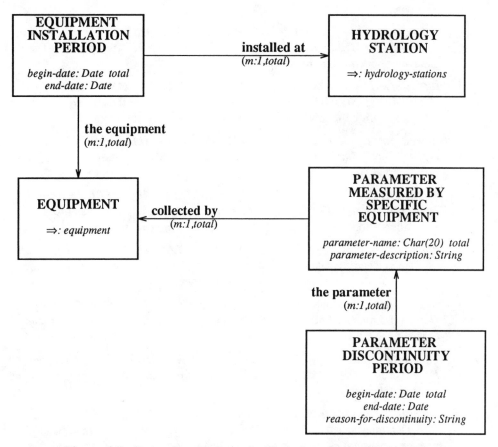

Figure 5-7. Semantic subschema for Hydrology Stations Equipment.

☐ *PARAMETER-MEASURED-BY-SPECIFIC-EQUIPMENT* — category (A catalog of parameters for which data are collected from various equipment installed at different hydrology stations.)

☐ *PARAMETER-DISCONTINUITY-PERIOD* — category (A catalog of periods during which a parameter is not collected.)

☐ *EQUIPMENT* — category (See subschema equipment.)

☐ *EQUIPMENT-INSTALLATION-PERIOD* — category (A catalog of time intervals indicating the station where an equipment has been installed during that interval.)

☐ *collected-by* — relation from *PARAMETER-MEASURED-BY-SPECIFIC-EQUIPMENT* to *EQUIPMENT* (*m:1,total*) (The equipment which collects the parameter.)

☐ *the-parameter* — relation from *PARAMETER-DISCONTINUITY-PERIOD* to *PARAMETER-MEASURED-BY-SPECIFIC-EQUIPMENT* (*m:1,total*) (The parameter not collected for the period.)

☐ *installed-at* — relation from *EQUIPMENT-INSTALLATION-PERIOD* to *HYDROLOGY-STATION* (*m:1,total*) (The station where the equipment was or is present during the time interval.)

☐ *the-equipment* — relation from *EQUIPMENT-INSTALLATION-PERIOD* to *EQUIPMENT* (*m:1,total*) (The equipment installed at a station during a given time interval.)

☐ *begin-date* — attribute of *EQUIPMENT-INSTALLATION-PERIOD*, range: *Date* (*m:1,total*) (The beginning date on which the equipment was installed at a specific station. May be omitted if unknown or irrelevant.)

☐ *end-date* — attribute of *EQUIPMENT-INSTALLATION-PERIOD*, range: *Date* (*m:1*) (The ending date on which the equipment was removed from a specific station. Omitted when the equipment is still there.)

☐ *begin-date* — attribute of *PARAMETER-DISCONTINUITY-PERIOD*, range: *Date* (*m:1,total*) (The beginning date on which data for a specific parameter ceased to be collected.)

☐ *end-date* — attribute of *PARAMETER-DISCONTINUITY-PERIOD*, range: *Date* (*m:1*) (The last day of a period during which data for a specific parameter was not collected.)

☐ *reason-for-discontinuity* — attribute of *PARAMETER-DISCONTINUITY-PERIOD*, range: *String* (*m:1*) (The reason for which data for a specific parameter was not collected during this time interval.)

☐ *parameter-name* — attribute of *PARAMETER-MEASURED-BY-SPECIFIC-EQUIPMENT*, range: *Char(20)* (*m:1,total*) (The name of the parameter collected by some specific equipment.)

☐ *parameter-description* — attribute of *PARAMETER-MEASURED-BY-SPECIFIC-EQUIPMENT*, range: *String* (*m:1*) (Designation of the parameter collected by some specific equipment.)

The objects of the category *EQUIPMENT-INSTALLATION-PERIOD* are identified by: begin-date installed-at the-equipment.

The objects of the category *PARAMETER-MEASURED-BY-SPECIFIC-EQUIPMENT* are identified by: parameter-name collected-by.

The objects of the category *PARAMETER-DISCONTINUITY-PERIOD* are identified by: begin-date the-parameter.

5.1.1.7. Fire history

Principal interviewer: Michael Alexopoulos. Client representatives interviewed: Sue Husari, Dave Lentz. Revised by Naphtali Rishe 03/19/91.

- ☐ *FIRE-INCIDENT* — category (A catalog of fire incidents which occur within the boundaries of the Everglades National Park.)

- ☐ *DAILY-DESCRIPTION* — category (Each fire occurring within the park may burn continuously for a number of days until it is put out. This category is a catalog of all the days for which a fire has lasted, for all fires.)

- ☐ *FIRE-WEATHER-OBSERVATION* — category (A catalog of fire-weather related observations for every day of interest to the Everglades Park authorities.)

- ☐ *HYDROLOGY-STATION* — category (See subschema hydrology.)

- ☐ *FIRE-WEATHER-STATION* — category (A catalog of fire-weather stations, where a fire-weather station is a collection of equipment used to measure various quantities pertaining to weather conditions within the Everglades Park area.)

- ☐ *YEAR* — category (A catalog of years during which various fire incidents occur.)

- ☐ *for* — relation from *DAILY-DESCRIPTION* to *FIRE-INCIDENT* (*m:1,total*) (The days during which a fire was burning.)

- ☐ *designated-hydrology-station* — relation from *FIRE-INCIDENT* to *HYDROLOGY-STATION* (*m:1*) (Closest hydrology station to the origin of the fire, designated by Park officials.)

- ☐ *observed-by* — relation from *FIRE-WEATHER-OBSERVATION* to *FIRE-WEATHER-STATION* (*m:1,total*) (The weather observations carried out by a fire-weather station every day.)

- ☐ *the-year* — relation from *FIRE-INCIDENT* to *YEAR* (*m:1,total*) (The year during which a fire incident has occurred.)

- ☐ *fire-number-within-year* — attribute of *FIRE-INCIDENT*, range: *1..999* (*m:1,total*) (A sequential integer value assigned to each fire incident within a calendar year. A fire incident occurs within a calendar year x if its starting date falls within x.)

- ☐ *fire-type* — attribute of *FIRE-INCIDENT*, range: *'incendiary'*, *'lightning'*, *'prescribed'*, *'research'* (*m:1*) (The possible type of a particular fire incident.)

☐ *fire-name* — attribute of *FIRE-INCIDENT*, range: *String* (*m:1*) (An arbitrary name assigned to each fire incident by the Everglades Park authorities.)

☐ *fire-origin-north* — attribute of *FIRE-INCIDENT*, range: *2746840..2865840* (*m:1*) (UTM coordinate for North. Together with *fire-origin-east* they indicate the geographical position of the origin of a fire incident. *May be overwritten by GIS.*)

☐ *fire-origin-east* — attribute of *FIRE-INCIDENT*, range: *446880..563280* (*m:1*) (UTM coordinate for East. Together with *fire-origin-north* they indicate the geographical position of the origin of a fire incident. *May be overwritten by GIS.*)

☐ *fuel-model* — attribute of *FIRE-INCIDENT*, range: *'n','d'* (*m:1*) (Dominant vegetation where fire incident occurred. n stands for Pine, and d for Grass.)

☐ *fine-fuel-load* — attribute of *FIRE-INCIDENT*, range: *0..9999* (*m:1*) (The amount of fuel per square meter for a fire incident, measured in grams per square meter.)

☐ *cost* — attribute of *FIRE-INCIDENT*, range: *0..99999999* (*m:1*) (Total cost in dollars to manage fire. Rounded to nearest dollar.)

☐ *year-number* — attribute of *YEAR*, range: *1940..2040* (*1:1,total*) (The year number.)

☐ *is-drought-year* — attribute of *YEAR*, range: *Boolean* (*m:1*)

☐ *has-crossed-perimeter* — attribute of *FIRE-INCIDENT*, range: *Boolean* (*m:1*)

☐ *fire-management-unit* — attribute of *FIRE-INCIDENT*, range: *1..44* (*m:1*) (Descriptor of geographical zones in the park or area surrounding it.)

☐ *date* — attribute of *DAILY-DESCRIPTION*, range: *Date* (*m:1,total*) (The date of a particular day during which a fire was still burning. The year in this date should be the same or one more than the year during which the fire incident occurred.)

☐ *new-acres-burned* — attribute of *DAILY-DESCRIPTION*, range: *0..99999* (*m:1*) (The number of acres burned only for that particular date indicated in the *Date* attribute.)

☐ *soil-moisture* — attribute of *DAILY-DESCRIPTION*, range: *0..100* (*m:1*) (Ratio ((wet in grams)–(dry in grams))/(dry in grams)*100%. Quantity indicating the soil moisture during a fire day. Percentage measure.)

☐ *date* — attribute of *FIRE-WEATHER-OBSERVATION*, range: *Date* (*m:1,total*) (The date of the day for which the weather observation has been

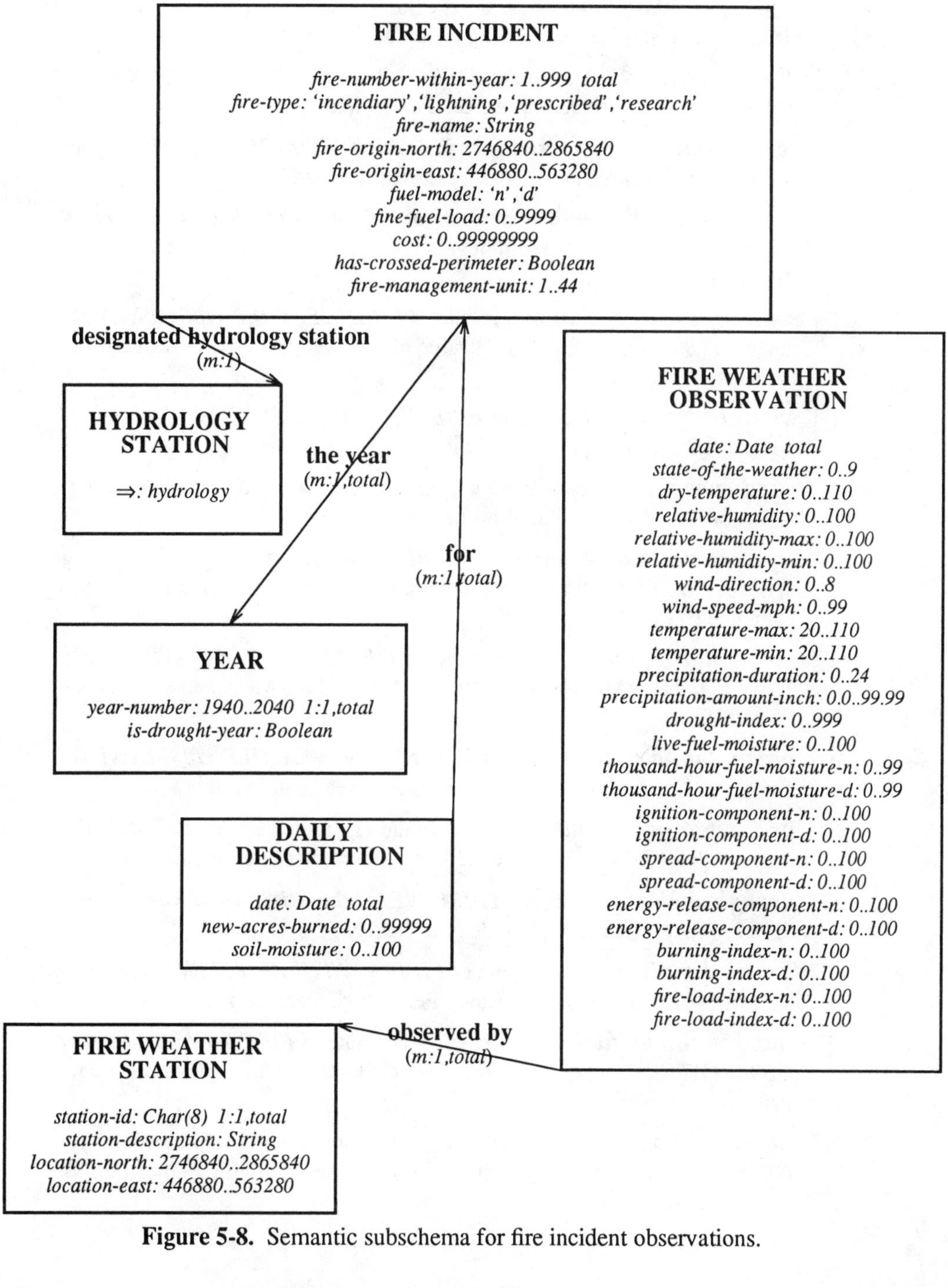

FIRE INCIDENT

fire-number-within-year: 1..999 total
fire-type: 'incendiary','lightning','prescribed','research'
fire-name: String
fire-origin-north: 2746840..2865840
fire-origin-east: 446880..563280
fuel-model: 'n','d'
fine-fuel-load: 0..9999
cost: 0..99999999
has-crossed-perimeter: Boolean
fire-management-unit: 1..44

designated hydrology station
(m:1)

**HYDROLOGY
STATION**

⇒: *hydrology*

the year
(m:1,total)

for
(m:1 total)

YEAR

year-number: 1940..2040 1:1,total
is-drought-year: Boolean

**FIRE WEATHER
OBSERVATION**

date: Date total
state-of-the-weather: 0..9
dry-temperature: 0..110
relative-humidity: 0..100
relative-humidity-max: 0..100
relative-humidity-min: 0..100
wind-direction: 0..8
wind-speed-mph: 0..99
temperature-max: 20..110
temperature-min: 20..110
precipitation-duration: 0..24
precipitation-amount-inch: 0.0..99.99
drought-index: 0..999
live-fuel-moisture: 0..100
thousand-hour-fuel-moisture-n: 0..99
thousand-hour-fuel-moisture-d: 0..99
ignition-component-n: 0..100
ignition-component-d: 0..100
spread-component-n: 0..100
spread-component-d: 0..100
energy-release-component-n: 0..100
energy-release-component-d: 0..100
burning-index-n: 0..100
burning-index-d: 0..100
fire-load-index-n: 0..100
fire-load-index-d: 0..100

**DAILY
DESCRIPTION**

date: Date total
new-acres-burned: 0..99999
soil-moisture: 0..100

observed by
(m:1,total)

**FIRE WEATHER
STATION**

station-id: Char(8) 1:1,total
station-description: String
location-north: 2746840..2865840
location-east: 446880..563280

Figure 5-8. Semantic subschema for fire incident observations.

☐ *state-of-the-weather* — attribute of *FIRE-WEATHER-OBSERVATION*, range: *0..9 (m:1)* (An arbitrarily assigned value for the state of the weather; 0 means clear, 9 means thunder, etc. Assigned by the Everglades Park personnel.)

☐ *dry-temperature* — attribute of *FIRE-WEATHER-OBSERVATION*, range: *0..110 (m:1)* (Measured in degrees Fahrenheit.)

☐ *relative-humidity* — attribute of *FIRE-WEATHER-OBSERVATION*, range: *0..100 (m:1)* (Percentage measure of relative humidity.)

☐ *relative-humidity-max* — attribute of *FIRE-WEATHER-OBSERVATION*, range: *0..100 (m:1)* (Maximum value of relative humidity for the day. Percentage measure.)

☐ *relative-humidity-min* — attribute of *FIRE-WEATHER-OBSERVATION*, range: *0..100 (m:1)* (Minimum value of relative humidity for the day. Percentage measure.)

☐ *wind-direction* — attribute of *FIRE-WEATHER-OBSERVATION*, range: *0..8 (m:1)* (0-8 compass point.)

☐ *wind-speed-mph* — attribute of *FIRE-WEATHER-OBSERVATION*, range: *0..99 (m:1)* (Measured in miles per hour.)

☐ *temperature-max* — attribute of *FIRE-WEATHER-OBSERVATION*, range: *20..110 (m:1)* (Maximum temperature for the day. Measured in degrees Fahrenheit.)

☐ *temperature-min* — attribute of *FIRE-WEATHER-OBSERVATION*, range: *20..110 (m:1)* (Minimum temperature for the day. Measured in degrees Fahrenheit.)

☐ *precipitation-duration* — attribute of *FIRE-WEATHER-OBSERVATION*, range: *0..24 (m:1)* (Precipitation duration measured in hours.)

☐ *precipitation-amount-inch* — attribute of *FIRE-WEATHER-OBSERVATION*, range: *0.0..99.99 (m:1)* (Precipitation amount measured in inches.)

☐ *drought-index* — attribute of *FIRE-WEATHER-OBSERVATION*, range: *0..999 (m:1)* (The drought index for the day.)

☐ *live-fuel-moisture* — attribute of *FIRE-WEATHER-OBSERVATION*, range: *0..100 (m:1)* (Live fuel moisture. Percentage measure.)

☐ *thousand-hour-fuel-moisture-n* — attribute of *FIRE-WEATHER-OBSERVATION*, range: *0..99 (m:1)* (One thousand hour fuel moisture for Pine. Percentage measure.)

☐ *thousand-hour-fuel-moisture-d* — attribute of *FIRE-WEATHER-OBSERVATION*, range: *0..99 (m:1)* (One thousand hour fuel moisture for Grass. Percentage measure.)

□ *ignition-component-n* — attribute of *FIRE-WEATHER-OBSERVATION*, range: *0..100* (*m:1*) (Fire ignition component for Pine.)

□ *ignition-component-d* — attribute of *FIRE-WEATHER-OBSERVATION*, range: *0..100* (*m:1*) (Fire ignition component for Grass.)

□ *spread-component-n* — attribute of *FIRE-WEATHER-OBSERVATION*, range: *0..100* (*m:1*) (Fire spread component for Pine.)

□ *spread-component-d* — attribute of *FIRE-WEATHER-OBSERVATION*, range: *0..100* (*m:1*) (Fire spread component for Grass.)

□ *energy-release-component-n* — attribute of *FIRE-WEATHER-OBSERVATION*, range: *0..100* (*m:1*) (Energy release component for Pine.)

□ *energy-release-component-d* — attribute of *FIRE-WEATHER-OBSERVATION*, range: *0..100* (*m:1*) (Energy release component for Grass.)

□ *burning-index-n* — attribute of *FIRE-WEATHER-OBSERVATION*, range: *0..100* (*m:1*) (Burning index for Pine.)

□ *burning-index-d* — attribute of *FIRE-WEATHER-OBSERVATION*, range: *0..100* (*m:1*) (Burning index for Grass.)

□ *fire-load-index-n* — attribute of *FIRE-WEATHER-OBSERVATION*, range: *0..100* (*m:1*) (Fire load index for Pine.)

□ *fire-load-index-d* — attribute of *FIRE-WEATHER-OBSERVATION*, range: *0..100* (*m:1*) (Fire load index for Grass.)

The objects of the category *FIRE-INCIDENT* are identified by: fire-number-within-year the-year.

The objects of the category *DAILY-DESCRIPTION* are identified by: date for.

The objects of the category *YEAR* are identified by: year-number.

The objects of the category *FIRE-WEATHER-STATION* are identified by: station-id.

The objects of the category *FIRE-WEATHER-OBSERVATION* are identified by: date observed-by.

□ *station-id* — attribute of *FIRE-WEATHER-STATION*, range: *Char(8)* (*1:1,total*) (A sequence of alphanumeric characters which is assigned to each fire-weather station and which uniquely identifies that station.)

□ *station-description* — attribute of *FIRE-WEATHER-STATION*, range: *String* (*m:1*) (English name or designation of the station.)

□ *location-north* — attribute of *FIRE-WEATHER-STATION*, range: *2746840..2865840* (*m:1*) (UTM north coordinate of a fire-weather station.)

□ *location-east* — attribute of *FIRE-WEATHER-STATION*, range: *446880..563280* (*m:1*) (UTM east coordinate of a fire-weather station.)

5.1.2. Relational schema of the application

BATTERY-CHANGE

in-equipment--park-service-number-in-key:Char(15); *battery-change-date-in-key*:Date;

Reference from *BATTERY-CHANGE* to *EQUIPMENT*: in-equipment--park-service-number-in-key→park-service-number-key.

CALIBRATION

equipment-calibrated--park-service-number-in-key:Char(15); *calibration-date-in-key*:Date;
calibration-method:'Field','Lab';   *is-calibration-using-other-technique*:Boolean;
technique-description:String;

Reference from *CALIBRATION* to *EQUIPMENT*: equipment-calibrated--park-service-number-in-key→park-service-number-key.

DAILY-DESCRIPTION

for--year-number-in-key:1940..2040;   *for--fire-number-within-year-in-key*:1..999;
date-in-key:Date; *new-acres-burned*:0..99999; *soil-moisture*:0..100;

Reference from *DAILY-DESCRIPTION* to *FIRE-INCIDENT*: for--year-number-in-key→year-number-in-key, for--fire-number-within-year-in-key→fire-number-within-year-in-key.

EQUIPMENT

park-service-number-key:Char(15) 1:1; *model-number*:Char(15); *serial-number*:Char(20);
type-descriptor:Char(30);

EQUIPMENT-INSTALLATION-PERIOD

equipment--park-service-number-in-key:Char(15); *installed-at--station-id-in-key*:Char(15);
begin-date-in-key:Date; *end-date*:Date;

Reference from *EQUIPMENT-INSTALLATION-PERIOD* to *HYDROLOGY-STATION*: installed-at--station-id-in-key→station-id-key.

Reference from *EQUIPMENT-INSTALLATION-PERIOD* to *EQUIPMENT*:
equipment--park-service-number-in-key→park-service-number-key.

FIRE-INCIDENT

year-number-in-key:1940..2040;   *fire-number-within-year-in-key*:1..999;
fine-fuel-load:0..9999; *fire-management-unit*:1..44; *fire-name*:String; *cost*:0..99999999;
fire-origin-east:446880..563280;   *fire-origin-north*:2746840..2865840;
fire-type:'incendiary','lightning','prescribed','research';   *fuel-model*:'n','d';
has-crossed-perimeter:Boolean; *designated-hydrology--station-id*:Char(15);

Reference from *FIRE-INCIDENT* to *HYDROLOGY-STATION*: designated-
hydrology--station-id→station-id-key.

Reference from *FIRE-INCIDENT* to *YEAR*: year-number-in-key→year-number-key.

FIRE-WEATHER-OBSERVATION

observed-by--station-id-in-key:Char(8);   *date-in-key*:Date;   *burning-index-n*:0..100;
burning-index-d:0..100;   *drought-index*:0..999;   *dry-temperature*:0..110;
energy-release-component-d:0..100;   *energy-release-component-n*:0..100;
fire-load-index-d:0..100;   *fire-load-index-n*:0..100;   *ignition-component-d*:0..100;
ignition-component-n:0..100;   *live-fuel-moisture*:0..100;
precipitation-amount-inch:0.0..99.99;   *precipitation-duration*:0..24;
relative-humidity:0..100;   *relative-humidity-max*:0..100;   *relative-humidity-min*:0..100;
spread-component-d:0..100;   *spread-component-n*:0..100;   *state-of-weather*:0..9;
temperature-max:20..110; *temperature-min*:20..110; *thousand-hour-fuel-moisture-d*:0..99;
thousand-hour-fuel-moisture-n:0..99; *wind-direction*:0..8; *wind-speed-mph*:0..99;

Reference from *FIRE-WEATHER-OBSERVATION* to *FIRE-WEATHER-STATION*:
observed-by--station-id-in-key→station-id-key.

FIRE-WEATHER-STATION

station-id-key:Char(8);   *location-north*:2746840..2865840;   *station-description*:String;
location-east:446880..563280;

HYDROLOGY-STATION

station-id-key:Char(15);   *method-used*:'standard-survey','loran','gps-equipment','map';
station-description:String;   *location-tolerance-ft*:0..1000;
station-location-east:446880..563280;   *station-location-north*:2746840..2865840;
station-owner:'everglades-national-park','usgs','sfwmd','us-coe';
is-continuous-station:Boolean;   *is-discontinuous-station*:Boolean;
benchmark-location-east:446880..563280;   *benchmark-location-north*:2746840..2865840;
housing-descriptor:String;   *platform-benchmark-height-difference*:0.00..10.00;
platform-height-ft:0.00..10.00;   *is-temporary-station*:Boolean;   *begin-date*:Date;
end-date:Date;

PARAMETER-DISCONTINUITY-PERIOD

parameter--collected-by--park-service-number-in-key:Char(15);
parameter-name-in-key:Char(20);   *begin-date-in-key*:Date;   *end-date*:Date;
reason-for-discontinuity:String;

Reference from *PARAMETER-DISCONTINUITY-PERIOD* to *PARAMETER-MEASURED-BY-SPECIFIC-EQUIPMENT*: parameter--collected-by--park-service-number-in-key→collected-by--park-service-number-in-key, parameter-name-in-key→parameter-name-in-key.

PARAMETER-MEASURED-BY-SPECIFIC-EQUIPMENT

collected-by--park-service-number-in-key:Char(15);   *parameter-name-in-key*:Char(20);
parameter-description:String;

Reference from *PARAMETER-MEASURED-BY-SPECIFIC-EQUIPMENT* to *EQUIPMENT*: collected-by--park-service-number-in-key→park-service-number-key.

REPAIR-PERIOD

equipment-repaired--park-service-number-in-key:Char(15);   *begin-date-in-key*:Date;
end-date:Date; *reason-for-repair*:String; *repair-entity*:String;

Reference from *REPAIR-PERIOD* to *EQUIPMENT*: equipment-repaired--park-service-number-in-key→park-service-number-key.

STATION-CONTINUITY-PERIOD

discontinuous--station-id-in-key:Char(15); *begin-date-in-key*:Date; *end-date*:Date;

Reference from *STATION-CONTINUITY-PERIOD* to *HYDROLOGY-STATION*: discontinuous--station-id-in-key→station-id-key.

YEAR

year-number-key:1940..2040; *is-drought-year*:Boolean;

DAILY-DISCHARGE

daily-produced-by--station-id-in-key:Char(15);   *date-in-key*:Date;
daily-downstream-stage-ft:0..12;   *daily-mean-discharge*:-99999.99..+99999.99;
daily-upstream-stage-ft:0..12; *formula*:'weir','rating-curves';

Reference from *DAILY-DISCHARGE* to *HYDROLOGY-STATION*: daily-produced-by--station-id-in-key→station-id-key.

DAILY-EVAPORATION

daily-produced-by--station-id-in-key:Char(15);   *date-in-key*:Date;
total-daily-evaporation-inch:0.00..12.00;

Reference from *DAILY-EVAPORATION* to *HYDROLOGY-STATION*: daily-produced-by--station-id-in-key→station-id-key.

DAILY-RAINFALL

daily-produced-by--station-id-in-key:Char(15);   *date-in-key*:Date;
daily-precipitation-inch:0.00..22.00;

Reference from *DAILY-RAINFALL* to *HYDROLOGY-STATION*: daily-produced-by--station-id-in-key→station-id-key.

DAILY-STAGE

daily-produced-by--station-id-in-key:Char(15);   *date-in-key*:Date;
daily-mean-stage:-99.99..+99.99;

Reference from *DAILY-STAGE* to *HYDROLOGY-STATION*: daily-produced-by--station-id-in-key→station-id-key.

DAILY-TEMPERATURE

daily-produced-by--station-id-in-key:Char(15);   *date-in-key*:Date;
daily-max-temperature:20.00..120.00;   *daily-mean-temperature*:20.00..120.00;
daily-min-temperature:20.00..120.00;

Reference from *DAILY-TEMPERATURE* to *HYDROLOGY-STATION*: daily-produced-by--station-id-in-key→station-id-key.

HOURLY-RAINFALL

hourly-produced-by--station-id-in-key:Char(15);   *hour-in-key*:0..23;   *date-in-key*:Date;
hourly-precipitation-inch:0.00..22.00;

Reference from *HOURLY-RAINFALL* to *HYDROLOGY-STATION*: hourly-produced-by--station-id-in-key→station-id-key.

HOURLY-STAGE

hourly-produced-by--station-id-in-key:Char(15);   *hour-in-key*:0..23;   *date-in-key*:Date;
hourly-mean-stage:-99.99..+99.99;

Reference from *HOURLY-STAGE* to *HYDROLOGY-STATION*: hourly-produced-by--station-id-in-key→station-id-key.

HOURLY-WIND

hourly-produced-by--station-id-in-key:Char(15);   *hour-in-key*:0..23;   *date-in-key*:Date;
hourly-mean-wind-speed-mph:0.00..200.00; *hourly-wind-direction*:1..360;

Reference from *HOURLY-WIND* to *HYDROLOGY-STATION*: hourly-produced-by--station-id-in-key→station-id-key.

MONTHLY-RAINFALL

monthly-produced-by--station-id-in-key:Char(15);   *month-in-key*:1..12;
year-in-key:1940..2040; *monthly-precipitation-inch*:0.00..22.00;

Reference from *MONTHLY-RAINFALL* to *HYDROLOGY-STATION*: monthly-produced-by--station-id-in-key→station-id-key.

MONTHLY-STAGE

monthly-produced-by--station-id-in-key:Char(15);   *month-in-key*:1..12;
year-in-key:1940..2040; *monthly-mean-stage*:-99.99..+99.99;

Reference from *MONTHLY-STAGE* to *HYDROLOGY-STATION*: monthly-produced-by--station-id-in-key→station-id-key.

CALIBRATION--HAS-USED--EQUIPMENT

calibration-equipment-calibrated--park-service-number-in-key:Char(15);
calibration-date-in-key:Date; *equipment--park-service-number-in-key*:Char(15);

Reference from *CALIBRATION HAS-USED EQUIPMENT* to *CALIBRATION*: calibration-equipment-calibrated--park-service-number-in-key→equipment-calibrated--park-service-number-in-key, calibration-date-in-key→calibration-date-in-key.

Reference from *CALIBRATION HAS-USED EQUIPMENT* to *EQUIPMENT*: equipment--park-service-number-in-key→park-service-number-key.

Some of the Integrity Constraints Generated During Schema Conversion

(**for every** x **in** *CALIBRATION*:   **if not** x *technique-description* **null**   **then** x.*is-calibration-using-other-technique*) **and**

(**for every** x **in** *HYDROLOGY-STATION*:   **if not** x *begin-date* **null**   **then** x.*is-temporary-station*) **and**

(**for every** x **in** *HYDROLOGY-STATION*:   **if not** x *end-date* **null**   **then** x.*is-temporary-station*) **and**

(**for every** x **in** *CALIBRATION--HAS-USED--EQUIPMENT*:   **exists** y **in** *CALIBRATION*: x.*the-calibration-equipment-calibrated--park-service-number-in-key* = y.*the-equipment-calibrated--park-service-number-in-key* and x.*the--calibration-date-in-key* = y.*calibration-date-in-key*) **and**

(**for every** x **in** *CALIBRATION--HAS-USED--EQUIPMENT*:   **exists** y **in** *EQUIPMENT*: x.*the-equipment--park-service-number-in-key* = y.*park-service-number-key*) **and**

(for every x **in** *PARAMETER-MEASURED-BY-SPECIFIC-EQUIPMENT*: **exists** y **in** *EQUIPMENT*: x.*collected-by--park-service-number-in-key* = y.*park-service-number-key*) and

(for every x **in** *FIRE-INCIDENT*: **exists** y **in** *HYDROLOGY-STATION*: x *designated-hydrology--station-id null or* x.*designated-hydrology--station-id* = y.*station-id-key*) and

(for every x **in** *DAILY-DESCRIPTION*: **exists** y **in** *FIRE-INCIDENT*: (x.*for--year-number-in-key* = y.*the--year-number-in-key* and x.*for--fire-number-within-year-in-key* = y.*fire-number-within-year-in-key*)) and

(for every x **in** *BATTERY-CHANGE*: **exists** y **in** *EQUIPMENT*: x.*in-equipment--park-service-number-in-key* = y.*park-service-number-key*) and

(for every x **in** *EQUIPMENT-INSTALLATION-PERIOD*: **exists** y **in** *HYDROLOGY-STATION*: x.*installed-at--station-id-in-key* = y.*station-id-key*) and

(for every x **in** *FIRE-WEATHER-OBSERVATION*: **exists** y **in** *FIRE-WEATHER-STATION*: x.*observed-by--station-id-in-key* = y.*station-id-key*) and

(for every x **in** *STATION-CONTINUITY-PERIOD*: **exists** y **in** *HYDROLOGY-STATION*: x.*the-discontinuous--station-id-in-key* = y.*station-id-key* and y.is-fixed-station) and

(for every x **in** *EQUIPMENT-INSTALLATION-PERIOD*: **exists** y **in** *EQUIPMENT*: x.*the-equipment--park-service-number-in-key* = y.*park-service-number-key*) and

(for every x **in** *CALIBRATION*: **exists** y **in** *EQUIPMENT*: x.*the-equipment-calibrated--park-service-number-in-key* = y.*park-service-number-key*) and

(for every x **in** *REPAIR-PERIOD*: **exists** y **in** *EQUIPMENT*: x.*the-equipment-repaired--park-service-number-in-key* = y.*park-service-number-key*) and

(for every x **in** *PARAMETER-DISCONTINUITY-PERIOD*: **exists** y **in** *PARAMETER-MEASURED-BY-SPECIFIC-EQUIPMENT*: (x.*the-parameter--collected-by--park-service-number-in-key* = y.*collected-by--park-service-number-in-key* and x.*the--parameter-name-in-key* = y.*parameter-name-in-key*)) and

(for every x **in** *FIRE-INCIDENT*: **exists** y **in** *YEAR*: x.*the--year-number-in-key* = y.*year-number-key*) and

(for every x **in** *DAILY-DISCHARGE*: **exists** y **in** *HYDROLOGY-STATION*: x.*daily-produced-by--station-id-in-key* = y.*station-id-key*) and (**for every** x **in** *DAILY-EVAPORATION*: **exists** y **in** *HYDROLOGY-STATION*: x.*daily-produced-by--station-id-in-key* = y.*station-id-key*) and

(**for every** x **in** *DAILY-RAINFALL*: **exists** y **in** *HYDROLOGY-STATION*: x.*daily-produced-by--station-id-in-key* = y.*station-id-key*) and

(**for every** x **in** *DAILY-STAGE*: **exists** y **in** *HYDROLOGY-STATION*: x.*daily-produced-by--station-id-in-key* = y.*station-id-key*) and

(**for every** x **in** *DAILY-TEMPERATURE*: **exists** y **in** *HYDROLOGY-STATION*: x.*daily-produced-by--station-id-in-key* = y.*station-id-key*) and

(**for every** x **in** *HOURLY-RAINFALL*: **exists** y **in** *HYDROLOGY-STATION*: x.*hourly-produced-by--station-id-in-key* = y.*station-id-key*) and

(**for every** x **in** *HOURLY-STAGE*: **exists** y **in** *HYDROLOGY-STATION*: x.*hourly-produced-by--station-id-in-key* = y.*station-id-key*) and

(**for every** x **in** *HOURLY-WIND*: **exists** y **in** *HYDROLOGY-STATION*: x.*hourly-produced-by--station-id-in-key* = y.*station-id-key*) and

(**for every** x **in** *MONTHLY-RAINFALL*: **exists** y **in** *HYDROLOGY-STATION*: x.*monthly-produced-by--station-id-in-key* = y.*station-id-key*) and

(**for every** x **in** *MONTHLY-STAGE*: **exists** y **in** *HYDROLOGY-STATION*: x.*monthly-produced-by--station-id-in-key* = y.*station-id-key*)

5.2. Flow of Database Design

Figure 5-9 is an information flow diagram that outlines the major steps of database application design, including the schema, integrity constraints, userviews, data manipulation programs, query forms, and ad hoc queries. The design proceeds in the direction of the arrows from semantic descriptions to descriptions in the conventions and languages supported by the available DBMS. Nodes marked in brackets are omitted for some DBMSs.

In the first step, a conceptual schema of an enterprise is designed using the Semantic Binary Model. Then the schema is converted into the relational, network, or hierarchical model by manual algorithms. According to the criteria described in the text to assess the quality of databases, these manual algorithms produce very high-quality results.

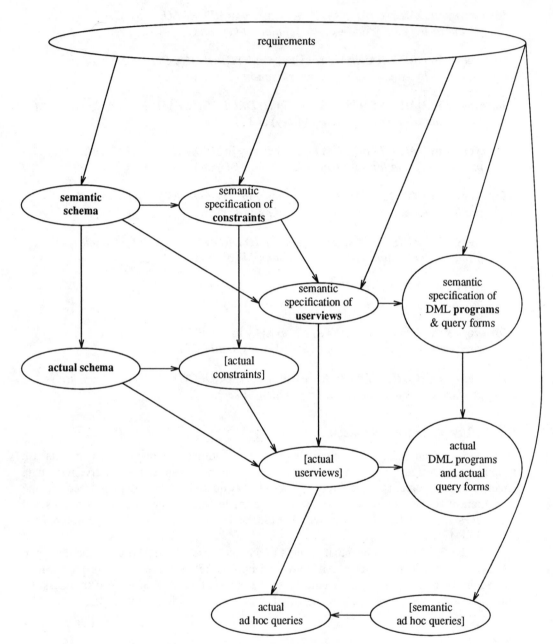

Figure 5-9. Flow of database design.

5.3. Other Methodolgies

5.3.1. An alternative methodology: normalization

Normalization is a methodology for the design of relational databases. This methodology used to be quite popular in the academic world. However, it has rarely been used in the application industry. One of the reasons for its lack of popularity in the industry is the mathematical sophistication of the normalization methodology.

This is a "bottom-up" methodology. The design proceeds as follows. First, a poor relational schema is designed directly from the requirements. Then, the schema is refined in steps by eliminating certain aspects of redundancy (and thus potential inconsistency and update anomalies). At every step the schema satisfies certain mathematically defined criteria of nonredundancy corresponding to that step. These criteria are called **normal forms**.

1.   The initial schema is said to be in the **first normal form**.

2.   The product of the first step, satisfying certain broad criteria, is in the **second normal form**.

3.   The product of the next step, satisfying certain stricter criteria, is in the **third normal form**.

4.   The normalization process can continue further until the arsenal of normal form definitions is exhausted.

After the design is completed, all the schemas but the last one are discarded. Programs, queries, and the like are designed directly in terms of the final schema. Figure 5-10 is a diagram of the flow of design by normalization.

5.3.1.1. *The third normal form defined

The following is a definition of the third normal form.

An attribute A of table T is said to be **functionally dependent** on a set of attributes $\{B_1, \ldots, B_k\}$ of T if for no tuple of values $(b_1, \ldots, b_k)$ of these attributes there may be two different values of A in the table at the same time.

A table T having exactly one key (possibly a multiattribute key) is said to be in the **third normal form** if:

No nonkey attribute A is functionally dependent on any set of attributes, unless the latter set of attributes contains A or contains the whole key.

(The definition is more complex for the unlikely case that the table has more than one key.)

For example, let T be a table with four attributes A, B, C, and D. Let the key of T be $\{A, B\}$. If T is in the third normal form then:

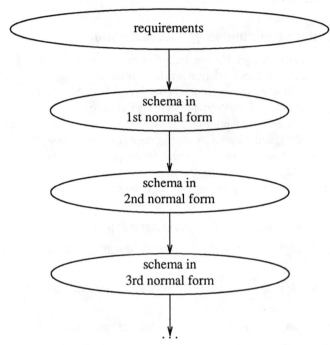

Figure 5-10. Alternative relational database design: Normalization.

a. A is not functionally dependent on $\{B, C, D\}$

b. B is not functionally dependent on $\{A, C, D\}$

c. C is not functionally dependent on $\{A, D\}$

d. C is not functionally dependent on $\{B, D\}$

e. D is not functionally dependent on $\{A, C\}$

f. D is not functionally dependent on $\{B, C\}$

If any of these conditions were violated, there would be a clear redundancy. For example, if D *is* functionally dependent on $\{B, C\}$, then observe the redundancy in the following instantaneous table. We can deduce from the constraint that the ? in the second row should read 45:

A	B	C	D
37	15	5	45
12	15	5	?

5.3.2. A comparison of methodologies

1. The normalization methodology captures only a few of the aspects of the semantic quality of databases, while the methodology suggested in this text attempts to capture all of the aspects.

2. The normalization methodology is too difficult to be used by most systems analysts and software engineers.

3. The normalization methodology is bottom-up: a "bad" database is designed, and then it is refined by normalization. This is analogous to writing a bad program and then improving its structure.

   This book's methodology is top-down: good semantic schemas are designed first and then they are downgraded to meet implementational restrictions, while the original semantic schemas remain to serve as documentation. This is analogous to writing an algorithm first and then translating it into a structured program, while the algorithm remains as documentation.

Figure 5-12 (page 232) is a "schema" of the world of relational database schemas and two database design processes: the binary-relational conversion according to the methodology of this book and the schema normalization according to the alternative methodology. This "methodology schema" shows:

- Every relational schema is a binary schema.

- Some of the binary schemas, which are not relational schemas, are high-quality schemas according to all the criteria of schema quality.

- Some of the relational schemas satisfy to a certain degree *some* of the nonredundancy criteria. These limited criteria are primarily concerned with the possible redundancy of a table which could be split into two tables. The relational schemas which satisfy these limited criteria to a certain minimal degree (at least) are called the second-normal-form schemas. Some of the second-normal-form schemas satisfy the limited criteria to a higher degree and correspondingly belong to the *THIRD-NORMAL-FORM, FOURTH-NORMAL-FORM*, etc., subcategories of the second-normal-form schemas.

- Every high-quality relational schema should be in the maximal known normal form, but the opposite is not true: some maximal-normal-form schemas are not of high quality, since they do not address all the quality criteria.

- The process of normalization begins with a very poor relational schema and converts it into a second-normal-form schema, then into a third normal form schema, and so on.

- The methodology of this book begins with a quality semantic schema and downgrades it to a quality relational schema.

Figure 5-11 outlines the "instantaneous database" under the "methodology schema." The individual schemas are points there in a coordinate system of schema quality.

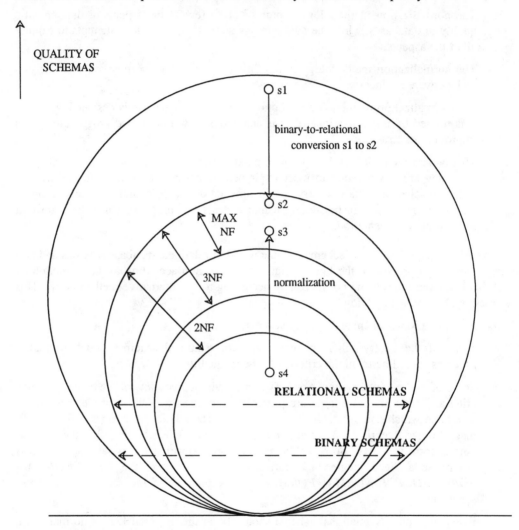

This diagram depicts the "instantaneous database" for the "schema" of conversion methodologies. The database schemas s_1, s_2, s_3, and s_4 are individual objects in that "instantaneous database."

Figure 5-11. A comparison between database design methodologies.

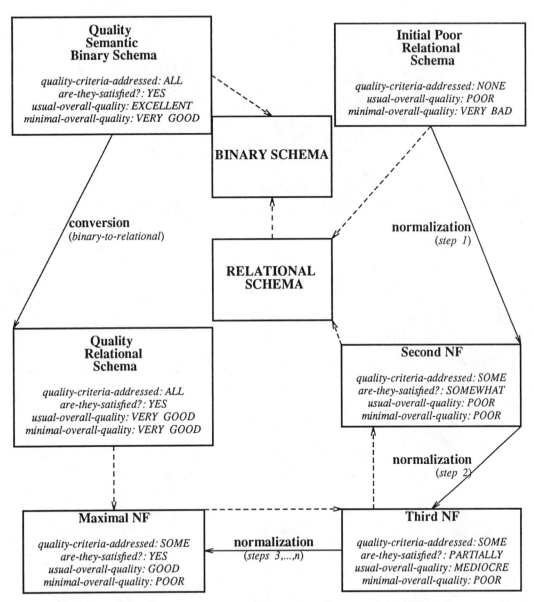

Figure 5-12. A "schema" of conversion methodologies: normalization versus semantic-to-relational conversion. The arrows with dashes show the subcategories among the categories of schemas.

CHAPTER 6

FROM THE SEMANTIC TO THE NETWORK MODEL

This chapter defines the Network Data Model and adapts the top-down database design methodology to network databases. Section 3 of this chapter discusses network database languages: application of the generic fourth-generation and logic-based languages and a special navigational language for the Network Model.

Since the 1970s, the Network Data Model has been very popular in the industry. An alternative name of the model is **CODASYL/DBTG**, after the name of the committee that produced a standard for the Network Model (CODASYL Data Base Task Group).

6.1. Definitions

Orderless network schema — a binary schema satisfying the following:

a. All the abstract categories are pairwise *disjoint*.

b. Every relation is either an *attribute* (an m:1 relation to a concrete category), or a 1:*m* relation between *different* abstract categories.

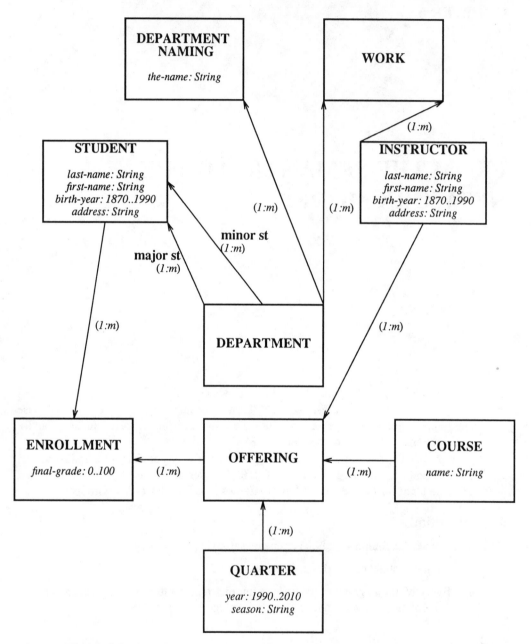

Figure 6-1. An orderless network schema for the university application.

> *Example:*
>
> The schema on Figure 6-1 could be an orderless network schema for a university, provided there are no persons but students and instructors, and the categories *INSTRUCTOR* and *STUDENT* are disjoint.

Default names of relations

It is customary in the network model to name relations as

$$domain \textbf{ hyphen } range$$

Of course, this convention may be used only when there is no other relation between the same domain and range.

In the graphic representation of network schemas we may omit some of the names of the relations. The omitted names by default conform to the above convention.

> *Example:*
>
> □ *instructor-work* — relation from *INSTRUCTOR* to *WORK*   (*1:m*)

Onto relation — a relation whose inverse is total.

This means that a relation R from C_1 to C_2 is onto if for every object y of C_2 there is an object x of C_1 such that xRy.

> *Example:*
>
> □ — relation from *STUDENT* to *ENROLLMENT*   (*1:m,onto*)
>
> (It is *onto* because every enrollment has a student related to it.)
>
> □ — relation from *INSTRUCTOR* to *WORK*   (*1:m,onto*)
>
> (It is *onto* because every event of work is related to an instructor.)

The phrase "relation R is **onto** category C" means:

$$R \text{ is an } onto \text{ relation, and its range is } C.$$

The phrase "category C_2 **depends on** category C_1" means:

$$\text{there is a } relation \text{ from } C_1 \text{ onto } C_2$$

(that is, there is a relation which relates every object of C_2 to an object of C_1).

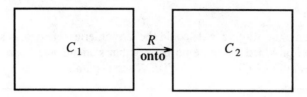

Figure 6-2. C_2 depends on C_1.

Example:

- *OFFERING* depends on *COURSE*
- *OFFERING* depends on *QUARTER*
- *OFFERING* depends on *INSTRUCTOR*
- *ENROLLMENT* depends on *OFFERING*
- *ENROLLMENT* depends on *STUDENT*
- *DEPARTMENT-NAMING* depends on *DEPARTMENT*
- *WORK* depends on *DEPARTMENT*
- *WORK* depends on *INSTRUCTOR*

The phrase "category C_1 **indirectly depends on** category C_2" means (recursively):

C_1 depends on C_2, or there exists C_3 such that C_1 depends on C_3 and C_3 indirectly depends on C_2.

Example:

- *ENROLLMENT* indirectly depends on *OFFERING*
  (since *ENROLLMENT* depends on *OFFERING*).
- *ENROLLMENT* indirectly depends on *COURSE*

Independent category — an abstract category which depends on no category.

Example:

Independent categories:

STUDENT, INSTRUCTOR, DEPARTMENT, COURSE, QUARTER.

Ordered network schema — a binary system consisting of:

a.   An orderless network schema.

b.   A category, called *SYSTEM*, in which at all times there is only one and the same object SYSTEM.

c.   Relations from *SYSTEM onto* some of the abstract categories of the orderless schema, such that every abstract category of the orderless schema would be indirectly dependent on *SYSTEM*.

Example:

☐   — relation from *SYSTEM* to *STUDENT*   (*1:m,onto*)

☐   — relation from *SYSTEM* to *INSTRUCTOR*   (*1:m,onto*)

☐   — relation from *SYSTEM* to *DEPARTMENT*   (*1:m,onto*)

☐   — relation from *SYSTEM* to *COURSE*   (*1:m,onto*)

☐   — relation from *SYSTEM* to *QUARTER*   (*1:m,onto*)

---

d.   For every relation R between different abstract categories C_1 and C_2 there is a relation $NEXT_R$ such that:

   •   The domain of $NEXT_R$ is C_2.

   •   The range of $NEXT_R$ is C_2.

   •   For every object x in C_1, $NEXT_R$ constitutes a linear order of C_2's objects connected by R to x.

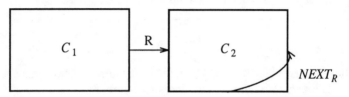

Example:

☐ *next-system-department* — relation from *DEPARTMENT* to *DEPARTMENT* (*1:1*)

This is a chain connecting all of the departments:

$$d_1 \rightarrow d_2 \rightarrow d_3 \rightarrow d_4$$

Example:

☐ *next-system-student* — relation from *STUDENT* to *STUDENT* (*1:1*)

This is a chain connecting all of the students:

$$s_1 \rightarrow s_2 \rightarrow s_3 \rightarrow \cdots \rightarrow s_{500}$$

Example:

☐ *next-major-st* — relation from *STUDENT* to *STUDENT* (*1:1*)

This is a set of chains, one chain per department, connecting all the majoring students of the department.

For department d_1: $s_{11} \rightarrow s_{25} \rightarrow s_3 \rightarrow s_{15}$

For department d_2: trivial chain because the department has only 1 majoring student.

For department d_3: empty chain because the department has no majoring students.

For department d_4: $s_1 \rightarrow s_{220} \rightarrow s_{31}$

(The remaining 492 students have not declared their majors.)

Network schema terminology

The following terms are frequently used in network database management systems. Most of them have synonyms in the binary terminology.

Record-type — abstract category.

> *Example:*
>
> *DEPARTMENT* is a record-type.

Field — attribute.

> *Example:*
>
> *LAST-NAME* is a field.

Set-type — a nonattribute relation between different categories.

> *Example:*
>
> ☐ *major-st* — relation from *DEPARTMENT* to *STUDENT*   (*1:m*)
>
> ☐ *instructor-work* — relation from *INSTRUCTOR* to *WORK*   (*1:m*)

Record occurrence — a part of an instantaneous database, consisting of exactly one abstract object and all its attributes.

> *Example:*
>
> A record occurrence of record-type *STUDENT*:
>
> | **ONE student** |
> | --- |
> | *last-name:* Jackson |
> | *first-name:* Mary |
> | *birth-year:* 1970 |
> | *address:* 123 Dorms |

Set occurrence of a set-type R for an object x — a part of an instantaneous database consisting only of x, all the objects related to x by R, and the relation $NEXT_R$ on these objects.

Example:

Let s_1, s_2, s_3, s_4 be the only majoring students of department d. Then the following may be a set occurrence:

$$d, s_1 \, NEXT_{\text{major-st}} \, s_2 \, NEXT_{\text{major-st}} \, s_3 \, NEXT_{\text{major-st}} \, s_4$$

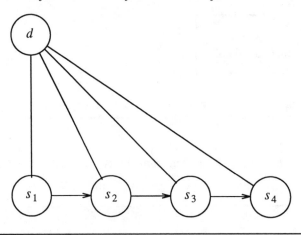

Each set-type whose domain is *SYSTEM* has exactly one set-occurrence, since there is only one object of the record-type *SYSTEM*.

Example:

The following is the set-occurrence of *SYSTEM-STUDENT* in an instantaneous database.

$$SYSTEM \xrightarrow{\textit{first}} student_1 \xrightarrow{\textit{next}} student_2 \xrightarrow{\textit{next}} student_3$$

Example:

The following figure shows a part of a network instantaneous database. This part contains all the record-occurrences of *STUDENT*, *DEPARTMENT*, and *DEPARTMENT-NAMING* and all the set-occurrences of *SYSTEM-STUDENT*, *SYSTEM-DEPARTMENT*,   *DEPARTMENT--DEPARTMENT-NAMING*, *MAJOR-ST*, and *MINOR-ST*.

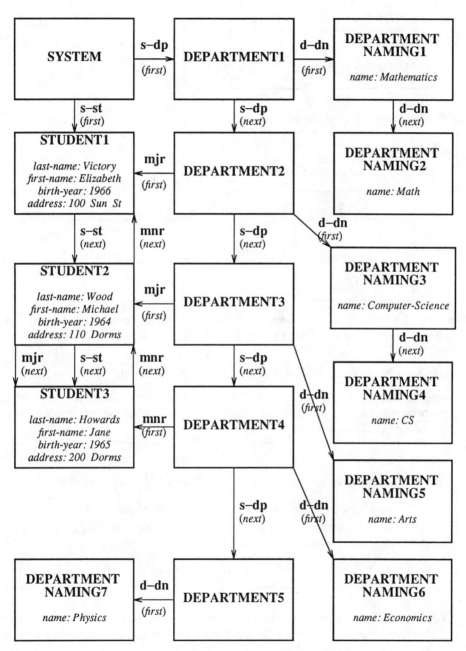

Figure 6-3. A part of a network instantaneous database.

Owner of a set-type R — its domain.

> *Example:*
>
> *DEPARTMENT* is the owner of *MAJOR-ST*.

Member of a set-type R — its range.

> *Example:*
>
> *STUDENT* is the member of *MAJOR-ST*.

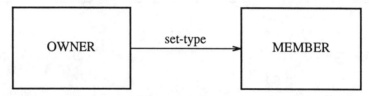

Order-type of a set type R — the integrity constraints, the implementational restrictions, or the inference rules regarding the ordering of a set-occurrence (as determined by the relation $NEXT_R$).

Many network database management systems recognize the following order types:

'order is last' — the member object last related (in time) to a given owner object becomes the last in the order among all the member objects related by the relation to the owner object.

> *Example:*
>
> Let the following be the set occurrence of *MAJOR-ST* for department d:
>
> $$d, s_1\ NEXT_{\text{major-st}}\ s_2\ NEXT_{\text{major-st}}\ s_3\ NEXT_{\text{major-st}}\ s_4$$
>
> Now assume that another student s becomes a majoring student of d. Then the new set occurrence would be
>
> $$d,\ s_1\ NEXT_{\text{major-st}}\ s_2\ NEXT_{\text{major-st}}\ s_3\ NEXT_{\text{major-st}}\ s_4\ NEXT_{\text{major-st}}\ s$$

'order is first' — the member object last (in time) related to a given owner object becomes the first in the order among all the member objects related by the relation to the owner object.

Example:

Let the following be the set occurrence of *MAJOR-ST* for department d:

$$d, s_1 \, NEXT_{\text{major-st}} \, s_2 \, NEXT_{\text{major-st}} \, s_3 \, NEXT_{\text{major-st}} \, s_4$$

Now assume that another student s becomes a majoring student of d. Then the new set occurrence would be

$$d,$$
$$s \, NEXT_{\text{major-st}} \, s_1 \, NEXT_{\text{major-st}} \, s_2 \, NEXT_{\text{major-st}} \, s_3 \, NEXT_{\text{major-st}} \, s_4$$

'order is ascending by field f **'** — the member object last related to a given owner object is put in a position within the order according to the following criterion for every two member objects y_1 and y_2:

$$\textbf{if } y_1 \, NEXT_R \, y_2 \textbf{ then } y_1.f \leq y_2.f$$

This order type is often also called **order by key**. This "key" has nothing to do with the concept of *key* as defined for the relational model. To avoid confusion, the "order by key" terminology is not used in this text.

'order is descending by field f **'** — the member object last related to a given owner object is put in a position within the order according to the following criterion for every two member objects y_1 and y_2:

$$\textbf{if } y_1 \, NEXT_R \, y_2 \textbf{ then } y_1.f \geq y_2.f$$

'order is $o_1, o_2, \ldots, o_k$ **'**, where each o_i is of the form

'ascending by field f_i **'** or **'descending by field** f_i **'**

— a lexicographic combination of ordering conditions on several fields.

'order is current' — no constraints, restrictions, or program-independent rules for the order. Pragmatically, the position of a new object is determined by the application program: the position will be right next to the last object accessed by the program within the same set-occurrence.

6.2. Database Design

Conversion algorithm of a semantic schema into a network schema whose quality is among the highest possible for the latter (provided the original semantic schema is of high quality):

1. **Convert all abstract categories into disjoint ones** as in the conversion for the Relational Model.

Note:

- In the Network Model, the categories need not have keys. Thus, when the solution **Events** is chosen, its redundancy cannot be controlled in terms of the key. If the supercategory has a 1:1 attribute, then we can specify an integrity constraint controlling the **Events** redundancy in terms of that attribute.

Example:

Suppose we had

☐ *ssn* — attribute of *PERSON*, range: *Integer*   *(1:1)*

After the conversion into **Events** we would have

☐ *ssn* — attribute of *STUDENT*, range: *Integer*   *(1:1)*

☐ *ssn* — attribute of *INSTRUCTOR*, range: *Integer*   *(1:1)*

In this case, we can specify a constraint for every relation whose domain or range was the category *PERSON*. For the relation *ADDRESS* such a constraint is:

for every s **in** *STUDENT*:

for every i **in** *INSTRUCTOR*:

    if s.*SSN*=i.*SSN*

      then

        s.*ADDRESS*=i.*ADDRESS* **or**

        (s *ADDRESS* **null and** i *ADDRESS* **null**)

- The available network database management systems usually do not support sophisticated userviews; they support only subschemas, which are trivial userviews. This means that normally the solution **Union+Events** should not be chosen in the design of a network schema.

2. **Convert every proper 1:m or m:m relation whose range is a concrete category** into a new abstract category and its two functional relations through a relation-split.

3. **Convert every proper many-to-many** relation into a category and two functional relations through a relation-split.

4. **Convert every m:1 nonattribute relation into a 1:m relation** by changing its direction and its name.

> *Example:*
>
> Instead of
>
> > ☐ *the-student* — relation from *ENROLLMENT* to *STUDENT*   (*m:1*)
>
> we have
>
> > ☐ *student-enrollment* — relation from *STUDENT* to *ENROLLMENT*   (*1:m*)

5. **Convert every 1:m relation whose domain and range are the same category** into a new category, a 1:1 onto relation, and a 1:m onto relation, through a relation-split.

> *Example:*
>
> If we had:
>
> > ☐ *subdepartment* — relation from *DEPARTMENT* to *DEPARTMENT*   (*1:m*)
>
> then we would convert it into:
>
> > ☐ *event-of-SUBDEPARTMENT* — category
> >
> > ☐ *the-event-of-the-same-department* — relation from *DEPARTMENT* to *event-of-SUBDEPARTMENT*   (*1:1,onto*)
> >
> > ☐ *department-subdepartment* — relation from *DEPARTMENT* to *event-of-SUBDEPARTMENT*   (*1:m,onto*)

> *Example:*
>
> The binary schema of the university has been converted so far into the orderless network schema of Figure 6-1 on page 236.

6. **Add the category** *SYSTEM,* which always has just one object — the enterprise or the world for which the database is being designed.

7. **Relate every independent category** *C* to the category *SYSTEM*:

> ☐ *system-C* — relation from *SYSTEM* to *C*   (*1:m,onto*)

> *Example:*
>
> □ *system-department* — relation from *SYSTEM* to *DEPARTMENT* (*1:m,onto*)

8. If there are still abstract categories *C* that do not indirectly depend on *SYSTEM* (a very rare case), then relate them to *SYSTEM*:

□ *system-C* — relation from *SYSTEM* to *C*   (*1:m,onto*)

> *Example:*
>
> There is no such problem in our schema. Let's spoil our schema a bit to have such a problem. If the relation *MAJOR-ST* were onto:
>
> □ *major-st* — relation from *DEPARTMENT* to *STUDENT* (*1:m,onto*)
>
> and in addition we had a relation assigning one student council liaison to several departments:
>
> □ *student-council-liaison-for-department* — relation from *STUDENT* to *DEPARTMENT*   (*1:m,onto*)
>
> then the categories *STUDENT* and *DEPARTMENT* would depend on each other. None of the categories would be independent. We have to link at least one of them to *SYSTEM*, so that they would indirectly depend on SYSTEM:
>
> □ *system-department* — relation from *SYSTEM* to *DEPARTMENT* (*1:m,onto*)

9. Define **order-type** of every nonattribute relation *R* as follows:

If the domain of the relation is *SYSTEM*

a.   *then* ("order is by ascendance or descendance by fields"):

   (1) Let *C* be the range of this relation. Pick an attribute of *C*, or a list of attributes, so that the application programs are most likely to access the objects of *C* in the order which can be defined by these attributes.

   (2) Specify the order-type to preserve the ascendance-descendance of the above attributes.

    (A *list* of attributes establishes precedence between them: the objects are ordered primarily according to the first attribute in the list. Two objects that have the same value of the first attribute in the list are ordered according to the second attribute, and so on.)

This need not be a *deterministic* (unambiguous) specification of the order — two distinct objects may have equal values in each of the attributes in the list. (In many DBMSs, such two objects are called **duplicates**.)

The list of attributes may be empty, as it is, for example, when C has no attributes at all.

Example:

- The order of *SYSTEM-COURSE* is ascending by *NAME*.

- The order of *SYSTEM-QUARTER* is ascending by *YEAR*, descending by *SEASON*. (Fortunately, the alphabetic order of seasons, 'Winter' > 'Spring' > 'Fall', coincides with their natural order.)

- The order of *SYSTEM-INSTRUCTOR* is ascending by *LAST-NAME*, ascending by *FIRST-NAME*.

- The order of *SYSTEM-STUDENT* is ascending by *LAST-NAME*, ascending by *FIRST-NAME*.

- The order of *SYSTEM-DEPARTMENT* has no constraint.

---

b. *else* (''order is last''):

Let the order be the order of insertion or connection, that is, there is a dynamic constraint (restriction) that when an object x becomes connected by R to an object y, this x becomes the last by $NEXT_R$ among the objects connected by R to y.

10. **Translate the integrity constraints** into the terms of the new schema:

a. The constraints of the original schema.

b. The additional constraints accumulated during the conversion process.

Problem 6-1.

Use the university/network reference schema at the end of this book. Specify in calculus all the integrity constraints which are not covered by this network schema but are covered by the binary schema, that is, the constraints generated during the conversion from the binary schema.

Problem 6-2.

Use the university/binary reference schema at the end of this book. Convert this schema into a network schema, assuming:

- 50 percent of the instructors are students and 40 percent of students are instructors.

- An instructor can give the same course several times during one quarter.

- The DBMS does not support userviews.

Specify the integrity constraints which are not covered by your network schema but are covered by the binary schema.

Problem 6-3.

Use the studio/binary schema (Figure 13-2 on page 389). Design a network schema for the studio application.

Solution on page 457.

Problem 6-4.

Use the medical/binary schema (Figure 13-6 on page 395).

1. Design a network schema for the medical application. Your database should be equivalent in the information content to the binary database described by the above binary schema.

2. Specify in calculus all the integrity constraints that have to be added to the schema during conversion.

3. Whenever the conversion algorithm allows a selection between alternatives, discuss the alternatives and justify your selection.

4. Specify one subschema of your schema.

5. According to your subschema draw the corresponding part of an instantaneous database.

In the following problems, design a network schema equivalent to the appropriate binary schema. Specify the integrity constraints incident to the conversion from the binary schema to the network schema.

Problem 6-5.

Use the clan/binary schema (Figure 13-3 on page 390).

Solution on page 458.

Problem 6-6.

Use the circuit/binary schema (Figure 13-5 on page 391).

Solution on page 459.

Problem 6-7.

Use the sales/binary schema (Figure 13-4 on page 390).

Solution on page 460.

Problem 6-8.

Use the cable/binary schema (Figure 13-10 on page 398).

Solution on page 461.

Problem 6-9.

Use the busstop/binary schema (Figure 13-11 on page 399).

Solution on page 462.

Problem 6-10.

Use the carsale/binary schema (Figure 13-12 on page 400).

Problem 6-11.

Use the clinic/binary schema (Figure 13-13 on page 401).

Solution on page 463.

Problem 6-12.

Use the newspaper/binary schema (Figure 13-28 on page 419).

Solution on page 465.

Problem 6-13.

Use the library/binary schema (Figure 13-7 on page 396).

Solution on page 466.

6.3. Network Languages

6.3.1. Fourth-generation programming

Syntactically, this language is the same as the binary extension of Pascal but is used for network schemas. Pragmatically, there is one difference:

- In the Binary and Relational models, there is no order between the objects. Thus, the **for** loops are performed in an arbitrary order, transparent to the application programmer. The DBMS would usually attempt to find the most efficient order dependent on the circumstances of the program run and the physical structure of the database.

- In the Network Model, the loops are performed in the order specified by the *NEXT* ordering relations. This reduces the flexibility of the application program by making it depend on information which is not strictly relevant for the program's goals. Also, this does not allow for optimization of the program by the DBMS.

> *Example:*
>
> The university has decided to expel all the students whose average grade is below 60 (out of 100). To prevent this wrong-doing to computer science students, the department offered a fictitious course, Computer-Pass, by Prof. Good, in which all computer science students are to receive a sufficient grade so as to not to be expelled, if possible.
>
> The following program fabricates Prof. Good and the Computer-Pass course, enrolls students in this course, grades them accordingly, and prints the names of those computer science students whom this measure cannot help.

```
program Pass (Input, Output, UNIVERSITY-DB, UNIVERSITY-MASTER-VIEW);
var        Computer-Pass-Course, Prof-Good, Good-Offer, comp-science,
              work, this-quarter, cs-student, her-enrollment, fictitious-enrollment:
              ABSTRACT;
var        the-grade, desired-grade, number-of-grades,
              total-of-grades, current-year: INTEGER;
begin
(* Get the current year from the standard input file.  *)

      read (current-year);

(* Fabricate the course, Prof. Good, and the offering.  *)

      transaction begin

              create new Computer-Pass-Course in COURSE;

              Computer-Pass-Course.NAME := 'Computer Pass';

              create new Prof-Good in INSTRUCTOR;

              Prof-Good.LAST-NAME := 'Good';

              create new Good-Offer in OFFERING;

              relate: Computer-Pass-Course COURSE-OFFERING Good-Offer;

              relate: Prof-Good INSTRUCTOR-OFFERING Good-Offer;

              for this-quarter in QUARTER

                      where (this-quarter.YEAR = current-year and this-quarter.SEASON =
                          'Winter') do

                      relate: this-quarter QUARTER-OFFERING Good-Offer;

      end;
```

(* The following two nested loops will be performed only once. Inside the body of the second loop, the variable *comp-science* will refer to the Computer Science Department. *)

for computer-science-name **in** *DEPARTMENT-NAMING*

> **where** (computer-science-name.*NAME*= 'COMPUTER SCIENCE') **do**

>> **for** comp-science **in** *DEPARTMENT*

>>> **where** (computer-science *DEPARTMENT–DEPARTMENT-NAMING* comp-science-name) **do**

begin

transaction begin

> **create new** work in *WORK*;

> **relate**: Prof-Good *INSTRUCTOR-WORK* work;

> **relate**: comp-science *DEPARTMENT-WORK* work

> **end**;

for cs-student **in** *STUDENT*

> **where** (comp-science *MAJOR-ST* cs-student) **do**

>> **begin**

>> (* calculate this student's current statistics: number-of-grades and total-of-grades *)

>> number-of-grades := 0;

>> total-of-grades := 0;

>> **for** her-enrollment **in** *ENROLLMENT*

>>> **where** (cs-student *STUDENT-ENROLLMENT* her-enrollment **and not** her-enrollment *FINAL-GRADE* **null**) **do**

>>> **begin**

>>> the-grade :=

>>> cs-student.*FINAL-GRADE*;

>>> number-of-grades := number-of-grades + 1;

>>> total-of-grades := total-of-grades + the-grade

>>> **end**;

>> (* calculate the minimal desired grade in the computer-pass course, solving the equation

$(total + x)/(number + 1) = 60$ *)

desired-grade := 60 * (number-of-grades + 1) – total-of-grades;

if desired-grade > 100

    then

        (* the student cannot be helped. Print a message *)

           writeln ('The student ', cs-student.*LAST-NAME*, ' cannot be helped. Sorry!')

    else

        if desired-grade > 60 **then**

           transaction begin

               create new fictitious-enrollment **in** *ENROLLMENT*;

               relate: cs-student *STUDENT-ENROLLMENT* fictitious-enrollment;

               relate: Good-Offer *OFFERING-ENROLLMENT* fictitious-enrollment;

               fictitious-enrollment.*FINAL-GRADE* := desired-grade

           end

    end

end

end.

6.3.2. Logic

Since every network schema is a binary schema, we can use the same language of Predicate Calculus as was defined for the Binary Model.

> *Example:*
>
> Has every student taken at least one course in 1990?
>
>   **for every** st **in** *STUDENT:*
>
>   **exists** enrl **in** *ENROLLMENT*:
>
>   ((st *STUDENT-ENROLLMENT* enrl) **and**
>
>   **exists** offer **in** *OFFERING*:
>
>   **exists** quarter **in** *QUARTER*:

> quarter *QUARTER-OFFERING* offer **and**
>
> offer *OFFERING-ENROLLMENT* enrl **and**
>
> quarter.*YEAR*=1990)

Example:

Who took Prof. Smith's courses?

> **get** student.*LAST-NAME* **where**
>
> > exists enrl **in** *ENROLLMENT:*
> >
> > > **exists** prof **in** *INSTRUCTOR*:
> > >
> > > > **exists** offer **in** *OFFERING*:
> > > >
> > > > > prof.*LAST-NAME*='Smith' **and**
> > > > >
> > > > > prof *INSTRUCTOR-OFFERING* offer **and**
> > > > >
> > > > > offer *OFFERING-ENROLLMENT* enrl **and**
> > > > >
> > > > > student *STUDENT-ENROLLMENT* enrl

In the following problems, translate the request into the Predicate Calculus using the network reference schema for the university application (at the end of this book).

Problem 6-14.

Find the names of the students born in 1967.

Solution on page 467.

Problem 6-15.

For every student, list the instructors of the student's major department.

Solution on page 467.

Problem 6-16.

What instructors work in every department?

Solution on page 467.

Problem 6-17.

What instructors taught all the students?

Solution on page 467.

Problem 6-18.

Has every student taken at least one course in 1991?

Solution on page 468.

Problem 6-19.

Print a table with two columns, which associates students to their teachers. Only last names are printed.

Solution on page 468.

Problem 6-20.

Print the average of grades for every computer science student.

Solution on page 468.

Problem 6-21.

Print the average of the grades given by Prof. Smith.

Solution on page 469.

Problem 6-22.

How many students are there in the university?

Solution on page 469.

Problem 6-23.

What students have their average grade below 60?

Solution on page 469.

Problem 6-24.

An integrity constraint: No student may be enrolled twice in the very same offering of a course.

Solution on page 469.

Problem 6-25.

Define an inferred category of students whose minor is Management.

Solution on page 470.

Problem 6-26.

Give the grade 100 to all computer science students enrolled in the *Databases* course given by Prof. Smith in Fall 1991.

Solution on page 470.

Problem 6-27.

Let 'CS' no longer be an (alternative) name of a department.

Solution on page 471.

Problem 6-28.

Give the grade 100 to the computer science student Jack Johnson enrolled in the *Databases* course given by Prof. Smith. If a grade has been previously given, replace it by the new grade.

Solution on page 471.

Problem 6-29.

Increase by 10 percent the grades of all students ever enrolled in the *Databases* course given by Prof. Smith.

Solution on page 472.

6.3.3. *Navigation

The language presented here is a lower-level extension of Pascal for network data manipulation. Unlike the structured extension of Pascal, here the user herself is responsible for the organization of loops and for navigating in the labyrinth of the database.

The model language presented in this section is an adaptation to Pascal of the logical features of the network data manipulation language proposed by the standard committee CODASYL/DBTG and used with minor variations in many commercial network database management systems.

1. *Program heading* — same as in the structured extension.

> *Example:*
>
> **program** MY (input, output, University-data-base, University-principal-
> subschema)

2. There are *automatically-generated Pascal record types* for every record-type of the subschema.

> *Example:*
>
> **type** DEPARTMENT-NAMING =
>
>   **record**
>   the-name : String   **end**;
>
> **type** STUDENT =
>
>   **record**
>   last-name, first-name : String;
>   birth-year : 1870..1990;
>   address : String   **end**;
>
> **type** INSTRUCTOR =

```
        record
              last-name, first-name : String;
              birth-year : 1870..1990;
              address : String        end;
type QUARTER =

        record
              year : 1990..2010;
              season : String        end;
type COURSE =

        record
              name : String        end;
type ENROLLMENT =

        record
              final-grade : 0..100        end;
type NULL-RECORD =

        record

        end;*
type WORK = NULL-RECORD;

type DEPARTMENT = NULL-RECORD;

type OFFERING = NULL-RECORD
```

3.   *Automatically generated Pascal record variables* for every record-type in the subschema.

These variables bear the same names as the corresponding types.

These variables are called **template variables**. The template variable for a database record-type is used as a buffer to store the attributes of record-occurrences when they are moved between the database and the program.

---

* Standard *Pascal* does not allow records without fields. So, a dummy field may have to be introduced:

```
type DEPARTMENT =

    record
          dummy : 0..0        end;
```

Example:

var student : STUDENT;

var enrollment : ENROLLMENT;

etc.

---

4. Pascal data type *ABSTRACT*.

    The variables of type *ABSTRACT* reference database objects.

    In many network database management systems this type is called *DBKEY*.

5. System variables (read-only).

    There are several automatically generated system variables. The user may not perform explicit assignments to these variables. These variables are updated by the system as a side effect of performing user commands.

    var Error-status : (ok, end-of-set, error)

    > After the execution of any database command, this variable is automatically assigned one of the following values:
    >
    > - **end-of-set** — if the user attempted to locate the next record occurrence in a particular set-occurrence and no next record-occurrence existed
    >
    > - **error** — if another logical or physical error occurred
    >
    > - **ok** — otherwise.

    var current-of-run-unit : ABSTRACT

    > This variable references the last accessed object. Initially, it is the object SYSTEM.

    var current-of-record-type-*record-type* : ABSTRACT

    > For every record-type in the subschema, there is a variable referencing the last accessed object of that record-type.

Example:

var   current-of-record-type-DEPARTMENT,   current-of-record-type-
STUDENT,   current-of-record-type-INSTRUCTOR,   current-of-record-type-
QUARTER,   current-of-record-type-COURSE,   current-of-record-type-
OFFERING, current-of-record-type-ENROLLMENT, current-of-record-type-
WORK, current-of-record-type-DEPARTMENT-NAMING : ABSTRACT

---

var current-of-set-type-*set-type*** : ABSTRACT**

> For every set-type in the subschema, there is a variable referencing the last accessed object of a record-type which is the owner or the member of this set-type. For the set-types whose owner is *SYSTEM*, these variables initially contain the object *SYSTEM*. Otherwise the variables are uninitialized.

Example:

var   current-of-set-type-SYSTEM-INSTRUCTOR,   current-of-set-type-SYSTEM-STUDENT,   current-of-set-type-SYSTEM-DEPARTMENT, current-of-set-type-SYSTEM-COURSE,   current-of-set-type-SYSTEM-QUARTER, current-of-set-type-INSTRUCTOR-WORK, current-of-set-type-DEPARTMENT-WORK,   current-of-set-type-DEPARTMENT-DEPARTMENT-NAMING, current-of-set-type-MAJOR-ST, current-of-set-type-MINOR-ST, current-of-set-type-INSTRUCTOR-OFFERING, current-of-set-type-COURSE-OFFERING, current-of-set-type-QUARTER-OFFERING, current-of-set-type-OFFERING-ENROLLMENT,   current-of-set-type-STUDENT-ENROLLMENT : ABSTRACT

---

6.   Expressions — there is *no* extension to the syntax of Pascal expressions.

Particularly, there are no operations on the objects of type ABSTRACT. For example, if x is a variable of type ABSTRACT, and A is an attribute, then $x.A$ would be an expression in the structured extension of Pascal but not in the navigational extension.

However, if x is not an abstract variable, but a variable of a Pascal type **record**, for example

> **var** x: **record**
>
> > A: Integer,
> >
> > B: Integer
>
> **end**

then $x.A$ would be a usual Pascal expression and thus can be used in the navigational language.

Statements

7.   **find first within** *set-name*

The first member object is located in the current set-occurrence of this set-type, the set occurrence to which the object **current-of-set-type-***set-type* belongs.

If there are no member-objects in the set-occurrence, the system variable Error-status is set to **end-of-set**. (Otherwise, if the instruction is successfully performed, the variable Error-status is set to **ok**.)

If an object is found, the currency variables are updated: the found object becomes

- The current of run-unit
- The current of this set-type
- The current of this object's record-type
- The current of every set-type whose owner or member is the category of this object

---

Example:

Are there any students in the database?

    find first within SYSTEM-STUDENT;

    if Error-status = **end-of-set**

        then writeln ('no');

    if Error-status = **ok**

        then writeln ('yes');

    if Error-status = **error**

        then writeln ('I do not know. I have system problems.');

---

8.   **get**

This instruction assigns the attributes' values of the current object of run-unit to the template variable corresponding to the category of the object.

Example:

Print the address of one student.

    (* locate one student, the one which happens to be the first in the order of *SYSTEM-STUDENT* *)

        find first within *SYSTEM-STUDENT*;

    (* assign the attribute values of the student to the variable *student* *)

        get;

    (* print *)

        writeln ('The address of a student is:', student.ADDRESS)

---

9.   **find next within** *set-name*

The next member object is located in the order of the set-type after the current object of the set-type.

If there are no next member-objects in the set-occurrence, the system variable Error-status is set to **end-of-set**.

If an object is found, the currency variables are updated: the found object becomes the current of run-unit, the current of this set-type, the current of this object's record-type, and the current of every set-type whose owner or member is the category of this object.

Example:

Print names and addresses of all the students.

    find first within *SYSTEM-STUDENT*;

    while (Error-status ≠ end-of-set) **do**

        begin

        (* assign the attribute values of the current student to the variable *student* *)

            get;

        (* print *)

            writeln ('The address of Student', student.*LAST-NAME*, ' is: ', student.ADDRESS)

        find next within *SYSTEM-STUDENT*

        end;

---

10.   **find owner within** *set-name*

The owner object of the set occurrence of the current object of the set-type is located.

The currency variables are updated: the found object becomes the current of run-unit, the current of this set-type, the current of this object's record-type, and the current of every set-type whose owner or member is the category of this object.

Example:

Print names and major departments of all the students.

    find first within *SYSTEM-STUDENT*;

    while (Error-status ≠ end-of-set) **do**

---

begin

(* assign the attribute values of the current student to the variable
student *)

get;

(* find the major department of the student *)

find owner within *MAJOR-ST*;

(* find the name of the department; if the department has more than
one name, the first found will do. *)

find first within *DEPARTMENT–DEPARTMENT-NAMING* ;

(* assign the attribute value of the current department-naming to the
variable *department-naming* *)

get

(* print *)

writeln ('The major department of Student', student.*LAST-
NAME*, ' is: ', department-naming.*NAME*);

find next within *SYSTEM-STUDENT*

end;

---

11. **find db-key is** *variable-of-type-ABSTRACT*

(This statement is used to find and restore the currency of an object which was
previously accessed by the program and whose reference was saved in a variable.)

The object referred to by the variable is located. The currency variables are updated:
the found object becomes the current of run-unit and the current of every set-type
whose owner or member is the category of this object.

Example:

For every student, print the names of the students of the same major.

var student-to-remember: ABSTRACT;

begin

find first within *SYSTEM-STUDENT*;

while (Error-status ≠ end-of-set) **do begin**

(* assign the attribute values of the current student to the variable
student *)

```
        get;
(* find the major department of the student  *)
        find owner within MAJOR-ST;
(* print a heading for the current student's list of co-majors.  *)
            writeln ('Student', student.LAST-NAME, ' has the same major
                as the following students: ');
(* remember the current student, so that we can return to her after we
        have finished processing the co-majors.  *)
            student-to-remember := current-of-set-type-SYSTEM-
                STUDENT;
(* process the students connected in the set-type MAJOR-ST to the
        current department  *)
        find first within MAJOR-ST;
        while (Error-status ≠ end-of-set) do
            begin
            get;
            write (student.LAST-NAME);
            find next within MAJOR-ST
            end;
(* restore the currency of the student of the principal loop.  *)
        find db-key is student-to-remember;
    find next within SYSTEM-STUDENT
    end;
end.
```

12. **find within** *set-name* **using** *attribute*

Among the member objects in the set occurrence of the current object of the set-type, find the first object whose value of the *attribute* is the same as in the template variable of the member record-type.

The currency variables are updated: the found object becomes the current of run-unit, the current of this set-type, the current of this object's record-type, and the current of every set-type whose owner or member is the category of this object.

This is roughly equivalent to the following program, where S is the set-type and *rec* is the member record-type:

attribute-to-compare := *rec.attribute*;

find first within S;

found := false;

while (Error-status $\neq$ end-of-set) **and** (**not** found) **do**

   begin

   get;

   found **:=** (*rec.attribute* = attribute-to-compare);

   if not found

       then   **find next within** S

   end;

Example:

How many times was the *Databases* course offered?

   (* find the *Databases* course *)

       course.NAME := 'Databases';

       find within *SYSTEM-COURSE* **using** *NAME*;

   (* count the offerings *)

       number := 0;

       find first within *COURSE-OFFERING*;

       while Error-status $\neq$ end-of-set **do**

           begin

           number := number+1;

           find next within *COURSE-OFFERING*;

           end

       writeln ('Databases was offered ', number, ' times.')

---

13. **modify** *record-type*

The attributes' values of the current object of this record-type are updated according to the values in the template variable of this record-type.

Example:

Change the name of every Fall quarter to *Autumn*.

> **find first within** *SYSTEM-QUARTER*;
>
> **while** (Error-status ≠ end-of-set) **do**
>
>> **begin**
>>
>> **if** Error-status = error **then begin**
>>
>>> writeln (' SYSTEM ERROR'); stop   **end**;
>>
>> **get**;
>>
>> **if** quarter.*SEASON* = 'Fall' **then**
>>
>>> **begin**
>>>
>>> quarter.*SEASON* := 'Autumn';
>>>
>>> **modify** *QUARTER*;
>>>
>>> **end**;
>>
>> **find next within** *SYSTEM-QUARTER*
>>
>> **end**;

14. **erase** *record-type*

The current object of the *record-type* is deleted from the database.

If the object is the owner of a set-occurrence of a set-type *onto* the member, then all the member objects of that set occurrence are automatically erased. This process is recursive: the deletion of some objects may trigger deletion of more objects.

Example:

Cancel everything that happened in any summer.

> **find first within** *SYSTEM-QUARTER*;
>
> **while** (Error-status ≠ end-of-set) **do**
>
>> **begin**
>>
>> **if** Error-status = error **then begin**
>>
>>> writeln (' SYSTEM ERROR'); stop   **end**;
>>
>> **get**;
>>
>> **if** quarter.*SEASON* = 'Summer' **then**

> **erase** *QUARTER*;
>
> **find next within** *SYSTEM-QUARTER*
>
> **end**;

15. **connect** *record-type* **to** *set-type*

The current object of the *record-type* is inserted as a member into the current set-occurrence of the set-type — the set-occurrence in which the current object of the set-type is the owner or a member.

Example:

Let every student have the same minor as his major, assuming that every student had (until now) a major and no minor department.

> **find first within** *SYSTEM-STUDENT*;
>
> **while** (Error-status ≠ end-of-set) **do**
>
> > **begin**
> >
> > **if** Error-status = error **then begin**
> >
> > > writeln (' SYSTEM ERROR'); stop   **end**;
> >
> > **get**;
> >
> > **find owner within** *MAJOR-ST*;
> >
> > **if** Error-status = error **then**
> >
> > > writeln (' Oh-oh. Wrong assumption about having a major
> > > department for ', student.*LAST-NAME*);
> >
> > **connect** *STUDENT* **to** *MINOR-ST*;
> >
> > **if** Error-status = error **then**
> >
> > > writeln (' Oh-oh. Wrong assumption about not having a minor
> > > department for ', student.*LAST-NAME*);
> >
> > **find next within** *SYSTEM-STUDENT*
> >
> > **end**;

---

16. **disconnect** *record-type* **from** *set-type*

The current object of the *record-type* will no longer be a member in the current set-occurrence of the set-type (the set-occurrence in which the current object of the set-type is the owner or a member).

Example:

Let every student have the same minor as his major, by canceling the present minors. Assume that every student had a major department.

> **find first within** *SYSTEM-STUDENT*;
>
> **while** (Error-status ≠ end-of-set) **do**
>
> > **begin**
> >
> > **if** Error-status = error **then begin**
> >
> > > writeln ('SYSTEM ERROR'); stop   **end**;
> >
> > **get**;
> >
> > **disconnect** *STUDENT* **from** *MINOR-ST*;
> >
> > **find owner within** *MAJOR-ST*;
> >
> > **if** Error-status = error **then**
> >
> > > writeln ('Oh-oh. Wrong assumption about having a major
> > > department for ', student.*LAST-NAME*);
> >
> > **connect** *STUDENT* **to** *MINOR-ST*;
> >
> > **find next within** *SYSTEM-STUDENT*
> >
> > **end**;

17. **reconnect** *record-type* **to** *set-type*

The current object of the *record-type* will no longer be a member in its former set-occurrence of the set-type.

Instead, the current object of the *record-type* is inserted as a member into the current set-occurrence of the set-type (the set-occurrence in which the current object of the set-type is the owner or a member).

Example:

Let every student have the same minor as his major, canceling the present minor, assuming that every student had a major department.

> **find first within** *SYSTEM-STUDENT*;
>
> **while** (Error-status ≠ end-of-set) **do**
>
> > **begin**
> >
> > **if** Error-status = error **then begin**

> writeln (' SYSTEM ERROR'); stop   **end**;
>
> **get**;
>
> **find owner within** *MAJOR-ST*;
>
> **if** Error-status = error **then**
>
>> writeln (' Oh-oh. Wrong assumption about having a major
>> department for ', student.*LAST-NAME*);
>
> **reconnect** *STUDENT* **to** *MINOR-ST*;
>
> **find next within** *SYSTEM-STUDENT*
>
> **end**;

18. **store** *record-type*

A new object of the *record-type* is created.

The object automatically gets the values of its attributes from the template variable of this record-type.

This object becomes the current of the *record-type*.

19. **transaction** *compound-statement*

— as in the structured extension of Pascal.

> *Example:*
>
> Let Prof. Asteroid (a unique name for this instructor, so no confusion with other instructors is possible) offer the course *Databases* every quarter.
>
> instructor.*LAST-NAME* = 'Asteroid';
>
> course.*NAME* := 'Databases';
>
> **find within** *SYSTEM-INSTRUCTOR* **using** *LAST-NAME*;
>
> **find within** *SYSTEM-COURSE* **using** *NAME*;
>
> **find first within** *SYSTEM-QUARTER*;
>
> **while** (Error-status ≠ end-of-set) **do**
>
>> **begin**
>>
>> **if** Error-status = error **then begin**
>>
>>> writeln (' SYSTEM ERROR'); stop   **end**;
>>
>> **get**;
>>
>> **transaction begin**

> **store** *OFFERING*;
>
> **connect** *OFFERING* **to** *QUARTER-OFFERING*;
>
> **connect** *OFFERING* **to** *COURSE-OFFERING*;
>
> **connect** *OFFERING* **to** *INSTRUCTOR-OFFERING*
>
> **end**
>
> **find next within** *SYSTEM-QUARTER*
>
> **end**;

Example:

A navigational program for the expulsion prevention problem which has been previously solved in the structured extension of Pascal.

---

program Pass (Input, Output, UNIVERSITY-DB, UNIVERSITY-PRINCIPAL-
SUBSCHEMA);

> (* The comments in the boxes are the corresponding program fragments in the structured extension of Pascal. It is recommended that when a program needs to be written in the navigational language, it should first be written in the higher-level language. Then, when the higher-level program is translated into the lower-level navigational language, the commands of the original program should become algorithmic comments within the navigational program. *)

var Good-Offer: *ABSTRACT*;

var the-grade, desired-grade, number-of-grades, total-of-grades, current-year:
INTEGER;

const null-year = 1870 (* to represent missing birth-year, assuming nobody was born in 1870*);

const null-name = '' (* to represent missing names *);

const null-address = '' (* to represent missing addresses *);

const null-grade = 0 (* to represent missing grades, assuming that 0 is never given as a real grade† *);

---

† If the type of the variable *enrollment.Final-grade* technically allows for negative values, then a better representation of the missing grade is −1.

begin (* Get the current year from the standard input file. *)

    read (current-year);

transaction begin

> (*
>
> **create new** Computer-Pass-Course **in** *COURSE*;
>
> Computer-Pass-Course.*NAME* := 'Computer Pass';   *)

course.*NAME* := 'Computer Pass';

store *COURSE*;

connect *COURSE* **to** *SYSTEM-COURSE*;

> (*
>
> **create new** instructor **in** *INSTRUCTOR*;
>
> instructor.*LAST-NAME* := 'Good';   *)

instructor.*LAST-NAME* := 'Good';

instructor.*FIRST-NAME* := null-name;

instructor.*BIRTH-YEAR* := null-year;

instructor.*ADDRESS* := null-address;

store *INSTRUCTOR*;

connect *INSTRUCTOR* **to** *SYSTEM-INSTRUCTOR*;

> (*
>
> **create new** Good-Offer **in** *OFFERING*;
>
> **relate**: Computer-Pass-Course *COURSE-OFFERING* Good-Offer;
>
> **relate**: Prod-Good *INSTRUCTOR-OFFERING* Good-Offer;   *)

store *OFFERING*;

connect *OFFERING* **to** *INSTRUCTOR-OFFERING*;

connect *OFFERING* **to** *COURSE-OFFERING*;

Good-Offer := current-of-record-type-OFFERING;

```
(*
for quarter in QUARTER
        where (quarter.YEAR = current-year and quarter.SEASON =
            'Winter') do
        relate: quarter QUARTER-OFFERING Good-Offer;
        *)
```

found := **false**;

find first within *SYSTEM-QUARTER*;

while (Error-status ≠ end-of-set **and not** found) **do**

     begin;

     if Error-status = error **then begin**

         writeln (' SYSTEM ERROR'); stop   **end**;

     get;

     found := (quarter.*YEAR* = current-year **and** quarter.*SEASON* = 'Winter');

     if not found **then**

     find next within *SYSTEM-QUARTER*

     end;

connect *OFFERING* **to** *QUARTER-OFFERING*;

end (* transaction*);

```
(* Prepare-Department:
for department-naming in DEPARTMENT-NAMING
        where (department-naming.NAME= 'COMPUTER SCIENCE') do
            for department in DEPARTMENT
                where (department DEPARTMENT–DEPARTMENT-NAMING
                    department-naming) do
        *)
```

found := **false**;

find first within *SYSTEM-DEPARTMENT*;

while (Error-status ≠ end-of-set **and not** found) **do**

     begin;

     if Error-status = error **then begin**

      writeln (' SYSTEM ERROR'); stop   **end**;

get;

found := **false**;

find first within *DEPARTMENT–DEPARTMENT-NAMING*;

while (Error-status ≠ end-of-set **and not** found) **do**

    begin;

    if Error-status = error **then begin**

        writeln (' SYSTEM ERROR'); stop   **end**;

    get;

    found := (department-naming.*NAME* = 'Computer Science');

    if not found **then**

    find next within *DEPARTMENT–DEPARTMENT-NAMING*

    end;

if not found **then**

find next within *SYSTEM-DEPARTMENT*

end;

(****end Prepare-department****)

transaction begin

> (*
> **create new** work in *WORK*;
> **relate**: instructor *INSTRUCTOR-WORK* work;
> **relate**: department *DEPARTMENT-WORK* work   *)

store *WORK*;

connect *WORK* **to** *INSTRUCTOR-WORK*;

connect *WORK* **to** *DEPARTMENT-WORK*;

end (* transaction *);

> (* Student-loop:
> **for** student **in** *STUDENT*
>   **where** (department *MAJOR-ST* student) **do**   *)

find first within *MAJOR-ST*;

```
while (Error-status ≠ end-of-set) do
    begin
    if Error-status = error then begin
        writeln (' SYSTEM ERROR'); stop      end;
    get;
        (**end of the opening of Student-loop **)
    (* calculate this student's current statistics: number-of-grades and total-of-grades  *)
        number-of-grades := 0;
        total-of-grades := 0;
```

```
        (* Enrollment-loop:
        for enrollment in ENROLLMENT
            where (student STUDENT-ENROLLMENT enrollment and not
                enrollment FINAL-GRADE null) do   *)
```

```
    find first within STUDENT-ENROLLMENT;
    while (Error-status ≠ end-of-set) do
        begin
        if Error-status = error then begin
            writeln (' SYSTEM ERROR'); stop      end;
        get;
        if student.FINAL-GRADE ≠ null-grade then
            begin
                (**end of the opening of Enrollment-loop **)
            the-grade := student.FINAL-GRADE;
            number-of-grades := number-of-grades + 1;
            total-of-grades := total-of-grades + the-grade
                (**closing Enrollment-loop **)
            end;
        find next within STUDENT-ENROLLMENT
        end;
        (**end Enrollment-loop **)
```

(* calculate the minimal desired grade in the computer-pass course, solving the equation $(total + x) / (number + 1) = 60$ *)

desired-grade := 60 * (number-of-grades + 1) − total-of-grades;

if desired-grade > 100

    then

        (* the student cannot be helped. Print a message *)

            writeln (' The student ', student.*LAST-NAME*, ' cannot be helped. Sorry!')

    else

        if desired-grade > 60 **then**

            transaction begin

```
(*
create new fictitious-enrollment in
    ENROLLMENT;
relate: student STUDENT-ENROLLMENT
    fictitious-enrollment;
relate: Good-Offer OFFERING-ENROLLMENT
    fictitious-enrollment;
fictitious-enrollment.FINAL-GRADE := desired-
    grade  *)
```

        enrollment.*FINAL-GRADE* := desired-grade;

        store *ENROLLMENT*;

        connect *ENROLLMENT* **to** *STUDENT-ENROLLMENT*;

        find db-key is Good-Offer; (* We have to restore the currency of the fabricated offering remembered in the variable Good-Offer, because the currency may have changed in the meantime. *)

        connect *ENROLLMENT* **to** *OFFERING-ENROLLMENT*;

        end

    (**closing Student-loop**)

find next within *MAJOR-ST*

end;

      (**end Student-loop **)

end.

Problem 6-30.

Use the university/binary reference schema at the end of this book. Write a navigational program to find the average teaching load of *full-time* computer science instructors this quarter. (*Full-time* means working for no other department.)

CHAPTER 7

FROM THE NETWORK TO THE HIERARCHICAL MODEL

This chapter defines the hierarchical data model and adapts the top-down database design methodology to hierarchical databases. Section 3 of this chapter discusses network database languages: application of the generic fourth-generation and logic-based languages.

The Hierarchical Model requires the schema and the instantaneous database to be trees. The Hierarchical Model is the oldest (albeit, not the best) major database model. However, it is still widely used in the industry.

This chapter presents a "modern view" of the hierarchical model. Some technicalities, particularly the clearly obsolete ones, are ignored.

7.1. Definitions

Hierarchical schema — a network schema such that for every category, excluding *SYSTEM,* there is exactly one relation coming into it from another category.

Example:

A hierarchical schema for the university application follows. Only the order-less part is shown in the figure.

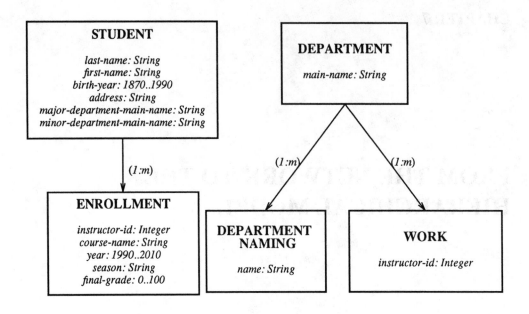

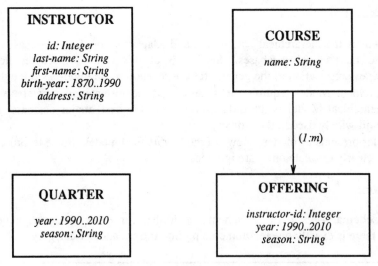

Figure 7-1. An orderless hierarchical schema for the university application.

Note: We can prove the truth of the following statements from the definition of the hierarchical schemas:

a.   The relations between the abstract categories of any orderless hierarchical schema form a set of directed trees.   (This is the reason for the name *Hierarchical.*)

b.   The root of every tree is an independent category.

c.   All the relations between distinct abstract categories are *onto*.

d.   Since every category C has only one entering relation R_C from another category, every category has only one order $NEXT_{R_C}$. Thus, we can speak about *the* order of the objects of a category.

Example:

The following figures represent an instantaneous database for the schema of Figure 7-1. This instantaneous database represents the same state of the application's real world as the binary instantaneous database of Figure 1-12 on page 22.

INSTRUCTOR

id	last-name	first-name	birth-year	address
11332	Brown	George	1956	112 Lucky Dr.
14352	Whatson	Mary	1953	231 Fortune Dr.
24453	Blue	John	1950	536 Orange Dr.

Figure 7-2. An instantaneous database for the hierarchical schema of the university application. Part I. The flat tree of *INSTRUCTOR*.

STUDENT

last-name	first-name	birth-year	address	major-dept-main-name	minor-dept-main-name
Victory	Elizabeth	1966	100 Sun St.	Computer Science	Economics

COURSE ENROLLMENT

instructor-id	course-name	year	season	final-grade
11332	Gastronomy	1990	Fall	100

STUDENT

last-name	first-name	birth-year	address	major-dept-main-name	minor-dept-main-name
Howards	Jane	1965	200 Dorms	Arts	Economics

COURSE ENROLLMENT

instructor-id	course-name	year	season	final-grade
11332	Gastronomy	1990	Fall	70
11332	Databases	1990	Fall	80

STUDENT

last-name	first-name	birth-year	address	major-dept-main-name	minor-dept-main-name
Wood	Michael	1964	110 Dorms	Arts	Economics

Figure 7-3. An instantaneous database for the hierarchical schema of the university application. Part II. The tree of *STUDENT*.

DEPARTMENT

main-name
Computer Science

DEPARTMENT NAMING

name
CS

WORK

instructor-id
11332

DEPARTMENT

main-name
Mathematics

DEPARTMENT NAMING

name
Math

WORK

instructor-id
11332
24453

DEPARTMENT

main-name
Physics

WORK

instructor-id
14352

DEPARTMENT

main-name
Arts
Economics

Figure 7-4. An instantaneous database for the hierarchical schema of the university application. Part III. The tree of *DEPARTMENT*.

COURSE

name
Databases

COURSE OFFERING

instructor-id	year	season
11332	1990	Fall

COURSE

name
Football

COURSE OFFERING

instructor-id	year	season
11332	1990	Fall

COURSE

name
Gastronomy

COURSE OFFERING

instructor-id	year	season
11332	1990	Fall

Figure 7-5. An instantaneous database for the hierarchical schema of the university application. Part IV. The tree of *COURSE*.

QUARTER

year	season
1990	Fall
1990	Winter
1990	Spring

Figure 7-6. An instantaneous database for the hierarchical schema of the university application. Part V. The flat tree of *QUARTER*.

Hierarchical schema terminology

Segment type — record type.

> *Example:*
>
> *DEPARTMENT.*

Segment occurrence — record occurrence.

> *Example:*
>
> One course and its name.

> *Example:*
>
> One student and his or her last name, first name, address, and the main names of his or her major and minor departments.

If there is a relation from a segment-type C_1 to another C_2, then C_1 is the **parent** of C_2 and C_2 is a **child** of C_1.

> *Example:*
>
> *DEPARTMENT* is the parent of *DEPARTMENT-NAMING.*
>
> *DEPARTMENT-NAMING* is a child of *DEPARTMENT.*

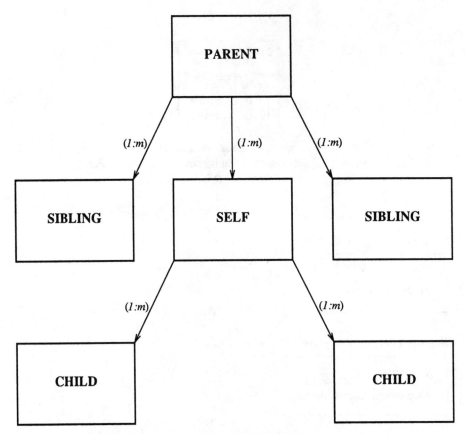

Figure 7-7. Family relations in a hierarchical schema.

Root segment type — a segment type whose *parent* is *SYSTEM*.

> *Example:*
> *DEPARTMENT, INSTRUCTOR, STUDENT, COURSE, QUARTER.*

The hierarchical model is not the most natural model to describe the real world of an application. One should notice that what is sometimes called "a hierarchical real world" usually implies a hierarchical *relation* between objects in the real world, not a hierarchical *schema*.

Example:

Consider an oversimplified military world, where every soldier has at most one commander. A binary schema for this world is:

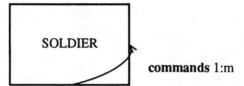

commands 1:m

This is not a hierarchical schema, since it contains a cycle. No hierarchical schema can represent this world in a *natural* way.

7.2. Database Design

Conversion algorithm of a semantic schema into a hierarchical schema whose quality is among the highest possible for the latter (provided the original semantic schema is of high quality).

1. Convert the binary schema into a *network schema*.

2. For every abstract category, excluding *SYSTEM*, choose its **parent-relation** R so that

    When all the relations, except the parent relations, are removed from the schema, every abstract category would still indirectly depend on *SYSTEM*.

Note: The parent relation for category C must be *onto* C.

Example:

The parent relation of *OFFERING* may be *COURSE-OFFERING* or *INSTRUCTOR-OFFERING* or *QUARTER-OFFERING*.

The parent relation for *ENROLLMENT* may be *OFFERING-ENROLLMENT* or *STUDENT-ENROLLMENT*.

The parent relation for *WORK* may be *DEPARTMENT-WORK* or *INSTRUCTOR-WORK*.

The parent relation for DEPARTMENT-NAMING is *DEPARTMENT–DEPARTMENT-NAMING*.

Note: The parent relations of independent categories are from *SYSTEM*.

Example:

The parent relation of *STUDENT* is *SYSTEM-STUDENT*.

The parent relation of *INSTRUCTOR* is *SYSTEM-INSTRUCTOR*.

The parent relation of *DEPARTMENT* is *SYSTEM-DEPARTMENT*.

The parent relation of *COURSE* is *SYSTEM-COURSE*.

The parent relation of *QUARTER* is *SYSTEM-QUARTER*.

3.   Convert the schema into a **tree**: for every abstract category C that has more than one entering relation, do the following.

Let R be its parent relation and $R_1, \ldots, R_n$ the other entering relations, whose domains are $C_1, \ldots, C_n$.

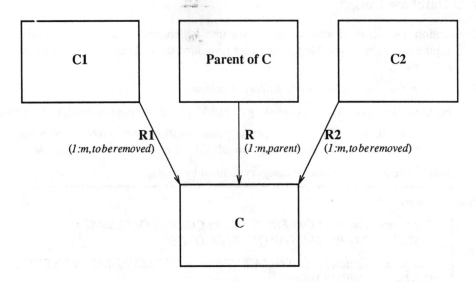

For each of the relations R_i perform the following:

a.   Find a key for the category C_i. (C_i is the domain of the relation R_i which we intend to eliminate.) Add the key to the schema (if this key has not been added yet).

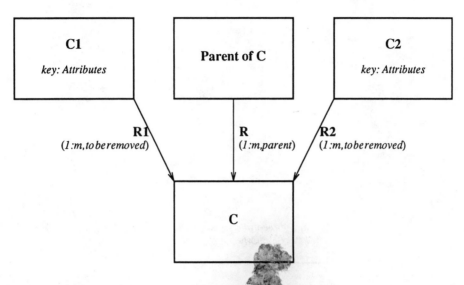

b.   Add to C a new attribute, or a group of attributes, that is the composition of the inverse of R_i on the key of C_i.

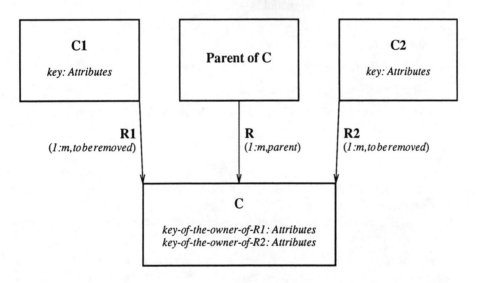

c.   Remove the relation R_i (and its order).

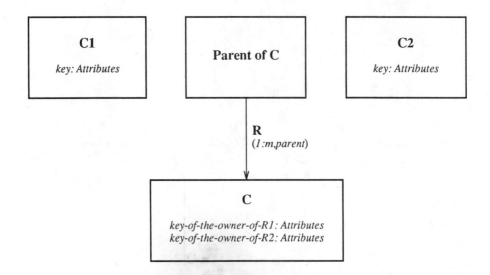

d.   Add the referential integrity constraints that the values of the new attributes of *C* must refer to the values of the keys of the categories C_i. (This is similar to what is done in the relational model.)

4.   Remove from every category attributes which can be *inferred* from other attributes of that category, its *parent*, or its *ancestors*.

5.   **Translate the integrity constraints** into the terms of the new schema:

a.   The constraints of the original schema.

b.   The additional constraints accumulated during the conversion process.

Note:

- In the first step, it is not strictly necessary to go all the way through in the conversion from the binary schema to the network schema. We can omit the substep where the 1:m relations from a category to itself are eliminated. Later, in Step 3 of the hierarchical conversion, these relations will be taken care of as all the nonparent relations.

  If we do this in Step 3 rather than in Step 1 we get a slightly better hierarchical schema. If we were to follow the network conversion in Step 1 fully, we could get one extra category for the relation-split of each 1:m relation from a category to itself.

In the following problems, design a hierarchical schema equivalent to the appropriate binary schema. Specify the integrity constraints incident to the conversion from the binary schema to the hierarchical schema.

Problem 7-1.
Use the clan/binary schema (Figure 13-3 on page 390).

Solution on page 473.

Problem 7-2.
Use the wholesaler/binary schema (Figure 13-1 on page 388).

Solution on page 474.

Problem 7-3.
Use the busstop/binary schema (Figure 13-11 on page 399).

Solution on page 476.

Problem 7-4.
Use the cable/binary schema (Figure 13-10 on page 398).

Solution on page 477.

Problem 7-5.
Use the circuit/binary schema (Figure 13-5 on page 391).

Solution on page 478.

Problem 7-6.
Use the clinic/binary schema (Figure 13-13 on page 401).

Solution on page 479.

Problem 7-7.
Use the library/binary schema (Figure 13-7 on page 396).

Solution on page 481.

Problem 7-8.
Use the sales/binary schema (Figure 13-4 on page 390).

Solution on page 482.

Problem 7-9.
Use the studio/binary schema (Figure 13-2 on page 389).

Solution on page 483.

7.3. Hierarchical Languages

7.3.1. Fourth-generation programming

Syntactically, this language is the same as the binary extension of Pascal but is used for the hierarchical schema (every hierarchical schema is a binary schema). Pragmatically, there is one difference: the **for** loops are performed in the order corresponding to the ordering of objects in the database. (In the Binary Model, the order in which a **for** loop is performed is transparent to the application programmer.)

Example:

The university has decided to expel all the students whose average grade is below 60 (out of 100). To prevent this wrong-doing to computer science students, the department offered a fictitious course, Computer-Pass, by Prof. Good, in which all computer science students are to receive a sufficient grade so as to not to be expelled, if possible.

The following program fabricates Prof. Good and the Computer-Pass course, enrolls students in this course, grades them accordingly, and prints the names of those computer science students whom this measure cannot help.

---

program Pass (Input, Output, UNIVERSITY-DB, UNIVERSITY-MASTER-VIEW);

var   Computer-Pass-Course, Prof-Good, Good-Offer, comp-science, comp-science-name, Good-employment, cs-student, her-enrollment, fictitious-enrollment: *ABSTRACT*;

var   the-grade, desired-grade, number-of-grades, total-of-grades, current-year: *INTEGER*;

begin (* Get the current year from the standard input file. *)

　　read (current-year);

transaction begin

　　create new Computer-Pass-Course **in** *COURSE*;

　　Computer-Pass-Course.*NAME* := 'Computer Pass';

　　create new Prof-Good **in** *INSTRUCTOR*;

　　Prof-Good.*LAST-NAME* := 'Good';

　　Prof-Good.*ID* := 1234;

　　create new Good-Offer **in** *OFFERING*;

　　relate: Computer-Pass-Course *OFFERING* Good-Offer;

　　Good-Offer.*INSTRUCTOR-ID* := 1234;

Good-Offer.*YEAR* := current-year;

Good-Offer.*SEASON* := 'Winter';

end

for   comp-science-name **in** *DEPARTMENT-NAMING*

        where (comp-science-name.*NAME*= 'COMPUTER SCIENCE') **do**

    for   comp-science **in** *DEPARTMENT*

            where (comp-science *DEPARTMENT–DEPARTMENT-NAME* comp-science-name) **do begin**

        transaction begin

            create new Good-employment in *WORK*;

            relate: comp-science *DEPARTMENT-WORK* Good-employment;

            Good-employment.*ID* := 1234

            end;

        for cs-student **in** *STUDENT*

                where (cs-student.*MAJOR-DEPARTMENT-MAIN-NAME* = comp-science.*MAIN-NAME*) **do begin**

            (* calculate this student's current statistics: number-of-grades and total-of-grades *)

            number-of-grades := 0;

            total-of-grades := 0;

            for her-enrollment **in** *ENROLLMENT*

                    where (cs-student *ENROLLMENT* her-enrollment **and not** her-enrollment *FINAL-GRADE* **null**) **do begin**

                the-grade :=

                her-enrollment.*FINAL-GRADE*;

                number-of-grades :=

                number-of-grades + 1;

                total-of-grades := total-of-grades + the-grade

                end;

            (* calculate the minimal desired grade in the computer-pass course, solving the equation $(total + x)/(number + 1) = 60$ *)

desired-grade := 60 * (number-of-grades + 1) — total-of-grades;

if desired-grade > 100

   then

   (* the student cannot be helped. Print a message *)

   writeln (' The student ', cs-student.*LAST-NAME*, ' cannot be helped. Sorry!')

   else if desired-grade > 60 **then**

   transaction begin

   create new fictitious-enrollment **in** *ENROLLMENT*;

   relate: cs-student *ENROLLMENT* fictitious-enrollment;

   fictitious-enrollment.*FINAL-GRADE* := desired-grade;

   fictitious-enrollment.*YEAR* := current-year;

   fictitious-enrollment.*SEASON* := 'Winter';

   fictitious-enrollment.*INSTRUCTOR-ID* := 1234;

   fictitious-enrollment.*COURSE-NAME* := 'Computer Pass'

   end

   end

   end

end.

7.3.2. Logic

Since every hierarchical schema is a binary schema, we can use the same language of Predicate Calculus as was defined for the Semantic Binary Model.

Example:

Has every student taken at least one course in 1990?

   for every st **in** *STUDENT:*

   exists enrl **in** *ENROLLMENT:*

((st *STUDENT-ENROLLMENT* enrl) **and**

(enrl.*YEAR*=1990))

Example:

Who took Prof. Smith's courses?

 get student.*LAST-NAME* **where**

  exists enrl **in** *ENROLLMENT*:

   (student *STUDENT-ENROLLMENT* enrl **and**

   exists inst **in** *INSTRUCTOR*:

    (inst.*LAST-NAME* = 'Smith' **and**

    enrl.*INSTRUCTOR-ID* = inst.*ID*))

Example:

What students have their average grade below 60?

 get std.*LAST-NAME*

 where 60 >

  average enrl.*FINAL-GRADE*

   where

    std *STUDENT-ENROLLMENT* enrl

Example:

Print the average of grades for every computer science student.

> **get** student.*LAST-NAME*,
>
> > (**average** enrollment.*FINAL-GRADE*
> >
> > > **where**
> > >
> > > > student *STUDENT-ENROLLMENT* enrollment)
> >
> > **where** student **is a** *STUDENT* and
> >
> > > (student.*MAJOR-DEPARTMENT-MAIN-NAME* = 'Computer
> > > Science')

Example:

How many students are there in the university?

> **get** (**count** std **where** std **is a** *STUDENT*)

Problem 7-10.

Solve the programming problems of Chapter 3 in the languages of the Hierarchical Model.

CHAPTER 8

THE PROGRESSION OF DATABASE MODELS

Four database models have been discussed in this text: Semantic, Relational, Network, and Hierarchical. This chapter compares aspects of theses models.

Each of the models provides a certain degree of **data independence** — the isolation of the application programmer from representational or implementational details. The following table illustrates five levels of data independence.

Level	What is transparent to the user?	Database model
V	The representation of *information* by *data*	**Semantic Binary**
IV	The organization of access to data	**Relational**
III	The physical implementation of the logical data-access structure	**Network**
II	The physical implementation of the special data structure *Hierarchy*	**Hierarchical**
I	The physical implementation of logical files by bytes on disks	File management systems

Figure 8-1. Levels of data independence.

The Relational, Network, and Hierarchical models were derived from the Binary Model as its subsets. A schema in any one of those models is a binary schema satisfying certain criteria. Those criteria are related to the implementational restrictions of the model. The following diagram shows the subsets of the Binary Model.

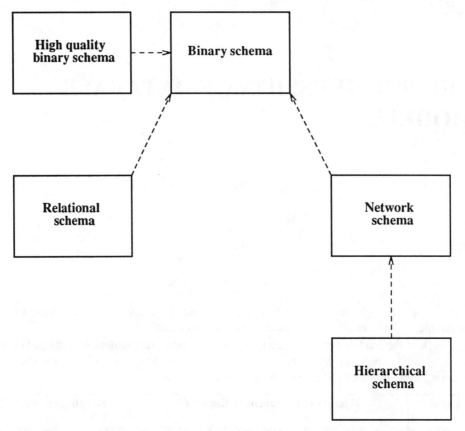

Figure 8-2. The generalization of data models. For example, the relational schemas form a subcategory of the binary schemas.

The following figure depicts the schema design methodologies presented in this text. The goal of the methodologies is to produce high-quality databases in the Relational, Network, and Hierarchical models.

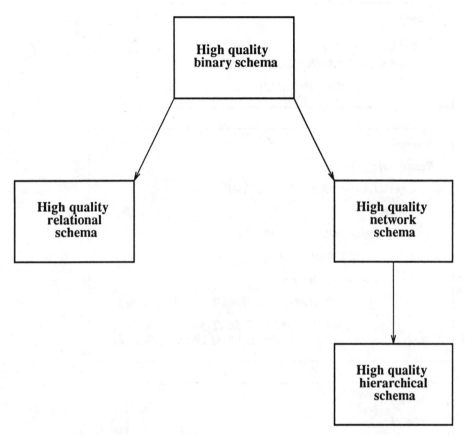

Figure 8-3. The schema-conversion methodologies studied in this text.

To review and compare some of the structural characteristics of the four database models studied in this text, the following series of examples solves the same query in the Predicate Calculus language, using, in turn, each of the four database models.

The examples use the four reference schemas of the university application at the end of this book. The query prints the pairs of the names of students and instructors, where the instructor works in the student's major department.

Example:

Binary:

  get s.*LAST-NAME*, i.*LAST-NAME*

  where i *WORKS-IN* s.*MAJOR-DEPARTMENT*

Example:

Relational:

  get s.*LAST-NAME*, i.*LAST-NAME*

  where

    i **is an** *INSTRUCTOR* **and**

    s **is a** *STUDENT* **and**

    exists w **in** *WORK*:

      (w.*INSTRUCTOR-ID-in-key* = i.*ID-key* **and**

      s.*MAJOR-DEPARTMENT-MAIN-NAME* =
        w.*DEPARTMENT-MAIN-NAME-in-key*)

Example:

Network:

  get s.*LAST-NAME*, i.*LAST-NAME*

  where

    i **is an** *INSTRUCTOR* **and**

    s **is a** *STUDENT* **and**

    exists w **in** *WORK*:

      (i *INSTRUCTOR-WORK* w **and**

      exists d **in** *DEPARTMENT*:

        (d *DEPARTMENT-WORK* w **and**

        d *MAJOR-ST* s))

Example:

Hierarchical :

    get s.*LAST-NAME*, i.*LAST-NAME*

    where

        i **is an** *INSTRUCTOR* **and**

        s **is a** *STUDENT* **and**

        exists w **in** *WORK*:

            (i.*ID* = w.*INSTRUCTOR-ID* **and**

            exists d **in** *DEPARTMENT*:

                (d *DEPARTMENT-WORK* w **and**

                d.*MAIN-NAME* = s.*MAJOR-DEPARTMENT-MAIN-NAME*))

CHAPTER 9

*ASPECTS OF DBMS IMPLEMENTATION

This chapter discusses aspects of DBMS implementation. Section 1 describes an efficient algorithm for the implementation of semantic databases. Section 2 addresses questions of transaction handling, including the enforcement of integrity constraints, backup and recovery, and concurrency control. Section 3 addresses issues of data definition languages and data dictionaries.

Chapter 10 addresses object-oriented databases. This chapter discusses the similarities and the minor difference between the semantic and object-oriented databases and augments the Semantic Binary Model (SBM) with object-oriented features related to modeling database behavior.

9.1. On the Implementation of Semantic Databases

This section presents a highly efficient file structure for the storage of semantic databases. A low-level access language is presented, such that an arbitrary query can be performed as one or several elementary queries of the language. Most elementary queries, including such nontrivial queries as range queries and others, can be performed in just one single access to the disk. The semantic models have a potential for a more efficient implementation than the conventional models for two reasons:

- All the physical aspects of representation of information by data are invisible to the user in the semantic models. This creates a greater potential for optimization: more things may be changed for efficiency considerations without affecting the user programs. The Relational Model has more data independence than the older models. For example, the order of rows in the tables (relations) is invisible to the user. The semantic models have even more data independence. For example, the representation of real-world entities by printable values is invisible to the user. One may recall that not long ago the Relational Model was criticized as being less efficient than the Network and Hierarchical Models. However, it is clear now that optimizing relational database systems have the potential to be much more efficient than the network and hierarchical systems due to the data independence of the relational model.

- In the semantic models, the system knows more about the meaning of the user's data and about the meaningful connections between such data. This knowledge can be utilized to organize the data so that meaningful operations can be performed faster at the expense of less meaningful or meaningless operations.

In the examples of this chapter we use the following database.

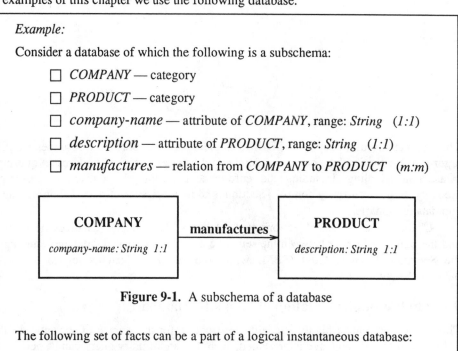

Example:

Consider a database of which the following is a subschema:

- ☐ *COMPANY* — category
- ☐ *PRODUCT* — category
- ☐ *company-name* — attribute of *COMPANY*, range: *String* *(1:1)*
- ☐ *description* — attribute of *PRODUCT*, range: *String* *(1:1)*
- ☐ *manufactures* — relation from *COMPANY* to *PRODUCT* *(m:m)*

COMPANY	**manufactures** →	**PRODUCT**
company-name: String 1:1		*description: String 1:1*

Figure 9-1. A subschema of a database

The following set of facts can be a part of a logical instantaneous database:

1.   object1 **COMPANY**

2.   object1 *COMPANY -NAME* 'IBM'

3.   object1 *MANUFACTURED* object2

4.   object1 *MANUFACTURED* object3

5.   object2 *PRODUCT*

6.   object2 *DESCRIPTION* 'IBM/SYSTEM-2'

> 7.   object3 *PRODUCT*
>
> 8.   object3 *DESCRIPTION* 'MONOCHROMATIC-MONITOR'

9.1.1. Storage structure

9.1.1.1. Abstracted level

Every abstract object in the database is represented by a unique integer identifier. The categories and relations of the schema are also treated as abstract objects and hence have unique identifiers associated with them. Information in the database can then be represented using two kinds of facts, denoted xC and xRy, where x is the identifier associated with an abstract object, C and R are the identifiers associated with a category or a relation respectively, and y is either an identifier corresponding to an abstract object or a concrete object (a number or a text string); xC indicates that the object x belongs to the category C; xRy indicates that the object x is associated with the object y by the relation R. Logically, the instantaneous database is a set of such facts.

9.1.1.2. Goals

9.1.1.2.1. Efficiency of retrieval requests

At the intermediate level of processing queries and program retrieval requests, the queries are decomposed into *atomic retrieval operations* of the types listed below. The primary goal of the physical file structure is to allow a very efficient performance for each of the atomic requests. Namely, *each atomic retrieval request normally requires only one disk access*, provided the output information is small enough to fit into one block. When the output is large, the number of blocks retrieved is close to the minimal number of blocks needed to store the output information.

1. **aC**   Verify the fact aC. (For a given abstract object a and category C, verify whether the object a is in the category C.)

2. **aRy**   Verify the fact aRy.

3. **a?**   For a given abstract object a, find all the categories to which a belongs.

4. **?C**   For a given category, find its objects.

5. **aR?**   For a given abstract object a and relation R, retrieve all y such that aRy. (The objects y may be abstract or concrete.)

6. **?Ra**   For a given abstract object a and relation R, retrieve all abstract objects x such that xRa.

7.   **a?+a??+??a**   Retrieve all the immediate information about an abstract object. (That is, for a given abstract object a, retrieve all of its direct and inverse relationships, that is, the relations R and objects y such that aRy or yRa, and the categories to which a belongs.)

(Although this request can be decomposed into a series of requests of the previous types, we wish to be able to treat it separately in order to ensure that the whole request will normally be performed in a single disk access. This will also allow a single-access performance of requests which require several, but not all, of the facts about an object, e.g., a query to find the first name, the last name, and the age of a given person.)

8.   **?Rv**   For a given relation (attribute) R and a given concrete object (value) v, find all abstract objects x such that xRv.

9.   **?R[v1,v2]**   For a given relation (attribute) R and a given range of concrete objects $[v_1, v_2]$, find all objects x and v such that xRv and $v_1 \leq v \leq v_2$. (The comparison "$\leq$" is appropriate to the type of v.)

The elementary queries defined above form a lower-level language of retrieval from semantic databases. Any query in any language can be solved by performing several elementary queries and processing their results in the memory.

Example:

Consider the following query in the Semantic Predicate Calculus:

get c.NAME, c.ADDRESS
where c **is an** *LTD –COMPANY* **and** c.YEAR-FOUNDED<1989 **and**
exists p **in** *PRODUCT* : c *MANUFACTURES* p **and** p.COST>=670 **and**
p.COST<=680

(This query prints the names and addresses of the limited companies founded before 1989 that manufacture products costing between \$670 and \$680. It is assumed that *LTD –COMPANY* is a subcategory of *COMPANY*.)

A query processor/optimizer can perform this as follows:

1.   Perform (? COSTS [670,680]) (resulting, say, in objects p_1, p_2, and p_3).

2.   For each of i in 1..3 perform (? MANUFACTURES p_i) (let us assume that the union of the results of the three queries is c_1, c_2, c_3, and c_4).

3.   For each j in 1..4 perform the elementary $(c_j ?+c_j ??+??c_j)$, obtaining the immediate information about the company c_j. This includes the information necessary to check (c.YEAR-FOUNDED<1989 **and** c **is an** *LTD –COMPANY*) as well as the values of *NAME* and *ADDRESS* to be

> printed if the result of the latter is positive.
>
> The total number of elementary queries here was eight.

9.1.1.2.2. Efficiency of update transactions

Efficient performance of update transactions is required, although more than one disk access per transaction is allowed.

A transaction is a set of interrelated update requests to be performed as one unit. Transactions are generated by programs and by interactive users. A transaction can be generated by a program fragment containing numerous update commands, interleaved with other computations. However, until the last command within a transaction is completed, the updates are not physically performed but rather are accumulated by the DBMS. Upon completion of the transaction, the DBMS checks its integrity and then physically performs the update. The partial effects of the transaction may be inconsistent. Every program and user sees the database in a consistent state: until the transaction is committed, its effects are invisible.

A completed transaction is composed of a set of facts to be deleted from the database, a set of facts to be inserted into the database, and additional information needed to verify that there is no interference between transactions of concurrent programs. If the verification produces a positive result, then the new instantaneous database is: ((the-old-instantaneous-database) − (the-set-of-facts-to-be-deleted)) $\cup$ (the-set-of-facts-to-be-inserted).

> *Example:*
>
> Consider the database of Example 9-1.
>
> The following is a transaction to rename *Burroughs* into *Unisys*, transfer all business from *Sperry* to *Unisys*, and delete *Sperry*.
>
> **transaction**
>   **for** b **where** b *COMPANY-NAME* 'Burroughs' **do**
>   **for** s **where** s *COMPANY-NAME* 'Sperry' **do**
>   **begin**
>   b.*COMPANY-NAME* := 'Unisys';
>   **for** p **where** s *MANUFACTURES* p **do**
>   **relate** b *MANUFACTURES* p;
>   **decategorize** s **from** *COMPANY*
>   **end**
>
> Let us assume that before the transaction the two companies are objects b_0 and s_0 respectively and Sperry manufactures products p_1 and p_2. The following queries were performed from within this transaction:
>
> 1.   ? *COMPANY-NAME* 'Burroughs' (results in b_0)

2.   ? *COMPANY-NAME* 'Sperry' (results in s_0)

3. s_0 *MANUFACTURES* ? (results in $\{ p_1, p_2 \}$)

At the end of the programmatic transaction, the accumulated transaction will be (V, D, I), where V, the verification specification, is the above three queries with their time-stamps; D is the following specification of the facts to be deleted:

s_0 *COMPANY*
s_0 *COMPANY-NAME* *
s_0 *MANUFACTURES* *
b_0 *NAME* *

and I is the following set of facts to be inserted:

b_0 *NAME* 'Unisys'
b_0 *MANUFACTURES* p_1
b_0 *MANUFACTURES* p_2

9.1.1.3.   Solution: a file structure achieving the goals

The following file structure supports the above requirements. The entire database is stored in a single file. This file contains all the facts of the database (xC and xRy) and additional information, called *inverted facts*, which are described below. The file is maintained as a B-tree. The variation of the B-tree used here allows both sequential access according to the lexicographic order of the items comprising the facts and the inverted facts, as well as random access by arbitrary prefixes of the facts and inverted facts.

The inverted facts do introduce some physical redundancy (no logical redundancy since they are invisible to the user), which results in a storage overhead and update-time overhead. However, as it is shown below, this overhead is not greater than if index structures were used. Of course, it is impossible to achieve any reasonable retrieval efficiency without physical redundancy, such as the indices in conventional implementations or the inverted facts proposed in this paper.

The facts which are close to each other in the lexicographic order reside close together in the file. (Notice, that although technically the B-tree-key is the entire fact, it is of varying length and on the average is only several bytes long, which is the average size of the encoded fact xRy. The total size of the data stored in the index-level blocks of the B-tree is less than 1 percent of the size of the database: e.g., each 10,000-byte data block may be represented in the index level by its first fact — 5 bytes — and block address — 3 bytes — which would amount to 0.08 percent of the data block. Thus, all the index blocks will fit into even a relatively small main memory.)

The file contains the original facts and additionally the following "inverted facts":

1. In addition to xC, we store its inverse $\overline{C}x$. ($\overline{C}$ is the system-chosen identifier to represent the inverse information about the category C. For example, it can be defined as $\overline{C} = 0 - C$.) (If a category C_1 is a subcategory of category C_2, an object a belongs to C_1 and, thus, also to C_2, then we choose to store both inverted facts $\overline{C_1}a$ and $\overline{C_2}a$. When the user requests the deletion of the fact aC_2, it triggers automatic deletion of the facts aC_1, $\overline{C_1}a$, and $\overline{C_2}a$ in order to guarantee consistency.) Thus, the elementary query ?C to find all the objects of the category C, can be answered by examining the (inverted) facts whose prefix is $\overline{C}$. The latter inverted facts are clustered together in the lexicographic order of the physical database.

2. In addition to xRv, where v is a concrete object (a number, a string, or a value of another type), we store $\overline{R}vx$. Thus, the range query "?R[v1,v2]" is satisfied by all and only the inverted facts which are positioned in the file between $\overline{R}v_1$ and $\overline{R}v_2$HighSuffix. (HighSuffix is a suffix which is lexicographically greater than any other possible suffix.) Thus, the result will most probably appear in one physical block, if it can fit into one block.

3. In addition to xRy, where both x and y are abstract objects, we store $y\overline{R}x$. Thus, for any abstract object x, all its relationships xRy, xRv, zRx, and xC can be found in one place in the file: the regular and inverted facts which begin with the prefix x. (The infixes are: categories for xC, relations for xRy and xRv, and inverse relations $x\overline{R}z$ from which we find z such that zRx.)

Example:

Consider the instantaneous database of Example 9-1. The additional inverted facts stored in the database are:

1. *COMPANY*^{inv} object1
2. *COMPANY -NAME*^{inv} 'IBM' object1
3. object2 *MANUFACTURED*^{inv} object1
4. object3 *MANUFACTURED*^{inv} object1
5. *PRODUCT*^{inv} object2
6. *DESCRIPTION*^{inv} 'IBM/SYSTEM-2' object2
7. *PRODUCT*^{inv} object3
8. *DESCRIPTION*^{inv} 'MONOCHROMATIC-MONITOR' object3

Notice that facts xRa and xRv (x and a are abstract objects, v is a value) are inverted dissimilarly. This is because we have different types of atomic retrieval requests concerning abstract and concrete objects:

- Concrete objects can be used to form range queries (e.g., "Find all persons with salaries between $40,000 and $50,000"). In such queries we know the identifier of the relation and partial information about the value. Therefore we need to use the inverted facts with the inverse of R as the prefix. Unlike concrete objects, ranges of abstract objects cannot form a meaningful range query.

- On the other hand, we have multiple-fact retrievals about an abstract object, that is, "Find all the immediate information about a given person p" (while such a request about a concrete object would be meaningless: "Find all the information about the number 5" makes no sense, as opposed to a meaningful query "Find information about item(s) whose price is $5"). Here we know the object but do not know the identifiers of the inverted relations. We need to cluster together all the inverted relations of one object. Therefore, the inverted relation should appear in the infix.

Example:

When the set of original facts is interleaved and lexicographically sorted with the inverted facts of the previous example, we obtain:

1. object1 **COMPANY**

2. object1 *COMPANY -NAME* 'IBM'

3. object1 *MANUFACTURED* object2

4. object1 *MANUFACTURED* object3

5. object2 *DESCRIPTION* 'IBM/SYSTEM-2'

6. object2 *PRODUCT*

7. object2 *MANUFACTURED*^{inv} object1

8. object3 *DESCRIPTION* 'MONOCHROMATIC-MONITOR'

9. object3 *PRODUCT*

10. object3 *MANUFACTURED*^{inv} object1

11. *COMPANY*^{inv} object1

12. *DESCRIPTION*^{inv} 'IBM/SYSTEM-2' object2

13. *DESCRIPTION*^{inv} 'MONOCHROMATIC-MONITOR' object3

14. *COMPANY -NAME*^{inv} 'IBM' object1

15. *PRODUCT*^{inv} object2

16. *PRODUCT*^{inv} object3

Example:

To answer the elementary query to find all the information about object3, including its direct and inverse relationships, we find all the entries whose prefix is object3. These entries are clustered together in the sorted order.

The elementary query "Find all objects manufactured by object1" we find all the facts whose prefix is object1_***MANUFACTURED*** . ('_' denotes concatenation.) These entries are clustered together in the sorted order.

The query to print the descriptions of the objects manufactured by the companies whose names are between 'IATA' and 'K-mart', we solve several elementary subqueries:

1. Find the companies whose names are in the above range strings. (We search for inverted facts which are lexicographically between
    COMPANY -NAME^{inv}_'IATA' and
    COMPANY -NAME^{inv}_'K-mart'_HighSuffix .
    For the instantaneous database given in the previous example we find only one inverted fact ***COMPANY -NAME***^{inv}_'IBM'_object1. The suffix object1 is the company we are looking for.)

2. Find the products manufactured by object1. (From facts with prefix object1_***MANUFACTURED*** we find suffixes {object2, object3}.)

3. Find the description of object2. (Prefix object2_***DESCRIPTION***);

4. Find the description of object3. (Prefix object3_***DESCRIPTION***);

The sorted file is maintained in a structure similar to a B-tree. The "records" of the B-tree are the regular and inverted facts. The records are of varying length. The B-tree-keys of the "records" are normally the entire B-tree-records (i.e., facts, regular and inverted). (An exception to this is when the record happens to be very long. The only potentially long records represent facts xRv where v is a very long character string. We employ a special handling algorithm for very long character strings.) Access to this B-tree does not require knowledge of the entire key: any prefix will do. All the index blocks of the B-tree can normally be held in cache.

At the most physical level, the data in the facts is compressed to minimal space. Also, since many consecutive facts share a prefix (e.g., an abstract object identifier), the prefix need not be repeated for each fact. In this way the facts are compressed further. The duplication in the number of facts due to the inverses is 100 percent, since there is only one inverse per each original fact (with a rare exception of the storage of redundant inverses of supercategories). The B-tree causes additional 30 percent overhead. (This overhead occurs because in a B-tree the data blocks are only 75 percent full on the average, though this can be improved by periodic reorganization. The overhead for the index blocks of the B-tree is no more than 1 to 2 percent since they contain only one short fact per every data block.) The total space used for the database is therefore only about 160 percent more than the amount of information in the database (i.e., the space minimally required to store the database in the most compressed form with no regard to the efficiency of data retrieval or update). Thus, the data structure described herein is more efficient in space and time than the conventional approach with separate secondary index files for numerous fields.

No separate index files are needed for the file structure described in this chapter. The duplication of data (i.e., inverted relations) together with the primary sparse index which is a part of the B-tree effectively eliminate the need for secondary (dense) indices. Furthermore, it eliminates the horrendous I/O operations caused by sequentially retrieving along a secondary index, since the sequence of information represented by our primary sparse index is also stored in consecutive physical locations. These claims are proven in the following section.

9.1.1.4. Proof of Time-efficiency of the file structure

Lemma 1. Let the file be logically perceived as a lexicographically ordered sequence of facts. Let *req* be an atomic retrieval request. Then there is a contiguous segment in the sequence, so that:

- All the facts in the segment satisfy the request *req*.

- No fact outside the segment satisfies the *req*.

- The boundaries $fact_{start}$ and $fact_{end}$ of the segment can be derived from the syntax of the request *req*. (Thus, all the output facts are lexicographically between $fact_{start}$ and $fact_{end}$. The boundaries may be inclusive or exclusive.)

Proof of Lemma 1.

The following are the ranges for the segments for each of the atomic requests (the symbol HighSuffix denotes the bit string "11111111111111 · · · " which is lexicographically greater than any possible suffix in a fact):

Request	Segment
1. **aC**	$aC \le fact \le aC$ (Verify the fact aC.)
2. **aRy**	$aRy \le fact \le aRy$ (Verify the fact aRy.)
3. **a?**	$aC_{min} \le fact \le aC_{max}$ (Here, it is assumed that all the categories of the schema are enumerated by identifiers between C_{min} and C_{max}.) (For a given abstract object a, find what categories the object belongs to.)
4. **?C**	$\bar{C} < fact \le \bar{C}\,\text{HighSuffix}$ (For a given category, find its objects.)

5.   **aR?** $aR < fact \leq aR$ HighSuffix

(For a given abstract object a and relation R, retrieve all y such that aRy.)

6.   **?Ra** $a\bar{R} < fact \leq a\bar{R}$ HighSuffix

(For a given abstract object a and relation R, retrieve all abstract objects x such that xRa.)

7.   **a?+a??+??a** $a < tuple \leq a$ HighSuffix

(Retrieve all the immediate information about an abstract object.)

8.   **?Rv** $\bar{R}v < fact \leq \bar{R}v$ HighSuffix

(For a given relation (attribute) R and a given concrete object v, find all abstract objects x such that xRv.)

9.   **?R[v1,v2]** $\bar{R}v_1 < fact \leq \bar{R}v_2$ HighSuffix

(For a given relation R and a given range of concrete objects [v_1, v_2], find all objects x and v such that: xRv and $v_1 \leq v \leq v_2$.)

• End of Lemma 1 •

In the following, an estimate is given for the number of disk accesses per atomic retrieval request. Two cases are considered.

A. One disk access per request of small output.

In the predominant case, the amount of information to be output for a given atomic request is much less than one block. According to the Lemma, all the information to be output comprises one contiguous segment. The segment has as many facts as there are items to be output. Therefore, the segment is much less than one block. (In the physical storage the facts are prefix-compressed, so the physical space for each fact is normally just a few bytes.) Hence, normally the segment fits into one block. We can find the address of this block in the cache-resident B-tree index with the key $fact_{start}$. Then, in a single access the block is brought to the memory. There is a small probability that the segment appears on the boundary of two blocks. In the latter case we may have to bring two blocks into the memory. On the other hand, the desired block(s) may have already been in cache and, thus, sometimes zero accesses are sufficient.

Thus, the retrieval efficiency for the atomic requests is the optimum, or very close to the optimum. (One cannot retrieve a memory-unavailable datum in less than one disk access.)

B. For large output, the efficiency is also close to the optimum.

When the output is larger than a block, so is the segment. If the output can be squeezed into n blocks, then n would be the theoretical optimum (not obtainable in any practical system) for the number of disk accesses per request. All the facts of the segment can be squeezed into slightly more than n blocks (depending on how much of the prefix can be compressed), say $1.1n$ blocks. Due the space maintenance policy of the B-tree, each physical data block is 75 percent full on the average. The segment may begin in the middle of one block and end in another; thus, on the average, one additional block has to be fetched (the actual overhead of this type ranges between 0 and 2 block fetches). Thus the total expected number of blocks to be fetched is $1.1n\,/\,0.75 + 1 = 1.47n + 1$. The number of disk accesses may be even less than that if some of the blocks are in cache.

9.1.2. Comparison to performance of implementations of the Relational Model

The system proposed herein is not less efficient, and is normally more efficient, in both time and storage space than the relational model's implementations with multiple dense indices.

Let us consider a simple relational database composed of one relation T with attributes $A_1, A_2, \ldots, A_n$. Let us assume that for each j there are queries of the type

$$\textbf{get } A_i \textbf{ where } A_j = c \qquad\qquad\qquad (Q1)$$

and that each of those queries is required to be performed in a reasonable time.

For the purpose of physical implementation, the Relational Model's databases can be technically represented (without affecting the user) as certain semantic binary databases. Specifically, the above relational schema can be regarded in the Semantic Binary Model as a category T and relations A_i between the objects of T and values.

To assure reasonable time performance in the Relational Model for each of the above queries, we need a dense index on each of the attributes A_i. There are n index files (or n indices combined in one file in some implementations). The total size of the indices thus exceeds the size of the table T itself. Therefore the space overhead in the Relational Model is greater than 100 percent and, thus, is greater than the space overhead in the proposed semantic implementation. Also, in the semantic implementation there is only one physical file, while there are many physical files in the relational implementations; in some implementations there are as many files as:

$$number\_of\_tables \times (1 + number\_of\_attributes\_per\_table)$$

The management of multiple files is not only a hassle but also contributes to additional space overhead due to allocation of growth areas for each file.

With respect to the time required to solve the simple queries of type Q1, it is the same in the best relational implementations and in the proposed semantic implementation. Namely, the time is:

$$(1 + number\_of\_values\_in\_the\_output) \times time\_to\_retrieve\_one\_block$$

(In the relational implementation, there will be one visit to the dense index on A_j, and for every $A_j = c$ found there, there will be one random access to the main table. In the semantic implementation, first the subquery $?A_j c$ will be solved, and then for every match x found the subquery $xA_i?$ will be evaluated.)

If in Query Q1 we desired to print many attributes A_i instead of just one, the same time results would be obtained in both implementations. Notice that in the semantic implementation proposed herein all the immediate information of an object, including all its attributes, is clustered together.

Now let us consider updates. Insertion of a row into the relational table takes replacement of one block in the main table and n blocks in the dense indices. In the semantic implementation there is insertion of the primary facts about the new object ob: $obA_1c_1, \ldots, obA_nc_n$ (all the primary facts will appear in contiguous storage in one block) and n inverse facts in possibly n different blocks. Thus, here, as well as in the other types of simple updates, the performance of the semantic implementation is not worse than that of the relational implementations supporting efficiency of queries.

The advantages in the semantic implementation's performance become even more significant for more complex queries and updates. Though the detailed analysis of these is beyond the space limit of this chapter, I would like to mention that, for example, queries requiring a natural join in the relational implementations would be more efficient in the semantic implementation because there are direct explicit relationships between the categories instead of relationships represented implicitly by foreign keys in the Relational Model. The gap in performance between the faster semantic implementation and the relational implementations is even greater when the relational keys are composed of more than one attribute and when the relationships between the tables are many-to-many, which requires an extra table to represent the many-to-many relationship in the relational implementations. The gap increases with the number of joins in the query. In general, the advantage in the efficiency of the proposed semantic implementation versus the relational implementations normally becomes greater as the complexity of the queries increases.

Of course, there are also major efficiency advantages in the semantic implementation in support of semantic complexities of the real world, which are very awkwardly and inefficiently implemented in the relational implementations. These complexities include intersecting categories, subcategories, categories with no keys, varying-length attributes, missing ("null") values, multiple values, etc.

9.2. Implementation of Transaction Control

This section addresses the questions of integrity constraints' enforcement, backup and recovery, and concurrency control. All those issues are related to the handling of transactions in databases. The material that follows pertains to semantic databases. However, since the other database models have been technically presented in this book as subsets of the Semantic Binary Model, the methods presented in this chapter are also applicable to the relational, network, hierarchical and object-oriented database models.

Since this book is primarily about *logical* database design, rather than about the implementational aspects of DBMSs, it is not my intention to present the full variety of the methods for dealing with integrity, recovery, and concurrency. Instead, each of the topics is represented by a sketch of one state-of-the-art technique.

9.2.1. The transaction model

A transaction is a set of interrelated update requests to be performed as one unit. In this presentation, we employ the deferred update scheme. Thus, until the last command within a transaction is completed, the updates are not physically performed but rather are accumulated by the DBMS. Upon completion of the transaction the DBMS checks its integrity and then physically performs the update. The partial effects of the transaction may be inconsistent. Every program and user see the database in a consistent state: until the transaction is committed, its effects are invisible (this is true in our transaction model even within the same transaction).

We use here the term **programmatic transaction** to denote the program fragment comprising a transaction. During its execution, a programmatic transaction may issue database queries. Queries which are performed from within a programmatic transaction are called here **transactional queries**.

The immediate outcome of a programmatic transaction is an **accumulated transaction**, which is composed of a set of facts to be deleted from the database, a set of facts to be inserted into the database, and additional information needed to verify that there is no interference between concurrent transactions. In the model described here, the updates are decomposed into inserts and deletes. If the verification produces a positive result, then the new instantaneous database is: ((the-old-instantaneous-database) − (the-set-of-facts-to-be-deleted)) $\cup$ (the-set-of-facts-to-be-inserted).

The execution of a transaction statement is composed of the following stages:

1. **Transaction accumulation** — this is a run of the program segment comprising the transaction. No updates are done physically in the database during this stage, but rather the results of the updating instructions are accumulated in the sets D (the set of facts to be deleted from the database) and I (the set of facts to be inserted into the database). Also, the *atomic* transactional queries performed on the database during this stage are accumulated in a set V (they will be verified to validate concurrency). The result of the transaction's accumulation, i.e. the outcome (V, D, I) of the program segment's run, is called the **accumulated transaction**.

2. **Integrity validation** — at this time the system checks to see that the database resulting from performing the update (i.e., with the set D deleted and I inserted) would not violate the integrity constraints. No actual update is done at this stage, but rather an algorithmic decision is made by examining the sets D, I, the constraints, and in some cases by getting some additional information from the database. (The integrity module may need to perform additional queries, which are also logged in V.)

3. **Concurrency validation** — it is verified that the results of inquiries logged in V are still the same (i.e., have not been changed by the concurrent transactions). (Verification implementation will be explained in a later section.) At this step we also check that this transaction is not interfering with the other concurrent accumulated transactions and queries. The set V contains specifications of the atomic

queries utilizing the algebraic notation of the section on the storage structure. (The results of the queries are not recorded in V; they are not needed for validation.) The set V also contains the time-stamps of the queries.

4. **Backup of the transaction** for the purpose of recovery from failures.

5. **Physical update of the accumulated transaction** — the new instantaneous database is: ((the-old-instantaneous-database) $-D$) $\cup I$.

No matter what the order and the mix of inserts, deletes, updates, and queries in the original programmatic transaction is, it can be shown, using the assumptions made above, that the transaction can be unambiguously converted into the execution of (V, D, I).

Example:

Transaction A. Increase by 10 percent the grades that are below 60.
  transaction
  for e **in** *COURSE-ENROLLMENT* **where** e.*FINAL-GRADE*<60 **do**
  e.*FINAL-GRADE* := e.*FINAL-GRADE**1.1

The above program fragment is performed as follows:

transaction begin

  Let query q = '(? FINAL-GRADE 0..60)'

  Perform the query q obtaining a set S of the resulting facts (e
      FINAL-GRADE g) from the database, where $0 \leq g \leq 60$

  For every fact (e FINAL-GRADE g) in S perform:

      let ng= g*1.1

      delete the old FINAL-GRADE of e

      insert the fact (e FINAL-GRADE ng)

  end

In the deferred update scheme, the delete and insert are not performed in the real time but are accumulated as follows. Here, it is assumed that the query was performed at time t_1 and that S consists of three facts with enrollments e_1, e_2, and e_3 and respective grades g_1, g_2, and g_3. For each of the three enrollments, the old grade must be deleted before the new one is inserted. The deletion of the old when it is irrelevant what the old is can be specified using the wild character '*':
                  delete (e_1 FINAL-GRADE *)

The accumulated transaction (V, D, I) is:

  $(V=\{(q, t_1)\}$,

D={ $(e_1$ FINAL-GRADE *), $(e_2$ FINAL-GRADE *), $(e_3$ FINAL-GRADE *) },

I={ $(e_1$ FINAL-GRADE $1.1*g_1)$, $(e_2$ FINAL-GRADE $1.1*g_2)$, $(e_3$ FINAL-GRADE $1.1*g_3)$ })

The resulting transaction is checked for its logical integrity. One of the integrity constraints to check is that the resulting grades are in the correct range of 0..100. This can be done simply by examining the accumulated transaction. Other constraints may require issuing queries to the database. In such a case, these additional queries would become a part of the verify set V.

The accumulation and integrity constraint checks of many transactions can proceed in parallel. The backup and concurrency control will be discussed in later sections.

9.2.2. Accumulation of a transaction

The updating instructions of the programmatic transaction are translated into updates to the sets D and I. These sets are empty when the programmatic transaction begins. The updates to D and I are shown here by considering a series of examples of commands from the programmatic transaction.

Example:

relate : i *WORKS-IN* d

Let i_0 be the object referred to by the variable i, and d_0 the object referred to by d. The change in I is:

$I := I \cup \{(i_0 \text{ WORKS-IN } d_0)\}$

Example:

unrelate : i *WORKS-IN* d

The change in D is:

$D := D \cup \{(i_0 \text{ WORKS-IN } d_0)\}$

The insertion set may have already contained this fact. Since the final database is the old database less D plus I, it must be assured that I does not reintroduce the fact:

$I := I - \{(i_0 \text{ WORKS-IN } d_0)\}$

Example:

(* Make d be the only department of i *)
    i:=*WORKS-IN* d

$$D := D \cup \{(i_0 \, WORKS\text{-}IN \, *)\}$$
$$I := I \cup \{(i_0 \, WORKS\text{-}IN \, d_0)\}$$

Example:

categorize : i **is an** *INSTRUCTOR*
$$I := I \cup \{(i_0 \, INSTRUCTOR)\}$$

The new object is also automatically inserted into the category *PERSON*:
$$I := I \cup \{(i_0 \, PERSON)\}$$

Example:

create new i **in** *INSTRUCTOR*

    A new object needs be created and inserted into the category *INSTRUCTOR*. In a single-user system, a global counter of objects could be incremented and its value would become an identifier of the new object. However, in conjunction with concurrency control, we cannot update a global counter at the time of transaction accumulation. We keep a local counter and temporarily denote the new objects as negative numbers: -1, -2, etc. At the time of physical transaction updates these numbers will be replaced by the new object identities. The local counter is 0 when the transaction begins.

    counter:=counter-1
$$I := I \cup \{(\text{counter} \, INSTRUCTOR)\}$$

The new object is also automatically inserted into the category *PERSON*:
$$I := I \cup \{(\text{counter} \, PERSON)\}$$

Example:

decategorize : i is no longer an *INSTRUCTOR*

The object must be removed from *INSTRUCTOR* . Also, all the facts that depended on the object being an instructor must be removed: the facts that the object works in departments and the facts that courses are offered by the object. These removal instructions need be added to D :

$D := D \cup \{(i_0 \; INSTRUCTOR), (i_0 \; WORKS\text{-}IN \; *), (* \; THE\text{-}INSTRUCTOR \; i_0)\}$

When a fact with the wild character * appears in D when the accumulated transaction comes to the physical update in the database, the system will interpret it as a command to remove all the relevant facts.

It is possible that prior to issuing the decategorization command the programmatic transaction has requested the insertion into I of some facts that are no longer valid due to the current command. Therefore, such facts must now be removed from I. Let us assume that I happens to contain facts that the instructor works in departments d_1 and d_2 and teaches course offerings o_1 and o_2. Then we should remove from I:

$I := I - \{(i_0 \; INSTRUCTOR), (i_0 \; WORKS\text{-}IN \; d_1), (i_0 \; WORKS\text{-}IN \; d_2), (o_1 \; THE\text{-}INSTRUCTOR \; i_0), (o_2 \; THE\text{-}INSTRUCTOR \; i_0)\}$

Note that unlike D, it would be meaningless for I to ever contain facts with wild characters like $(i_0 \; WORKS\text{-}IN \; *)$; I can contain only the actual facts to be inserted into the database.

Problem 9-1.

How should the accumulated transaction be changed by the command:

decategorize : i is no longer a *PERSON*

Solution on page 484.

9.2.3. Integrity constraint enforcement

We will discuss here an example of the enforcement of some of the integrity constraints expressed in the schema. The primary expense in integrity verification are the extra queries to be performed. Therefore, the algorithm should minimize the amount of queries. In many cases, the integrity of a transaction can be confirmed without performing any queries at all.

The following algorithm checks the correctness of the **domains, ranges, and types of relations**.

for $(x\ R\ y)$ **in** I **do**

    let d = the domain of R

    let r = the range of R

    (* Check that x is in the correct domain *)

        if $(x\ d)$ is in I **then** (* OK *)

        else if $(x\ d)$ is in D **then** error

        else (* check that x is in the category d in the current database *)

            perform query $(x\ d)$, if the result is false — error

    (* Check that y is in the correct range *)

        if r is a concrete category **then** check that y conforms to the specification of r

        else if $(y\ r)$ is in I **then** (* OK *)

        else if $(y\ r)$ is in D **then** error

        else perform query $(y\ r)$, if the result is false — error

    if R is m:1 (including 1:1) **then** (* check m:1 *):

        if there is $(x\ R\ z)$ in I where $y \neq z$ **then** error

        else if $x < 0$, that is, x is a new object, **then** (* OK *)

        else if $(x\ R\ *)$ is in D **then** (* OK *)

        else perform the query $(x\ R\ ?)$, if there is a result $(x\ R\ z)$ where $z \neq y$ and $(x\ R\ z)$ is not in D **then** error

    if R is 1:m (including 1:1) **then** (* check 1:m *):

        if there is $(z\ R\ y)$ in I where $x \neq z$ **then** error

        else if y is an abstract object and $y < 0$, that is, y is a new object, **then** (* OK *)

        else if $(*\ R\ y)$ is in D **then** (* OK *)

        else perform the query $(?\ R\ y)$, if there is a result $(z\ R\ y)$ where $z \neq x$ and $(z\ R\ y)$ is not in D **then** error

---

Example:

Consider:

- □ *birth-year* — attribute of *PERSON*, range: *1870..1992*   *(m:1)*
- □ *works-in* — relation from *PERSON* to *DEPARTMENT*   *(m:m)*

Check that the domain is correct:

If $(o_1$ WORKS-IN $o_2)$ is in I, then o_1 must be a PERSON: o_1 is either being put into this category in this transaction or was a person before and not removed by this transaction.

Check that the range is correct:

If $(o_1$ BIRTH-YEAR 1500) is in I, then an error will be produced when 1500 is checked against the range 1870..1992.

If $(o_1$ WORKS-IN $o_2)$ is in I, then o_2 must be a DEPARTMENT: either being put into this category in this transaction or was a department before and not removed by this transaction.

Check that the relation stays many-to-one:

If $(o_1$ BIRTH-YEAR 1950) is in I, then I should contain no other $(o_1$ BIRTH-YEAR $y)$. Further, if o_1 is an old object for which there is another fact $(o_1$ BIRTH-YEAR $y)$ in the database, and this fact is not deleted by this transaction, then an error should be produced.

During the verification of integrity constraints certain information may be requested from the database by means of queries. The atomic queries are added to the the set V of the transaction. The concurrency control algorithm, discussed later, will assure that, once the integrity constraints are checked, the information upon which the correctness depends will not be changed until the physical update of the transaction. The integrity constraint enforcement algorithm tend to minimize the number of additional queries performed. When a query does have to be performed, its cost is normally small because the data block accessed by a query verifying integrity is likely to already have been brought into the memory by a prior query executed during the programmatic transaction.

Problem 9-2.

Write an algorithm to check the accumulated transaction (V, D, I) against the integrity constraints of disjointness of categories in the schema.

Solution on page 484.

Problem 9-3.

Write an algorithm to check the accumulated transaction (V, D, I) against the integrity constraints of totality of relations in the schema.

9.2.4. Backup and recovery

The following is one possible procedure for **backup** for the deferred update scheme.

At the time of the physical update, the accumulated transaction is added to the **log**, which is a sequential file. This file can be maintained on a tape or a disk other than the disk on which the primary database resides. Periodically, a backup tape of the entire database is made. At that point the log is restarted.

Every log entry consists of the sets I and D of a transaction and a timestamp. The sets I and D are written on the log just before the physical update. The timestamp is added right after the physical update. A transaction for which a time-stamp has been issued is declared **committed** at that time.

The **recovery** depends on the cause of failure:

1. User's **program error**, for example, a division by zero during the execution of a programmatic transaction. The transaction is killed and its (V, D, I) is discarded. No harm has been done to the database.

2. **Violation of integrity constraints** — same as above.

3. The user decides to **abandon the transaction** in progress (e.g., by performing a "goto" to outside the body of the transaction) — same as above.

4. Other causes related to the user's program — same as above.

5. Problems in concurrency control — same as above, but the system will attempt to re-execute the programmatic transaction.

6. **Media failure** — a physical hardware problem on the disk. This type of failure is often called a **hard crash**. The disk is replaced. The last full backup is copied into the new disk. Then the committed transactions on the log are reapplied to the database.

Example:

Let B be the backup of the entire database made at time t_0. Let the log contain:
$(I_1, D_1, t_1), (I_2, D_2, t_2), (I_3, D_3, t_3), \cdots, (I_n, D_n, t_n)$.

Then the reconstructed database is:
$$B - D_1 \cup I_1 - D_2 \cup I_2 - D_3 \cup I_3 \cdots - D_n \cup I_n$$

The reapplication of the log can be done in a single sequential scan of the database. To do this, the log can be first processed into a cumulative transaction (I, D).

Example:

The cumulative transaction equivalent to the sum of transactions on the log is:
$$D = D_1 - I_1 \cup D_2 - I_2 \cup D_3 - I_3 \cup \cdots \cup D_n$$
$$I = I_1 - D_2 \cup I_2 - D_3 \cup I_3 - D_4 \cup \cdots \cup I_n$$

The resulting transaction (I, D) can be sorted in the same way the database is sorted and then merged with the database.

The reapplication of an accumulated transaction (I_k, D_k) is called a **roll forward**.

7. **System failure**, also called a **soft crash**. An example of this is a **power failure**. Other system failures include disk overflow, a run time error in the DBMS or the operating system, etc.

A simple, though not the most efficient, way to handle a soft crash is the same way as handling a hard crash. This is reasonable when power failures are rare or when an **uninterruptible power supply device** is installed. If, however, the soft crashes are very frequent, the above method of recovery may be too expensive.

A more efficient method of soft crash recovery involves a fast purge of problems caused by a soft crash. There are three types of such problems to be considered in the deferred update scheme:

a. Loss of physical integrity in the database file: an incorrect pointer between blocks in the B-tree, a block or a record whose writing on the disk has begun but has not been completed due to a power failure, etc.

b. In the virtual storage file management paradigm, some of the disk blocks are updated in their copies held in buffers in memory; it is possible that some committed transactions have been reflected in those blocks held in memory buffers and not yet copied into the disk before the soft crash.

c. Loss of logical integrity of the database: some of the facts of the sets D and I of the last transaction have been deleted from or inserted into the database, while others have not — after the crash the database is partially updated by the transaction, in violation of the atomicity principle of transactions.

Assuming that the DBMS is built on top of a B-tree virtual-storage file management system, problems a and b can be handled by the recovery mechanism of the file management system itself. Various simple algorithms exist for this purpose. (Of course, if the file management system does not provide a physical recovery mechanism, these algorithms should be implemented at the DBMS level.)

Problem c pertains only to the last accumulated transaction on the log: since the physical update of the accumulated transactions in the deferred update scheme is sequential (assuming a single-processor multiuser architecture), there is at most one transaction on the log that has not yet been committed. There are two possible solutions:

(i) **Roll forward** (i.e., reapply the uncommitted accumulated transaction on the log, if there is one). This will bring the database to a consistent state. However, a problem in this approach is that the user's program may have died during the soft crash and, therefore, the transaction cannot be acknowledged. Not knowing that the transaction has actually been performed, the user may repeat the programmatic transaction, with unexpected result.

Example:

Consider the transaction
> **transaction**
> **for** e **in** *COURSE-ENROLLMENT* **where** e.*FINAL-GRADE*<60 **do**
> e.*FINAL-GRADE* := e.*FINAL-GRADE**1.1

If this transaction is successfully performed twice, the result will be the increase of the grades by 21 percent — not what the user intended.

(ii) **Roll backward** (i.e., undo the uncommitted accumulated transaction on the log, if there is one). This will be tantamount to killing the transaction and restoring the database to state before the transaction. To be able to undo a transaction we need to assume that the transaction is written on the log in a normalized form as follows: the wild character * in the delete set D is replaced by the actual objects from the database; facts that appear in both D and I are removed from D. Then we can calculate the new database after the roll backward as follows:

$$\text{new-database} := \text{old-database} - I \cup D$$

Example:

The accumulated transaction at the end of the run of the programmatic transaction is:
> $D = \{(e_1 \text{ FINAL-GRADE *}), (e_2 \text{ FINAL-GRADE *})\}$
> $I = \{(e_1 \text{ FINAL-GRADE 54}), (e_2 \text{ FINAL-GRADE 65})\}$

After consultation with the database, D is normalized:
> $D = \{(e_1 \text{ FINAL-GRADE 40}), (e_2 \text{ FINAL-GRADE 50})\}$

The soft crash may have left the database with the facts about e_1 updated while the facts about e_2 not updated. To remove all of the effects of the transaction, it is undone:

new-database = old-database −
$\{(e_1 \text{ FINAL-GRADE 54}), (e_2 \text{ FINAL-GRADE 65})\} \cup$
$\{(e_1 \text{ FINAL-GRADE 40}), (e_2 \text{ FINAL-GRADE 50})\}$

9.2.5. Concurrency control

Every multiuser database management system must implement a strategy to alleviate the interference between transactions (and queries) executed in parallel.

Example:

Consider the following two transactions.

Transaction A. Increase by 10 percent the grades that are below 60.
> **transaction**
> **for** e **in** *COURSE-ENROLLMENT* **where** e.*FINAL-GRADE*<60 **do**
> e.*FINAL-GRADE* := e.*FINAL-GRADE**1.1

Transaction B. Add 10 to the grades that are below 60.
> **transaction**
> **for** e **in** *COURSE-ENROLLMENT* **where** e.*FINAL-GRADE*<60 **do**
> e.*FINAL-GRADE* := e.*FINAL-GRADE*+10

To consider the simplest case of transactions, let us assume that there is only one enrollment in the database with a grade under 60; let this enrollment be the object o_1 and the grade be 30.

Assume that the above two transactions are executed in parallel. Under a correct concurrency scheme the final result should be the same as if the transactions were executed serially in *some* order. Therefore, the new grade should be either $30 \times 1.1 + 10 = 43$ or $(30 + 10) \times 1.1 = 44$.

Now assume that there is no concurrency control and the following chain of events happens:

1. A finds the old value of the grade, 30;

2. B finds the old value of the grade, 30;

3. A calculates the new value as 30×1.1 and updates;

4. B calculates the new value as $30 + 10$ and updates.

The resulting value, 40, is incorrect. Let us call this chain of events C_1.

9.2.5.1. Orthogonal classifications of the database concurrency control strategies

This subsection briefly discusses various aspects of concurrency control strategies. The concurrency control strategies can be distinguished according to any of the following issues.

1. Types of parallelism:

   a. **Single-processor multiuser time-sharing database systems** — the DBMS runs on a single processor but handles many concurrent users.

   b. **Multiprocessor centralized database systems** — there is a parallel computer with several CPU's accessing the DBMS simultaneously.

   c. **Distributed database systems** — the database is partitioned between several independent computers, each of which can remotely access information held by other computers.

2. The pessimistic approach versus the optimistic approach:

   a. In the **pessimistic approach**, a transaction expecting to use or update some information locks it; a transaction trying to access the locked information is put on hold until the locks are released. There is some overhead cost for **locking** and **unlocking**. Deadlocks — situations where two transactions wait for each other — should be detected and resolved by aborting and restarting one of the transactions.

   b. The **optimistic approach** works better when the frequency of actual interference between transactions is low. Transactions are not put on hold and no locks are imposed. When a transaction is completed, the system checks whether any interference has occurred during the execution of the transaction. If interference has been detected, the transaction is aborted and restarted. **Livelocks** — situations where a transaction gets aborted and restarted repeatedly — should be taken care of. Livelocks may also occur in the deadlock resolution of the pessimistic approach but are rarer there.

3. When are the updates done?

   a. The updates generated by a transaction can be physically performed as they are requested by the user's program, without waiting for the completion of the transaction. When the transaction fails, or there is a system failure, the partial updates have to be physically removed from the database. Also, the system should take great pains to assure that partial updates are invisible to concurrent transactions.

   b. In the **deferred update scheme**, the updates are accumulated in the memory and are physically performed in the database only when the transaction has been successfully completed.

Example:

Each of the above transactions A and B issues one query during the transaction's run. This is an atomic query with a range of values for the attribute FINAL-GRADE:

$$q=(? \text{ FINAL-GRADE } 0..60)$$

Assuming that A issued this query at time t_1 finding the grade g_1, and B — at t_2 finding g_2, the accumulated transactions are:

Accumulated A =

$(V=\{(q,t_1)\}, \quad D=\{(o_1 \quad \text{FINAL-GRADE} \quad *)\}, \quad I=\{(o_1 \quad \text{FINAL-GRADE}$
$1.1*g_1)\})$

Accumulated B =

$(V=\{(q,t_2)\}, \quad D=\{(o_1 \quad \text{FINAL-GRADE} \quad *)\}, \quad I=\{(o_1 \quad \text{FINAL-GRADE}$
$10+g_2)\})$

---

4.   Approaches to the meaning of *interference*:

a.   At a high logical level, in the information-oriented approach, interference is said to occur when the result of any query issued by a transaction would be different if the query were issued at the very end of the transaction.

b.   In the data-oriented approach, interference is said to occur when a transaction attempts to update some data that has already been seen by another transaction in progress. This approach is problematic in its handling of transactions that insert new data rather than update existing data. For example, if a transaction A has queried the database and found that it contains 500 students, and transaction B is creating a new student, interference should be detected. Typical solutions for this problem provide for the correct resolution of only *some* cases.

5.   In Case *b* above, if locks or some other strategies are used, there is a choice of how big a chunk of information is to be locked. This is called the **lock granularity**. If the chunks are too big, the system will determine that transactions touching different parts of the chunk are interfering, even if they are not interfering on a logical level. Unnecessary holds and aborts of transactions result. If the chunks are made smaller, there is a higher overhead of locking. The typical granularities are:

a.   **Field granularity** in relational databases, or, equivalently, **fact granularity** in the semantic databases. Here, a single fact is locked.

b.   **Record granularity** or **row granularity** in relational databases, or **abstract object granularity** in the semantic databases. Here the unit of locking is an abstract object with all of its facts.

    c.   **Relation granularity** or **table granularity** in the relational databases, or **category granularity** in the semantic databases. Here, one locking unit is a category with all of its objects and all of their facts.

    d.   **Entire database granularity** — in this case a transaction locks the entire databases; de facto serial processing results.

    e.   Mixed or varying granularities.

6.   Criterion of correctness of a concurrency control scheme. The prevalent criterion is:

    a.   **Serializability of transactions** — The cumulative result of a load of concurrent transactions and queries should be the same as if they were executed serially in *some* order. The result here is composed of the final state of the database and all of the outputs delivered to the end users.

9.2.5.2. Optimistic concurrency control

We can summarize now the **optimistic scheme** for concurrency control:

- When an accumulated transaction (V, D, I) is committed, that is, allowed to be updated physically, its I and D parts are written on the log together with the current time.

- Before a transaction $T = (V, D, I)$ is committed, the system checks for every atomic* query (q, t) in the verification set V to see whether the log contains another transaction whose time is greater than t and whose insert or delete sets, I' or D', interfere with q. A set of facts interferes with a query q if it contain a fact satisfying the query. (In other words, the application of q on that set as if it were a database would produce a nonempty result.)

> *Example:*
>
> Let us consider again the chain of events C_1.
>
>   Transaction A successfully commits at time t_3 and writes on the log: (D={$(o_1$ FINAL-GRADE $g_1)$}, I={$(o_1$ FINAL-GRADE $1.1*g_1)$}, time=t_3)
>
>   Now transaction B is verified at time t_4. Its verification set contains (q,t_2) where $t_2 < t_3$ and q interferes with the transaction on the log. Therefore, B must be aborted and restarted.

It can be assumed that the file management system provides virtual storage management, so the physical memory is likely to contain a copy of the recently written information. The optimistic concurrency verification algorithm needs to examine the latest part of the log.

---

  * At this point the reader is reminded that every query is decomposed into a set of atomic queries. The atomic queries are: aC, aRy, a?, ?C, ?Ra, a?+a??+??a, ?rV, and ?R[v1..v2].

This latest part is thus likely to be in memory. The checking can proceed fact by fact from the current top of the log until it encounters a timestamp younger than that of the queries being verified. Since the queries in V are atomic retrieval request syntaxed as facts with wild cards ? and value-ranges, the check of a fact against a query is trivial.

9.2.5.3. Pessimistic concurrency control

Pessimistic concurrency control involves imposition of two kinds of locks:

- **Read locks, or shared locks** — when a transaction or query wants to assure that certain data it is reading will remain unaltered by competing transactions until a certain future time;

- **Write locks, or exclusive locks** — when a transaction intends to modify some data and wants to assure that other processes would not see or interfere with partially updated information.

Two processes are allowed to simultaneously hold read locks on the same data, but an exclusive lock cannot be simultaneous with another exclusive or shared lock on the same data.

The remainder of this section exemplifies one aspect of pessimistic concurrency control: read locks imposed by a complex query to prevent updating transactions from changing the relevant data during the execution of the query.

Example:

Let the following nonupdating transaction T_1 calculate the sum of money in all of the accounts:

transaction begin
s:=0
for a in *ACCOUNT* **do** s:=s+a.*AMOUNT*
end

At the same time a transaction T_2 moves \$100 from account a_1 to a_2. If this is done after T_1 read account a_1 but before it read a_2, the result will be incorrect. To prevent this, the system can put transaction T_2 on hold until T_1 finishes.

Every query performed by a nonupdating transaction is remembered by the system until the transaction completes or aborts. These remembered atomic queries become **logical read locks** in the sense that while they are remembered the system will not allow the physical update of the database capable of altering the results of those atomic queries.

Example:

The atomic queries issued by T_1 are:

1.   ? ACCOUNT

2. a_1 AMOUNT ?

3. a_2 AMOUNT ?

4. a_3 AMOUNT ?

5. a_4 AMOUNT ?

Let us assume that the transaction T_2 has been accumulated and is ready for physical update after T_1 has issued query 2 but before query 3. Assuming that the old values in the accounts a_1 and a_2 were \$100 and \$200, respectively, the sets I and D of T_2 are:

$$I = \{(a_1 \text{ AMOUNT } 0), (a_2 \text{ AMOUNT } 300)\}$$
$$D = \{(a_1 \text{ AMOUNT } *), (a_2 \text{ AMOUNT } *)\}$$

The system will put T_2 on hold because there is an active read-lock (a_1 AMOUNT ?) imposed by T_1. This atomic query has intersection with both sets I and D.

9.3. Meta-Schema, Data Dictionary, and DDL

A **data dictionary**, as described in Chapter 1, contains information about the application's schema. The data dictionary can be updated automatically by the system when it interprets DDL statements (the Data Definition Language), as well as manually by the Database Administrator. The dictionary contains all the names of the categories and relations of the application's schema, the structure of the schema, and other information. This additional information may include text explaining the informal meaning of every schema concept.

The data dictionary is used by the system when compiling and executing DML programs, when interacting with the users, etc. The dictionary can also be queried by the user. The user queries may be specific (e.g., What is the range of a given attribute?) or more global (e.g., How many categories and attributes are there in the schema? How many attributes are there per category on the average?)

The data dictionary can be maintained by the DBMS as an additional database. Since the data dictionary as a database describes the types of information that can be represented in the application database, it is often called a **meta-database**. As a database, the data dictionary requires a schema, called a **meta-schema**. The categories and relations of the meta-schema are called **meta-categories** and **meta-relations**. For example, the meta-category *CONCEPT* is a catalog of all the categories and relations of the schema. For every concept, there is a name and an optional comment:

```
┌─────────────────────────┐
│                         │
│        CONCEPT          │
│                         │
│   name,comment: String  │
│                         │
└─────────────────────────┘
```

9.3.1. A semantic binary Meta-schema

☐ *CONCEPT* — category (A catalog of all the categories and relations of the schema.)

☐ *CATEGORY* — subcategory of *CONCEPT*

☐ *ABSTRACT-CATEGORY* — subcategory of *CATEGORY* (Abstract categories are identified by their names.)

☐ *VALUE-CATEGORY* — subcategory of *CATEGORY* (This is a catalog of concrete categories that are ranges of relations.)

☐ *RELATION* — subcategory of *CONCEPT*

☐ *MANY-TO-ONE* — subcategory of *RELATION* (This meta-category includes m:1 and 1:1 relations.)

☐ *ONE-TO-MANY* — subcategory of *RELATION* (This meta-category includes 1:m and 1:1 relations. There is an inferred userview subcategory ONE-TO-ONE, which is the intersection of MANY-TO-ONE and ONE-TO-MANY.)

☐ *subcategory* — relation from *ABSTRACT-CATEGORY* to *ABSTRACT-CATEGORY* (m:m) (Relates between immediate subcategories. This meta-relation forms a direct acyclic graph of categories.)

☐ *name* — attribute of *CONCEPT*, range: *String* (m:1) (Names of categories and relations. This is 1:1 on categories.)

☐ *comment* — attribute of *CONCEPT*, range: *String* (m:1) (When defining a schema, the database designer should be able to comment on the meaning and use of every concept being defined.)

☐ *STRINGS-RANGE* — subcategory of *VALUE-CATEGORY* (One member of this meta-category is the concrete category of all the character strings, *String*; other members are subsets thereof having restrictions on maximal lengths of strings and allowable characters.)

☐ *NUMBERS-RANGE* — subcategory of *VALUE-CATEGORY* (One member of this meta-category is the concrete category of all the numbers, *Number*; other

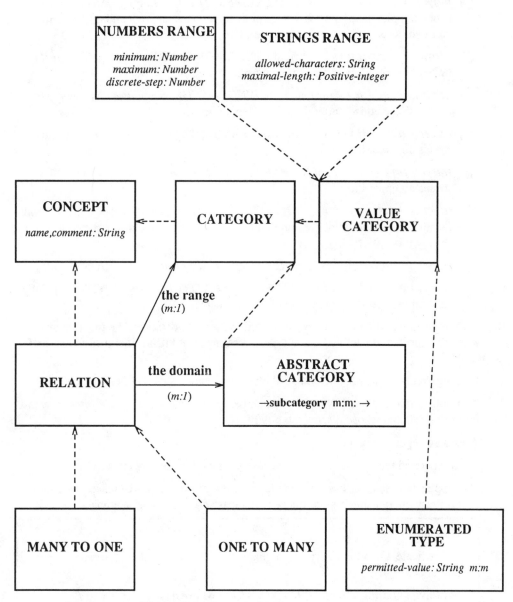

Figure 9-2. A semantic binary meta-schema

members are subsets thereof having various restrictions.)

☐ *ENUMERATED-TYPE* — subcategory of *VALUE-CATEGORY*   (Corresponds to the enumerated type in Pascal.)

☐ *permitted-value* — attribute of *ENUMERATED-TYPE*, range: *String* (*m:m*) (For example, the permitted values of the type Boolean are y and n; the permitted values of seasons are Spring, Summer, Fall, Winter.)

☐ *allowed-characters* — attribute of *STRINGS-RANGE*, range: *String* (*m:1*) (When this is null, all 256 characters are allowed.)

☐ *maximal-length* — attribute of *STRINGS-RANGE*, range: *Positive-integer* (*m:1*) (When this is null, there is no length limit.)

☐ *minimum* — attribute of *NUMBERS-RANGE*, range: *Number* (*m:1*) (Null means no lower limit.)

☐ *maximum* — attribute of *NUMBERS-RANGE*, range: *Number* (*m:1*) (Null means no upper limit.)

☐ *discrete-step* — attribute of *NUMBERS-RANGE*, range: *Number* (*m:1*) (Null means the continuum of the real numbers. For integers the discrete step is 1; for money it is 0.01.)

☐ *the-domain* — relation from *RELATION* to *ABSTRACT-CATEGORY* (*m:1*)

☐ *the-range* — relation from *RELATION* to *CATEGORY* (*m:1*) (The range of a relation may be abstract or concrete (value category).)

Before an application schema is entered as data into the meta-database, the meta-database is empty except for the predefined data types, forming the **initial instantaneous meta-database**:

1.   A strings-range named *String* whose allowed-characters is the ASCII character set

2.   A numbers-range named *Number*; a numbers-range named *Positive-integer* whose minimum is 0 and whose discrete-step is 1

3.   A value-category named *Date*.

4.   An enumerated type named *Boolean* whose permitted values are 'y' and 'n'.

Once the application schema has been loaded as data into the meta-database, the user can perform arbitrary query using regular query or database programming languages.

Example:

A Predicate Calculus query to calculate the average number of relations per domain category.

get (**avg** (**count** r **where** r *THE-DOMAIN* c) **where** c **is an** *ABSTRACT-CATEGORY*)

9.3.2. DML on Meta-schema = DDL

When the schema of an application is stored in a meta-database, described by a meta-schema, the development of the DBMS requires less effort. The vendor can save on developing a stand-alone support for the data definition language (DDL): the schemas can be defined and modified using the data manipulation languages (DML) applied to the meta-database.

Example:

Consider the following schema:

PERSON

name,address: String

It can be generated in Extended Pascal as follows:

create new p **in** *CATEGORY*

p.*NAME*:='PERSON'

create new n **in** *RELATION*

n.*NAME*:='NAME'

create new a **in** *MANY–TO–ONE*

a.*NAME*:='ADDRESS'

n.*THE-DOMAIN*:=p

a.*THE-DOMAIN*:=p

for s **in** *STRINGS-RANGE* **where** s *NAME* 'String' **do**

    begin

    n.*THE-RANGE*:=s

    a.*THE-RANGE*:=s

    end

Example:

The same schema can be defined in the Predicate Calculus as follows:

insert into *ABSTRACT-CATEGORY* (*NAME*: 'PERSON')

insert into *MANY-TO-ONE* (*NAME*: 'NAME', *THE-DOMAIN*: p, *THE-RANGE*: s)

> **where** p **is an** *ABSTRACT-CATEGORY* **and** p.*NAME*='PERSON' **and** s **is a** *STRINGS-RANGE* **and** s.*NAME*='String'

insert into *MANY-TO-ONE* (*NAME*: 'ADDRESS', *THE-DOMAIN*: p, *THE-RANGE*: s)

> **where** p **is an** *ABSTRACT-CATEGORY* **and** p.*NAME*='PERSON' **and** s **is a** *STRINGS-RANGE* **and** s.*NAME*='String'

Of course, the above specifications are not as user friendly as a straightforward DDL. This problem can be easily overcome by writing a simple translator from DDL to one of the above data manipulation languages.

9.3.3. Relational data dictionary and Meta-schema

A relational meta-schema is a relational schema which describes all the relational schemas. Therefore, we will design it the way we design any relational schema: first we design a semantic schema for it and then convert it into a relational schema. The semantic schema of the relational meta-schema follows.

☐ *TABLE* — category   (Tables (abstract categories) are identified by their names.)

☐ *name* — attribute of *TABLE*, range: *String*   (*1:1,total*)

☐ *comment* — attribute of *TABLE*, range: *String*   (*m:1*) (When defining a schema, the database designer should be able to comment on the meaning and use of every table being defined.)

☐ *ATTRIBUTE* — category   (Attributes of tables.)

☐ *name* — attribute of *ATTRIBUTE*, range: *String*   (*m:1,total*) (Attribute names are unique within one table. An attribute that is a part of the key must have the suffix -in-key in its name; an attribute that is the key must have the suffix -key.)

☐ *of-table* — relation from *ATTRIBUTE* to *TABLE*   (*m:1,total*)

☐ *comment* — attribute of *ATTRIBUTE*, range: *String*   (*m:1*) (When defining a schema, the database designer should be able to comment on the meaning and use of every attribute being defined.)

☐ *VALUE-CATEGORY* — category   (Descriptions of ranges of various attributes.)

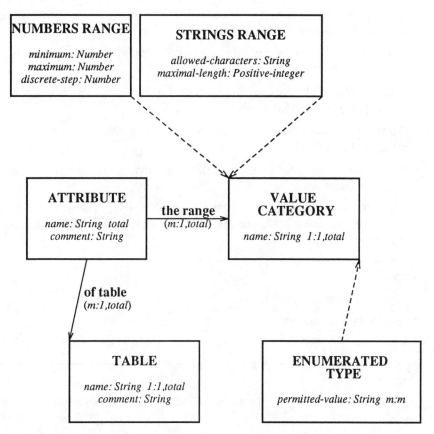

Figure 9-3. A semantic schema for the relational meta-schema

☐ *name* — attribute of *VALUE-CATEGORY*, range: *String*   (*1:1,total*)

☐ *the-range* — relation from *ATTRIBUTE* to *VALUE-CATEGORY*   (*m:1,total*)

☐ *STRINGS-RANGE* — subcategory of *VALUE-CATEGORY*   (One member of this meta-category is the concrete category of all the character strings, *String*; other members are subsets thereof having restrictions on maximal lengths of strings and allowable characters.)

☐ *NUMBERS-RANGE* — subcategory of *VALUE-CATEGORY*   (One member of this meta-category is the concrete category of all the numbers, *Number*; other members are subsets thereof having various restrictions.)

☐ *ENUMERATED-TYPE* — subcategory of *VALUE-CATEGORY*   (Corresponds to the enumerated type in Pascal.)

☐ *permitted-value* — attribute of *ENUMERATED-TYPE*, range: *String*   (*m:m*)
(For example, the permitted values of type Boolean are y and n; the permitted
values of seasons are Spring, Summer, Fall, Winter.)

☐ *allowed-characters* — attribute of *STRINGS-RANGE*, range: *String*   (*m:1*)
(When this is null, all 256 characters are allowed.)

☐ *maximal-length* — attribute of *STRINGS-RANGE*, range: *Positive-integer*
(*m:1*)   (When this is null, there is no length limit.)

☐ *minimum* — attribute of *NUMBERS-RANGE*, range: *Number*   (*m:1*)   (Null
means no lower limit.)

☐ *maximum* — attribute of *NUMBERS-RANGE*, range: *Number*   (*m:1*)   (Null
means no upper limit.)

☐ *discrete-step* — attribute of *NUMBERS-RANGE*, range: *Number*   (*m:1*)   (Null
means the continuum of the real numbers. For integers the discrete step is 1; for
money it is 0.01.)

Example:

A Predicate Calculus query to print the attributes of every table.

get c.*NAME*, r.*NAME* **where** r *OF-TABLE* c

Example:

A Predicate Calculus query to calculate the average number of attributes per
table.

get (**avg** (**count** r **where** r *OF-TABLE* c) **where** c **is a** *TABLE)*

The information about keys of tables is implicit in this meta-schema: the key attributes are
distinguished by the suffix of their names. It may be convenient to have a category of keys
in the meta-schema. However such a category would be redundant with the information
contained in the suffix. While such a redundancy is not acceptable in a schema, the
convenience of the user can be assured by having a redundant inferred category in a
userview:

☐ *KEY-ATTRIBUTE* — subcategory of *ATTRIBUTE*   (An inferred (userview)
meta-subcategory containing the attributes that are the keys of or are in the keys
of their tables. An attribute belongs to this inferred meta-subcategory if and only
if its name's suffix is -key or -in-key.)

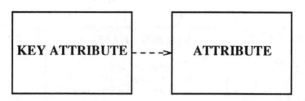

Figure 9-4. The inferred meta-subcategory
KEY-ATTRIBUTE

Our implicit representation of keys in the schema follows our relational schema conventions of Chapter 3. Under a different convention, it may make sense to have the meta-subcategory *KEY-ATTRIBUTE* in the meta-schema itself rather than in a userview.

We can now convert this semantic binary schema into a relational schema using the methodology of Chapter 3. The resulting relational meta-schema is in the following figure.

Example:

A Predicate Calculus query to calculate the average number of attributes per table using the relational meta-schema.

get (**avg** (**count** r **where** r.*OF-TABLE--NAME-in-key*=c.*NAME-key*) **where** c **is a** *TABLE*)

Example:

An SQL query to print the maxima of the numeric attributes.

select a.*OF-TABLE-NAME-in-key*, a.*NAME-in-key*, n.*MAXIMUM*
    from *ATTRIBUTE* a, *NUMBERS-RANGE* n
    where a.*THE-RANGE-NAME*=n.*NAME-KEY*

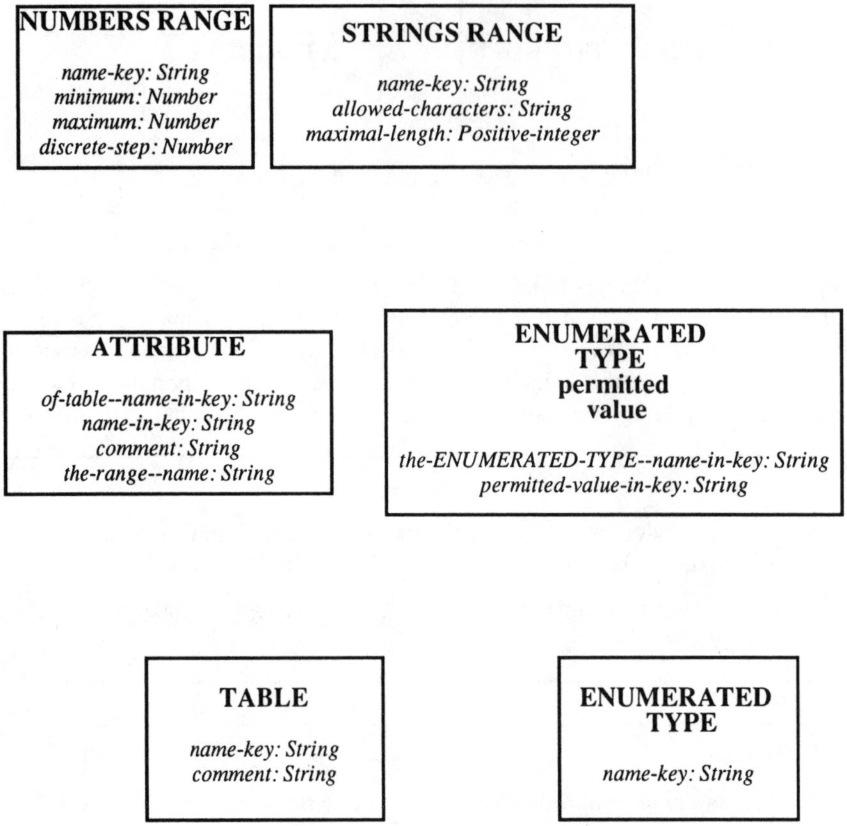

NUMBERS RANGE

name-key: String
minimum: Number
maximum: Number
discrete-step: Number

STRINGS RANGE

name-key: String
allowed-characters: String
maximal-length: Positive-integer

ATTRIBUTE

of-table--name-in-key: String
name-in-key: String
comment: String
the-range--name: String

**ENUMERATED
TYPE
permitted
value**

the-ENUMERATED-TYPE--name-in-key: String
permitted-value-in-key: String

TABLE

name-key: String
comment: String

**ENUMERATED
TYPE**

name-key: String

Figure 9-5. A relational meta-schema

CHAPTER 10

THE OBJECT-ORIENTED DATA MODELS

By Naphtali Rishe and Michael Alexopoulos

During the past several years the computer research community has undertaken a number of efforts to produce tools and methodologies that are needed to overcome the software crisis. The combined outcome of a number of such efforts is the *object-oriented programming paradigm*.

The concepts embodied in the object-oriented programming paradigm have received tremendous attention from many disciplines of computer science. In particular, the database research community has concentrated its efforts on extending database systems with object-oriented capabilities. A number of prototype and commercial systems have been built as a result of this activity (Orion, Gemstone, etc). These systems provide all the traditional DBMS services, but the data models that they support are based on object-oriented concepts. Such database systems have been termed **object-oriented database systems** (henceforth **OODBS**).

Despite the popularity that OODBSs have attained, no standard has yet been established for the object-oriented data model — as it is the case with previous data models (e.g., the network data model). Usually, the term **object-oriented** is used to refer collectively to a set of semantic modeling mechanisms for capturing the information of an application's real world. However, there appears to emerge a consensus among database researchers regarding a minimal set of features that a database model must exhibit if it is to be termed object-oriented. These features are the following:

- Object and object identity
- Semantic primitives for the modeling of the structure of information
- Object behavior and encapsulation

The first two features can be ascribed to the semantic database models which in general exhibit an orientation toward modeling the structure of the information in an application's real world. They suggest that an object-oriented database model should provide explicit semantic abstraction primitives for *direct object representation*, *object categorization*, *integrity constraints*, etc. Although a plethora of semantic modeling primitives can be found among various database systems, most of the object-oriented data models adopt only a handful of them that best fit the needs of the application domains for which they are intended. Two of the most common semantic modeling primitives encountered in object-oriented data models are:

- **Classification** of objects by categories.

- **Inheritance** — if an object is a member of a category (e.g., *STUDENT*), then it is automatically a member of its supercategories (e.g., *PERSON*). Therefore, the properties of the supercategories (e.g., the attribute last *LAST-NAME*) automatically apply to the subcategories. Note, however, that supercategory-subcategory is not a relation between objects of the two categories; rather objects of a category are simultaneously members of all of its supercategories. In some data models, due to implementational restrictions, categories must be disjoint. In those models, inheritance can be introduced indirectly by establishing *is-a* relations among objects and "**rules of inheritance.**"

The last feature, **object behavior**, means that an object-oriented model should provide abstraction mechanisms for modeling the behavior of objects in an application's real world.

Example:

When a student is registered for courses, a certain series of steps is to be followed, such as checking if a course is offered, adding the student into the list of students taking a course, etc. The same series of steps is followed every time that a student is registered for a new term. Such steps constitute a student's behavior during registration.

Various approaches can be found in the OODBSs for modeling object behavior. The most common of these are *methods* which are discussed later in this chapter.

Finally, **encapsulation** means that the values associated with objects in an object-oriented database can only be accessed via specific predefined operations which implement their behavioral characteristics (i.e., methods). Consequently, users should not be concerned about the implementation details of such operations but rather with their functional specification. Applications which access the values associated with certain objects do not have to be rewritten every time that the programs which implement the behavioral characteristics of these objects are modified. This increases the degree of data independence of applications and enforces a near uniform treatment of objects throughout applications.

Example:

Consider the schema for the University database. In an object-oriented system one could define a program P whose input is an object in *PERSON* and whose output is a printout of all the concrete values associated with that object. Any modifications in the implementation of P should not have any effect on the applications which use P as long as P conforms to its original input and output specifications.

An object-oriented data model, therefore, is a semantic model which provides mechanisms for modeling not only the structural but also the behavioral characteristics of an application's real world.

In this chapter we describe the object-oriented paradigm for database modeling from the perspective of the Semantic Binary Model. For the purposes of this presentation we use our example of an object-oriented data model. We call this model the *Semantic Binary Object-Oriented Data Model* (henceforth **SBOODM**).

10.1. The Semantic Binary Object-Oriented Data Model

This section introduces SBOODM, which is an example of an object-oriented data model. SBOODM has been defined with the intention to expose the basics of the object-oriented paradigm to the readers already familiar with semantic modeling. It is a semantic binary model augmented with an abstraction mechanism to model the behavior of objects.

10.1.1. Object-Oriented schemas

An object-oriented schema must capture not only the structural properties of an application's real world but also its behavioral properties. In the SBOODM, a schema lists all aspects of an application's real world in graphical form and in the appendix. More formally a SBOODM schema is defined as follows:

SBOODM schema — a semantic binary schema whose appendix lists the methods defined for each of the categories and the interface to each category. The concepts of *method* and *category interface* are defined in the sections that follow.

10.1.2. Methods

In the object-oriented paradigm it is possible to predefine a library of operations (procedures and functions) for a given schema. These operations are called **methods** and are the primary means for modeling the behavioral characteristics of an application's real world. Methods can be constructed by data manipulation primitives. Of special interest are the *object methods* and *category methods*.

In the SBOODM methods are implemented via Extended Pascal procedures or functions and are defined as follows:

Object method — an extended Pascal **function** or **procedure** which satisfies the following:

- The first formal parameter of the method is of type *ABSTRACT* and must be a value parameter. When a method *m* is invoked and an object *o* is assigned to its first parameter, then we say that *m* **is invoked on** *o*.

- The method restricts the first argument to belong to a particular category. When that is a category *C*, we say that the method **is defined on** *C*.

We allow for the following convenient syntactic abbreviation for the header of a procedure method *m* defined on a category *C*:

procedure *m*(first-argument:*C*; other-arguments);

(and similarly for function methods.)

Example:

The method

      procedure print-name(i:*INSTRUCTOR*);

      begin

          writeln(i.*LAST-NAME*, i.*FIRST-NAME*)

      end

can be regarded as a syntactic abbreviation for

      procedure print-name(i:*ABSTRACT*);

      begin

          if not (i **is an** *INSTRUCTOR)* **then**

             writeln('Error: The input object is not of the category *INSTRUCTOR*')

> **else** writeln(i.*LAST-NAME*, i.*FIRST-NAME*)
>
> **end**

Example:

An object method which computes and returns the age of a person.

> **function** get-approximate-age(person: *PERSON*): *INTEGER*;
>
> **var** current-year: *INTEGER*;
>
> **begin**
>
> > read(current-year);
> >
> > get-age := current-year - person.*BIRTH-YEAR*;
>
> **end**;

Example:

An object method which updates the major of a student.

> **procedure** change-major(student-to-change: *STUDENT*; new-major: *STRING*);
>
> **var** dept: *ABSTRACT*;
>
> **begin**
>
> > **transaction**
> >
> > > **for** dept **in** *DEPARTMENT* **where** dept *NAME* new-major **do**
> > >
> > > > student-to-change.*MAJOR* := dept;
>
> **end**;

Example:

An object method which enrolls a student in a course.

>**procedure** enroll(student-to-enroll: *STUDENT*; course-name: *STRING*;
>>quarter: *STRING*; year: *INTEGER*);
>
>**var** offer, enrollment : *ABSTRACT*;
>
>**begin**
>
>>**transaction**
>>
>>>**for** offer **in** *COURSE-OFFERING* **where** offer.*THE-
>>>COURSE.NAME* = course-name **and** offer.*THE-
>>>QUARTER.YEAR* = year **and** offer.*THE-
>>>QUARTER.SEASON* = quarter **do**
>>
>>**begin**
>>
>>>**create new** enrollment **in** *COURSE-ENROLLMENT*;
>>>
>>>enrollment.*THE-STUDENT* := student-to-enroll;
>>>
>>>enrollment.*THE-OFFER* := offer;
>>
>>**end**
>
>**end;**

Example:

An example of an object method which interactively registers a student into up to five courses.

>**procedure** register(student-to-register: *STUDENT*);
>
>**var** enrollment: *ABSTRACT*;
>>course-name, quarter: *STRING*;
>>
>>nbr-courses, year: *INTEGER*;
>>
>>answer: *CHAR*;
>
>**begin**
>
>>**transaction**
>>
>>>**begin**

```
            nbr-courses := 0;
            writeln('Please enter the current year and quarter');
            readln(year, quarter);
        repeat
                writeln('Please enter the course name');
                readln(course-name);
                enroll(student-to-enroll, course-name, quarter, year);
                nbr-courses := nbr-courses + 1;
                writeln('Register for another course (y/n) ?');
                readln(answer);
        until (answer = 'n' or nbr-courses >= 5) ;
        end;
    end;
```

Example:

An example of an object method which gets all the information pertaining to a particular person from the standard input and then it inserts it into the database.

```
    procedure get-person-data(person-object: PERSON);
    var first-name, last-name, address: STRING;
            birth-year: 1870..1990;
    begin
        transaction
            begin
            writeln('Please enter the first and last name and the birth year');
            readln(first-name, last-name, birth-year);
            person-object.FIRST-NAME := first-name;
            person-object.LAST-NAME := last-name;
            person-object.BIRTH-YEAR := birth-year;
            writeln('Please enter the address');
```

```
          readln(address);

          person-object.ADDRESS := address;

          end;

     end;
```

Example:

A new student has arrived at the Computer Science department and he or she must be registered in several courses. The following program will request all the information pertaining to the new student and the courses that he or she would like to be registered for, and then it will insert them into the University database.

program New-Student-Registration(Input, Output, UNIVERSITY-DB,
       UNIVERSITY-MASTER-VIEW);

var new-student, student-category: *ABSTRACT*;

begin

   (* Create a new student *)

       create new new-student **in** *STUDENT*;

   (* Get all the personal information about the new student *)

       get-person-data(new-student);

   (* Update the student's major *)

       update-major(new-student, 'Computer Science');

   (* Get the course names for the courses that the student is interested
       in taking and register the student in these courses *)

       register-student(new-student);

end.

Sometimes, it is of interest to the users of a database to retrieve or store global information about a category rather than specific information about its objects. Such information about categories can be manipulated by methods which are called **category methods**, and are a special case of object methods in that the objects upon which they are invoked are categories themselves. Category methods are defined within the SBOODM by considering a special category *CATEGORY* whose objects are the categories of the schema. The category *CATEGORY* is an example of a special type of categories called **meta-categories**. Meta-categories are used together with meta-relations to manipulate the concepts of a schema. Formally, category methods are defined as follows:

Category method — an object method such that the category for which it is defined is the meta-category *CATEGORY*.

Example:

The following is an example of a category method which counts the number of objects contained in a given category.

function category-size(category-object: *CATEGORY*): *INTEGER*;

var object: *ABSTRACT*;

    count: *INTEGER*;

begin

    count := 0;

    for object **in** category-object **do** count := count + 1;

    category-size := count;

end;

In the example above, the method *category-size* had to repeatedly read the database in order to determine the number of objects that are members of some particular category. Obviously, *category-size* is an expensive operation in terms of number of times that the database must be accessed, especially if the size of the database is large. An alternative to this implementation is to have all global information that is of concern to the users of a category (e.g., the number of objects which are members of a category) associated with the category object itself via some relation.

Example:

Suppose that for some users of the University database it is necessary to know the number of objects that are recorded in the instantaneous database for each category. Instead of computing this number by the method *category-size*, it is possible to alter the schema so that this information is directly recorded in the instantaneous database and it does not have to be recomputed every time that it is needed. By adding the relation *number-objects* from the category *CATEGORY* to the category of integer numbers, it is possible to record the number of objects which are members of a category in the instantaneous database. Each time that a new object is inserted into the database, the integer value associated with *number-objects* must be incremented by 1. The following is an example of a category method to increment the *number-objects* counter.

procedure increment-object-counter(category-object: *CATEGORY*);

begin

category-object.*NUMBER-OBJECTS* := category-object.*NUMBER-OBJECTS* + 1;

end;

Example:

The following is an example of a category method which returns the number of objects which are members of a given category in the instantaneous database.

function get-number-objects(category-object: *CATEGORY*): *INTEGER*;

begin

get-number-objects := category-object.*NUMBER-OBJECTS*;

end;

The database designer can provide the users with a library of methods attached to the schema. The bodies of the methods are not visible to the users, only the headers of the methods are visible. For some methods which are used only as subroutines in other methods, neither the headers nor bodies are visible to the users. The schema's *interface* is the the headers of the methods that may be used by the users. For any category *C*, the user-visible headers of the schema object methods defined on C are called the **category interface of** C.

In SBOODM, a method defined for a category can invoke any of the other methods defined for the categories in the schema. However, it should be noted that in some object-oriented models, the methods defined for a specific category cannot indiscriminately invoke any other methods defined in the schema. In these models various mechanisms are provided to restrict the visibility of the methods defined for a particular category to only a subset of the categories defined in the schema.

10.1.2.1. Overloading and late binding

It is often convenient to use the same name for different methods. Such a need arises primarily when the functional specification of a method resembles that of other methods. Consider the following example, which illustrates this point.

Example:

A method needs to be defined for the University schema which given an object in *PERSON* will display its name and address. The following procedure may be used to implement this method.

    procedure display(person: *PERSON*);

    begin

        writeln('Name:', person.*FIRST-NAME*, ' ', person.*LAST-NAME*);

        writeln('Address:', person.*ADDRESS*);

    end;

Similarly, for persons who are students another method is to be defined which given an object in *PERSON* it displays its name, address, and major. A convenient choice for the name of this method is also *display*. The following is a procedure to implement this method:

    procedure display(student-object: *STUDENT*);

    begin

        writeln('Name:', student-object.*FIRST-NAME*, student-object.*LAST-NAME*);

        writeln('Address:', student-object.*ADDRESS*);

        display-dept-name(student-object.*MAJOR*);

> **end**;
>
> Here, *display-dept-name* is a method defined on *DEPARTMENT*: given an
> object in *DEPARTMENT* it displays the department's name.

In the above example two methods are defined and both are to display the values associated
with abstract objects which are members of the category *PERSON*. Their functional
specifications present a lot of similarities, which justifies the choice for sharing the same
name. A method name shared by more than one method is called an **overloaded method
name**.

> *Example:*
>
> A user's program can be as follows:
>
>   **for** p **in** *PERSON* **do** display(p);
>
> For persons that happen to be students the second method will be automatically
> used.

A reference to an overloaded method name cannot be bound to a specific function or
procedure body at compile time. Therefore, the code that is to be bound to an overloaded
method name is determined during execution time (this practice is called **late binding**). If
late binding were not available, then a programmer would have to use different names for
the display methods above, such as *display-person* and *display-student*, and then test for the
category where each object belongs before referencing any of the method names.

> *Example:*
>
> An equivalent user program without overloading would be:
>
> **for** p **in** *PERSON* **do**
>
>   **if** p **is a** *STUDENT* **then** display-student(p)
>
>   **else** display-person(p);

However, with late binding the programmer is free from such constraints and he or she can
simply reference the name *display* where needed.

In SBOODM the following algorithm is used to determine the procedure or function body which is to be bound to an overloaded method name reference.

10.1.2.2. A late binding algorithm

Let $C_1, C_2, \ldots, C_n$ be categories in a schema and let m be a method name which is shared by methods defined for each of the categories $C_1, C_2, \ldots, C_n$ (i.e., m is an overloaded method name). Let $b_1, b_2, \ldots, b_n$ be the method bodies where b_i is the body of a method with name m defined for category C_i (for $i = 1, 2, \ldots, n$). Finally, let o be the object identifier that is assigned to the first parameter of m during some invocation of m.

The algorithm will test the object o for membership in each of the categories $C_1, C_2, \ldots, C_n$. If o belongs to the category C_i, then m is bound to the body b_i (where $1 \leq i \leq n$). However, the following two special cases must be considered if the algorithm is to work properly:

1.   If a category C_i is a subcategory of some other category C_j, where $1 \leq i,j \leq n$, then if the object o is in C_i then the object's membership in C_j is ignored.

2.   It is possible that o belongs to the intersection of two or more categories so that all have a method named m and none of them is a subcategory of any of the others. If this is the case, the late binding algorithm cannot unambiguously determine which procedure or function body should be bound to the name m. In order to avoid such problems the data definition language processor must warn users of such ambiguities if they are detected within a schema being defined.

The following two examples illustrate the late binding algorithm.

Example:

Assume that some application on the University database has referenced the method name *display*. Since *display* is an overloaded method name, it must be determined at run time which of the two method bodies defined in the schema is to be invoked. The algorithm to determine this is the following:

if (o **is a** *STUDENT*) **then**

(* Bind *display* to the body of the method *display* defined on *STUDENT* *)

else if (o **is a** *PERSON*) **then**

(* Bind *display* to the body of the method *display* defined on *PERSON* *)

else (* Error : *display* can not be bound to any method body. *)

where o is the object assigned to the first parameter of *display*. The algorithm first tests o for membership in *STUDENT* and then in *PERSON*. If the test were performed in the reverse order and o is in *STUDENT*, then the major associated with o would not be printed.

Example:

Assume that a new method has been added to the University application schema. This new method is also named *display* and it is defined on the category *INSTRUCTOR*. Given an object in *INSTRUCTOR*, *display* will print the name, address, and the name of the department where the instructor works.

Consider now a reference to the name *display* by some application program. It is possible that the object assigned to the first parameter of *display* is a member of both *STUDENT* and *INSTRUCTOR* (i.e., it lies in the intersection of categories *STUDENT* and *INSTRUCTOR*). Hence, there are two possible procedure bodies that can be bound to the name *display*, one defined on *STUDENT* and another defined on *INSTRUCTOR*. Obviously, the system cannot unambiguously bind any method body to *display* and it should generate a run-time error message indicating that.

10.2. Object-Oriented Terminology

The following are definitions of terms which are common to many object-oriented models.

Attribute — synonymous with the SBOODM term *binary relation*.

In some object-oriented models (e.g., the O_2 model) an object is not only represented by its object identifier but as a grouping of all the facts in which the object is the domain value. We call this an **OO-object** and it is defined as follows:

OO-Object — is a pair *(I, V)* where *I* is an object identifier and *V* is set of pairs of the form *(A:v)*. *A* is an attribute and *v* can be a concrete value or an object identifier or the symbol **nil**. *(A:v)* means that there exists a fact *"I A v"* in the database.

Example:

The following is an example of an *OO-object* in the category *STUDENT* whose object identifier is *o1*.

(*o1* ,

{ (*FIRST-NAME* : 'Roberta'),

> (*LAST-NAME* : 'Jackson'),
>
> (*BIRTH-YEAR* : 1950),
>
> (*ADDRESS* : '111 Park Ave., New York, NY, 22233, U.S.A.'),
>
> (*MAJOR* : *o2*),
>
> (*MINOR* : *o3*) }
>
>)
>
> *o2* and *o3* are object identifiers for the departments which constitute the major and the minor of the student named *Roberta Jackson*.

Class — synonymous with the term *category*.

Class instance — an object is an instance of class C if it is a member of *C*.

Message — a method invocation on some object. In some object-oriented data models, the invocation of a method *m* on some object *o* (i.e., "a message *m* sent to *o*") is denoted as:

> *o.m(parameter-list)*

Method signature — the specification of a method header.

Class method — synonymous with the term *category method*.

Instance method — synonymous with the term *object method*.

Public method — any method which appears in the interface of a category.

Private method — any method which is defined for a category and does not appear in the interface of that category. That is, the method is used by the database designer only as a subroutine in defining other methods, but the method is not made available to the other users.

Class type — is a triple *(N,T,M)* where

- *N* is the name of the class for which the type is defined.

- *T* is a set of pairs *(A:C)* where *A* is an attribute and *C* is a class name. *(A:C)* means that objects in class *N* can relate through *A* with objects in class *C*.

- *M* is a set of methods defined for the class whose name is *C*.

is-a relationship — equivalent to the *subcategory-supercategory* relationship which may exist between two categories.

Inheritance — all the properties, such as methods and attributes, of a category *C* automatically apply to all of its subcategories. We say that all the subcategories of *C* *inherit* its properties.

Class lattice — a graph showing the inclusion of categories. It is a directed acyclic graph $H = (V, A)$ where

- V is a set of nodes, and each node represents a class in a database schema.

- A is a set of arcs representing *is-a* relationships between classes. An arc from C_1 to C_2 means that C_1 is a subclass of C_2.

In some object-oriented models, a class cannot be an immediate subclass of more than one class. In such models, H is a set of trees.

Problem 10-1.

Use the university/binary reference schema at the end of this book. The departments of Mathematics and Computer Science have decided to merge their operations for economic reasons. Write an Extended Pascal program that merges the two departments by performing all of the following tasks. Create a new department and assign it the name *Dept. of Mathematical and Computing Sciences*. All the instructors working in either department should be transferred to the new department. Finally, if the major or minor of any student is *Mathematics* or *Computer Science*, then it should be updated to the new department.

Assume that the following methods are already defined in the University schema:

procedure insert-name(dept: *DEPARTMENT*; new-name: *STRING*); (* Insert a new name for a department object. *)

procedure update-major(student-object: *STUDENT*; new-major: *ABSTRACT*); (* Update the major of a student object. *)

procedure update-minor(student-object: *STUDENT*; new-major: *ABSTRACT*); (* Update the minor of a student object. *)

procedure update-work-dept(instructor-object: *INSTRUCTOR*; new-dept, old-dept: *ABSTRACT*); (* Assign a professor to work for another department. *)

Solution on page 485.

Problem 10-2.

Use the studio-multimedia/binary schema (Figure 13-15 on page 403). Assume that there is a method *show* which displays images on the monitor. The method *show* on other character strings converts them into images and then shows them. The method *show* applied to several character strings shows them in one image of several lines. The method *show* on the category *FRAME* shows its picture. The method *show* on the category *SCENE* sequentially shows its frames with appropriate time delay. The procedure *wait* freezes all activities for a specified number of seconds.

Write the methods *show* on *FRAME* and *SCENE*. Write a method *audition* on the category *ACTOR* that shows his or her information, photograph, and plays the video of all his or her scenes, preceded by the movie titles.

The purpose of this problem is to the exemplify an important application of the object-oriented approach to *multimedia databases*.

Solution on page 486.

CHAPTER 11

*FIFTH-GENERATION LANGUAGES

This chapter discusses several fifth-generation languages. Sections 1-3 address issues of expressive power of logic-based database languages and discuss Prolog-like languages and a logic-based language which attains computational completeness. Section 4 discusses user-friendly interfaces, using the Query-By-Example language as an example.

The optional sections of Chapter 3 are prerequisite to reading this chapter.

11.1. Limitations of Nonprocedural Database Languages

Not every query can be specified in the languages based on Predicate Calculus.

Example:

A person x *can improve grades of* a person y if x teaches y or x teaches a person who *can improve grades of y*. A query to find whether x can improve grades of y cannot be specified in the calculus.

Example:

Consider the following relational subschema of the bill of materiel of items. Each row in the table contains the names of two items where one item has the other as its immediate component.

COMPONENT

contained-item: String
containing-item: String

We cannot specify in Predicate Calculus or in SQL or in the Relational Algebra the following query:

'Print a list of all the pairs of items which directly or indirectly contain one another.'

The queries in the examples above are *recursive* queries. Some unexpressible recursive queries would become expressible if we extend the calculus with additional constructs, such as the so-called *transitive closure* operator or the more powerful *fixed-point* operator. But no matter what additional constructs we add to the Predicate Calculus, it will still be possible to encounter a query which cannot be specified in the extended language. A solution to this problem will be suggested in a later section.

11.2. Prolog-Like Languages

In the section on the calculus for transactions we have used an *insert* operation with the following syntax:

> **insert into** *category* (*relation*$_1$: *expression*$_1$, . . . , *relation*$_k$: *expression*$_k$)
> **where** *condition*

Let us consider now a program which iteratively performs a set of **insert** statements and terminates when there is nothing more to insert.

Example:

Let *ITEM-NAME* be a concrete category of strings.

The following program augments the table *COMPONENT* by all the pairs of items which directly or indirectly contain one another.

> **repeat**
>
> > **insert into** *COMPONENT*

> (*CONTAINING-ITEM*: containing,
>
> *CONTAINED-ITEM*: contained)
>
> **where**
>
> > **exists** intermediate **in** *ITEM-NAME*:
> >
> > > *COMPONENT* (*CONTAINING-ITEM*: containing,
> > > *CONTAINED-ITEM*: intermediate) **and**
> > >
> > > *COMPONENT* (*CONTAINING-ITEM*: intermediate,
> > > *CONTAINED-ITEM*: contained)
>
> **until** nothing new has been inserted in the last iteration

A **Prolog-like database program** is an equivalent of a program with one *repeat* loop enclosing several *insert* statements:

> **repeat**
>
> > *insert-statements*
>
> **until** nothing new has been inserted in the last iteration

(We interpret the *insert* operation as adding only information which is not already there.)

Normally, Prolog-like languages allow only very primitive conditions within the *insert* statements: they do not allow the quantifier "**for every**" or complex expressions within those conditions. In exchange for this limitation, the Prolog-like languages can perform the program by a much faster algorithm than the obvious straightforward implementation of the loop.

A Prolog-like program can be used for retrieval of information from the database if instead of inserting new objects into the existing categories in the database we perform insertion into output tables.

> *Example:*
>
> The following program will produce a table *OUTPUT-COMPONENT* which will be composed of all the pairs of items which directly or indirectly contain one another. The input is the original table COMPONENT, which is composed of the pairs of items directly containing one another.
>
> > **repeat**
> >
> > > **insert into** *OUTPUT-COMPONENT*
> > >
> > > > (*CONTAINING-ITEM*: containing,
> > > >
> > > > *CONTAINED-ITEM*: contained)
> > >
> > > **where**

>   *COMPONENT* (*CONTAINING-ITEM*: containing,
>   *CONTAINED-ITEM*: contained);
>
>   **insert into** *OUTPUT-COMPONENT*
>
>   (*CONTAINING-ITEM*: containing,
>
>   *CONTAINED-ITEM*: contained)
>
>   **where**
>
>   **exists** intermediate **in** *ITEM-NAME*:
>
>   *COMPONENT* (*CONTAINING-ITEM*: containing,
>   *CONTAINED-ITEM*: intermediate) **and**
>
>   *OUTPUT-COMPONENT* (*CONTAINING-ITEM*:
>   intermediate, *CONTAINED-ITEM*: contained)
>
>   **until** nothing new has been inserted in the last iteration
>
>   (* The first insert statement will be performed only once. *)

The above description of Prolog-like languages has a strong procedural flavor because of the "**repeat** · · · **until**" loop. We can describe a Prolog-like program nonprocedurally — as an assertion which links the relations of the input database and the relations to be produced as the output of the query.

> *Example:*
>
> The above query can be nonprocedurally regarded as the following assertion:
>
> **for every** containing **in** *ITEM-NAME*:
>
>   **for every** contained **in** *ITEM-NAME*:
>
>   **if** *COMPONENT*
>
>   (*CONTAINING-ITEM*: containing,
>
>   *CONTAINED-ITEM*: contained)
>
>   **then** *OUTPUT-COMPONENT*
>
>   (*CONTAINING-ITEM*: containing,
>
>   *CONTAINED-ITEM*: contained)
>
> **and**
>
> **for every** containing **in** *ITEM-NAME*:
>
>   **for every** contained **in** *ITEM-NAME*:

for every intermediate **in** *ITEM-NAME*:

if

> *COMPONENT* (*CONTAINING-ITEM*: containing,
> *CONTAINED-ITEM*: intermediate) **and**

> *OUTPUT-COMPONENT* (*CONTAINING-ITEM*: intermediate,
> *CONTAINED-ITEM*: contained)

then *OUTPUT-COMPONENT*

(*CONTAINING-ITEM*: containing,

CONTAINED-ITEM: contained)

The pragmatic meaning of such an assertion is:

> Output a set of tuples which, when regarded as a table *OUTPUT-COMPONENT*, would make the above assertion come true. Do not output any extra tuples which are not needed to make the assertion *true*.

The Prolog-like languages described above are sometimes referred to as **fifth-generation database languages**, although this term can be broadly applied to all powerful nonprocedural database languages, particularly the languages based on Predicate Calculus.

The actual syntax of Prolog-like languages is usually somewhat different from the "insert" notation shown above, but it is equivalent to that notation. The loop specification is omitted. The quantifiers "exists" in the conditions are implicit. (No ambiguity arises since the "for every" quantifier is normally not allowed as a part of the insert conditions in Prolog-like languages.)

Example:

The above program would be written as follows in some Prolog-like languages:

> *OUTPUT-COMPONENT*(*CONTAINING-ITEM*: containing,
> *CONTAINED-ITEM*: contained) ←

> > *COMPONENT* (*CONTAINING-ITEM*: containing,
> > *CONTAINED-ITEM*: contained);

> *OUTPUT-COMPONENT* (*CONTAINING-ITEM*: containing,
> *CONTAINED-ITEM*: contained) ←

> > *COMPONENT* (*CONTAINING-ITEM*: containing,
> > *CONTAINED-ITEM*: intermediate),

> *OUTPUT-COMPONENT* (*CONTAINING-ITEM*: intermediate,
> *CONTAINED-ITEM*: contained)

The expressive power of Prolog-like database languages, that is, the ability of these languages to express a wide range of queries, depends, in part, on what is allowed to appear on the right side of the ← statement. However, even if we allow arbitrary first-order Predicate Calculus assertions on the right side of the statements, there would still be many reasonable queries which cannot be specified in the Prolog-like database languages without sacrificing the nonprocedurality of the language.* The cause of such limitation is the limit to what one can do with the "insert until nothing new comes" construct.

11.3. The Maximal Expressive Power

A nonprocedural language more powerful than the Prolog-like database languages has been proposed by N. Rishe.†

In this language, a query is specified simply as an assertion about the relations to appear in the output, linking those relations to the information in the input instantaneous database.

Example:

The previously considered example on page 358, which was an assertion equivalent to a Prolog program producing the table of the pairs of components indirectly containing one another, is also an example of a query specification in the language discussed in this section.

Example:

The following is an assertion stating that the output shall display the item which indirectly contains all the items (if such a superitem exists).

We assume that the userview has

☐ *contains* — relation from *ITEM-NAME* to *ITEM-NAME*   (*m:m*)

The output is the category *SUPERITEM-OUTPUT*. This category will have at most one object — the superitem. In the formulation of the query we define a

---

* Some Prolog-like languages allow specification of functions, which increases their expressive power. However, the use of those functions, which act like subroutines logically defined by the user, greatly reduces the nonprocedurality of the language.

† N. Rishe. "Postconditional Semantics of Data Base Queries." *Mathematical Foundations of Programming Semantics*. A. Melton (ed.). Lecture Notes in Computer Science, vol. 239. Springer-Verlag, New York, 1986.

temporary relation *INDIRECTLY-CONTAINS*. The assertion states that this temporary relation relates all the pairs of items indirectly containing one another. (This includes an item containing itself.)   This temporary relation will not become a part of the output.

for every item **in** *ITEM-NAME*:

>   item *INDIRECTLY-CONTAINS* item

and

for every containing **in** *ITEM-NAME*:

>   **for every** contained **in** *ITEM-NAME*:

>>   **for every** intermediate **in** *ITEM-NAME*:

>>>   **if**   containing *CONTAINS* intermediate **and**
>>>   intermediate *INDIRECTLY-CONTAINS* contained

>>   **then** containing *INDIRECTLY-CONTAINS* contained

and

for every si **in** *ITEM-NAME*:

>   **if**

>>   (**for every** item **in** *ITEM-NAME*:

>>>   si *INDIRECTLY-CONTAINS* item)

>   **then** si **is a** *SUPERITEM-OUTPUT*

The pragmatic meaning of such an assertion is:

>   Create an instantaneous relation *INDIRECTLY-CONTAINS* and an instantaneous category *SUPERITEM-OUTPUT*, which would make the above assertion come true. Output the *SUPERITEM-OUTPUT* category and discard the temporary relation *INDIRECTLY-CONTAINS*. Do not output any extra objects or relationships which are not needed to make the assertion *true*.

Example:

The following is an assertion specifying the relation *CAN-IMPROVE-THE-GRADES-OF*.

for every s **in** *STUDENT*:

    for every i **in** *INSTRUCTOR*:

        (**if** i *TAUGHT* s

            then i *CAN-IMPROVE-THE-GRADES-OF* s) **and**

        for every middleman **in** *STUDENT*:

            if   i *TAUGHT* middleman **and**
                  middleman *CAN-IMPROVE-THE-GRADES-OF* s

            then i *CAN-IMPROVE-THE-GRADES-OF* s

In a sense, this language is a superset of the Prolog-like database languages. A Prolog-like database program can also be regarded as an assertion about the output relations. However, the Prolog-like languages allow only *some* assertions: those assertions which are equivalent to the "insert until nothing new comes" interpretation.

Example:

It is known that several items have more components than the item CAR. Display one of those items.

    exists output-item **in** *OUTPUT-ITEM*:

        (**count** car-component **where** 'Car' *CONTAINS*: car-component) <

        (**count** item-component **where** output-item *CONTAINS* item-
           component)

The aggregate functions, like the function **count** in the above example, are not strictly necessary in the language. Every query can be expressed without aggregate functions.* The aggregate function can be regarded as convenient abbreviations for nonaggregate constructs.

---

  * The following is a specification of the query of the previous example without the aggregate function count.

exists output-item **in** *OUTPUT-ITEM*:

    (* There is a relation *MATCHES* between the components of CAR and the components of the output-item. It is m:1 and "total," but not "onto" the components of the output-item: there exists at least one extra component of the output-item not matched by a component of CAR. *)

The following is an informal description of the semantics of a query in this language. This is also a description of the semantics of the Prolog-like languages (since every Prolog-like program can be regarded as an assertion, the Prolog-like programs are a subset of all queries expressed by assertions).

- A query is an assertion about a virtual instantaneous database. This virtual database exists only in the programmer's mind. The virtual database contains all of the information of the input instantaneous database and, in addition, the output which the query should produce. Thus, the schema of the virtual database consists of all the relations (including the categories) of the input database and all the relations of the output. The output relations may form the headings of columns and tables in the output. One query can produce several tables in its output or, in general, any interrelated information, like a whole instantaneous database.

  In addition to the input and output relations, the virtual database may contain intermediate relations which are not in the input or the output but which are needed to establish connection between the input and the output.

- Now, consider all the potential virtual databases which satisfy the assertion. It is possible that there is no such database at all. Then there is no output. Pragmatically, this means that the program goes into an infinite loop.

- It is possible that there is exactly one such virtual database. The output relations are then extracted from the virtual database and delivered to the user.

- It is possible that there are several such virtual databases satisfying the assertion, $vdb_1, vdb_2, \ldots$, but all the information contained in vdb_1 is also contained in the rest of them. That means that, in addition to the minimally required output, the other

---

(**for every** cc **in** *ITEM-NAME*:   **if** 'CAR' *CONTAINS* cc **then**

    exists oc **in** *ITEM-NAME*:

        output-item *CONTAINS* oc **and** cc *MATCHES* oc **and**

        (* The car-component cc matches with nothing else but oc *)

            for every z **in** *ITEM-NAME*:   **if** cc *MATCHES* z **then** z=oc)

  and

  (* There is at least one *extra* component of the output item *)

    exists oc **in** *ITEM-NAME*:   output-item *CONTAINS* oc **and**

      not exists cc **in** *ITEM-NAME*:   cc MATCHES oc

The pragmatic meaning of such an assertion is:

Create an instantaneous relation *MATCHES* and an instantaneous category *OUTPUT-ITEM* which would make the above assertion come true. Output the *OUTPUT-ITEM* category and discard the temporary relation *MATCHES*. Do not output any extra objects or relationships which are not needed to make the assertion *true*.

virtual databases contain some extra, possibly irrelevant, information. The database vdb_1 is minimal in the sense of information content. Only the minimal possible virtual database will be taken into account by the language interpreter.

- It is possible that there are several possible virtual databases satisfying the assertion where none of the virtual databases contains all the information of any other. This means that there is no single minimal database. In this case, all of those databases are regarded as equally suitable to produce the output for the user. The system will select one of them.

The last case appears in **nondeterministic** queries — the queries in which the user does not wish to bother to specify what exact output should be received, but only specifies some requirements to be satisfied by the output.

Example:

Display the last name of *one* student.

     exists s **in** *STUDENT*:

          s.*LAST-NAME* **is an** *OUTPUT-STUDENT-NAME*

The capability of nondeterministic specification saves the user's effort and also allows for a greater optimization potential.

Example:

In the above example, the system will fetch one student which happens to the first in the physical access path to the database. Had the user specified a specific student, it would take longer to deliver that student from the database.

This language has no limitation of expressive power — every query that can be programmed in any procedural data manipulation language also can be specified nonprocedurally in Rishe's language.[*]

While the language can express any query, this generality might also allow for unreasonable queries, that is, queries which would not make any sense.

---

[*] Formally, this means that if we encode the databases by integers, then every partial recursive function would be expressible. The encoding, though, is not trivial, since the databases are unordered sets of information, and moreover, contain abstract objects which can be distinguished from each other only by relations in which the objects participate.

> *Example:*
>
> A query to find the average social security number of two persons makes no sense.
>
> A query to find the average between two persons, as if they were integers, makes even less sense.

It may be desirable to prevent the user from asking such queries. Such a constraint would both eliminate some user errors and improve the efficiency of the system. An interesting feature of the language is the capability to restrict itself to the reasonable queries by accepting criteria of reasonability as a parameter. When such criteria are given as a parameter, those queries which are unreasonable according to the criteria are syntactically screened out. The criteria are defined in terms of the scalar operators which make sense in different concrete categories.

> *Example:*
>
> The operators meaningful on the final grades are $+$, $-$, $>$, $<$, and so on. There are no operators except the equality verification $(=, \neq)$ on the IDs of the students. Constants of the type *STUDENT-ID* are allowed. (Unlike that, there are no constants in the abstract categories.)

The sublanguage restricted according to the reasonability criteria can express *every* reasonable query that can be programmed in any procedural language.†

The language can also be used to specify integrity constraints, inference rules, userviews, and update transactions. An update transaction can be specified as two sets of facts: a set of old facts to remove from the database and a set of new facts to insert into the database. Those two sets of facts are extracted from an output of a query. The output of a query (specified as an assertion) may contain relations marked with a suffix -insert. The facts of those relations are to be inserted. The facts of the relations marked with the suffix -delete are to be deleted.

---

† Formally, the set of *reasonable* queries is defined in terms of isomorphisms of databases. Two instantaneous databases are isomorphic if they cannot be distinguished by means of the available operators. A query is reasonable if for isomorphic inputs it produces isomorphic outputs.

Example:

Remove all the grades.

> **for every** e **in** *ENROLLMENT*:
>
> > e   *FINAL-GRADE-delete*   s.*FINAL-GRADE*

Example:

Create a new student Veronica. Assume that the category *EXISTING-OBJECT* is the supercategory of all the categories.

> **exists** s **in** *STUDENT-insert*:
>
> > **not** (s **is an** *EXISTING-OBJECT*) **and**
> >
> > s   *FIRST-NAME-insert*   'Veronica'

(The condition '**not** (s **is an** *EXISTING-OBJECT*)' can be stated implicitly.)

Example:

Enroll every student in the *Databases* course. It is assumed that at least one offering of the course exists.

> **for every** s **in** *STUDENT*:
>
> > **exists** e **in** *ENROLLMENT-insert*:
> >
> > > **not** (e **is an** *EXISTING-OBJECT*) **and**
> > >
> > > e.*THE-STUDENT-insert*=s **and**
> > >
> > > e.*THE-OFFERING-insert.THE-COURSE.NAME* = 'Databases'

A problem with this language is that there is no practical efficient implementation for the language. Nevertheless, the language is useful for the following purposes:

- As a high-level language in which to write the specification of a problem before that specification is translated into a lower-level program in the language supported by the actual DBMS

- As a language model from which sublanguages can be derived and efficiently implemented

- As a tool to compare and evaluate the power of practical database languages

- As a tool to reason about databases

11.4. User-Friendly Interfaces

The Predicate Calculus languages may be unfriendly to the unsophisticated user. However, user-friendly **"syntactic sugar"** can, and has been, added to some Predicate Calculus languages to enhance their usability. This "sugar" can range from simple syntactic abbreviations to menu-driven languages and to natural language interfaces in which the user can enter a query in what might look like plain English or Swahili.

An interesting user interface to a Relational Calculus-based language is the **Query-By-Example** language developed by M. Zloof and now used commercially. In this language, the user specifies a query by drawing, with the system's assistance, tables on a two-dimensional screen.

Example:

The following table will be an on-the-screen specification of the query

'Print the names and the seasons of the course offerings prior to 1900.'

COURSE OFFERING

INSTRUCTOR-ID	COURSE-NAME	YEAR	SEASON
	print	<1990	**print**

Example:

The following table will be an on-the-screen specification of the query

'Print the names and the seasons of the course offerings by the instructors who also taught *Databases*.'

This query uses a variable _dbinstructor in order to specify a relationship (join) between different rows of the table, so that the related rows have the same value in the column *INSTRUCTOR-ID*. The variables in this language are preceded by an underscore (_).

COURSE OFFERING

INSTRUCTOR-ID	COURSE-NAME	YEAR	SEASON
_dbinstructor _dbinstructor	**print** Databases	<1990	**print**

Some Prolog-based languages have user-friendly interfaces to subsets of the languages. The Rishe language described in the previous section also has a user-friendly interface which can be used only for intermediate specifications of data manipulation tasks — it is not used to write the actual programs since there is no efficient implementation.

CHAPTER 12

BIBLIOGRAPHY

Section 1 of this chapter gives annotated references to papers on issues of semantic modeling addressed in this book. Section 2 is a listing of recent books on databases.

12.1. References to Semantic Modeling Papers

The cornerstone of the contemporary theory and technology of databases was the development of the Relational Data Model in [Codd-70]. The use of the predicate calculus for relational databases was proposed in [Codd-71].

The recent development of the new generation of data models — the semantic models — offers a simple, natural, implementation-independent, flexible, and nonredundant specification of information and its semantic aspects. Since the original idea of [Abrial-74], many semantic data models have been studied in the computer science literature. Many semantic models have been surveyed in [Hull&King-87] and [Peckham&Maryanski-88]. Although somewhat differing in their terminology and their selection of tools used to describe the semantics of the real world, the various semantic models are roughly equivalent and have several common principles:

- The entities ("abstract objects") of the real world are represented in the database in a manner transparent to the user.

- The entities are classified into types, or categories, which need not be disjoint. Meta-relations of inclusion are defined between the categories, implying inheritance of properties.

- Logically explicit relationships are specified among abstract objects (e.g., "person p_1 is the mother of person p2") and between abstract and concrete objects (e.g., "person p_1 has first name 'Jack'"). There are no direct relationships among the concrete objects. In most semantic models, only binary relations are allowed, since they provide the full power of semantic expressiveness.

This book is based on the Semantic Binary Model (SBM) ([Rishe-87-RM], [Rishe-89-SD], [Rishe-90-SB]), a descendant of the model of [Abrial-74]. Models similar to SBM have been studied in: [Bracchi&al.-76], [Nijssen-77], [Nijssen-81], [Breutman&al.-79], [Senko-78], [Mark-83], [Mark-87], [Mark-89], [Meersman&Assche-83], [Vermeir-83], and others. SBM does not have as rich an arsenal of tools for semantic description as can be found in some other semantic models, such as the IFO model [Abiteboul&Hull-84], SDM [Hammer&McLeod-81], the Functional Model ([Kerschberg&Pacheco-76], [Shipman-81], [Chan&al.-82]), SEMBASE [King-84], NIAM ([Nijssen-81], [Verheijen&VanBekkum-82], [Leung&Nijssen-87]), Taxis [Nixon&al.-87], SIM [Jagannathan&al.-88], SAM [Su&Lo-80], OSAM* [Su-88-OS], GEM [Tsur&Zaniolo-84], GENESIS [Batory&al.-88], ER [Chen-76]. Nevertheless, the SBM has a small set of sufficient simple tools by which all of the semantic descriptors of the other models can be constructed. This makes SBM easier to use for the novice, easier to implement, and usable for delineation and study of the common properties of the semantic models.

Typically, semantic data models have been experimentally implemented as interfaces to database management systems in other data models, (e.g., the relational or the network model). (Although, there are less typical, direct implementations, e.g., [Lien&al.-81], [Chan&al.-82], [Benneworth&al.-81].) The efficiency of an interface implementation is limited to that of the conventional DBMS and is normally much worse due to the interface overhead. The direct implementations were previously believed to be less efficient than the conventional systems. However, the semantic models have potential for much more efficient implementation than the conventional data models, as was shown in [Lin&al.-89], [Rishe-89-EO], and [Rishe-91-FS].

The use of semantic models for the design of relational schemas has been studied in [Brodie&al.-84-CM], [Chen-76], [King&McLeod-85], [Teorey&al.-86], [Leung&Nijssen-87], [Shoval/Even-Chaime-87], [Verheijen&VanBekkum-82], [DeTroyer&Meersman-86], [Shoval-85], and other works. A graphical interactive system for the design of semantic databases is discussed in [Shoval&al.-88],

Nonprocedural languages for semantic databases have been studied in [Meersman-81], [Shipman-81], [Senko-78], [Rishe-86-PS], [Rishe-91-PC], and others. Extended Pascal for semantic databases is defined in [Rishe-88-TM]. Data definition languages integrated with data manipulation languages for semantic databases have been studied in [Roussopoulos&Mark-85].

[Abiteboul&Hull-84] S. Abiteboul and R. Hull. "IFO: A Formal Semantic Database Model," *Proceedings of ACM SIGACT-SIGMOD Symposium on Principles of Database Systems*, 1984.

[Abrial-74] J.R. Abrial, "Data Semantics," in J.W. Klimbie and K.L. Koffeman (eds.), *Data Base Management*. North Holland, 1974.

[Batory&*al.*-88] D.S. Batory, T.Y. Leung, and T.E. Wise. "Implementation Concepts for an Extensible Data Model and Data Language." *ACM Transactions on Database Systems*, vol. 13, no. 3, September 1988, pp. 231-262.

[Benneworth&*al.*-81] R.L. Benneworth, C.D. Bishop, C.J.M. Turnbull, W.D. Holman, F.M. Monette. "The Implementation of GERM, an Entity-Relationship Data Base Management System." *Proceedings of the Seventh International Conference on Very Large Data Bases*. (C. Zaniolo & C. Delobel, eds.) IEEE Computer Society Press, 1981, pp. 465-477.

[Bracchi&*al.*-76] G. Bracchi, P. Paolini, G. Pelagatti. "Binary Logical Associations in Data Modelings." In G.M. Nijssen (ed.), *Modeling in Data Base Management Systems*. IFIP Working Conference on Modeling in DBMSs, 1976.

[Breutman&*al.*-79] B. Breutman, E. Falkenberg, and R. Mauer. "CSL: A Conceptual Schema Language." *Proceedings IFIP TC 2 WG 2.6 Working Conference*, March 1979.

[Brodie&*al.*-84-CM] M.L. Brodie, J. Mylopoulos, and J.W. Schmidt (eds.). *On Conceptual Modelling*. Springer-Verlag, New York, 1984.

[Chan&*al.*-82] A. Chan, S. Danberg, S. Fox, W. Lin, A. Nori, and D.R. Ries. "Storage and Access Structures to Support a Semantic Data Model." *Proceedings of the Eighth International Conference on Very Large Data Bases*. IEEE Computer Society Press, 1982.

[Chen-76] P. Chen. "The Entity-Relationship Model: Toward a Unified View of Data." *ACM Trans. Database Syst. 1*, 1, pp. 9-36.

[Codd-70] E. Codd. "A Relational Model for Large Shared Data Banks." *Communications of ACM*, 13:6.

[Codd-71] E. Codd. "A Data Base Sublanguage Founded on the Relational Calculus." *Proceedings of the ACM SIGFIDET Workshop on Data Description, Access, and Control*, ACM, 1971.

[DeTroyer&Meersman-86] O. de Troyer and R. Meersman. "Transforming Conceptual Schema Semantics to Relational Database Applications." *Fourth Scandinavian Research Seminar on Information Modeling and Data Base Management*, 1986.

[Hammer&McLeod-81] M. Hammer and D. McLeod. "Database Description with SDM: A Semantic Database Model," *ACM Transactions on Database Systems*, vol. 6, no. 3, 1981, pp. 351-386.

[Hull&King-87] R. Hull and R. King. "Semantic Data Models." *ACM Computing Surveys, 20*, 3, pp. 153-189.

[Jagannathan&*al.*-88] D. Jagannathan, R.L. Guck, B.L. Fritchman, J.P. Thompson, D.M. Tolbert. "SIM: A Database System Based on Semantic Model." *Proceedings of SIGMOD International Conference on Management of Data.* Chicago, June 1-3, 1988. ACM-Press, 1988.

[Kerschberg&Pacheco-76] L. Kerschberg and J.E.S. Pacheco. "A Functional Data Base Model." Tech. Rep., Pontificia Univ. Catolica do Rio de Janeiro, Brazil, 1976.

[King-84] R. King. "SEMBASE: A Semantic DBMS." *Proceedings of the First Workshop on Expert Database Systems.* Univ. of South Carolina, 1984, pp. 151-171.

[King&McLeod-85] R. King and D. McLeod. "A Database Design Methodology and Tool for Information Systems." *ACM Transactions on Office Information Systems, 3,* 1, pp. 2-21.

[Leung&Nijssen-87] C.M.R. Leung and G.M. Nijssen. "From a NIAM Conceptual Schema into the Optimal SQL Relational Database Schema." *Aust. Comput. J.*, vol. 19, no. 2.

[Lien&*al.*-81] Y.E. Lien, J.E. Shopiro, S. Tsur. "DSIS — A Database System with Interrelational Semantics." *Proceedings of the Seventh International Conference on Very Large Data Bases.* (C. Zaniolo & C. Delobel, eds.) IEEE Computer Society Press, 1981, pp 465-477.

[Lin&*al.*-89] C. Lin, L. Mark, T. Sellis, and C. Faloutsos. "Query Optimization in the Binary Relationship Model." *Data and Knowledge Engineering.* September 1989, pp. 195-221.

[Mark-83] L. Mark. "What Is Binary Relationship Approach?" *Entity-Relationship Approach to Software Engineering.* North-Holland, 1983.

[Mark-87] L. Mark. "Defining Views in the Binary Relationship Model." *Information Systems*, vol. 12, no. 3, 1987.

[Mark-89] L. Mark. "A Graphical Query Language for the Binary Relationship Model" *Information Systems*, vol. 14, no. 3, 1989.

[Meersman-81] R. Meersman. "RIDL: A Query System as Support for Information Analysis." *ECODO 32*, September 1981.

[Meersman&Assche-83] R. Meersman and F. Van Assche. "Modeling and Manipulating Production Data Bases in Terms of Semantic Nets." *8th International Joint Conference on Artificial Intelligence, Karlsruhe,* 1983, pp. 325-329.

[Nijssen-77] G.M. Nijssen. "Current Issues in Conceptual Schema Concepts." *Architecture and Models in Data Base Management Systems* North-Holland, 1977.

[Nijssen-81] G.M. Nijssen "An architecture for knowledge base systems," Proceedings, SPOT-2 Conference, Stockholm, 1981.

[Nixon&*al.*-87] B. Nixon, L. Chung, I. Lauzen, A. Borgida, and M. Stanley. "Implementation of a Compiler for a Semantic Data Model: Experience with Taxis."

In *Proceedings of the ACM SIGMOD Conference* ACM, 1987.

[Peckham&Maryanski-88] J. Peckham and F. Maryanski. "Semantic Database Modeling: Survey, Applications, and Research Issues." *ACM Computing Surveys, 19*, 3, pp. 201-260.

[Rishe-86-PS] N. Rishe. "Postconditional Semantics of Data Base Queries." *Lecture Notes in Computer Science, vol. 239 (Mathematical Foundations of Programming Semantics.* A. Melton, ed.), Springer-Verlag, 1986, pp. 275-295.

[Rishe-87-RM] N. Rishe. "On Representation of Medical Knowledge by a Binary Data Model." *Journal of Mathematical and Computer Modelling,* vol. 8 (1987), pp. 623-626.

[Rishe-88-TM] N. Rishe. "Transaction-Management System in a Fourth-Generation Language for Semantic Databases." In: *Mini and Microcomputers: From Micros to Supercomputers* (Proceedings of the ISMM International Conference on Mini and Microcomputers, Miami Beach, December 14-16, 1988; M.H. Hamza, ed.), Acta Press, 1988, pp. 92-95.

[Rishe-89-EO] N. Rishe. "Efficient Organization of Semantic Databases" *Foundations of Data Organization and Algorithms.* (FODO-89) W. Litwin and H.-J. Schek, eds. *Springer-Verlag Lecture Notes in Computer Science*, vol. 367, pp. 114-127, 1989.

[Rishe-89-SD] N. Rishe. "Semantic Database Management: From Microcomputers to Massively Parallel Database Machines." Keynote Paper, *Proceedings of the Sixth Symposium on Microcomputer and Microprocessor Applications*, Budapest, October 17-19, 1989, pp 1-12.

[Rishe-90-SB] N. Rishe. "Semantic Binary Database Model." *HK Computer Journal, 6, 11* (1990), pp. 30-34.

[Rishe-91-FS] N. Rishe. "A File Structure for Semantic Databases." *Information Systems,* 16, *4* (1991), pp. 375-385.

[Rishe-91-PC] N. Rishe and W. Sun. "A Predicate Calculus Language for Queries and Transactions in Semantic Databases." In: *Databases: Theory, Design and Applications.* IEEE Computer Society Press, 1991 (N. Rishe, S. Navathe, and D. Tal, eds.) pp. 204-221.

[Roussopoulos&Mark-85] N. Roussopoulos and L. Mark. "Schema Manipulation in Self-Describing and Self-Documenting Data Models." *International Journal of Computer and Information Sciences*, vol.14, no.1, 1985.

[Senko-78] M.F. Senko. "Foral LP: Design and Implementation." *Proceedings of Very Large Data Base Conference*, 1978.

[Shipman-81] D.W. Shipman. "The Functional Data Model and the Data Language DAPLEX." *ACM Transactions on Database Systems*, vol. 6, no. 1, pp. 140-173, 1981.

[Shoval-85] P. Shoval. "Essential Information Structure Diagrams and Database Schema Design." *Information Systems*, vol. 10, no. 4, 1985.

[Shoval&*al.*-88] P. Shoval, E. Gudes, and M. Goldstein. "GISD: A Graphical Interactive System for Conceptual Database Design." *Information Systems*, vol. 13, no.1, 1988.

[Shoval/Even-Chaime-87] P. Shoval and M. Even-Chaime. "ADDS: A Systems for Automatic Database Schema Design Based on the Binary-Relationship Model." *Data and Knowledge Engineering 2*, 1987.

[Su-88-OS] S. Su. "An Object-Oriented Semantic Association Model (OSAM*) for CAD/CAM Databases." In: *AI in Industrial Engineering and Manufacturing: Theoretical Issues and Applications* (Soyster and Kashyap, eds.), 1988.

[Su&Lo-80] S.Y.W. Su and D.H. Lo. "A Semantic Association Model for Conceptual Database Design." In: P.P. Chen (ed.), *Entity-Relationship Approach to Systems Analysis and Design*, North-Holland, Amsterdam, 1980, pp. 147-171.

[Teorey&*al.*-86] T.J. Teorey, D. Yang, and J.P. Fry. "A Logical Design Methodology for Relational Databases using the Extended Entity-Relationship Model." *ACM Computing Surveys, 18*, 2, pp. 197-222.

[Tsur&Zaniolo-84] S. Tsur and C. Zaniolo. "An Implementation of GEM — Supporting a Semantic Data Model on a Relational Backend." In: *Proceedings of ACM SIGMOD Intl. Conference on Management of Data, May 1984*.

[Verheijen&VanBekkum-82] G.M.A. Verheijen and J. Van Bekkum. "NIAM - An Information Analysis Method," In: *Information Systems Design Methodologies: A Comparative Review*, T.W. Olle et al., eds., IFIP, North-Holland, 1982.

[Vermeir-83] D. Vermeir. "Semantic Hierarchies and Abstraction in Conceptual Schemata" *Information Systems*, vol.8, no.2, 1983.

12.2. General Database Bibliography

ACM. *Proceedings of the 1989 ACM SIGMOD International Conference on the Management of Data, Portland, Oregon.* Baltimore, MD: Association of Computing Machinery, 1989.

ACM. *Proceedings of the Eighth ACM SIGACT-SIGMOD-SIGART Symposium on Principles of Database Systems, March 29-31, 1989, Philadelphia, Pennsylvania.* Baltimore, MD: Association of Computing Machinery, 1989.

ACM. *Proceedings of the Ninth ACM SIGACT-SIGMOD-SIGART Symposium on Principles of Database Systems, April 2-4, 1990, Nashville, Tennessee.* Baltimore, MD: Association of Computing Machinery, 1990.

ACM. *Proceedings of the Sixth ACM SIGACT-SIGMOD-SIGART Symposium on Principles of Database Systems, March 23-25, 1987, San Diego, California.* Baltimore, MD: Association of Computing Machinery, 1987.

ACM. *Proceedings, Second International Symposium on Databases in Parallel and Distributed Systems: July 2-4, 1990, Trinity College, Dublin, Ireland.* Baltimore, MD: Association of Computing Machinery, 1990.

ACM. *SIGIR 89: Proceedings of the Twelfth Annual International ACMSIGIR Conference on Research and Development in Information Retrieval, Cambridge, Massachusetts, U.S.A., June 25-28, 1989.* Baltimore, MD: Association of Computing Machinery, 1989.

Abiteboul, S., P.C. Fischer, H.J. Schek. *Nested relations and complex objects in databases.* Berlin; New York: Springer-Verlag, 1989.

Abiteboul, S., P.C. Kanellakis (edit.) *ICDT 90: Third International Conference on Database Theory, Paris, France, December 12-14, 1990: proceedings.* Berlin; New York: Springer-Verlag, 1990.

Alagic, Suad. *Object-oriented database programming.* New York: Springer-Verlag, 1989.

Andersen, Dick, Bill Weil. *1-2-3 database techniques.* Carmel, IN: Que Corp., 1989.

Armenskii, A.E. *Tenzornye metody postroeniia informatsionnykh sistem.* Moskva: Nauka, 1989.

Atkinson, Malcolm P., Peter Buneman, Ronald Morrison (edit.) *Data types and persistence.* Berlin; New York: Springer-Verlag, 1988.

Atre, Shaku. *Data base: structured techniques for design, performance, and management.* 2d ed. New York: Wiley, 1988.

Austing, Richard H., Lillian N. Cassel. *File organization and access, from data to information.* Lexington, MA: DC Heath, 1988.

Bagchi, Tapan P., Vinay K. Chaudhri. *Interactive relational database design: a logic programming implementation.* Berlin; New York: Springer-Verlag, 1989.

Bancilhon, Francois, Peter Buneman (edit.) *Advances in database programming languages.* New York, NY: ACM Press: Reading, MA: Addison-Wesley, 1990.

Barker, Richard. *CASE*Method: entity relationship modelling.* Wokingham, England: Reading, MA: Addison-Wesley, 1990.

Barker, Richard. *CASE*Method: tasks and deliverables.* Wokingham, England: Reading, MA: Addison-Wesley, 1990.

Batini, C., S. Ceri, and S.B. Navathe. *Database design: an entity relationship approach.* Benjamin-Cummings, 1990.

Batini, Carlo (edit.) *Entity-relationship approach: a bridge to the user: proceedings of the Seventh International Conference on Entity-Relationship Approach, Rome, Italy, November 16-18, 1988.* Amsterdam; New York: North-Holland; New York, NY: Elsevier, 1989.

Beeri, C., J.W. Schmidt, U. Dayal (edit.) *Proceedings of the Third International Conference on Data and Knowledge Bases — Improving Usability and Responsiveness: June 28-30, 1988, Jerusalem, Israel.* San Matheo, CA: Morgan Kaufmann, 1988.

Benson, James A., Bella Hass Weinberg (edit.) *Gateway software and natural language interfaces: options for online searching.* Ann Arbor, MI: Pierian Press, 1988.

Benyon, David. *Information and data modelling.* Oxford; Boston: Blackwell Scientific
    Publications: Brookline Village, MA: Distributors, U.S.A., Publishers' Business
    Services, 1990.

Bernstein, Philip A., Vassos Hadzilacos, Nathan Goodman. *Concurrency control and
    recovery in database systems.* Reading, MA: Addison-Wesley, 1987.

Bielawski, Larry, Robert Lewand. *Intelligent systems design: expert systems, hypermedia,
    and database technologies.* New York: Wiley, 1991.

Birrell, Andrew D., Michael B. Jones, and Edward P. Wobber. *A simple and efficient
    implementation for small databases.* Palo Alto, CA: Digital Systems Research Center,
    1988.

Biskup, J., et al. *MFDBS 87: 1st Symposium on Mathematical Fundamentals of Database
    Systems, Dresden, GDR, January 19-23, 1987: proceedings.* Berlin; New York:
    Springer-Verlag, 1988.

Blaser, A. (edit.) *Database systems of the 90s: international symposium, Muggelsee,
    Berlin, FRG, November 5-7, 1990: proceedings.* Berlin; New York: Springer-Verlag,
    1990.

Boisgontier, J., and C. Donay. *File handling in Turbo Pascal.* London: Paradigm, 1988.

Boral, H., P. Faudemay (edit.) *Database machines: sixth international workshop, IWDM
    89, Deauville, France, June 19-21, 1989: proceedings.* Berlin; New York: Springer-
    Verlag, 1989.

Brackett, Michael H. *Developing data structured databases.* Englewood Cliffs, NJ:
    Prentice-Hall, 1987.

Brackett, Michael H. *Practical data design.* Englewood Cliffs, NJ: Prentice Hall, 1990.

Braithwaite, Kenmore S. *Database management and control.* New York: Intertext
    Publications: McGraw-Hill, 1990.

Brathwaite, Kenneth S. *Analysis, design, and implementation of data dictionaries.* New
    York: McGraw-Hill, 1988.

Brathwaite, Kenneth S. *Systems design in a database environment.* New York: Intertext
    Publications: McGraw-Hill, 1989.

Brathwaite, Kenneth S. *The data base environment: concepts and applications.* New
    York: Van Nostrand, 1990.

Burns, George. *Database applications in engineering.* Wilmslow: Sigma, 1989.

Cabrera, Luis-Felipe, and Darrell D.E. Long. *Swift: a storage architecture for very large
    objects.* Santa Cruz, CA: University of California, Santa Cruz, Computer Research
    Laboratory, 1989.

Cardenas, A., and D. McLeod (edit.) *Research foundations in object-oriented and
    semantic database systems.* Englewood Cliffs, NJ: Prentice-Hall, 1990.

Ceri, S., G. Gottlob, L. Tanca. *Logic programming and databases.* Berlin; New York:
    Springer-Verlag, 1990.

Cesarini, Francesca, and Silvio Salza (edit.) *Database machine performance: modeling
    methodologies and evaluation strategies.* Berlin; New York: Springer-Verlag, 1987.

Chorafas, Dimitris N. *Handbook of database management and distributed relational
    databases.* 1st ed. Blue Ridge Summit, PA: TAB Books, 1989.

Cobb, Douglas, and Jeff Yocom, et al. *Douglas Cobb's Paradox 3 handbook*. 2d ed. New York: Bantam Books, 1989.

Cobb, Stephen. *Using Reflex: the database manager*. Berkeley, CA: Osborne McGraw-Hill, 1987.

Codd, E.F. *The relational model for database management: version 2*. Reading, MA: Addison-Wesley, 1990.

Condliffe, Susa. *Paradox: a business user's guide*. New York: Wiley, 1989.

Cronin, Daniel J. *Mastering ORACLE: featuring ORACLE's SQL standard*. 1st ed. Indianapolis, IN, U.S.A.: Hayden Books, 1988, 1989.

Date, C.J. *Relational database writings 1985-1989*. Reading, MA: Addison-Wesley, 1990.

Date, C.J. *A guide to INGRES: a user's guide to the INGRES product from Relational Technology Inc*. Reading, MA: Addison-Wesley, 1987.

Date, C.J. *A guide to the SQL standard: a user's guide to the standard relational language SQL*. 2d ed. Reading, MA: Addison-Wesley, 1989.

Date, C.J., and Colin J. White. *A guide to DB2*. 3d ed. Reading, MA: Addison-Wesley, 1989.

Date, C.J., and Colin J. White. *A guide to SQL/DS*. Reading, MA: Addison-Wesley, 1989.

Dayal, Umeshwar, and Irv Traiger (edit.) *Proceedings of Association for Computing Machinery Special Interest Group on Management of Data: 1987 Annual Conference San Francisco May 27-29, 1987*. New York: Association for Computing Machinery, 1987.

DeMaria, Rusel, and Gregory B. Salcedo. *Elementary Paradox*. Radnor, PA: Compute! Books, 1990.

DeVita, Joseph. *The database experts' guide to FOCUS*. New York, NY: Intertext Publications: McGraw-Hill, 1988.

Debenham, John K. *Knowledge systems design*. Englewood Cliffs, NJ: Prentice Hall, 1989.

Deen, S.M., G.P. Thomas (edit.) *Data & knowledge base integration*. London: Pitman, 1990.

Deen, S.M., G.P. Thomas (edit.) *Data and knowledge base integration: proceedings of the Working Conference on Data and Knowledge Base Integration held at the University of Keele, England on October 4-5, 1989*. London: Pitman, 1990.

Demetrovics, J., B. Thalheim (edit.) *MFDBS 89: 2d Symposium on Mathematical Fundamentals of Database Systems, Visegrad, Hungary, June 26-30, 1989: proceedings*. Berlin; New York: Springer-Verlag, 1989.

Desai, Bipin C. *An introduction to database systems*. West Publishing Co., 1990.

Diener, Andreas R. *An architecture for distributed databases on workstations*. Zurich: Verlag der Fachvereine, 1987.

Dittrich, K.R. (edit.) *Advances in object-oriented database systems: 2d International Workshop on Object-oriented Database Systems, Bad Munster am Stein-Ebernburg, FRG, September 27-30, 1988, proceedings*. Berlin; New York: Springer-Verlag, 1988.

Downes, P.M. *Practical data analysis.* London: Blenheim, 1989.

Dunlop, Neil. *Working with Q & A: practical techniques in database design.* Glenview, IL: Scott, Foresman, 1987.

Dutka, Alan F., Howard H. Hanson. *Fundamentals of data normalization.* Reading, MA: Addison-Wesley, 1989.

Eliassen, Frank, Jari Veijalainen. *An S-transaction definition language and execution mechanism.* Sankt Augustin: Gesellschaft fur Mathematik und Datenverarbeitung, 1987.

Elmasri, Ramez, Shamkant B. Navathe. *Fundamentals of database systems.* Redwood City, CA: Benjamin/Cummings, 1989.

Fabbri, Tony, A. Robert Schwab, Jr. *Working with DB2, SQL/DS, SQL, and QMF.* 1st ed. Blue Ridge Summit, PA: TAB Books, 1990.

Fidel, Raya. *Database design for information retrieval: a conceptual approach.* New York: Wiley, 1987.

Finkelstein, Clive. *An introduction to information engineering: from strategic planning to information systems.* Sydney; Reading, MA: Addison-Wesley, 1989.

Fitch, Carl, Charles Hinchey, James Larson. *DB2 applications development handbook.* New York: Intertext Publications: McGraw-Hill, 1989.

Fleming, Candace C., Barbara von Halle. *Handbook of relational database design.* Reading, MA: Addison-Wesley, 1989.

Fong, Elizabeth N., and Bruce K. Rosen. *Guide to distributed database management.* Gaithersburg, MD: U.S. Dept. of Commerce, National Bureau of Standards: Washington, DC: For sale: the Supt. of Docs., US GPO., 1988.

Fosdick, Howard. *OS/2 database manager: a developer's guide.* New York: Wiley, 1989.

Fosdick, Howard. *The best book of OS/2 database manager.* 1st ed. Indianapolis, IN: Hayden Books, 1989.

Frank, Lars. *Database: theory and practice.* Workingham, England: Reading, MA: Addison-Wesley, 1988.

Gardarin, Georges, Patrick Valduriez. *Relational databases and knowledge bases.* Reading, MA: Addison-Wesley, 1989.

Gaydasch, Alexander, Jr. *Effective database management.* Englewood Cliffs, NJ: Prentice Hall, 1988.

Geller, Joseph R. *IMS administration, programming, and data base design.* New York: J Wiley, 1989.

Ghosh, Sakti P., Yahiko Kambayashi, and Katsumi Tanaka (edit.) *Foundations of data organization.* New York: Plenum Press, 1987.

Gillenson, Mark L. *Database: step-by-step.* 2d ed. New York: Wiley, 1990.

Gilor, Dov. *SQL/DS performance: techniques for improvement.* New York: Wiley, 1991.

Ginsberg, Allen. *Automatic refinement of expert system knowledge bases.* London: Pitman: San Mateo, CA: Morgan Kaufmann, 1988.

Goley, George F., I.V. *Dynamics of FoxBASE+ programming.* Homewood, IL: Dow Jones-Irwin, 1988.

Grant, John. *Logical introduction to databases.* San Diego: Harcourt Brace Jovanovich, 1987.

Gray, W.A. (edit.) *Proceedings of the Sixth British National Conference on Databases.* Cambridge: New York: Cambridge University Press on behalf of the British Computer Society, 1988.

Gunther, Oliver. *Efficient structures for geometric data management.* Berlin; New York: Springer-Verlag, 1988.

Gupta, Amar (edit.) *Integration of information systems: bridging heterogeneous databases.* New York: IEEE Press, 1989.

Gupta, R., and E. Horowitz (edit.) *Object-oriented databases with applications to CASE, networks, and VLSI CAD.* Englewood Cliffs, NJ: Prentice-Hall, 1990.

Gyssens, M., J. Paredaens, D. Van Gucht. *ICDT 88: 2d International Conference on Database Theory, Bruges, Belgium, August 31-September 2, 1988: proceedings.* Berlin; New York: Springer-Verlag, 1988.

Hansen, Gary W. *Database processing with fourth generation languages.* Cincinnati, OH: South-Western, 1988.

Harrington, Jan L. *Database management with Double Helix 3.0.* New York: Brady: Distributed Prentice Hall Trade, 1990.

Harrington, Jan L. *Database management with Double Helix II for the Macintosh and VAX.* New York: Brady: Distributed Prentice Hall Trade, 1988.

Hartman, Patricia A., Cary N. Prague, and James E. Hammitt. *Paradox programming.* 1st ed. Blue Ridge Summit, PA: Windcrest, 1991.

Hawryszkiewcz, Igor Titus. *The art of database design.* New York: Macmillan, 1990.

Hennerkes, Wilhelm A. *MAXDATA: a time series data base system.* Berlin; New York: Springer-Verlag, 1990.

Heydt, Robert, and Diane Heydt. *DB2 database design and administration: version 2.* New York: Wiley, 1989.

Hinterberger, Hans. *Data density: a powerful abstraction to manage and analyze multivariate data.* Zurich: Verlag der Fachvereine, 1987.

Hixson, Amanda C. *Rapidfile for business users.* Toronto; New York: Bantam, 1987.

Hoechst, Tim, Nicole Melander, Christopher Chabris. *Guide to ORACLE.* New York: Intertext Publications: McGraw-Hill, 1990.

Holloway, Simon. *Data administration.* Aldershot, Hants, England: Gower Technical Press: Brookfield, VT: Gower, 1988.

Howe, D.R. *Data analysis for data base design.* 2d ed. London; New York: E Arnold: New York, NY: Distributed in the U.S.A. Routledge, Chapman, and Hall, 1989.

Hughes, John G. *Database technology: a software engineering approach.* Englewood Cliffs, NJ: Prentice-Hall, 1988.

Hull, Richard, Ron Morrison, David Stemple. *Proceedings of the Second International Workshop on Database Programming Languages, June 4-8, 1989 Salishan Lodge, Gleneden, Beach, Oregon.* San Mateo, CA: Morgan Kaufmann, 1989.

Hursch, Carolyn J., and Jack L. Hursch. *SQL, the structured query language.* 1st ed. Blue Ridge Summit, PA: TAB Books, 1988.

Hurson, A.R., L.L. Miller, and S.H. Pakzad. *Tutorial: parallel architectures for database systems*. Washington, DC: IEEE Computer Society Press: Los Angeles, CA: Order from IEEE Computer Society, 1989.

IEEE. *Data engineering: proceedings of the Fifth International Conference on Data Engineering, February 6-10, 1989, Los Angeles, California, U.S.A.* Washington, DC: IEEE Computer Society Press, 1989.

IEEE. *Data engineering: proceedings of the Fourth International Conference on Data Engineering, February 1-5, 1988, Los Angeles Airport Hilton and Towers, Los Angeles, California, U.S.A.* Washington, DC: Computer Society Press of the IEEE: Los Angeles, CA:

IEEE. *Proceedings, Third International Conference on Data Engineering, February 3-5, 1987, Pacifica Hotel, Los Angeles, California U.S.A.* Washington, DC: IEEE Computer Society Press: 1987.

Inmon, W.H. *Advanced topics in information engineering*. Wellesley, MA: Information Sciences, 1989.

Inmon, W.H. *Information engineering for the practitioner: putting theory into practice*. Englewood Cliffs, NJ: Prentice Hall, 1988.

Inmon, W.H. *ORACLE: building high performance online systems*. Wellesley, MA: Information Sciences, 1989.

Inmon, W.H. *Optimizing performance in DB2 software*. Englewood Cliffs, NJ: Prentice Hall, 1988.

Inmon, W.H. *Using DB2 to build decision support systems*. Wellesley, MA: Information Sciences, 1990.

Ivanov, I.U.N. *Teoriia informatsionnykh obektov i sistemy upravleniia bazami dannykh*. Moskva: Nauka, Glav. red. fiziko-matematicheskoi lit-ry, 1988.

Jackson, Glenn A. *Relational database design with microcomputer applications*. Englewood Cliffs, NJ: Prentice Hall, 1988.

Jones, Edward. *Paradox*. Berkeley, CA: Osborne McGraw-Hill, 1988.

Jones, Paul E., Robert M. Curtice. *Logical data base design*. 2d ed. Wellesley, MA: Information Sciences, 1988.

Kamin, Jonathan. *The first book of Paradox 3*. 1st ed. Carmel, IN: Sams, 1990.

Keogh, James. *Paradox 3: the complete reference*. Berkeley: Osborne/McGraw-Hill, 1989.

Keogh, James. *Paradox: the complete reference*. Berkeley, CA: Osborne McGraw-Hill, 1988.

Kerry, Ruth. *Integrating knowledge-based and database management systems*. New York: Published on behalf of Central Computer and Telecommunications Agency Ellis Horwood, 1990.

Kerschberg, Larry (edit.) *Proceedings from the First International Conference on Expert Database Systems*. Menlo Park, CA: Benjamin/Cummings, 1987.

Kerschberg, Larry (edit.) *Proceedings from the Second International Conference on Expert Database Systems*. Redwood City, CA: Benjamin/Cummings, 1989.

Kitagawa, H., T.L. Kunii. *The unnormalized relational data model: for office form processor design.* Tokyo; New York: Springer-Verlag, 1989.

Kitsuregawa, Masaru, Hidehiko Tanaka (edit.) *Database machines and knowledge base machines.* Boston: Kluwer Academic, 1988.

Kliewer, Bradley D. *Guide to Paradox 386.* New York: Intertext Publications: McGraw Hill, 1989.

Knight, Tim. *4th dimension: a complete guide to database development.* Glenview, IL: Scott, Foresman, 1989.

Kotz, Angelika M. *Triggermechanismen in Datenbanksystemen.* Berlin; New York: Springer-Verlag, 1989.

Kroenke, David M., Kathleen A. Dolan. *Database processing: fundamentals, design, implementation.* 3d ed. Chicago: Science Research Associates, 1988.

Kunii, Hideko S. *Graph data model and its data language.* Tokyo; New York: Springer-Verlag, 1990.

Larson, Bruce L. *The database experts' guide to Database 2.* New York, NY: Intertext Publications: McGraw-Hill, 1988.

Larson, James A. (edit.) *Tutorial — database management.* Washington, DC: IEEE Computer Society Press: 1987.

Law, Margaret Henderson. *Guide to information resource dictionary system applications: general concepts and strategic systems planning.* Gaithersburg, MD: U.S. Dept. of Commerce, National Bureau of Standards, 1988.

Lenat, D., and R.V. Guha. *Building large knowledge-based systems.* Reading, MA: Addison-Wesley, 1990.

Li, Deyi, and Dongbo Liu. *A fuzzy PROLOG database system.* Taunton, Somerset, England: Research Studies Press; New York: Wiley, 1990.

Lim, Pacifico Amarga. *DB2 for application programmers.* Englewood Cliffs, NJ: Prentice Hall, 1990.

Litton, Gerry M. *Introduction to database management: a practical approach.* Dubuque, Iowa: WC Brown, 1987.

Litton, Gerry. *Understanding Professional file.* San Francisco: Sybex, 1990.

Litwin, W., H.J. Schek (edit.) *Foundations of data organization and algorithms: 3d international conference, FODO 1989, Paris, France, June 21-23, 1989: proceedings.* Berlin; New York: Springer-Verlag, 1989.

Lochovsky, Frederick H. (edit.) *Entity-relationship approach to database design and querying: proceedings of the Eighth International Conference on Entity-Relationship Approach, Toronto, Canada, 18-20 October 1989.* Amsterdam; New York: North-Holland; New York: Distributors for the U.S. and Canada, Elsevier, 1990.

Loomis, Mary E.S. *Data management and file structures.* 2d ed. Englewood Cliffs, NJ: Prentice-Hall, 1989.

Loomis, Mary E.S. *The database book.* New York: Macmillan; London: Collier Macmillan, 1987.

Lorie, Raymond A., Jean-Jacques Daudenarde. *SQL and its applications.* Englewood Cliffs, NJ: Prentice Hall, 1991.

Lucas, Robert. *Database applications using Prolog.* Chichester, West Sussex, England: E. Horwood; New York: Halsted Press, 1988.

Lusardi, Frank. *The database experts' guide to SQL.* New York, NY: Intertext Publications/Multiscience Press: McGraw-Hill, 1988.

Lyon, Lockwood. *The IMS/VS expert's guide.* New York: Van Nostrand Reinhold, 1990.

Lyon, Lockwood. *The database expert's guide to IMS.* New York: Van Nostrand Reinhold, 1990.

Maciaszek, L.A. *Database design and implementation.* Englewood Cliffs, NJ: Prentice Hall, 1990.

Malamud, Carl. *INGRES: tools for building an information architecture.* New York: Van Nostrand Reinhold, 1989.

Martin, Charles Fontaine. *User-centered requirements analysis.* Englewood Cliffs, NJ: Prentice-Hall, 1988.

Martin, James, and Joe Leben. *Strategic information planning methodologies.* 2d ed. Englewood Cliffs, NJ: Prentice Hall, 1989.

Martin, James, Kathleen Kavanagh Chapman, and Joe Leben. *DB2, concepts, design, and programming.* Englewood Cliffs, NJ: Prentice Hall, 1989.

Martin, James, Richard Derer, and Joe Leben. *IDMS/R: concepts, design, and programming.* Englewood Cliffs, NJ: Prentice Hall, 1990.

Martin, Tim, and Tim Hartley. *DB2/SQL: a professional programmer's guide.* New York: Intertext: McGraw-Hill, 1989.

McClelland, Trish. *Dynamics of Reflex.* Homewood, IL: Dow Jones-Irwin, 1987.

McFadden, Fred R., Jeffrey A. Hoffer. *Database management.* 3d ed. Redwood City, CA: Benjamin/Cummings, 1991.

McNichols, Charles W., Sara F. Rushinek. *Data base management: a microcomputer approach.* Englewood Cliffs, NJ: Prentice Hall, 1988.

Meersman, R.A., A.C. Sernadas (edit.) *Data and knowledge, Albufeira, Portugal, November, 3-7, 1986.* Amsterdam; New York: North-Holland; New York: Elsevier, 1988.

Meersman, Robert A., Zhongzhi Shi, Chen-Ho Kung (edit.) *Artificial intelligence in databases and information systems: proceedings of the IFIP TC2/TC8/WG2.6/WG8.1 Working Conference on the Role of Artificial Intelligence in Databases and Information Systems, Guangzhou, PR China, July 4-8, 1988.* Amsterdam; New York: North-Holland; Distributors for the U.S. and Canada: Elsevier, 1990.

Montgomery, Stephen L. *Relational database design and implementation using DB2.* New York: Van Nostrand Reinhold, 1990.

Mounsey, Helen (edit.) *Building databases for global science: the proceedings of the first Meeting of the International Geographical Union Global Database Planning Project, held at Tylney Hall, Hampshire, UK, May, 9-13, 1988.* London: New York: Taylor & Francis, 1988.

Mount, Ellis (edit.) *End-user training for sci-tech databases.* New York: Haworth Press, 1990.

Murdoch, S., and L. Johnson. *Intelligent data handling.* 1st ed. London: New York: Chapman and Hall, 1990.

Mylopolous, John, and Michael L. Brodie (edit.) *Readings in artificial intelligence and databases.* San Mateo, CA: M Kaufmann, 1989.

NBS. *Guideline on functional specifications for database management systems..* Gaithersburg, MD: U.S. Dept. of Commerce/National Bureau of Standards; Springfield, VA: National Technical Information Service, 1987.

Naqvi, Shamim, Shalom Tsur. *A logical language for data and knowledge bases.* New York: Computer Science Press, 1989.

Narayan, Rom. *Data dictionary: implementation, use, and maintenance.* Englewood Cliffs, NJ: Prentice Hall, 1988.

Nath, Aloke. *The guide to SQL Server.* Reading, MA: Addison-Wesley, 1990.

Newton, Judith J. *Guide on data entity naming conventions.* Gaithersburg, Md. U.S. Dept. of Commerce, National Bureau of Standards. For sale the Supt. of Docs., USGPO., 1987.

Newton, Judith, Frankie E. Spielman (edit.) *Data administration management and practice: proceedings of the first DAMA Symposium.* Gaithersburg, Md. National Institute of Standards and Technology, 1988.

Nijssen, G.M., T.A. Halpin. *Conceptual schema and relational database design: a fact oriented approach.* Englewood Cliffs, NJ: Prentice Hall, 1989.

Ozkarahan, Esen. *Database management: concepts, design, and practice.* Englewood Cliffs, NJ: Prentice Hall, 1990.

Ozsu, M.T., and P. Valduriez. *Principles of distributed database systems.* Englewood Cliffs, NJ: Prentice-Hall, 1991.

Page, A.J. *Relational databases: concepts, selection, and implementation.* Wilmslow: Sigma, 1990.

Papazoglou, M., and W. Valder. *Relational database management: a systems programming approach.* Englewood Cliffs, NJ: Prentice Hall, 1989.

Paredaens, J. (edit.) *Databases.* London; Orlando: Academic Press, 1987.

Paredaens, Jan, et al. *The structure of the relational database model.* Berlin; New York: Springer-Verlag, 1989.

Parsaye, Kamran, et al. *Intelligent databases: object-oriented, deductive hypermedia technologies.* New York: Wiley, 1989.

Peinl, Peter. *Synchronisation in zentralisierten Datenbanksystemen: Algorithmen, Realisierungsmoglichkeiten und quantitative Analyse.* Berlin; New York: Springer-Verlag, 1987.

Perry, William E. *A standard for auditing computer applications.* Pennsauken, NJ: Auerbach, 1988.

Piggott, Stephen. *CICS: a practical guide to system fine tuning.* New York: Intertext Publications: McGraw-Hill, 1989.

Prague, Cary N., James E. Hammitt, and Mark R. Nowacki. *Programming with Paradox.* 1st ed. Blue Ridge Summit, PA: TAB Books, 1987.

Pratt, Philip J., Joseph J. Adamski. *Database systems: management and design.* Boston: Boyd & Fraser, 1987.

Rada, Roy. *HYPERTEXT: from Text to Expertext.* 1990.

Rafanelli, M., J.C. Klensin, P. Svensson (edit.) *Statistical and scientific database management: Fourth International Working Conference SSDBM, Rome, Italy, June 21-23, 1988: proceedings.* Berlin; New York: Springer-Verlag, 1989.

Ranade, Jay, et al. *DB2 — concepts, programming, and design.* New York: McGraw-Hill, 1991.

Ricardo, Catherine M. *Database systems: principles, design, and implementation.* New York: Macmillan; London: Collier Macmillan, 1990.

Rishe, N., S. Navathe, and D. Tal (edit.) *Databases: theory, design and applications.* IEEE Computer Society Press, 1991.

Rishe, N., S. Navathe, and D. Tal (edit.) *Proceedings of the PARBASE-90: International Conference on Databases, Parallel Architectures, and their Applications.* IEEE Computer Society Press, 1990.

Rodgers, Ulka. *UNIX database management systems.* Englewood Cliffs, NJ: Prentice Hall, 1990.

Rolland, C., F. Bodart, M. Leonard (edit.) *Temporal aspects in information systems: proceedings of the IFIP TC 8/WG 8.1 Working Conference on Temporal Aspects in Information Systems, Sophia-Antipolis, France, May, 13-15, 1987.* Amsterdam; New York: North Holland; New York: Elsevier, 1988.

Rolland, Fr (edit.) *Relational database management with Oracle.* Reading, MA: Addison-Wesley, 1990.

Rothstein, Michael F., Burt Rosner. *The professional's guide to database systems project management.* New York: Wiley, 1990.

Rudd, Anthony S. *Implementing practical DB2 applications.* New York: E Horwood, 1990.

Rumble, J.R., Jr., and F.J. Smith. *Database systems in science and engineering.* Bristol; Philadelphia: Adam Hilger, 1990.

Sayles, Jonathan S. *Embedded SQL for DB2: application design and programming.* Wellesley, MA: Information Sciences, 1990.

Sayles, Jonathan. *SQL for DB2 and SQL/DS application developers.* Wellesley, MA: Information Sciences, 1990.

Sayles, Jonathan. *SQL spoken here.* Wellesley, MA: Information Sciences, 1989.

Schmidt, J.W., S. Ceri, M. Missikoff (edit.) *Advances in database technology, EDBT 88: International Conference on Extending Database Technology, Venice, Italy, March 14-18, 1988, proceedings.* Berlin; New York: Springer-Verlag, 1988.

Schmidt, Joachim W., Costantino Thanos. *Foundations of knowledge base management: contributions from logic, databases, and artificial intelligence applications.* Berlin; New York: Springer-Verlag, 1989.

Sherif, M.A. *Database projects: a framework for effective management.* Chichester, West Sussex, England: E. Horwood; New York: Halsted Press, 1988.

Shortliffe, E., L. Perrault, G. Wiederhold, and L. Fagan (edit.) *Medical informatics: computer applications in health care.* Reading, MA: Addison-Wesley, 1990.

Siegel, Charles. *Mastering FoxPro.* San Francisco, CA: Sybex, 1990.

Siegel, Charles. *The ABC's of Paradox.* San Francisco, CA: Sybex, 1989.

Simpson, Alan. *Mastering Paradox.* 4th ed. San Francisco, CA: Sybex, 1989.

Slusky, Ludwig. *Cases in database design.* St. Louis, MO: Times Mirror/Mosby College Pub., 1988.

Smith, Peter D., G. Michael Barnes. *Files and databases: an introduction.* Reading, MA: Addison-Wesley, 1987.

Sosinsky, Barrie. *Using FileMaker.* Carmel, IN: Que, 1990.

Spooner, D.L., and C. Landwehr (edit.) *Database security III, status and prospects.* North-Holland, 1990.

Srinivasan, B., J. Zeleznikow (edit.) *Databases in the 1990s: proceedings of the Australian Database Research Conference, Melbourne, February, 6, 1990.* Singapore; New Jersey: World Scientific, 1990.

Stanczyk, Stefan K. *Theory and practice of relational databases.* London: Pitman, 1990.

Steele, Philip. *66 FoxBASE+ user-defined functions.* 1st ed. Blue Ridge Summit, PA: TAB Books Inc., 1989.

Stonebraker, Michael (edit.) *Readings in database systems.* San Mateo, CA: Morgan Kaufmann, 1988.

Storey, Veda Catherine. *View creation: an expert system for database design.* Washington, DC: ICIT Press, 1988.

Su, Stanley Y.W. *Database computers: principles, architectures, and techniques.* 1st ed. New York: McGraw-Hill, 1988.

Swanson, E. Burton, and Cynthia Mathis Beath. *Maintaining information systems in organizations.* Chichester : New York: Wiley, 1989.

Tare, Ramkrishna S. *Data processing in the UNIX environment: with INFORMIX-SQL, Embedded-SQL, C-ISAM, and TURBO.* New York: McGraw-Hill, 1989.

Tasker, Dan. *Fourth generation data: a guide to data analysis for new and old systems.* Englewood Cliffs, NJ: Prentice Hall, 1989.

Tay, Y.C. *Locking performance in centralized databases.* Boston: Academic Press, 1987.

Tenopir, Carol, and Gerald Lundeen. *Managing your information: how to design and create a textual database on your microcomputer.* New York: Neal-Schuman, 1988.

Tenopir, Carol, and Jung Soon Ro. *Full text databases.* Foreword by Stephen Harter. New York: Greenwood Press, 1990.

Teorey, Toby J. *Database modeling and design: the entity-relationship approach.* San Mateo, CA: Morgan Kaufman, 1990.

Thompson, J. Patrick. *Data with semantics: data models and data management.* New York: Van Nostrand Reinhold, 1989.

Towner, Larry E. *IDMS/R: a professional's guide to concepts, design and programming.* New York, NY: Intertext Publications, 1989.

Tsai, Alice Y.H. *Database systems: management and use.* Scarborough, Ont.: Prentice-Hall Canada; Englewood Cliffs, NJ: Prentice-Hall, 1988.

Ullman, Jeffrey D. *Principles of database and knowledge-base systems.* Rockville, Md.: Computer Science Press, vol. 1, 1988, vol. 2, 1989.

Vasta, Joseph A. *Understanding database management systems.* 2d ed. Belmont, CA: Wadsworth, 1989.

Vidick, Jean-Luc (edit.) *Proceedings of the 13th International Conference on Research and Development in Information Retrieval.* September 5-7, 1990 in Brussels, Belgium. New York, NY: Association for Computing Machinery, 1989.

Vinden, Robin J. *Data dictionaries for database administrators.* Blue Ridge Summit, PA: TAB Books, 1990.

Vossen, Gottfried. *Datenmodelle, Datenbanksprachen und Datenbank-Management-Systeme.* Bonn: Reading, MA: Addison-Wesley, 1987.

Vowell, Jeff D., Jr. *DB2: the complete guide to implementation and use.* 2d ed. Wellesley, MA: Information Sciences, 1990.

Vuong, Ziep N. *IMS/VS data communications programming using message format service.* 1st ed. Blue Ridge Summit, PA: TAB Books, 1990.

Walters, Richard F. *Database principles for personal computers.* Englewood Cliffs, NJ: Prentice-Hall, 1987.

Wertz, Charles J. *The data dictionary: concepts and uses.* 2d ed. Wellesley, MA: Information Sciences, 1989.

Whittington, R.P. *Database systems engineering.* Oxford: Clarendon Press; New York: Oxford University Press, 1988.

Wiederhold, Gio. *File organization for database design.* New York: McGraw-Hill, 1987.

Williams, M.H. (edit.) *Proceedings of the seventh British National Conference on Databases: Heriot-Watt University, July, 12-14, 1989.* Cambridge; New York: Cambridge University Press on behalf of the British Computer Society, 1989.

Winslett, Marianne. *Updating logical databases.* Cambridge; New York: Cambridge University Press, 1990.

Wiorkowski, Gabrielle, David Kull. *DB2: design & development guide.* 2d ed. Reading, MA: Addison-Wesley, 1990.

Wipper, Fritz. *Guide to DB2 & SQL/DS.* New York: McGraw-Hill, 1989.

Yannakoudakis, E.J. *The architectural logic of database systems.* London; New York: Springer-Verlag, 1988.

Yannakoudakis, E.J., and C.P. Cheng. *Standard relational and network database languages.* London; New York: Springer-Verlag, 1988.

Zdonik, Stanley, and David Maier (edit.) *Readings in object-oriented databases.* San Mateo, CA: Morgan Kaufmann, 1990.

CHAPTER 13

SOLVED CASE STUDY PROBLEMS

This chapter contains solutions for most of the case-study problems. For many problems, only a part of the problem is solved here — the reader is expected to complete the rest.

Solution for Problem 1-1 on page 13

Works-in m:m, name of DEPARTMENT 1:m (department may have several names, but every name is unique), last-name m:1, address m:1, major m:1, minor m:1, year m:1, season m:1, name of COURSE 1:1.

Solution for Problem 1-2 on page 13

$\{ \}$; $\{(a_1 \text{ R } a_1)\}$; $\{(a_1 \text{ R } a_2)\}$; $\{(a_1 \text{ R } a_1), (a_1 \text{ R } a_2)\}$
$\{(a_2 \text{ R } a_1)\}$; $\{(a_2 \text{ R } a_2)\}$; $\{(a_2 \text{ R } a_1), (a_2 \text{ R } a_2)\}$;
$\{(a_1 \text{ R } a_1), (a_2 \text{ R } a_1)\}$; $\{(a_1 \text{ R } a_1), (a_2 \text{ R } a_2)\}$; $\{(a_1 \text{ R } a_1), (a_2 \text{ R } a_1), (a_2 \text{ R } a_2)\}$;
$\{(a_1 \text{ R } a_2), (a_2 \text{ R } a_1)\}$; $\{(a_1 \text{ R } a_2), (a_2 \text{ R } a_2)\}$; $\{(a_1 \text{ R } a_2), (a_2 \text{ R } a_1), (a_2 \text{ R } a_2)\}$;
$\{(a_1 \text{ R } a_1), (a_1 \text{ R } a_2), (a_2 \text{ R } a_1)\}$; $\{(a_1 \text{ R } a_1), (a_1 \text{ R } a_2), (a_2 \text{ R } a_2)\}$; $\{(a_1 \text{ R } a_1), (a_1 \text{ R } a_2), (a_2 \text{ R } a_1), (a_2 \text{ R } a_2)\}$;

Solution for Problem 1-3 on page 13

Each object of *A* has four choices to be paired with one of the objects (including itself). Thus, the total number of choices is $4 \times 4 \times 4 \times 4 = 256$. Thus, 256 different sets of pairs are possible.

Solution for Problem 1-4 on page 14

Each object of *A* has five choices: to be paired with one of the four objects (including itself) or to be paired with no object. Thus, a total number of choices is $5 \times 5 \times 5 \times 5 = 625$. Thus, 625 different sets of pairs are possible.

Solution for Problem 1-5 on page 24

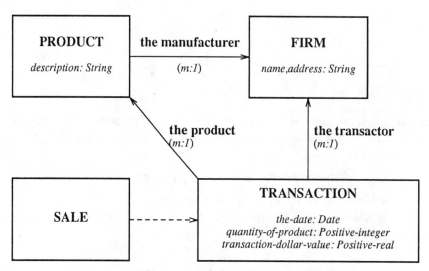

Figure 13-1. A semantic schema for a wholesaler. The transactions which are not *sales* are purchases.

Solution for Problem 1-6 on page 24

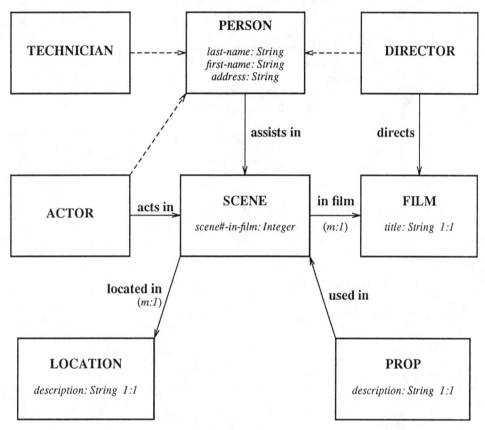

Figure 13-2. A semantic schema for a movie studio.

Solution for Problem 1-7 on page 24

All the members of the clan have the same last name, so it is absent from the schema. *MARRIED* is a many-to-many relation (between current and exspouses). If the society described by the database does not allow divorce and a widower may not remarry, then the relation MARRIED would be one-to-one.

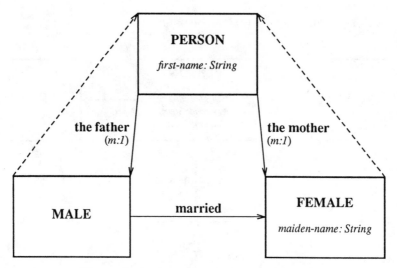

Figure 13-3. A semantic schema for a clan.

Solution for Problem 1-8 on page 24

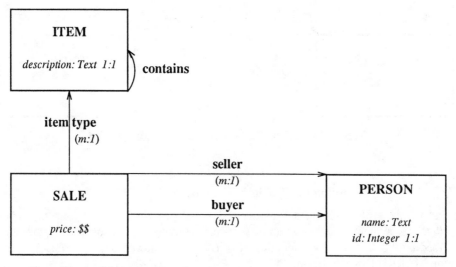

Figure 13-4. A semantic schema to record sale transactions.

A *sale* is a transaction of a merchandise of the *item-type* for the *price* between the *seller* and the *buyer*. The many-to-many relation *contains* forms a bill of material of item-types.

Solution for Problem 1-9 on page 24

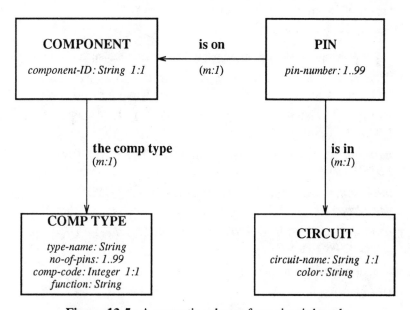

Figure 13-5. A semantic schema for a circuit board.

Note: No pin is in two circuits because a circuit is defined as containing a full set of electrically common wires.

Solution for Problem 1-10 on page 31

The concepts incorporated in the semantic schema are marked with " ☐ ".

1. A catalog of names of known diseases.

    ☐ *DISEASE* — category

    ☐ *name* — attribute of *DISEASE*, range: *String* (*m:1*)

2. A catalog of descriptions of known symptoms: their names and the units in which the magnitude of their intensity or acuteness is measured.

    ☐ *SYMPTOM-TYPE* — category

    ☐ *name* — attribute of *SYMPTOM-TYPE*, range: *String* (*m:1*)

    ☐ *magnitude-unit* — attribute of *SYMPTOM-TYPE*, range: *String* (*m:1*)

3.   For every disease there is a list of its possible symptoms, in which

    for every possible symptom

    for some magnitudes of its acuteness

    there is a probability estimation whether

        the symptom should accompany the disease with such magnitude at least.

☐ *SYMPTOM'S-POSSIBILITY-FOR-A-DISEASE* — category (Every object of this category is an event of the possibility of a symptom for a disease.)

☐ *may-have* — relation from *DISEASE* to *SYMPTOM'S-POSSIBILITY-FOR-A-DISEASE* (*1:m*)

☐ *may-indicate* — relation from *SYMPTOM-TYPE* to *SYMPTOM'S-POSSIBILITY-FOR-A-DISEASE* (*1:m*)

☐ *magnitude* — attribute of *SYMPTOM'S-POSSIBILITY-FOR-A-DISEASE*, range: *Number* (*m:1*)

☐ *probability* — attribute of *SYMPTOM'S-POSSIBILITY-FOR-A-DISEASE*, range: *0-100%* (*m:1*)

4.   A catalog of names of known drugs.

☐ *DRUG* — category

☐ *name* — attribute of *DRUG*, range: *String* (*m:1*)

5.   For every disease there are lists of factors which may aggravate, cause, or cure the disease: drugs, drug combinations, other diseases.

☐ *FACTOR-INFLUENCING-DISEASES* — category (Every factor is either DRUG or DRUG-INTERACTION or DISEASE. The three subcategories are disjoint.)

☐ *DRUG* — subcategory of *FACTOR-INFLUENCING-DISEASES*

☐ *DISEASE* — subcategory of *FACTOR-INFLUENCING-DISEASES*

☐ *DRUG-INTERACTION* — subcategory of *FACTOR-INFLUENCING-DISEASES* (Every object of the category DRUG-INTERACTION stands for a combination of drugs which jointly can produce influence.)

☐ *in* — relation from *DRUG* to *DRUG-INTERACTION* (*m:m*) (A drug may participate **in** several drug-interactions)

☐ *may-cure* — relation from *FACTOR-INFLUENCING-DISEASES* to *DISEASE* (*m:m*)

☐ *may-aggravate* — relation from *FACTOR-INFLUENCING-DISEASES* to *DISEASE* (*m:m*)

☐ *may-cause* — relation from *FACTOR-INFLUENCING-DISEASES* to *DISEASE* (*m:m*)

6.   Names, addresses, and dates of birth of patients, names and addresses of physicians. Some physicians are also known as patients. Some persons relevant to the database are neither patients nor physicians. For these persons we have names and addresses.

☐ *PERSON* — category

☐ *name* — attribute of *PERSON*, range: *String* (*m:1*)

☐ *address* — attribute of *PERSON*, range: *String* (*m:1*)

☐ *PATIENT* — subcategory of *PERSON*

☐ *PHYSICIAN* — subcategory of *PERSON*

☐ *born* — attribute of *PATIENT*, range: *Date* (*m:1*)

7.   Physicians' areas of specialization (diseases).

☐ *specializes-in* — relation from *PHYSICIAN* to *DISEASE* (*m:m*)

8.   Every patient's medical history, including

a.   all his or her present and past illnesses

- Their duration

- Their diagnosing physicians

- Drugs prescribed for them

☐ *PATIENT'S-SICKNESS* — category (Every object of this category is an event of a patient having a disease during a period of time.)

☐ *had* — relation from *PATIENT* to *PATIENT'S-SICKNESS* (*1:m*)

☐ *occurred* — relation from *DISEASE* to *PATIENT'S-SICKNESS* (*1:m*)

☐ *from* — attribute of *PATIENT'S-SICKNESS*, range: *Date* (*m:1*)

☐ *to* — attribute of *PATIENT'S-SICKNESS*, range: *Date* (*m:1*)

☐ *diagnosed* — relation from *PHYSICIAN* to *PATIENT'S-SICKNESS* (*m:m*)

b.   all his or her reported symptoms with

- The duration of the symptom's occurrences

- An indication of the magnitude of intensity or acuteness of the symptom's occurrence

- A record of the persons (names and addresses) who reported or measured the symptom's occurrence (the occurrence can be reported, for example, by the patient, relatives, or medical personnel)

- The physicians who confirmed the symptom's occurrence

☐ *SYMPTOM'S-INSTANCE-FOR-A-PATIENT* — category (Every object of this category is an event of a patient having a certain symptom with a certain magnitude during a certain period of time.)

☐ *had* — relation from *PATIENT* to *SYMPTOM'S-INSTANCE-FOR-A-PATIENT* (*1:m*)

☐ *appeared* — relation from *SYMPTOM-TYPE* to *SYMPTOM'S-INSTANCE-FOR-A-PATIENT* (*1:m*)

☐ *from* — attribute of *SYMPTOM'S-INSTANCE-FOR-A-PATIENT*, range: *Date* (*m:1*)

☐ *to* — attribute of *SYMPTOM'S-INSTANCE-FOR-A-PATIENT*, range: *Date* (*m:1*)

☐ *magnitude* — attribute of *SYMPTOM'S-INSTANCE-FOR-A-PATIENT*, range: *Number* (*m:1*)

☐ *reported* — relation from *PERSON* to *SYMPTOM'S-INSTANCE-FOR-A-PATIENT* (*m:m*)

☐ *confirmed* — relation from *PHYSICIAN* to *SYMPTOM'S-INSTANCE-FOR-A-PATIENT* (*m:m*)

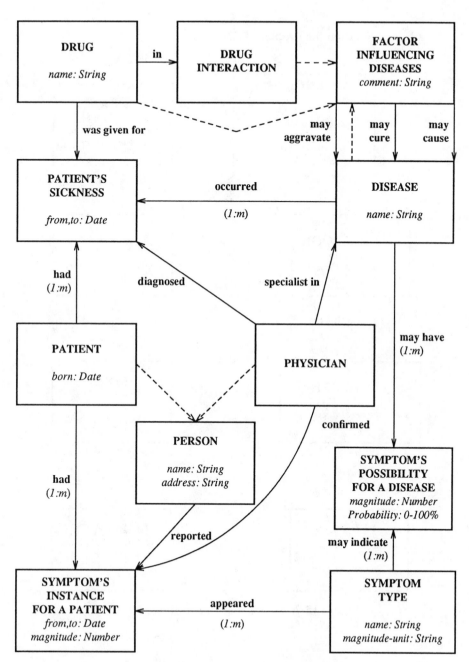

Figure 13-6. A semantic schema for a medical application.

Solution for Problem 1-12 on page 42

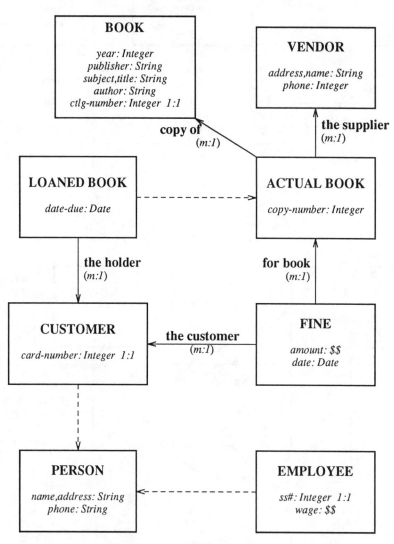

Figure 13-7. A semantic schema for a library.

FINE

violator's-name: String
violator's-address: String
violator's-phone: String
violator's-card-number: Integer (m:1, unlike in the schema)
amount: $$
date: Date
ctlg-number: Integer (m:1, unlike in the schema)
book-copy-number: Integer

Figure 13-8. A userview of the library schema for billing of customers.

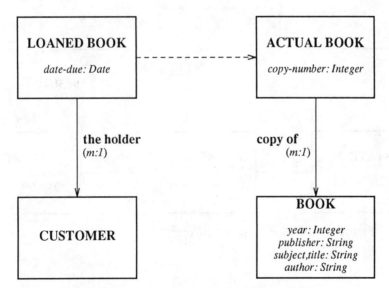

Figure 13-9. A subschema of the library schema for statistical analysis of reading habits. All the information that can help identify a particular person is concealed from this subschema.

Solution for Problem 1-13 on page 49

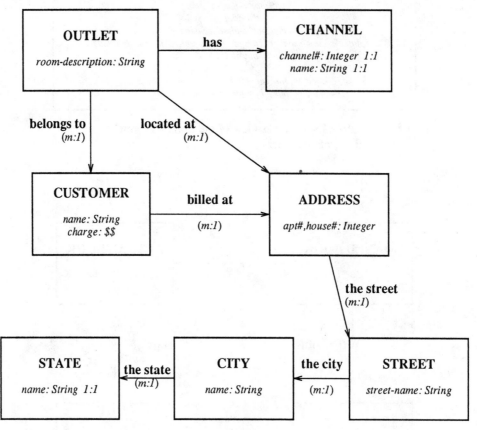

Figure 13-10. A semantic schema for a cable distribution network.

Solution for Problem 1-14 on page 49

The schema appears on the following page.

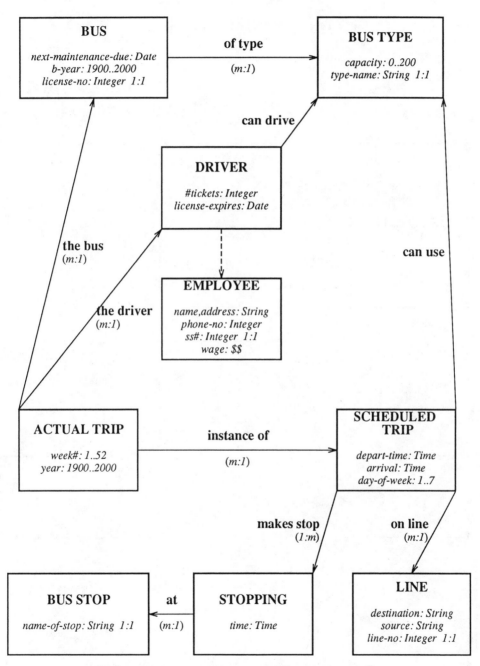

Figure 13-11. A semantic schema for a bus company.

Solution for Problem 1-15 on page 50

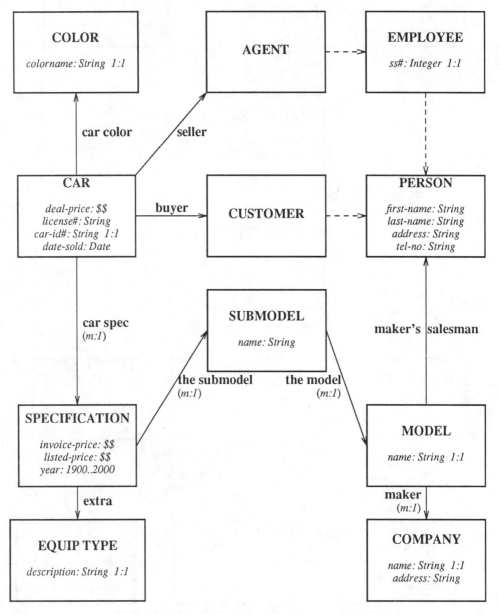

Figure 13-12. A semantic schema for a car dealer.

Solution for Problem 1-16 on page 51

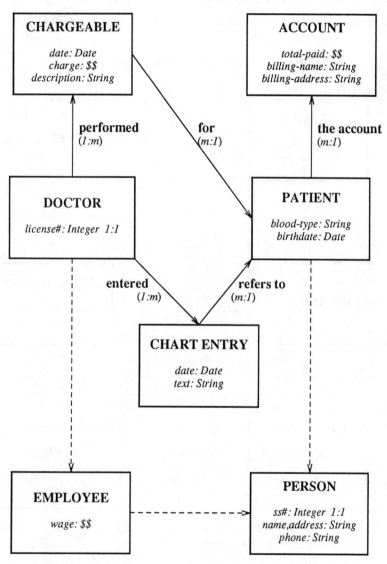

Figure 13-13. A semantic schema for a medical clinic.

Explanation follows.

- Several patients, such as a family, can use a joint account with the clinic. No patient has two accounts — otherwise we would not know where to send bills.

- A chart entry is a doctor's memo written during a patient's visit.

- A chargeable is any activity which is performed by a doctor and is billable to a patient.

Solution for Problem 1-17 on page 51

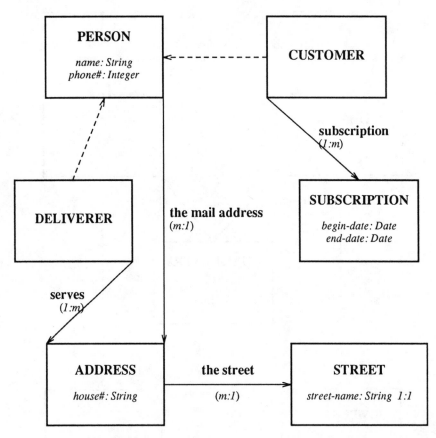

Figure 13-14. A semantic schema for a newspaper distribution department.

Assumptions follow.

- All the subscriptions of one person are delivered to that person's mailing address. Otherwise, we would have a separate relation from *SUBSCRIPTION* to *ADDRESS*.

- For any address, there is only one deliverer who serves it.

- It is a local newspaper. All its customers and deliverers reside within one city. Thus, the name of the city does not appear in the address. All the addresses in the city are composed of a street name and house number.

- For the distribution department, the addresses are more than just character strings: they are topographical locations which are grouped into sets according to the streets of the city. Thus, there is a separate abstract category *ADDRESS*.

Solution for Problem 1-23 on page 53

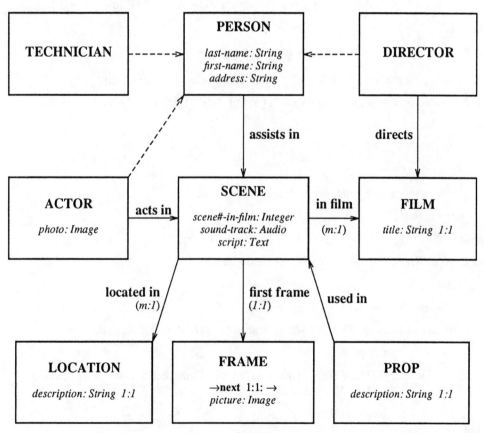

Figure 13-15. A semantic schema for a movie studio, a multimedia version.

- *next* — relation from *FRAME* to *FRAME*   (*1:1*)   (This relation establishes a linear order among the frames of a scene.)

Solution for Problem 2-4 on page 71

(* Normalization formula:

$$\text{new grade} := \text{old grade} + \text{factor}*(100 - \text{old grade})$$

where

$$75 = \text{AVERAGE (new grade)} =$$
$$\text{AVERAGE (old grade)} + \text{factor}*(100 - \text{AVERAGE(old grade)})$$

Thus:

$$\text{factor} = (75 - \text{average})/ (100 - \text{average})$$

(For simplification, the effect of a grade going below 0 is neglected.)   *)

Program Normalize (output, UNIVERSITY-DB, UNIVERSITY-MASTER-VIEW) ;

var

    co,ce : ABSTRACT ;

    iscsmajor : Boolean ;

    number-of-grades, total, average: Integer ;

    factor: Real;

begin

for co **in** *COURSE-OFFERING* **where** true **do begin**

    total := 0;

    number-of-grades :=0;

    for ce **in** *COURSE-ENROLLMENT* **where** (ce.*THE-OFFER* = co) **do begin**

        iscsmajor := false ;

        for d **in** *DEPARTMENT* **where** (d *NAME* 'Computer Science' **and** ce.*THE-STUDENT MAJOR* d) **do**

            iscsmajor := true ;

        if (**not** iscsmajor) **and not** (ce *FINAL-GRADE* **null**) **then begin**

            total := total + ce.*FINAL-GRADE* ;

            number-of-grades := number-of-grades + 1 ;

        end

     end (* enrollment loop *)

  if number-of-grades>0 **then begin**

     average := total/number-of-grades ;

     factor := (75. – average)/ (100 – average)

     transaction begin

       for ce **in** *COURSE-ENROLLMENT* **where** (ce.*THE-OFFER* = co) **do begin**

         iscsmajor := false ;

         for d **in** *DEPARTMENT* **where** (d *NAME* 'Computer Science' **and**
            ce.*THE-STUDENT MAJOR* d) **do**

          iscsmajor := true ;

         if (**not** iscsmajor) **and not** (ce *FINAL-GRADE* null) **then**

           ce.*FINAL-GRADE* := ce.*FINAL-GRADE* + factor * (100 –
             ce.*FINAL-GRADE*);

        end (* enrollment loop *)

      end (* transaction *)

    end

  end (* course offering loop *)

end. (* program *)

Solution for Problem 2-7 on page 101

A.   A simplified solution. We assume that *TO-DATE* is a total relation on the category *SICKNESS*.

get sickness.*THE-PATIENT.NAME*, sickness.*THE-DISEASE.NAME*

where

  sickness **is a** *SICKNESS* **and**

  exists possibility **in** *SYMPTOM'S-POSSIBILITY*:

     possibility.*THE-DISEASE*=sickness.*THE-DISEASE* **and**

     possibility.*PROBABILITY* ≥ 0.9 **and**

     not exists instance **in** *SYMPTOM'S-INSTANCE*:

          instance.*THE-PATIENT*=sickness.*THE-PATIENT* **and**

          instance.*THE-SYMPTOM*=possibility.*THE-SYMPTOM* **and**

          instance.*FROM-DATE*≤sickness.*FROM-DATE* **and**

          instance.*TO-DATE*≥sickness.*FROM-DATE*

B.   A full solution. It is possible that a sickness has no *TO-DATE*, which means that the sickness has not ended yet.

get sickness.*THE-PATIENT.NAME, sickness.THE-DISEASE.NAME*

where

   sickness **is a** *SICKNESS* **and**

   exists possibility **in** *SYMPTOM'S-POSSIBILITY*:

          possibility.*THE-DISEASE*=sickness.*THE-DISEASE* **and**

          possibility.*PROBABILITY* ≥ 0.9 **and**

          not exists instance **in** *SYMPTOM'S-INSTANCE*:

               instance.*THE-PATIENT*=sickness.*THE-PATIENT* **and**

               instance.*THE-SYMPTOM*=possibility.*THE-SYMPTOM* **and**

               instance.*FROM-DATE*≤sickness.*FROM-DATE***and**

               (instance.*TO-DATE*≥sickness.*FROM-DATE* **or**

               not exists d **in** *DATE*: instance *TO-DATE* d)

            Solution for Problem 3-1 on page 113

> EMPLOYEE [id-key: Integer, name: Text, boss-id: Integer]
>
> PROJECT [proj-name-key: Text]
>
> WORK [empl-id-in-key: Integer, proj-name-in-key: Text]
>
> SUBPROJECT [subproj-name-in-key: Text, proj-name-in-key: Text]

Figure 13-16. A relational schema for project information.

Solution for Problem 3-6 on page 148

```
+-------------------------------------+        +-------------------------------------+
|                MALE                 |        |               FEMALE                |
|                                     |        |                                     |
|         first-name: String          |        |         first-name: String          |
|   the-mother--person-id: Integer    |        |   the-mother--person-id: Integer    |
|   the-father--person-id: Integer    |        |   the-father--person-id: Integer    |
|       person-id-key: Integer        |        |       person-id-key: Integer        |
|                                     |        |        maiden-name: String          |
+-------------------------------------+        +-------------------------------------+
```

```
+-------------------------------------+
|              MARRIAGE               |
|                                     |
|  husband--person-id-in-key: Integer |
|   wife--person-id-in-key: Integer   |
+-------------------------------------+
```

Figure 13-17. A relational schema for a clan.

Some of the Integrity Constraints Generated During Schema Conversion

(**for every** x **in** *MARRIAGE*:

    exists y **in** *MALE*:

        x.*husband--person-id-in-key* = y.*person-id-key*)

    and

(**for every** x **in** *FEMALE*:

    x *the-mother-person-id* **null or**

    exists y **in** *FEMALE*:

        x.*the-mother--person-id* = y.*person-id-key*)

    and

(**for every** x **in** *FEMALE*:

    x *the-father-person-id* **null or**

    exists y **in** *MALE*:

        x.*the-father--person-id* = y.*person-id-key*)

Solution for Problem 3-7 on page 148

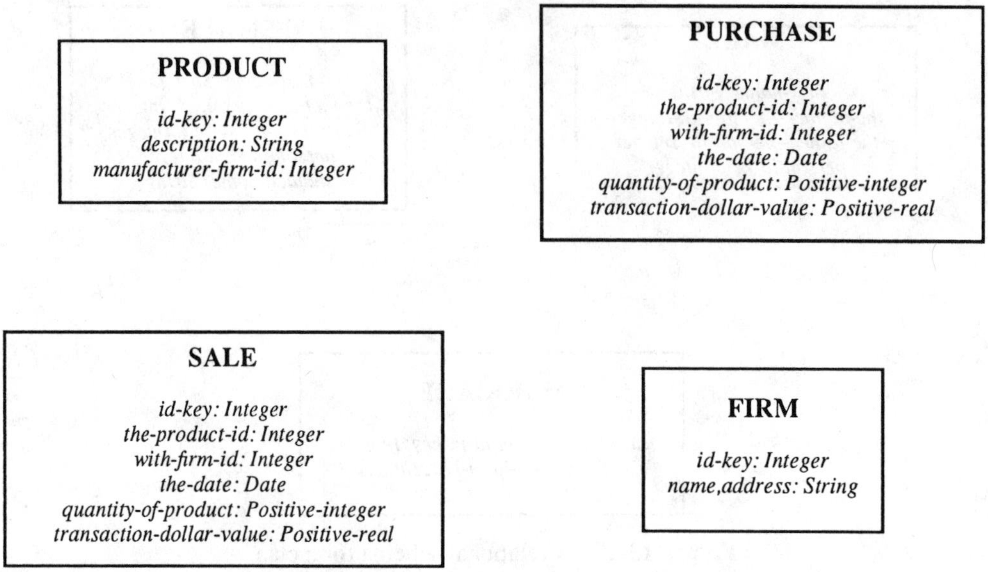

```
┌─────────────────────────────┐        ┌──────────────────────────────────────────┐
│           PRODUCT           │        │                 PURCHASE                   │
│                             │        │                                            │
│       id-key: Integer       │        │              id-key: Integer               │
│     description: String     │        │          the-product-id: Integer           │
│  manufacturer-firm-id: Integer │     │           with-firm-id: Integer            │
│                             │        │              the-date: Date                │
└─────────────────────────────┘        │      quantity-of-product: Positive-integer │
                                       │  transaction-dollar-value: Positive-real   │
                                       └──────────────────────────────────────────┘


┌──────────────────────────────────────────┐
│                   SALE                     │        ┌────────────────────────────┐
│                                            │        │            FIRM            │
│              id-key: Integer               │        │                            │
│          the-product-id: Integer           │        │       id-key: Integer      │
│           with-firm-id: Integer            │        │    name,address: String    │
│              the-date: Date                │        │                            │
│      quantity-of-product: Positive-integer │        └────────────────────────────┘
│  transaction-dollar-value: Positive-real   │
└──────────────────────────────────────────┘
```

Figure 13-18. A relational schema for a wholesaler. Alternative I.

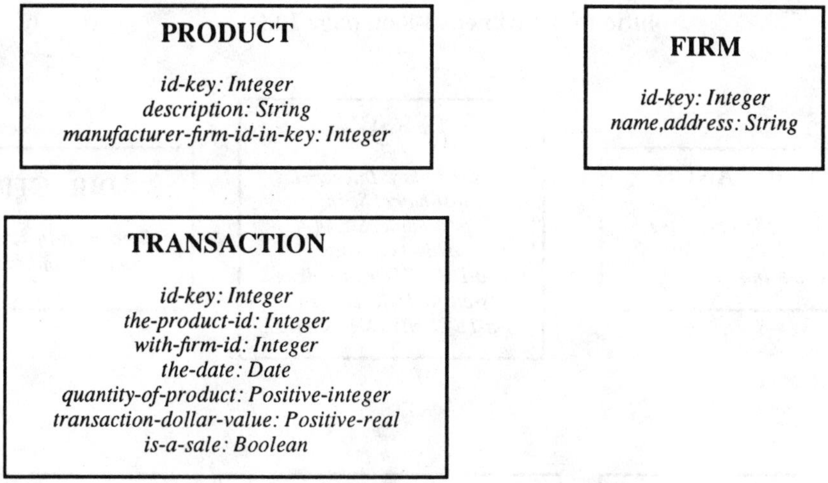

PRODUCT

id-key: Integer
description: String
manufacturer-firm-id-in-key: Integer

FIRM

id-key: Integer
name,address: String

TRANSACTION

id-key: Integer
the-product-id: Integer
with-firm-id: Integer
the-date: Date
quantity-of-product: Positive-integer
transaction-dollar-value: Positive-real
is-a-sale: Boolean

Figure 13-19. A relational schema for a wholesaler.
Alternative II.

PRODUCT

product-id-key: Integer
description: String
the-manufacturer--firm-id: Integer

FIRM

firm-id-key: Integer
address,name: String

SALE

transaction-id-key: Integer

TRANSACTION

transaction-id-key: Integer
quantity-of-product: Positive-integer
transaction-dollar-value: Positive-real
the-date: Date
the-product--product-id: Integer
the-transactor--firm-id: Integer

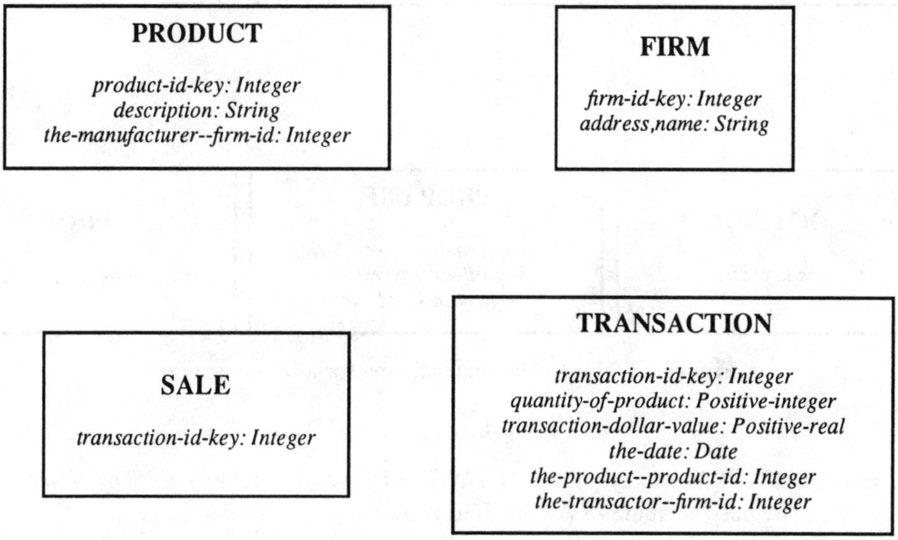

Figure 13-20. A relational schema for a wholesaler.
Alternative III.

Solution for Problem 3-8 on page 148

PERSON
person-id-key: Integer 1:1
last-name: String
first-name: String
address: String
is-a-DIRECTOR: Boolean
is-an-ACTOR: Boolean
is-a-TECHNICIAN: Boolean

ASSISTANCE
person-id-in-key: Integer
film-title-in-key: String
scene-#-in-key: Integer

DIRECTION
director-id-in-key: Integer
film-title-in-key: String

ACTING
actor-id-in-key: Integer
film-title-in-key: String
scene-#-in-key: Integer

SCENE
film-title-in-key: String
scene#-in-film-in-key: Integer
location-description: String

FILM
title-key: String 1:1

LOCATION
description-key: String 1:1

PROP USE
prop-description-in-key: String
film-title-in-key: String
scene-#-in-key: String

PROP
description-key: String 1:1

Figure 13-21. A relational schema for a movie studio.

Integrity Constraints

1. Every *ACTOR-ID-in-key* of an *ACTING* corresponds to the *PERSON-ID-key* of a *PERSON* whose attribute *IS-AN-ACTOR* is *true*.

2. Every *DIRECTOR-ID-in-key* of a *DIRECTION* corresponds to the *PERSON-ID-key* of a *PERSON* whose attribute *IS-A-DIRECTOR* is *true*.

3. Every *PERSON-ID-in-key* of an *ASSISTANCE* corresponds to the *PERSON-ID-key* of a *PERSON*.

4.   Every *FILM-TITLE-in-key* of a *DIRECTION* corresponds to the *FILM-TITLE-key* of a *FILM*.

5.   Every *PROP-DESCRIPTION-in-key* of a *PROP-USE* corresponds to the *PROP-DESCRIPTION-key* of a *PROP*.

6.   Every *LOCATION-DESCRIPTION-in-key* of a *SCENE* corresponds to the *LOCATION-DESCRIPTION-key* of a *LOCATION*.

7.   For every *ACTING*, its *FILM-TITLE-in-key* and *SCENE-#-in-key* correspond to the *FILM-TITLE-in-key* and *SCENE-#-in-key* of one *SCENE*.

8.   For every *PROP-USE*, its *FILM-TITLE-in-key* and *SCENE-#-in-key* correspond to the *FILM-TITLE-in-key* and *SCENE-#-in-key* of one *SCENE*.

Solution for Problem 3-9 on page 148

COMPONENT
component-ID-key: String *the-comp-type--comp-code: Integer*

PIN
is-on--component-ID-in-key: String *pin-number-in-key: 1..99* *is-in--circuit-name: String*

COMP TYPE
comp-code-key: Integer *no-of-pins: 1..99* *type-name: String* *function: String*

CIRCUIT
circuit-name-key: String *color: String*

Figure 13-22. A relational schema for a circuit board.

Some of the Integrity Constraints Generated During Schema Conversion

(**for every** x **in** *PIN*:

   x *is-in--circuit-name* **null or**

   exists y **in** *CIRCUIT*: x.*is-in--circuit-name* = y.*circuit-name-key*) **and**

(**for every** x **in** *COMPONENT*:

   exists y **in** *COMP-TYPE*: x.*the-comp-type--comp-code* = y.*comp-code-key*)

A Constraint Translated from an Original Constraint

for every p **in** *PIN*:

    exists cmp **in** *COMPONENT*:

        p.*is-on-component-ID-in-key* = cmp.*component-ID-key* **and**

        exists ct **in** *COMP-TYPE*:

            x.*the-comp-type--comp-code* = ct.*comp-code-key* **and**

            p.*pin-number-in-key* ≤ ct.*no-of-pins*

Solution for Problem 3-10 on page 148

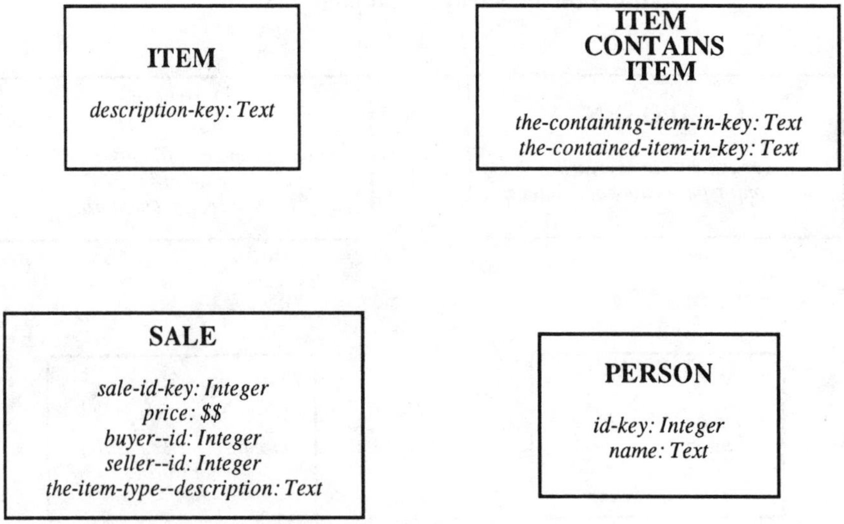

Figure 13-23. A relational schema of sale transactions.

Some of the Integrity Constraints Generated During Schema Conversion

(**for every** x **in** *SALE*:

    exists y **in** *PERSON*:   x.*seller--id* = y.*id-key*) **and**

(**for every** x **in** *SALE*:

    exists y **in** *ITEM*:   x.*the-item-type--description* = y.*description-key*)

Solution for Problem 3-11 on page 148

SYMPTOM'S INSTANCE	SYMPTOM'S POSSIBILITY
symptom's-instance-id-key: Integer *to,from: Date* *magnitude: Number* *the-patient-had--person-id: Integer* *the-symptom-appeared--name: String*	*symptom's-possibility-id-key: Integer* *probability: 0-100%* *magnitude: Number* *the-disease-may-have--factor-id: Integer* *the-symptom-may-indicate--name: String*

FACTOR	DRUG	DISEASE
factor-id-key: Integer *comment: Text*	*factor-id-key: Integer* *name: String*	*factor-id-key: Integer* *name: String*

PERSON	PHYSICIAN	PATIENT
person-id-key: Integer *address,name: String*	*person-id-key: Integer*	*person-id-key: Integer* *born: Date*

DRUG INTERACTION	SYMPTOM
factor-id-key: Integer	*name-key: String* *magnitude-unit: String*

SICKNESS
sickness-id-key: Integer *to,from: Date* *the-patient-had--person-id: Integer* *the-disease-occurred--factor-id: Integer*

Figure 13-24. A relational schema for a medical application. Part I: tables representing the categories.

**DRUG
PARTICIPATES
DRUG
INTERACTION**

the-drug--factor-id-in-key: Integer
the-drug-interaction--factor-id-in-key: Integer

**FACTOR
MAY-CURE
DISEASE**

the-factor--factor-id-in-key: Integer
the-disease--factor-id-in-key: Integer

**FACTOR
MAY-AGGRAVATE
DISEASE**

the-factor--factor-id-in-key: Integer
the-disease--factor-id-in-key: Integer

**FACTOR
MAY-CAUSE
DISEASE**

the-factor--factor-id-in-key: Integer
the-disease--factor-id-in-key: Integer

**PHYSICIAN
DIAGNOSED
SICKNESS**

the-physician--person-id-in-key: Integer
the-sickness-id-in-key: Integer

```
┌─────────────────────────────────────────┐
│              PERSON                      │
│             REPORTED                     │
│            SYMPTOM'S                     │
│             INSTANCE                     │
│                                          │
│       the-person-id-in-key: Integer      │
│   the-symptom's-instance-id-in-key: Integer │
└─────────────────────────────────────────┘
```

```
┌─────────────────────────────────────────┐
│             PHYSICIAN                    │
│             CONFIRMED                    │
│            SYMPTOM'S                     │
│             INSTANCE                     │
│                                          │
│  the-physician--person-id-in-key: Integer │
│   the-symptom's-instance-id-in-key: Integer │
└─────────────────────────────────────────┘
```

```
┌─────────────────────────────────────────┐
│               DRUG                       │
│           WAS-GIVEN-FOR                  │
│             SICKNESS                     │
│                                          │
│    the-drug--factor-id-in-key: Integer   │
│       the-sickness-id-in-key: Integer    │
└─────────────────────────────────────────┘
```

```
┌─────────────────────────────────────────┐
│             PHYSICIAN                    │
│           SPECIALIZES-IN                 │
│              DISEASE                     │
│                                          │
│  the-physician--person-id-in-key: Integer │
│   the-disease--factor-id-in-key: Integer  │
└─────────────────────────────────────────┘
```

Figure 13-25. A relational schema for a medical application. Part II: tables representing the m:m relationships.

Solution for Problem 3-12 on page 149

BUS

license-no-key: Integer
b-year: 1900..2000
next-maintenance-due: Date
type-name: String

BUS TYPE

type-name-key: String
capacity: 0..200

DRIVER

ss#-key: Integer
#tickets: Integer
license-expires: Date

**DRIVER
CAN-DRIVE
BUS TYPE**

ss#-in-key: Integer
type-name-in-key: String

EMPLOYEE

ss#-key: Integer
address,name: String
phone-no: Integer
wage: $$

**SCHEDULED
TRIP
CAN-USE
BUS TYPE**

scheduled-trip-id-in-key: Integer
type-name-in-key: String

ACTUAL TRIP

actual-trip-id-key: Integer
year: 1900..2000
week#: 1..52
the-driver--ss#: Integer
the-bus--license-no: Integer
instance-of--scheduled-trip-id: Integer

**SCHEDULED
TRIP**

scheduled-trip-id-key: Integer
arrival: Time
day-of-week: 1..7
depart-time: Time
on-line--line-no: Integer

BUS STOP

name-of-stop-key: String

STOPPING

stopping-id-key: Integer
time: Time
scheduled-trip-id: Integer
at--name-of-stop: String

LINE

line-no-key: Integer
source: String
destination: String

Solution for Problem 3-13 on page 149

COLOR

colorname-key: String

AGENT

person-id-key: Integer

EMPLOYEE

person-id-key: Integer
ss#: Integer

CAR

car-id#-key: String
license#: String
deal-price: $$
date-sold: Date
car-spec--specification-id: Integer

CUSTOMER

person-id-key: Integer

PERSON

person-id-key: Integer
last-name: String
address: String
tel-no: String
first-name: String

SUBMODEL

name-key: String
the-model--name: String

SPECIFICATION

specification-id-key: Integer
listed-price: $$
year: 1900..2000
invoice-price: $$
the-submodel--name: String

MODEL

name-key: String
maker--name: String

EQUIP TYPE

description-key: String

COMPANY

name-key: String
address: String

Figure 13-26. A relational schema for a car dealer. Part I: tables representing the categories.

```
┌─────────────────────────────┐   ┌─────────────────────────────┐
│         PURCHASE            │   │           SALE              │
│                            │   │                            │
│   the-car-id#-in-key: String   │   │   the-car-id#-in-key: String   │
│ the-customer--person-id-in-key: Integer │ │ the-agent--person-id-in-key: Integer │
└─────────────────────────────┘   └─────────────────────────────┘
```

```
┌─────────────────────────────┐   ┌─────────────────────────────┐
│        CAR  COLOR           │   │      SPECIFICATION          │
│                            │   │      EXTRA  EQUIP           │
│   the-car-id#-in-key: String   │   │          TYPE               │
│ the-color--colorname-in-key: String │ │                            │
│                            │   │  the-specification--id-in-key: Integer │
│                            │   │ the-equip-type--description-in-key: String │
└─────────────────────────────┘   └─────────────────────────────┘
```

```
┌─────────────────────────────┐
│          MODEL              │
│     MAKER'S-SALESMAN        │
│          PERSON             │
│                            │
│  the-model--name-in-key: String │
│   the-person-id-in-key: Integer │
└─────────────────────────────┘
```

Figure 13-27. A relational schema for a car dealer. Part II: tables representing the m:m relationships.

Some of the Integrity Constraints Generated During Schema Conversion

(**for every** x **in** *CUSTOMER*:

    exists y **in** *PERSON*: x.*person-id-key* = y.*person-id-key*) **and**

(**for every** x **in** *EMPLOYEE*:

    exists y **in** *PERSON*: x.*person-id-key* = y.*person-id-key*) **and**

(**for every** x **in** *AGENT*:

    exists y **in** *PERSON*: x.*person-id-key* = y.*person-id-key*) **and**

(**for every** x **in** *PURCHASE*:

    exists y **in** *CAR*: x.*the-car-id#-in-key* = y.*car-id#-key*)

Solution for Problem 3-14 on page 149

```
┌─────────────────────────────────────────────┐
│                   PERSON                       │
│                                                │
│            person-id-key: Integer              │
│                phone#: Integer                 │
│                  name: String                  │
│ the-mail-address--the-street--street-name: String │
│       the-mail-address--house#: String         │
└─────────────────────────────────────────────┘
```

```
┌──────────────────────────┐
│         CUSTOMER          │
│                           │
│    person-id-key: Integer │
└──────────────────────────┘
```

```
┌──────────────────────────┐
│        DELIVERER          │
│                           │
│    person-id-key: Integer │
└──────────────────────────┘
```

```
┌────────────────────────────────────────────┐
│                SUBSCRIPTION                   │
│                                               │
│         subscription-id-key: Integer          │
│                end-date: Date                 │
│               begin-date: Date                │
│ the-customer-subscription--person-id: Integer │
└────────────────────────────────────────────┘
```

```
┌──────────────────────────────────────────┐
│                 ADDRESS                    │
│                                            │
│  the-street--street-name-in-key: String   │
│           house#-in-key: String            │
│  the-deliverer-serves--person-id: Integer  │
└──────────────────────────────────────────┘
```

```
┌──────────────────────────┐
│          STREET           │
│                           │
│   street-name-key: String │
└──────────────────────────┘
```

Figure 13-28. A relational schema for a newspaper distribution department.

Some of the Integrity Constraints Generated During Schema Conversion

(for every x **in** *DELIVERER*:

    exists y **in** *PERSON*:

        x.*person-id-key* = y.*person-id-key*)

Solution for Problem 3-15 on page 149

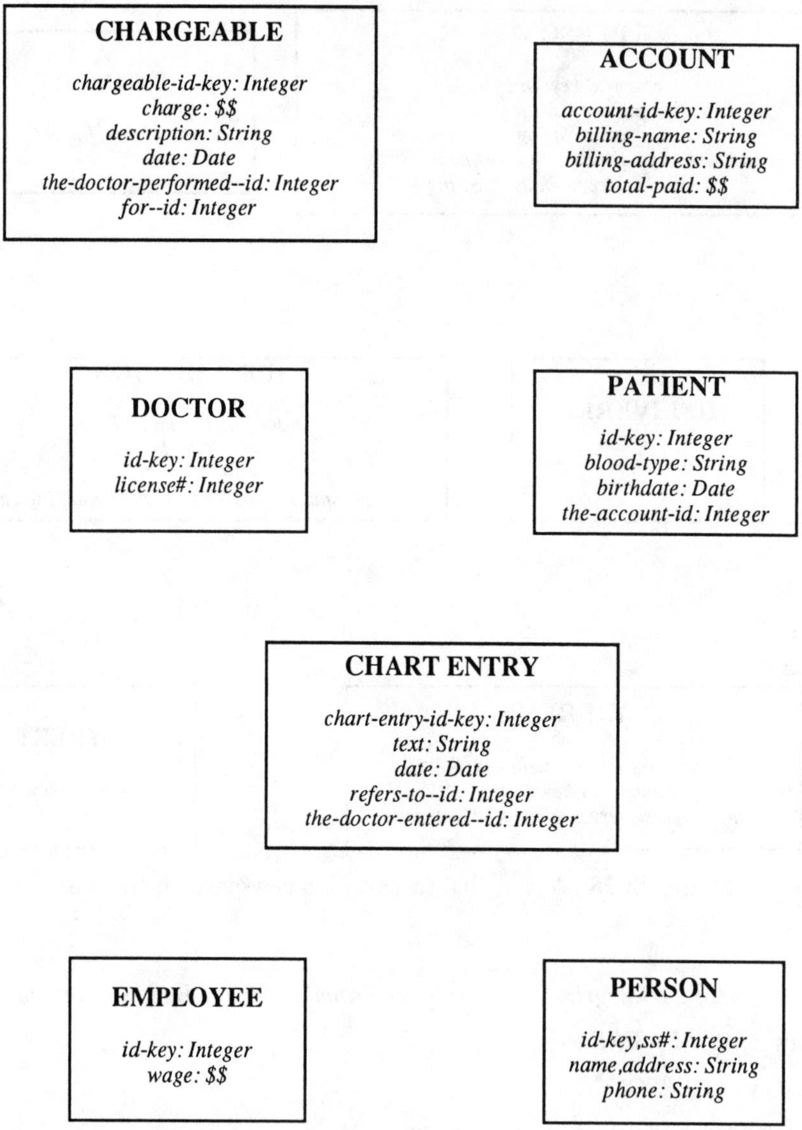

CHARGEABLE

chargeable-id-key: Integer
charge: $$
description: String
date: Date
the-doctor-performed--id: Integer
for--id: Integer

ACCOUNT

account-id-key: Integer
billing-name: String
billing-address: String
total-paid: $$

DOCTOR

id-key: Integer
license#: Integer

PATIENT

id-key: Integer
blood-type: String
birthdate: Date
the-account-id: Integer

CHART ENTRY

chart-entry-id-key: Integer
text: String
date: Date
refers-to--id: Integer
the-doctor-entered--id: Integer

EMPLOYEE

id-key: Integer
wage: $$

PERSON

id-key,ss#: Integer
name,address: String
phone: String

Figure 13-29. A relational schema for a medical clinic.

Solution for Problem 3-16 on page 149

BOOK

ctlg-number-key: Integer
publisher: String
subject,title: String
author: String
year: Integer

VENDOR

vendor-id-key: Integer
name,address: String
phone: Integer

EMPLOYEE

person-id-key: Integer
address,phone: String
name: String
ss#: Integer
wage: $$

ACTUAL BOOK

ctlg-number-in-key: Integer
copy-number-in-key: Integer
is-loaned-book: Boolean
date-due: Date
the-holder--person-id: Integer
the-supplier--vendor-id: Integer

CUSTOMER

person-id-key: Integer
address,phone: String
name: String
card-number: Integer

FINE

fine-id-key: Integer
date: Date
amount: $$
the-customer--person-id: Integer
for-book--ctlg-number: Integer
for-book--copy-number: Integer

Figure 13-30. A relational schema for a library.
Alternative I.

Some of the Integrity Constraints Generated During Schema Conversion

(for every x **in** *ACTUAL-BOOK*: **if not** x *date-due* **null   then** x.*is-loaned-book*) **and**

(for every x **in** *ACTUAL-BOOK*: **if not** x *the-holder--person-id* **null   then** x.*is-loaned-book*) **and**

(for every x **in** *EMPLOYEE*:

for every y **in** *CUSTOMER*:

(* if x and y have equal keys, then all their other attributes are respectively equal or
null *)

if

    (x.*address* ≠ y.*address* **or**

    x.*phone* ≠ y.*phone* **or**

    x.*name* ≠ y.*name*)

then

    x.*person-id-key* ≠ y.*person-id-key*)

and

(for every x **in** *FINE*:

    exists y **in** *CUSTOMER*:

        x.*the-customer--person-id* = y.*person-id-key*)

    and

(for every x **in** *ACTUAL-BOOK*:

    x *the-holder--person-id* **null or**

    exists y **in** *CUSTOMER*:

        x.*the-holder--person-id* = y.*person-id-key*)

    and

(for every x **in** *FINE*:

    exists y **in** *ACTUAL-BOOK*:

        (x.*for-book--ctlg-number* = y.*ctlg-number-in-key* **and**

        x.*for-book--copy-number* = y.*copy-number-in-key*))

    and

(for every x **in** *ACTUAL-BOOK*:

    exists y **in** *VENDOR*:

        x.*the-supplier--vendor-id* = y.*vendor-id-key*)

    and

(for every x **in** *ACTUAL-BOOK*:

    exists y **in** *BOOK*:

        x.*ctlg-number-in-key* = y.*ctlg-number-key*)

```
┌─────────────────────────────┐
│            BOOK             │
│                             │
│   ctlg-number-key: Number   │
│     publisher: String       │
│    subject,title: String    │
│      author: String         │
│       year: Integer         │
└─────────────────────────────┘
```

```
┌─────────────────────────────┐
│           VENDOR            │
│                             │
│   vendor-id-key: Integer    │
│   name,address: String      │
│      phone: Integer         │
└─────────────────────────────┘
```

```
┌─────────────────────────────────┐
│          LOANED BOOK            │
│                                 │
│ copy-of--ctlg-number-in-key: Number │
│  copy-number-in-key: Integer    │
│       date-due: Date            │
│ the-holder--person-id: Integer  │
└─────────────────────────────────┘
```

```
┌─────────────────────────────────┐
│          ACTUAL BOOK            │
│                                 │
│ copy-of--ctlg-number-in-key: Number │
│   copy-number-in-key: Integer   │
│ the-supplier--vendor-id: Integer │
└─────────────────────────────────┘
```

```
┌─────────────────────────────┐
│          CUSTOMER           │
│                             │
│   person-id-key: Integer    │
│    card-number: Integer     │
└─────────────────────────────┘
```

```
┌───────────────────────────────────────┐
│                 FINE                  │
│                                       │
│          fine-id-key: Integer         │
│              date: Date               │
│             amount: $$                │
│   the-customer--person-id: Integer    │
│ for-book--copy-of--ctlg-number: Number │
│    for-book--copy-number: Integer     │
└───────────────────────────────────────┘
```

```
┌─────────────────────────────┐
│           PERSON            │
│                             │
│   person-id-key: Integer    │
│   address,phone: String     │
│       name: String          │
└─────────────────────────────┘
```

```
┌─────────────────────────────┐
│          EMPLOYEE           │
│                             │
│   person-id-key: Integer    │
│       ss#: Integer          │
│       wage: $$              │
└─────────────────────────────┘
```

Figure 13-31. A relational schema for a library. Alternative II.

Some of the Integrity Constraints Generated During Schema Conversion

(**for every** x **in** *EMPLOYEE*:

exists y **in** *PERSON*:

x.*person-id-key* = y.*person-id-key*)

and

(**for** every x in *CUSTOMER*:

    exists y **in** *PERSON*:

        x.*person-id-key* = y.*person-id-key*)

    and

(**for** every x in *LOANED-BOOK*:

    exists y **in** *ACTUAL-BOOK*:

        x.*copy-of--ctlg-number-in-key* = y.*copy-of--ctlg-number-in-key* and

        x.*copy-number-in-key* = y.*copy-number-in-key*)

    and

(**for** every x in *FINE*:

    exists y **in** *CUSTOMER*:

        x.*the-customer--person-id* = y.*person-id-key*)

    and

(**for** every x in *LOANED-BOOK*:

    exists y **in** *CUSTOMER*:

        x.*the-holder--person-id* = y.*person-id-key*)

    and

(**for** every x in *FINE*:

    exists y **in** *ACTUAL-BOOK*:

        x.*for-book--copy-of--ctlg-number* = y.*copy-of--ctlg-number-in-key* and

        x.*for-book--copy-number* = y.*copy-number-in-key*)

    and

(**for** every x in *ACTUAL-BOOK*:

    exists y **in** *VENDOR*:

        x.*the-supplier--vendor-id* = y.*vendor-id-key*)

Solution for Problem 4-1 on page 158

program Jane (STUDIO-DB, STUDIO-FULL-SCHEMA);

var Jane, memories, new-scene, old-acting: ABSTRACT;

var current-new-scene-#: Integer;

begin

for Jane **in** *PERSON*

        where (Jane.*LAST-NAME* = 'Smith' **and** Jane.*FIRST-NAME* = 'Jane' **and** Jane.-*IS-AN-ACTOR*)

    do

    transaction begin

        create new memories **in** *FILM*;

        memories.*FILM-TITLE-key* := 'Memories of Actress Jane Smith';

        current-new-scene-# := 0

        for old-acting **in** *ACTING* **where** (old-acting.*ACTOR-ID-in-key* = Jane.-*PERSON-ID-key*) **do**

        begin

            create new new-scene **in** *SCENE*;

            current-new-scene-# := current-new-scene-# +1;

            new-scene.*SCENE-#-in-key* := current-new-scene-#;

            new-scene.*FILM-TITLE-in-key* := 'Memories of Actress Jane Smith';

            new-scene.*LOCATION-DESCRIPTION* := Jane.*ADDRESS*

            end

        end

    end.

Solution for Problem 4-2 on page 158

for e **in** *EMPLOYEE* **where** (e.*BOSS-ID-in-key*=555) **do**

    for w **in** *WORK* **where** (w.*EMPL-ID-in-key*=e.*ID-key*) **do**

      begin

      present:= false

      for w_1 **in** *WORK* **where**

          (w_1.*PROP-NAME-in-key* = w.*PROP-NAME-in-key* **and**

          w_1.*EMPL-ID-in-key* = 555)

          do present:= true

      if not present **then transaction**

      begin

        create new w_1 **in** *WORK*;

        w_1.*PROJ-NAME-in-key*:= w.*PROJ-NAME-in-key*;

        w_1.*EMPL-ID-in-key*:= 555

      end

end

Solution for Problem 4-3 on page 161

get p.*NAME*
where p **is a** *PERSON* **and**
exists act **in** *ACTING*:
    exists ast **in** *ASSISTANCE*:
        act.*ACTOR-ID-in-key* = p.*PERSON-ID-key* **and**
        ast.*PERSON-ID-in-key* = p.*PERSON-ID-key* **and**
        ast.*FILM-TITLE-in-key* = act.*FILM-TITLE-key*
    or exists dir **in** *DIRECTION*:
        act.*ACTOR-ID-in-key* = p.*PERSON-ID-key* **and**
        dir.*PERSON-ID-in-key* = p.*PERSON-ID-key* **and**
        dir.*FILM-TITLE-in-key* = act.*FILM-TITLE-key*

Solution for Problem 4-4 on page 161

get e.*NAME* **where** e **is an** *EMPLOYEE* **and**
    exists s **in** *EMPLOYEE*: s.*BOSS-ID* = e.*ID-key* **and**
    not exists w **in** *WORK*: w.*EMPL-ID-in-key* = e.*ID-key*

Solution for Problem 4-6 on page 161

for every x **in** *T*:
for every y **in** *T*:
    if (x.*A* =y.*A* **and** x.*B* =y.*B*) **then** x.*D* =y.*D*

Solution for Problem 4-7 on page 169

PERSON

[PERSON-ID = DIRECTOR-ID-in-key]

DIRECTION

☐

PROP-USE [PROP-DESCRIPTION-in-key = 'Helicopter']

[LAST-NAME]

Solution for Problem 4-8 on page 170

(EMPLOYEE[name='Smith']) [EMPLOYEE.id-key=WORK.empl-id-in-key] WORK
[proj-name-in-key > 'Z'] [proj-name-in-key]

Solution for Problem 4-9 on page 191

select *DIRECTION.FILM-TITLE-in-key*

from *DIRECTION, PERSON*

where

    PERSON.LAST-NAME = 'Fellini' **and**

    PERSON.PERSON-ID-key =

    DIRECTION.DIRECTOR-ID-in-key

Solution for Problem 4-10 on page 191

select distinct *PROJ-NAME-in-key*

from *SUBPROJECT*

where TRUE

Solution for Problem 4-11 on page 191

    select *ID-key*

    from *PERSON*

    where *NAME* = 'Johnson'

Solution for Problem 4-12 on page 191

    select *ITEM-TYPE-DESCRIPTION*

    from *SALE, PERSON*

    where *SALE.BUYER-ID* = *PERSON.ID-KEY* **and** *PERSON.NAME* = 'Johnson'

Solution for Problem 4-13 on page 191

select p.*NAME*

from *PERSON* p, *SALE* s, *PERSON* r

where r.*NAME* = 'Rothschild' **and** s.*SELLER-ID* = r.*ID-key* **and** s.*BUYER-ID* = p.*ID-key*

Solution for Problem 4-14 on page 191

select *PRICE*

from *SALE*

where *ITEM-TYPE-DESCRIPTION* = 'nail'

Solution for Problem 4-15 on page 192

select *

from *SALE*

where *PRICE* > 100

Solution for Problem 4-16 on page 192

select *NAME, ID-key*

from *PERSON, SALE* s1, *SALE* s2

where *PERSON.ID-key* = s1.*SELLER-ID* **and** *PERSON.ID-key* = s2.*BUYER-ID* **and** s_1.*PRICE* < s_2.*PRICE* **and** s_1.*THE-ITEM-TYPE--DESCRIPTION* = s_2.*THE-ITEM-TYPE--DESCRIPTION*

Solution for Problem 4-17 on page 192

select count (∗)

from *SALE*

where *PRICE* = 1

Solution for Problem 4-18 on page 192

select avg(*PRICE*)

from *SALE*

where *ITEM-TYPE-DESCRIPTION* = 'nail'

Solution for Problem 4-19 on page 192

select distinct *ITEM-TYPE-DESCRIPTION*

from *SALE, PERSON*

where *PERSON.NAME* = *'Tsai'* **and** *PERSON.ID-key* = *SALE.BUYER-ID*

Solution for Problem 4-20 on page 192

select count(**distinct** *ITEM-TYPE-DESCRIPTION*)

from *SALE, PERSON*

where *PERSON.NAME* = *'Tsai'* **and** *PERSON.ID-key* = *SALE.BUYER-ID*

Solution for Problem 4-21 on page 192

select *ITEM-TYPE-DESCRIPTION*, avg(*PRICE*)

from *SALE*

group by *ITEM-TYPE-DESCRIPTION*

Solution for Problem 4-22 on page 192

select *ITEM-TYPE-DESCRIPTION*

from *SALE*

group by *ITEM-TYPE-DESCRIPTION*

having avg(*PRICE*) > 1000

Solution for Problem 4-23 on page 193

select *ITEM-TYPE-DESCRIPTION*

from *SALE*

where *PRICE* > 10

group by *ITEM-TYPE-DESCRIPTION*
having avg(*PRICE***) >** 1000

Solution for Problem 4-24 on page 193

select *
from *PERSON*
order by *NAME*

Solution for Problem 4-25 on page 193

delete from *PERSON*
where *ID-key = 555*

Solution for Problem 4-26 on page 193

delete from *SALE*
where *ITEM-TYPE-DESCRIPTION = 'car'*

Solution for Problem 4-27 on page 193

insert into *PERSON*

ID-key, NAME

values

333, 'Vasudha'

Solution for Problem 4-28 on page 193

insert into *SALE*
SALE-ID-key, BUYER-ID, SELLER-ID, ITEM-TYPE-DESCRIPTION, PRICE
select *SALE-ID-key+100000, BUYER-ID, SELLER-ID, 'Nail', PRICE*.01*
from *SALE*
where *ITEM-TYPE-DESCRIPTION = 'Hammer'*

Solution for Problem 4-29 on page 193

update *SALE*
   set *PRICE = PRICE * .90*
   where *PRICE > 90*

Solution for Problem 4-30 on page 193

create table *PERSON*

ID-key	Integer
NAME	String

Solution for Problem 4-31 on page 194

create view *BOUGHT*
PERSON, ITEM
as
   select *BUYER-ID, ITEM-TYPE-DESCRIPTION*
   from *SALE*

Solution for Problem 4-32 on page 194

insert into *ITEM*
DESCRIPTION-key
values :item

Solution for Problem 4-33 on page 194

var item: String;
begin
while not eof(Input) **do begin**
   readln (item);
   insert into *ITEM*

DESCRIPTION-key **values** :item

    end

end.

Solution for Problem 4-34 on page 194

select count (✳)

from *SALE*

where PRICE < 10

into :total

Solution for Problem 4-35 on page 194

declare current-sale **cursor for**

    select *ITEM-TYPE-DESCRIPTION*

    from *SALE*

    where *PRICE* = 20;

open current-sale;

repeat

    fetch current-sale **into** :item;

    if sqlstatus ≠ not-found **then** writeln(item)

until sqlstatus = not-found

Solution for Problem 4-36 on page 194

declare current-sale **cursor for**

    select *PRICE*

    from *SALE;*

open current-sale;

repeat

    fetch current-sale **into** :price;

    price := modify(price);

if sqlstatus ≠ not-found **then**

      update *SALE*

           set *PRICE* := price

           where current of current-sale

until sqlstatus = not-found

Solution for Problem 4-37 on page 194

declare current-item **cursor for**

      select *DESCRIPTION-key*

      from *ITEM*

open current-item;

repeat

    fetch current-item **into** :item;

    if sqlstatus ≠ not-found **then begin**

        writeln (' Would you like to delete ', item, '?');

        readln (answer);

        if answer='yes' **then**

            delete from *ITEM*

                where current of current-item

      end

until sqlstatus = not-found

Solution for Problem 4-38 on page 194

select P.*THE_COMP_ID_KEY*, P.*PIN_NUMBER_KEY*, F.*FUNCTION*

from *PIN* P, *COMPONENT* C, *COMP_TYPE* F

where P.*THE_CKT_NAME* = 'DATABIT01' **and** P.*THE_COMP_ID_KEY* = C.*COMP_ID_KEY* **and** C.*THE_COMP_CODE* = F.*COMP_CODE_KEY*

order by *THE_COMP_ID_KEY*, *PIN_NUMBER_KEY*

Solution for Problem 4-39 on page 195

select *THE_CKT_NAME, THE_COMP_ID_KEY, PIN_NUMBER_KEY*
from *PIN*
order by *THE_CKT_NAME, THE_COMP_ID_KEY, PIN_NUMBER_KEY*

Solution for Problem 4-40 on page 195

select *THE_CKT_NAME*
from *PIN*
group by *THE_CKT_NAME*
having count(∗) = 1

Solution for Problem 4-41 on page 195

select distinct CT.*TYPE_NAME*
from *COMP_TYPE* CT, *COMPONENT* C, *PIN* P, *CIRCUIT* CI
where CI.COLOR = 'RED' and CI.*CIRCUIT_NAME_KEY* = P.*THE_CKT_NAME* and
    P.*PIN_NUMBER_KEY* = 14 and P.*THE_COMP_ID_KEY* = C.*COMP_ID_KEY* and
    C.*THE_COMP_CODE* = CT.*COMP_CODE_KEY*

Solution for Problem 4-42 on page 195

select *COMP_ID_KEY, TYPE_NAME, FUNCTION*
from *COMPONENT* X, *COMP_TYPE* Y
where X.*THE_COMP_CODE* = Y.*COMP_CODE_KEY*
order by *COMP_ID_KEY*

Solution for Problem 4-43 on page 195

update *CIRCUIT*
set *CIRCUIT_NAME_KEY* = 'databit02'
where *CIRCUIT_NAME_KEY* = 'databit01';

update *PIN*

set *THE_CKT_NAME* = 'databit02'

where *THE_CKT_NAME* = 'databit01'

Solution for Problem 4-44 on page 196

Find the names of the persons born in 1967.

Calculus for the semantic schema

get person.*LAST-NAME*

   where (person.*BIRTH-YEAR* = 1967)

Calculus for the relational schema

get person.*LAST-NAME*

   where ((person **is a** *STUDENT*) **and** (person.*BIRTH-YEAR* = 1967)) **or**

   ((person **is an** *INSTRUCTOR*) **and** (person.*BIRTH-YEAR* = 1967))

Ext. Pascal for the relational schema

A. If duplicates may be printed

for s **in** *STUDENT* **where** s.*BIRTH-YEAR* = 1967 **do**

   writeln(s.*LAST-NAME*);

for i **in** *INSTRUCTOR* **where** i.*BIRTH-YEAR* = 1967 **do**

   writeln(i.*LAST-NAME*);

B. Without duplicates

for s **in** *STUDENT* **where** s.*BIRTH-YEAR* = 1967 **do**

   writeln(s.*LAST-NAME*);

for i **in** *INSTRUCTOR*

   where i.*BIRTH-YEAR* = 1967

   do begin

      already-printed := **false**;

      for s **in** *STUDENT*

         where i.*ID-key* = s.*ID-key*

         do already-printed := **true**;

      if not already-printed **then writeln**(i.*LAST-NAME*)

end

Algebra for the relational schema

(*STUDENT* [*BIRTH-YEAR* = 1967] [*LAST-NAME*]) ∪

(*INSTRUCTOR* [*BIRTH-YEAR* = 1967] [*LAST-NAME*])

SQL for the relational schema

(* The following pair of queries will print duplicates; it's too hard to eliminate
  duplication *)

select *LAST-NAME* **from** *STUDENT* **where** *BIRTH-YEAR* = 1967;

select *LAST-NAME* **from** *INSTRUCTOR* **where** *BIRTH-YEAR* = 1967

Solution for Problem 4-45 on page 196

For every student, list the instructors of the student's major department.

Calculus for the semantic schema

get student.*FIRST-NAME*, student.*LAST-NAME*, instructor.*FIRST-NAME*, instructor.-
    LAST-NAME

where (instructor   *WORKS-IN*   student.*MAJOR*)

Calculus for the relational schema

get s.*FIRST-NAME*, s.*LAST-NAME*, i.*FIRST-NAME*, i.*LAST-NAME*

where

(s **is a** *STUDENT*) **and** (i **is an** *INSTRUCTOR*) **and**

(**exists** w **in** *WORK*:

i.*ID-key* = w.*INSTRUCTOR-ID-in-key* **and** s.*MAJOR-DEPT-MAIN-NAME*
= w.*DEPT-MAIN-NAME-in-key*)

Ext. Pascal for the relational schema

for s **in** *STUDENT*

where true

do

for w **in** *WORK*

where (w.*DEPT-MAIN-NAME-in-key* = s.*MAJOR-DEPT-MAIN-NAME*)

> **do**
>> **for** i **in** *INSTRUCTOR*
>>> **where** w.*INSTRUCTOR-ID-in-key* = i.*ID-key*
>>>> **do writeln**(s.*FIRST-NAME*, s.*LAST-NAME*, i.*FIRST-NAME*, i.*LAST-NAME*)

Algebra for the relational schema

All-instructors-with-renamed-attributes =
    INSTRUCTOR [*ID-key/INSTR-ID-key*] [*FIRST-NAME/INSTR-FIRST-NAME*] [*LAST-NAME/INSTR-LAST-NAME*]

All-instructors-and-their-departments =
    All-instructors-with-renamed-attributes [*INSTR-ID-key = INSTRUCTOR-ID-in-key*]
    WORK

Pairs-student-instructor =
    STUDENT [*MAJOR-DEPT-MAIN-NAME = DEPT-MAIN-NAME-in-key*] All-instructors-and-their-departments

Result =
    Pairs-student-instructor [*FIRST-NAME, LAST-NAME, INSTR-FIRST-NAME, INSTR-LAST-NAME*]

SQL for the relational schema

select s.*FIRST-NAME*, s.*LAST-NAME*, i.*FIRST-NAME*, i.*LAST-NAME*

from *STUDENT* s, *INSTRUCTOR* i

where <i.*ID-key*, s.*MAJOR-DEPT-MAIN-NAME*> **in**

> **select** *INSTRUCTOR-ID-in-key*, *DEPT-MAIN-NAME-in-key*

> **from** *WORK*

> **where** TRUE

Solution for Problem 4-46 on page 196

What instructors work in every department? (Each relevant instructor shares her time between all the departments.)

Calculus for the semantic schema

get instructor.*LAST-NAME* **where**

> (**for every** d **in** *DEPARTMENT*:

instructor *WORKS-IN* d)

Calculus for the relational schema

get instructor.*LAST-NAME*

    where (instructor **is an** *INSTRUCTOR*) **and**

        for every d **in** *DEPARTMENT*:

            (**exists** w **in** *WORK*:

                instructor.*ID-key* = w.*INSTRUCTOR-ID-in-key* **and** d.*MAIN-NAME-key* = w.*DEPT-MAIN-NAME-in-key*)

Ext. Pascal for the relational schema

for i **in** *INSTRUCTOR*

    where true

    do begin

        instructor-OK := **true**;

        for d **in** *DEPARTMENT*

            where instructor-OK

            do begin

                works-in := **false**;

                for w **in** *WORK*

                    where (w.*INSTRUCTOR-ID-in-key* = i.*ID-key*) **and** (w.*DEPT-MAIN-NAME-in-key* = d.*MAIN-NAME-key*) **and** (**not** works-in)

                do works-in := **true**;

                if not works-in **then** instructor-OK := **false**

            end;

        if instructor-OK **then writeln**(i.*LAST-NAME*)

        end

Algebra for the relational schema

(* {all instructors} − {instructors who do not work in every department} *)

Pairs-inst-dpt-where-the-instructor-does-not-work-in-the-department = (*INSTRUCTOR* [*ID-key*] × *DEPARTMENT*) −
    (*WORK* [*INSTRUCTOR-ID-in-key/ID-key*] [*DEPARTMENT-MAIN-NAME-in-*

key/MAIN-NAME-key])

Instructors-who-do-not-work-every-department =
   Pairs-inst-dpt-where-the-instructor-does-not-work-in-the-department [*INSTRUCTOR-ID-in-key*]

Instructors-who-work-in-every-department =
   INSTRUCTOR [*ID-key*] – Instructors-who-do-not-work-every-department

Names-of-instructors-who-work-in-every-department =
   (Instructors-who-work-in-every-department ☐ *INSTRUCTOR*) [*LAST-NAME*]

SQL for the relational schema

select i.*LAST-NAME*

from *INSTRUCTOR* i

where

       select w.*DEPT-MAIN-NAME-in-key*

       from *WORK* w

       where w.*INSTRUCTOR-ID-in-key* = i.*ID-key*

contains

       select d.*MAIN-NAME-key*

       from *DEPARTMENT* d

       where true

Solution for Problem 4-47 on page 196

What instructors taught every student?

Calculus for the semantic schema

get instructor.*LAST-NAME* **where**

    for every s **in** *STUDENT*:

      exists enrl **in** *COURSE-ENROLLMENT*:

        (enrl *THE-STUDENT* s **and**

        enrl.*THE-OFFERING.THE-INSTRUCTOR* = instructor)

Calculus for the relational schema

get instructor.*LAST-NAME*

where (instructor **is an** *INSTRUCTOR*) **and**

    (**for every** s **in** *STUDENT*:

        exists enrl **in** *COURSE-ENROLLMENT*:

            enrl.*STUDENT-ID-in-key* = s.*ID-key* **and** enrl.*INSTRUCTOR-ID-in-key* = instructor.*ID-key*)

                                  Ext. Pascal for the relational schema

for i **in** *INSTRUCTOR*

    where true

    do begin

        instructor-OK := **true**;

        for s **in** *STUDENT*

            where instructor-OK

            do begin

                has-taught-the-student := **false**;

                for enrl **in** *COURSE-ENROLLMENT*

                    where (enrl.*INSTRUCTOR-ID-in-key* = i.*ID-key*) **and** (enrl.*STUDENT-ID-in-key* = s.*ID-key*) **and** (**not** has-taught-the-student)

                    do has-taught-the-student := **true**;

                if not has-taught-the-student **then** instructor-OK := **false**

            end;

        if instructor-OK **then writeln**(i.*LAST-NAME*)

    end

                                Algebra for the relational schema

All-pairs-instructor-teaching-student =
    COURSE-ENROLLMENT [*INSTRUCTOR-ID-in-key, STUDENT-ID-in-key*]

All-pairs-instructor-student =
    (*INSTRUCTOR* [*ID-key*][*ID-key/INSTRUCTOR-ID-in*-key]) × (*STUDENT* [*ID-key*]
    [*ID-key/STUDENT-ID-in-key*])

All-pairs-instructor-not-teaching-student =
    All-pairs-instructor-student − All-pairs-instructor-teaching-student

The-instructors-not-teaching-all-students =
  All-pairs-instructor-not-teaching-student [*INSTRUCTOR-ID-in-key*]

The-instructors-teaching-all-students =
  INSTRUCTOR [*ID-key*] – The-instructors-not-teaching-all-students

The-names-of-the-instructors-teaching-all-students =
  (The-instructors-teaching-all-students □ *INSTRUCTOR*) [*LAST-NAME*]

                                                    SQL for the relational schema

select i.*LAST-NAME*

from *INSTRUCTOR* i

where

> **select** enrl.*STUDENT-ID-in-key*
>
> **from** COURSE-ENROLLMENT enrl
>
> **where** enrl.*INSTRUCTOR-ID-in-key* = i.*ID-key*

contains

> **select** s.*ID-key*
>
> **from** *STUDENT* s
>
> **where true**

Solution for Problem 4-48 on page 196

Who took Prof. Smith's courses?

                                                    Calculus for the semantic schema

get student.*LAST-NAME* **where**

> **exists** enrl **in** *COURSE-ENROLLMENT*:
>
> > (enrl.*THE-STUDENT*=student **and** enrl.*THE-OFFERING. THE-INSTRUCTOR.*
> > *LAST-NAME*='Smith')

                                                    Calculus for the relational schema

get s.*LAST-NAME*

> **where** s **is a** *STUDENT* **and**
>
> > **exists** enrl **in** *COURSE-ENROLLMENT*:
> >
> > > enrl.*STUDENT-ID-in-key* = s.*ID-key* **and**

(exists i **in** *INSTRUCTOR*:

enrl.*INSTRUCTOR-ID-in-key* = i.*ID-key* **and** i.*LAST-NAME* = 'Smith')

Ext. Pascal for the relational schema

(* This program is allowed to print a student's name twice *)

for i **in** *INSTRUCTOR*

    where i.*LAST-NAME* = 'Smith'

    do begin

        for enrl **in** *COURSE-ENROLLMENT*

            where enrl.*INSTRUCTOR-ID-in-key* = i.*ID-key*

            do begin

                for s **in** *STUDENT*

                    where enrl.*STUDENT-ID-in-key* = s.*ID-key*

                    do writeln(s.*LAST-NAME*)

                end

        end

Algebra for the relational schema

The-enrollments-of-instructor-Smith =
    INSTRUCTOR [*LAST-NAME* = 'Smith'] [*ID-key*] [*ID-key/INSTRUCTOR-ID-in-key*]
    □ *COURSE-ENROLLMENT*

The-enrollments-and-students-of-instructor-Smith =
    The-enrollments-of-instructor-Smith [*STUDENT-ID-in-key* = *ID-key*] *STUDENT*

The-students-of-instructor-Smith =
    The-enrollments-and-students-of-instructor-Smith [*LAST-NAME*]

SQL for the relational schema

select s.*LAST-NAME*

from *STUDENT* s

where s.*ID-key* **in**

    select enrl.*STUDENT-ID-in-key*

    from *COURSE-ENROLLMENT* enrl

    where enrl.*INSTRUCTOR-ID-in-key* **in**

        select i.*ID-key*

        from *INSTRUCTOR* i

        where i.*LAST-NAME* = 'Smith'

Solution for Problem 4-49 on page 196

Display 'TRUE' if every student took at least one course.

Calculus for the semantic schema

get

    (for every s **in** *STUDENT*:

        exists enrl **in** *COURSE-ENROLLMENT*:

            s=enrl.*THE-STUDENT*)

Calculus for the relational schema

get

    (for every s **in** *STUDENT*:

        exists enrl **in** *COURSE-ENROLLMENT*:

            s.*ID-key* = enrl.*STUDENT-ID-in-key*)

Ext. Pascal for the relational schema

```
OK := true;
for s in STUDENT
    where OK
    do begin
        student-OK := false;
        for enrl in COURSE-ENROLLMENT
            where not student-OK
            do if enrl.STUDENT-ID-in-key = s.ID-key then student-OK := true;
        if not student-OK then OK := false
    end;
if OK then writeln('TRUE')
```

SQL for the relational schema

select distinct 'TRUE' (* This constant is printed if the **where** condition is satisfied. Otherwise, nothing is printed. *)

from *DEPARTMENT* (* The table *DEPARTMENT* is irrelevant, but we have to specify a table. We are "retrieving" a constant. *)

where

         select *STUDENT-ID-in-key*

         from *COURSE-ENROLLMENT*

         where true

contains

         select *ID-key*

         from *STUDENT*

         where true

Solution for Problem 4-50 on page 197

Print a table with two columns, which associates students to their teachers. Only last names are printed.

Calculus for the semantic schema

get Teacher: instructor.*LAST-NAME*, Student-taught: student.*LAST-NAME* **where**

     exists enrl **in** *COURSE-ENROLLMENT*:

         enrl.*THE-STUDENT* = student **and**

         enrl.*THE-OFFER. THE-INSTRUCTOR* = instructor

Calculus for the relational schema

get Teacher: i.*LAST-NAME*, Student-taught: s.*LAST-NAME*

     where (s **is a** *STUDENT*) **and** (i **is an** *INSTRUCTOR*) **and**

         (**exists** enrl **in** *COURSE-ENROLLMENT*:

            enrl.*STUDENT-ID-in-key* = s.*ID-key* **and** enrl.*INSTRUCTOR-ID-in-key* = i.*ID-key*)

Ext. Pascal for the relational schema

(* It is a rather inefficient program, but other possibilities are either very hard to program or produce redundant output *)

writeln('Teacher', 'Student-taught');

for i **in** *INSTRUCTOR*

    where true

    do

        for s **in** *STUDENT*

            where true

            do begin

                (* find whether i taught s *)

                taught := **false**;

                for enrl **in** *COURSE-ENROLLMENT*

                    where (enrl.*INSTRUCTOR-ID-in-key* = i.*ID-key* **and**
                        enrl.*STUDENT-ID-in-key* = s.*ID-key*)

                    do taught := **true**;

                if taught **then writeln**(i.*LAST-NAME*, s.*LAST-NAME*)

                end

Algebra for the relational schema

(*INSTRUCTOR* [*ID-key, LAST-NAME*] [*ID-key*/*INSTRUCTOR-ID-in-key*])

□

COURSE-ENROLLMENT

□

(*STUDENT* [*ID-key*/*STUDENT-ID-in-key*] [*LAST-NAME*/*ST-LAST-NAME*])

[*LAST-NAME, ST-LAST-NAME*]

SQL for the relational schema

select i.*LAST-NAME*, s.*LAST-NAME*

from *INSTRUCTOR* i, *STUDENT* s

where <i.*ID-key*, s.*ID-key*> **in**

    select enrl.*INSTRUCTOR-ID-in-key*, enrl.*STUDENT-ID-in-key*,

    from *COURSE-ENROLLMENT* enrl

    where true

Solution for Problem 4-51 on page 197

Find the average birth year of the students.

Calculus for the relational schema

get (average s.*BIRTH-YEAR* **where** s **is a** *STUDENT*)

Ext. Pascal for the relational schema

number := 0;

sum-of-birthyear := 0;

for s **in** *STUDENT*

    where true

    do begin

        number := number + 1;

        sum-of-birthyear := sum-of-birthyear + s.*BIRTH-YEAR*

        end;

writeln(sum-of-birthyear/number)

SQL for the relational schema

select avg (*BIRTH-YEAR*)

from *STUDENT*

where true

Solution for Problem 4-52 on page 197

Find the number of pairs (*INSTRUCTOR, DEPARTMENT*) where the instructor works in the department.

Calculus for the relational schema

get (count w

    where w **is a** *WORK*)

Ext. Pascal for the relational schema

pair-count := 0;

for w **in** *WORK*

where true

    do pair-count := pair-count + 1;

writeln(pair-count)

SQL for the relational schema

select count (*)

from *WORK*

where true

Solution for Problem 4-53 on page 197

Find the average of grades of student Jane Howard.

Calculus for the relational schema

get average enrl.*FINAL-GRADE*

    where (enrl **is a** *COURSE-ENROLLMENT*) **and**

        (**exists** s **in** *STUDENT*:

            s.*LAST-NAME* = 'Howard' **and** s.*FIRST-NAME* = 'Jane' **and**

            s.*ID-key* = enrl.*STUDENT-ID-in-key*)

Ext. Pascal for the relational schema

for s **in** *STUDENT*

    where (s.*LAST-NAME* = 'Howard') **and** (s.*FIRST-NAME* = 'Jane')

    do begin

        sum-grade := 0;

        number-grade := 0;

        for enrl **in** *COURSE-ENROLLMENT*

            where s.*ID-key* = enrl.*STUDENT-ID-in-key*

            do begin

                sum-grade := sum-grade + enrl.*FINAL-GRADE*;

                number-grade := number-grade + 1

            end;

        writeln(sum-grade/number-grade)

end

SQL for the relational schema

select avg (enrl.*FINAL-GRADE*)

from *COURSE-ENROLLMENT* enrl

where

    exists

        (**select ***

        from *STUDENT* s

        where

            s.*LAST-NAME* = 'Howards' **and** s.*FIRST-NAME* = 'Jane' **and**

            s.*ID-key* = enrl.*STUDENT-ID-in-key*)

Solution for Problem 4-54 on page 197

Print the average of all grades given by Prof. Brown.

Calculus for the relational schema

get (**average** enrl.*FINAL-GRADE*

    where (enrl **is a** *COURSE-ENROLLMENT*) **and**

        (**exists** i **in** *INSTRUCTOR*:

            i.*LAST-NAME* = 'Brown' **and**

            i.*ID-key* = enrl.*INSTRUCTOR-ID-in-key*))

Ext. Pascal for the relational schema

for i **in** *INSTRUCTOR*

    where i.*LAST-NAME* = 'Brown'

    do begin

        sum-grade := 0;

        number-grade := 0;

        for enrl **in** *COURSE-ENROLLMENT*

            where i.*ID-key* = enrl.*INSTRUCTOR-ID-in-key*

            do begin

sum-grade := sum-grade + enrl.*FINAL-GRADE*;

number-grade := number-grade + 1

end;

writeln(sum-grade/number-grade)

end

SQL for the relational schema

select avg (enrl.*FINAL-GRADE*)

from *COURSE-ENROLLMENT* enrl

where exists

(**select** *

from *INSTRUCTOR* i

where i.*LAST-NAME* = 'Brown' **and**

i.*ID-key* = enrl.*INSTRUCTOR-ID-in-key*)

Solution for Problem 4-55 on page 197

How many students are there in the university?

Calculus for the relational schema

get (**count** s

where s **is a** *STUDENT*)

Ext. Pascal for the relational schema

total := 0;

for s **in** *STUDENT*

where true

do total := total + 1;

writeln(total)

SQL for the relational schema

select count (*)

from *STUDENT*

where true

Solution for Problem 4-56 on page 197

What students have their average grade above 90?

Calculus for the relational schema

get s.*FIRST-NAME*, s.*LAST-NAME*

    where s **is a** *STUDENT* **and** $90 \leq$

        (**average** enrl.*FINAL-GRADE*

            where enrl **is a** *COURSE-ENROLLMENT* **and** s.*ID-key* = enrl.*STUDENT-ID-in-key*)

Ext. Pascal for the relational schema

for s **in** *STUDENT*

    where true

    do begin

        total := 0;

        count := 0;

        for enrl **in** *COURSE-ENROLLMENT*

            where s.*ID-key* = enrl.*STUDENT-ID-in-key*

            do begin

                total := total + enrl.*FINAL-GRADE*;

                count := count + 1

                end;

        if (90 <= total/count) **then writeln**(s.*FIRST-NAME*, s.*LAST-NAME*)

    end

SQL for the relational schema

select s.*FIRST-NAME*, s.*LAST-NAME*

from *STUDENT* s

where 90 <=

    (**select avg** enrl.*FINAL-GRADE*

    from *COURSE-ENROLLMENT* enrl

where s.*ID-key* = enrl.*STUDENT-ID-in-key*)

Solution for Problem 4-57 on page 197

What are the last names of all the students?

Calculus for the relational schema

get s.*LAST-NAME*
　　where s **is a** *STUDENT*

Ext. Pascal for the relational schema

for s **in** *STUDENT*
　　where true
　　do writeln(s.*LAST-NAME*)

Algebra for the relational schema

(* distinct *LAST-NAME*s *)
STUDENT [*LAST-NAME*]

SQL for the relational schema

select *LAST-NAME*
from *STUDENT*
where true

Solution for Problem 4-58 on page 197

When was student Russel born?

Calculus for the relational schema

get s.*BIRTH-YEAR*
　　where (s **is a** *STUDENT*) **and** (s.*LAST-NAME* = 'Russel')

Ext. Pascal for the relational schema

for s **in** *STUDENT*
　　where s.*LAST-NAME* = 'Russel'
　　do writeln(s.*BIRTH-YEAR*)

Algebra for the relational schema

($STUDENT$ [$LAST$-$NAME$ = 'Russel']) [$BIRTH$-$YEAR$]

Solution for Problem 4-59 on page 197

What courses has Prof. Graham taught?

Calculus for the relational schema

get enrl.$COURSE$-$NAME$-in-key

    where (enrl **is a** $COURSE$-$ENROLLMENT$) **and**

        (**exists** i **in** $INSTRUCTOR$:

            i.ID-key = enrl.$INSTRUCTOR$-ID-in-key **and** i.$LAST$-$NAME$ = 'Graham')

Ext. Pascal for the relational schema

(* a very inefficient program in order to eliminate duplicates *)

for c **in** $COURSE$

    where true

    do begin

        OK := false;

        for i **in** $INSTRUCTOR$

            where i.$LAST$-$NAME$ = 'Graham'

            do

                for enrl **in** $COURSE$-$ENROLLMENT$

                    where (enrl.$INSTRUCTOR$-ID-in-key = i.ID-key) **and** (c.$NAME$-key = enrl.COURSE-NAME-in-key)

                    do OK := true;

        if OK **then writeln**(c.$NAME$-key)

    end

Algebra for the relational schema

(($INSTRUCTOR$ [$LAST$-$NAME$ = 'Graham']) [ID-key = $INSTRUCTOR$-ID-in-key]
    $COURSE$-$OFFERING$) [$COURSE$-$NAME$-in-key]

Solution for Problem 4-60 on page 198

Print the names of the pairs of students who live together.

Calculus for the relational schema

get s_1.*LAST-NAME*, s_2.*LAST-NAME*

    where (s_1 **is a** *STUDENT*) **and** (s_2 **is a** *STUDENT*) **and** (s_1.*ADDRESS* =
    s_2.*ADDRESS*) **and not**(s_1.*ID-key* = s_2.*ID-key*)

Ext. Pascal for the relational schema

(* Both (s_1, s_2) and (s_2, s_1) are printed *)

for s_1 **in** *STUDENT*

where true

do

    for s_2 **in** *STUDENT*

    where s_1.*ADDRESS* = s_2.*ADDRESS* **and** s_1.*ID-key* <> s_2.*ID-key*

    do writeln(s_1.*LAST-NAME*, s_2.*LAST-NAME*)

Algebra for the relational schema

STUDENT [*ID-key/ID-key1*] [*LAST-NAME/LAST-NAME1*]
(* rename columns to prepare for join with another copy of table STUDENT *)
[*ID-key1*, *ADDRESS*, *LAST-NAME1*]
(* the attribute ADDRESS is for natural join, the others are to produce the results *)
☐
STUDENT
(* natural join: two students are paired if their addresses are equal *)
[*ID-key* ≠ *ID-key1*]
(* remove the trivial pairs of a student with himself *)
[*LAST-NAME1*, *LAST-NAME*]
(* produce the names of the pairs of students *)

Solution for Problem 4-61 on page 198

Print the names and the addresses of all computer science students.

Calculus for the relational schema

get s.*LAST-NAME*, s.*ADDRESS*

where (s **is a** *STUDENT*) **and** (s.*MAJOR-DEPT-MAIN-NAME* = 'Computer Science')

Ext. Pascal for the relational schema

for s **in** *STUDENT*

where s.*MAJOR-DEPT-MAIN-NAME* = 'Computer Science'

do writeln(s.*LAST-NAME*, s.*ADDRESS*)

Algebra for the relational schema

(*STUDENT* [MAJOR-DEPT-MAIN-NAME = 'Computer Science']) [*LAST-NAME*, *ADDRESS*]

Solution for Problem 4-62 on page 198

How many computer science students are there in the database?

Calculus for the relational schema

get (**count** s

where (s **is a** *STUDENT*) **and** (s.*MAJOR-DEPT-MAIN-NAME* = 'Computer Science'))

Ext. Pascal for the relational schema

sum := 0;

for s **in** *STUDENT*

where s.*MAJOR-DEPT-MAIN-NAME* = 'Computer Science'

do sum := sum + 1;

writeln(sum)

Solution for Problem 4-63 on page 198

What is the average grade in the *Databases* course?

Calculus for the relational schema

get (**average** enrl.*FINAL-GRADE*

where (enrl **is a** *COURSE-ENROLLMENT*) **and** (enrl.*COURSE-NAME-in-key* = 'DATABASES'))

Ext. Pascal for the relational schema

```
sum := 0;
grades := 0;
for enrl in COURSE-ENROLLMENT
      where enrl.COURSE-NAME-in-key = 'DATABASES'
      do begin
            sum := sum + 1;
            grades := grades + enrl.FINAL-GRADE
            end;
writeln(grades/sum)
```

Solution for Problem 4-64 on page 198

List the distinct addresses of the students.

Calculus for the relational schema

get n **where** (**exists** s **in** *STUDENT*:   n = s.*ADDRESS*)

Algebra for the relational schema

STUDENT [*ADDRESS*]

Solution for Problem 4-65 on page 198

Find the names of the students who never took a course.

Calculus for the relational schema

```
get s.LAST-NAME
      where (s is a STUDENT) and
            (not exists enrl in COURSE-ENROLLMENT:
                  enrl.STUDENT-ID-in-key = s.ID-key)
```

Ext. Pascal for the relational schema

```
for s in STUDENT do begin
            OK := true;
            for enrl in COURSE-ENROLLMENT
```

```
        where enrl.STUDENT-ID-in-key = s.ID-key
        do OK := false;
    if OK then writeln(s.LAST-NAME)
    end
```

Solution for Problem 6-3 on page 250

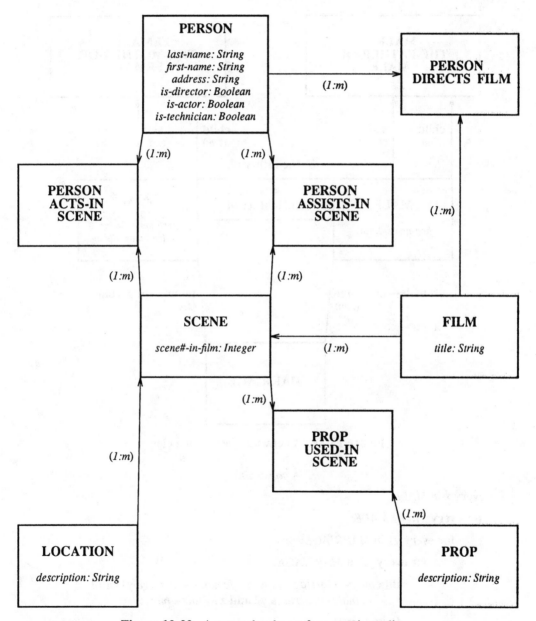

Figure 13-32. A network schema for a movie studio.

Solution for Problem 6-5 on page 250

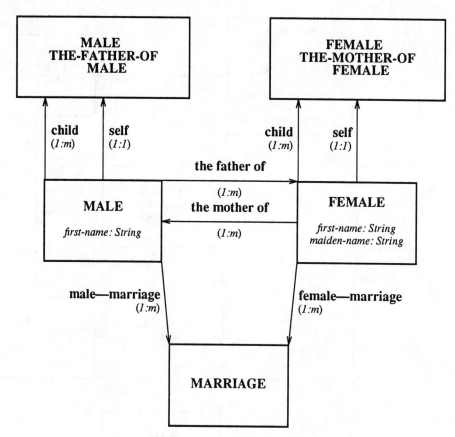

Figure 13-33. A network schema for a clan.

A constraint

(**for every** x **in** *MALE*:

    for every z **in** *FEMALE*:

        for every y1 **in** *MARRIAGE*:

            for every y2 **in** *MARRIAGE*:

                if (x *male—marriage* y1 **and** z *female—marriage* y1) **and**

                    (x *male—marriage* y2 **and** z *female—marriage* y2)

                then y1=y2)

Solution for Problem 6-6 on page 250

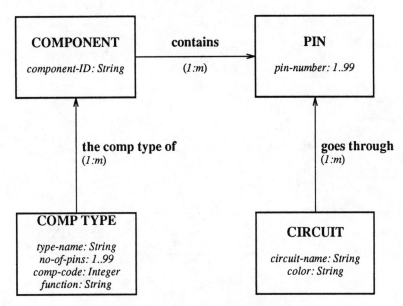

Figure 13-34. A network schema for a circuit board.

Some of the Integrity Constraints Generated During Schema Conversion

(**for every** x1 **in** *COMPONENT*:

    for every x2 **in** *COMPONENT*:

        if x1.*component-ID*=x2.*component-ID* **then** x1=x2)
    and

(**for every** x1 **in** *CIRCUIT*:

    for every x2 **in** *CIRCUIT*:

        if x1.*circuit-name*=x2.*circuit-name* **then** x1=x2)
    and

(**for every** x1 **in** *COMP-TYPE*:

    for every x2 **in** *COMP-TYPE*:

        if x1.*comp-code*=x2.*comp-code* **then** x1=x2)

Solution for Problem 6-7 on page 250

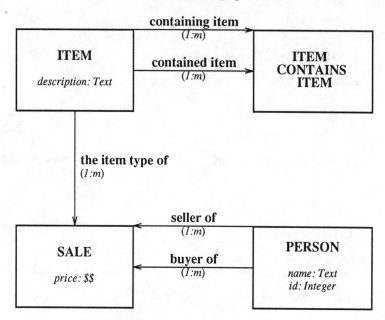

Figure 13-35. A network schema of sale transactions.

Some of the Integrity Constraints Generated During Schema Conversion

(**for every** x1 **in** *PERSON*:

    for every x2 **in** *PERSON*:

        if x1.*id*=x2.*id* **then** x1=x2)

    and

(**for every** x1 **in** *ITEM*:

    for every x2 **in** *ITEM*:

        if x1.*description*=x2.*description* **then** x1=x2)

    and

(**for every** x **in** *ITEM*:

    for every z **in** *ITEM*:

        for every y1 **in** *ITEM--CONTAINS--ITEM*:

            for every y2 **in** *ITEM--CONTAINS--ITEM*:

if (x *containing-item* y1 **and** z *contained-item* y1) **and**
(x *containing-item* y2 **and** z *contained-item* y2)

then y1=y2)

Solution for Problem 6-8 on page 251

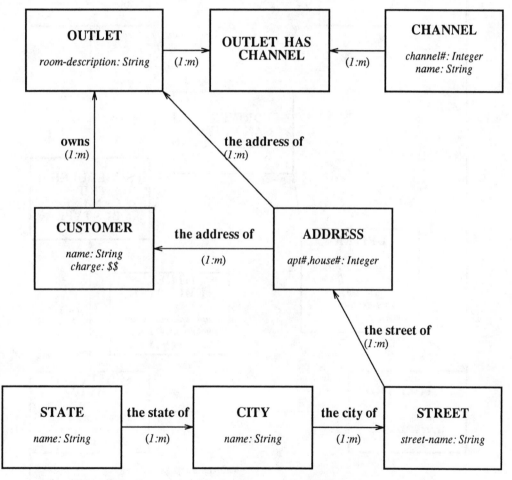

Figure 13-36. A network schema for a cable distribution network.

Solution for Problem 6-9 on page 251

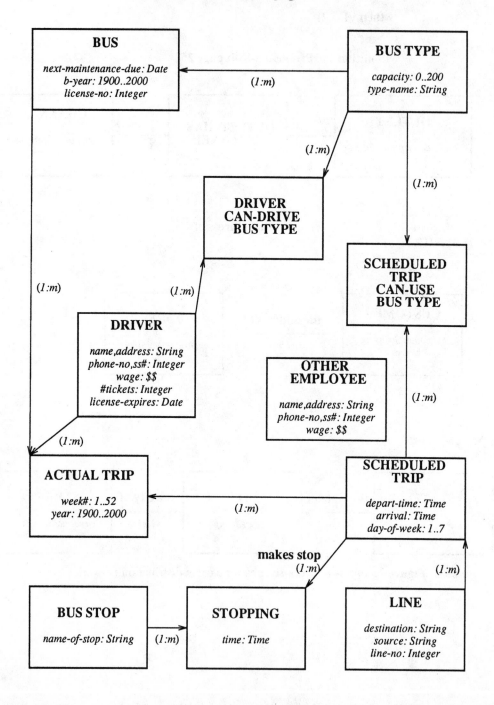

Solution for Problem 6-11 on page 251

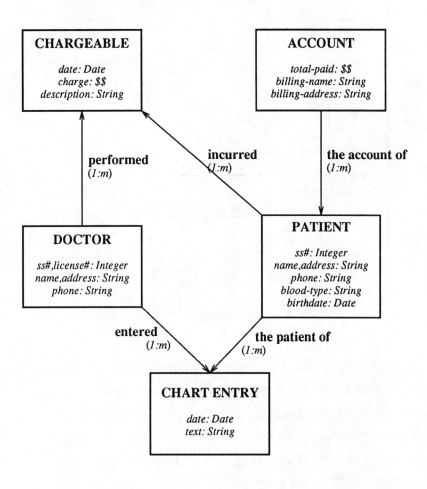

Figure 13-37. A network schema for a medical clinic. Alternative I.

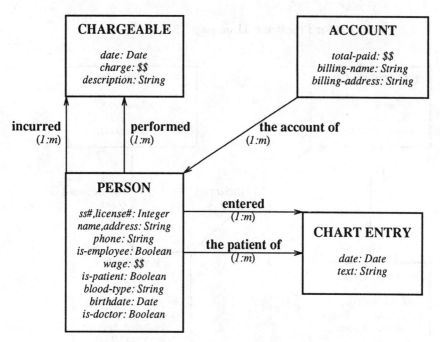

Figure 13-38. A network schema for a medical clinic. Alternative II.

Some of the Integrity Constraints Generated During Schema Conversion

(**for every** x **in** *PERSON*:   **if** x.*is-doctor* **then** x.*is-employee*) **and**

(**for every** x **in** *PERSON*:   **if not** x *wage* **null**   **then** x.*is-employee*) **and**

(**for every** x **in** *PERSON*:   **if not** x *blood-type* **null**   **then** x.*is-patient*) **and**

(**for every** x **in** *PERSON*:   **if not** x *birthdate* **null**   **then** x.*is-patient*) **and**

(**for every** x **in** *PERSON*:   **for every** y **in** *CHART-ENTRY*:
   if x *the-patient-of* y **then** x.*is-patient*) **and**

(**for every** x **in** *PERSON*:

   for every y **in** *ACCOUNT*:

      if y *the-account-of* x **then** x.*is-patient*)
   and

(**for every** x **in** *PERSON*:   **for every** y **in** *CHARGEABLE*:
   if x *incurred* y **then** x.*is-patient*) **and**

(**for every** x **in** *PERSON*:   **if not** x *license#* **null**   **then** x.*is-doctor*) **and**

(**for every** x **in** *PERSON*:   **for every** y **in** *CHART-ENTRY*:
    if x *entered* y **then** x.*is-doctor*) **and**

(**for every** x **in** *PERSON*:   **for every** y **in** *CHARGEABLE*:
    if x *performed* y **then** x.*is-doctor*)

Solution for Problem 6-12 on page 251

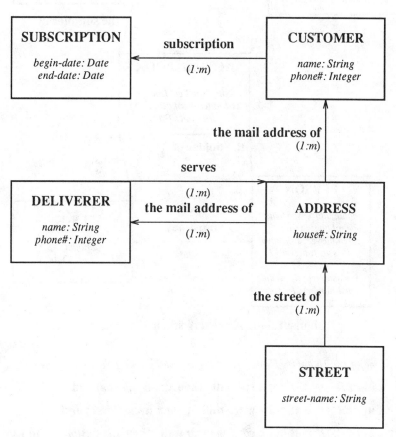

Figure 13-39. A network schema for a newspaper
distribution department.

Solution for Problem 6-13 on page 251

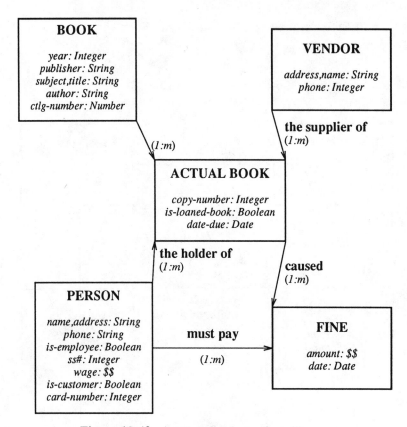

Figure 13-40. A network schema for a library.

Some of the Integrity Constraints Generated During Schema Conversion

(for every x **in** *PERSON*: **if not** x *ss#* **null   then** x.*is-employee*) **and**

(for every x **in** *PERSON*: **if not** x *wage* **null   then** x.*is-employee*) **and**

(for every x **in** *PERSON*: **if not** x *card-number* **null   then** x.*is-customer*) **and**

(for every x **in** *PERSON*: **for every** y **in** *FINE*:
    if x *must-pay* y **then** x.*is-customer*) **and**

(for every x **in** *ACTUAL-BOOK*: **if not** x *date-due* **null   then** x.*is-loaned-book*) **and**

(for every x **in** *PERSON*:

for every y **in** *ACTUAL-BOOK*:

    if x *the-holder-of* y

    then x.*is-customer* **and** y.*is-loaned-book*)

Solution for Problem 6-14 on page 255

get student.*LAST-NAME*

    where student.*BIRTH-YEAR* = 1967

Solution for Problem 6-15 on page 255

get student.*FIRST-NAME*, student.*LAST-NAME*,
instructor.*FIRST-NAME*, instructor.*LAST-NAME*

    where

        exists work **in** *WORK*:

        exists dept **in** *DEPARTMENT*:

            instructor *INSTRUCTOR-WORK* work **and**

            dept *DEPARTMENT-WORK* work **and**

            dept *MAJOR-ST* student

Solution for Problem 6-16 on page 255

get instructor.*LAST-NAME* **where**

    (**for every** dept **in** *DEPARTMENT*:

        exists work **in** *WORK*:

            instructor *INSTRUCTOR-WORK* work **and**

            dept *DEPARTMENT-WORK* work)

Solution for Problem 6-17 on page 255

get instructor.*LAST-NAME* **where**

    (**for every** student **in** *STUDENT*:

        exists enrl **in** *ENROLLMENT*:

        exists offer **in** *OFFERING*:

          student *STUDENT-ENROLLMENT* enrl **and**

          instructor *INSTRUCTOR-OFFERING* offer **and**

          offer *OFFERING-ENROLLMENT* enrl)

Solution for Problem 6-18 on page 256

get

    for every student **in** *STUDENT*:

        exists enrl **in** *ENROLLMENT*:

            exists quarter **in** *QUARTER*:

            exists offer **in** *OFFERING*:

                student *STUDENT-ENROLLMENT* enrl **and**

                quarter.*YEAR* = 1991 **and**

                quarter *QUARTER-OFFERING* offer **and**

                offer *OFFERING-ENROLLMENT* enrl

Solution for Problem 6-19 on page 256

get Teacher: instructor.*LAST-NAME*, Student-taught: student.*LAST-NAME* **where**

    exists enrl **in** *ENROLLMENT*:

    exists offer **in** *OFFERING*:

        instructor *INSTRUCTOR-OFFERING* offer **and**

        offer *OFFERING-ENROLLMENT* enrl **and**

        student *STUDENT-ENROLLMENT* enrl

Solution for Problem 6-20 on page 256

get student.*LAST-NAME*,

        (**average** enrl.*FINAL-GRADE* **where**

            student *STUDENT-ENROLLMENT* enrl)

    where student **is a** *STUDENT* **and**

        exists dept **in** *DEPARTMENT*:

   exists dept-name **in** *DEPARTMENT-NAMING*:

     dept-name.*THE-NAME* = 'Computer Science' **and**

     dept *DEPARTMENT—DEPARTMENT-NAMING* dept-name **and**

     dept *MAJOR-ST* student

    Solution for Problem 6-21 on page 256

get (**average** enrl.*FINAL-GRADE*

  where enrl **is an** *ENROLLMENT* **and**

    exists prof **in** *INSTRUCTOR*:

    exists offer **in** *OFFERING*:

     prof.*LAST-NAME* = 'Smith' **and**

     prof *INSTRUCTOR-OFFERING* offer **and**

     offer *OFFFERING-ENROLLMENT* enrl)

    Solution for Problem 6-22 on page 256

get (**count** student **where** student **is a** *STUDENT*)

    Solution for Problem 6-23 on page 256

get student.*LAST-NAME*

  where student **is a** *STUDENT* **and**

   60 >

     (**average** enrl.*FINAL-GRADE* **where**

     enrl **is an** *ENROLLMENT* **and**

     enrl *THE-STUDENT* student)

    Solution for Problem 6-24 on page 256

for every enrl **in** *ENROLLMENT*:

for every enrl2 **in** *ENROLLMENT*:

if

student *STUDENT-ENROLLMENT* enrl **and**

student *STUDENT-ENROLLMENT* enrl2 **and**

offer *OFFERING-ENROLLMENT* enrl **and**

offer *OFFERING-ENROLLMENT* enrl2 **then** enrl=enrl2

Solution for Problem 6-25 on page 256

userview subcategory: student *COMPUTER-SCIENCE-MAJOR*
where

student **is a** *STUDENT* **and**

exists dept **in** *DEPARTMENT*:

exists dept-name **in** *DEPARTMENT-NAMING*:

dept-name.*THE-NAME* = 'Management' **and**

dept *DEPARTMENT-DEPARTMENT-NAMING* dept-name **and**

dept *MINOR-ST* student

Solution for Problem 6-26 on page 256

connect enrl *FINAL-GRADE* 100
where

enrl **is an** *ENROLLMENT* **and**

exists dept-name **in** *DEPARTMENT-NAMING*:

exists dept **in** *DEPARTMENT*:

exists student **in** *STUDENT*:

exists prof **in** *INSTRUCTOR*:

exists offer **in** *OFFERING*:

exists quarter **in** *QUARTER*:

exists course **in** *COURSE*:

dept-name.*THE-NAME* = 'Computer Science' **and**

dept *DEPARTMENT—DEPARTMENT-NAMING* dept-name **and**

dept *MAJOR-ST* student **and**

        student *STUDENT-ENROLLMENT* enrl **and**

        prof.*LAST-NAME* = 'Smith' **and**

        prof *INSTRUCTOR-OFFERING* offer **and**

        quarter.*YEAR* = 1991 **and**

        quarter.*SEASON* = 'Fall' **and**

        quarter *QUARTER-OFFERING* offer **and**

        course.*NAME* = 'Databases' **and**

        course *COURSE-OFFERING* offer **and**

        offer *OFFERING-ENROLLMENT* enrl

Solution for Problem 6-27 on page 256

disconnect dn   *DEPARTMENT-NAMING*

    where dn.*NAME*='CS' **and**

    dn **is a** *DEPARTMENT-NAMING*

Solution for Problem 6-28 on page 257

update enrl *FINAL-GRADE* 100

    where

        enrl **is an** *ENROLLMENT* **and**

            exists dept-name **in** *DEPARTMENT-NAMING*:

            exists dept **in** *DEPARTMENT*:

            exists student **in** *STUDENT*:

            exists prof **in** *INSTRUCTOR*:

            exists offer **in** *OFFERING*:

            exists course **in** *COURSE*:

                dept-name.*THE-NAME* = 'Computer Science' **and**

                dept *DEPARTMENT—DEPARTMENT-NAMING* dept-name **and**

                dept *MAJOR-ST* student **and**

                student.*LAST-NAME* = 'Johnson' **and**

student.*FIRST-NAME* = 'Jack' **and**

student *STUDENT-ENROLLMENT* enrl **and**

prof.*LAST-NAME* = 'Smith' **and**

prof *INSTRUCTOR-OFFERING* offer **and**

course.*NAME* = 'Databases' **and**

course *COURSE-OFFERING* offer **and**

offer *OFFERING-ENROLLMENT* enrl

Solution for Problem 6-29 on page 257

update enrl   *FINAL-GRADE*   1.1*enrl.*FINAL-GRADE*

   where

       enrl **is an** *ENROLLMENT* **and**

          exists prof **in** *INSTRUCTOR*:

          exists offer **in** *OFFERING*:

          exists course **in** *COURSE*:

              prof.*LAST-NAME* = 'Smith' **and**

              prof *INSTRUCTOR-OFFERING* offer **and**

              course.*NAME* = 'Databases' **and**

              course *COURSE-OFFERING* offer **and**

              offer *OFFERING-ENROLLMENT* enrl

Solution for Problem 7-1 on page 289

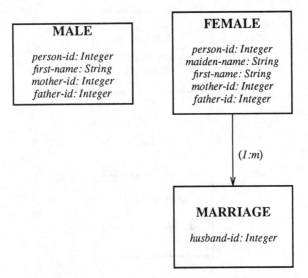

Figure 13-41. A hierarchical schema for a clan.

Some of the Integrity Constraints Generated During Schema Conversion

(**for every** x **in** *FEMALE*:

    x *mother-id* **null or**

    exists y **in** *FEMALE*: x.*mother-id* = y.*person-id*) **and**

(**for every** x **in** *MARRIAGE*:

    exists y **in** *MALE*: y.person-id = x.husband-id) **and**

(**for every** x **in** *FEMALE*:

    for every y1 **in** *MARRIAGE*:

        for every y2 **in** *MARRIAGE*:

            if x *female—marriage* y_1 **and** x *female—marriage* y_2 **and** y_1.husband-id = y_2.husband-id **then** $y_1 = y_2$)

Solution for Problem 7-2 on page 289

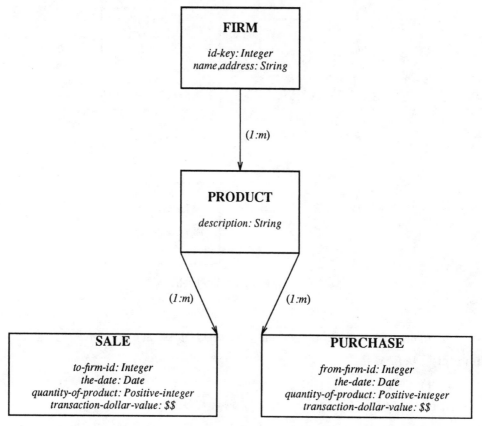

Figure 13-42. A hierarchical schema for a wholesaler. Alternative I.

The relation from the root segment *FIRM* means:

•   *manufactures* — relation from *FIRM* to *PRODUCT*   (*1:m,onto*)

     Some of the Integrity Constraints Generated During Schema Conversion

(**for every** x **in** *SALE*:

    exists y **in** *FIRM*:   x.*to-firm-id* = y.*id-key*) **and**

(**for every** x **in** *PURCHASE*:

    exists y **in** *FIRM*:   x.*from-firm-id* = y.*id-key*)

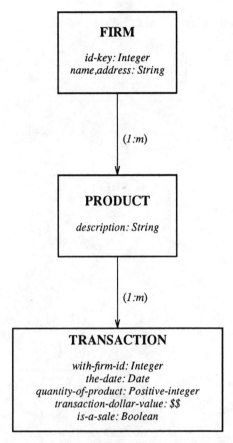

Figure 13-43. A hierarchical schema for a wholesaler. Alternative II.

Some of the Integrity Constraints Generated During Schema Conversion

(for every x **in** *TRANSACTION*:

   exists y **in** *FIRM*:

      x.*with-firm-id* = y.*id-key*)

Solution for Problem 7-3 on page 289

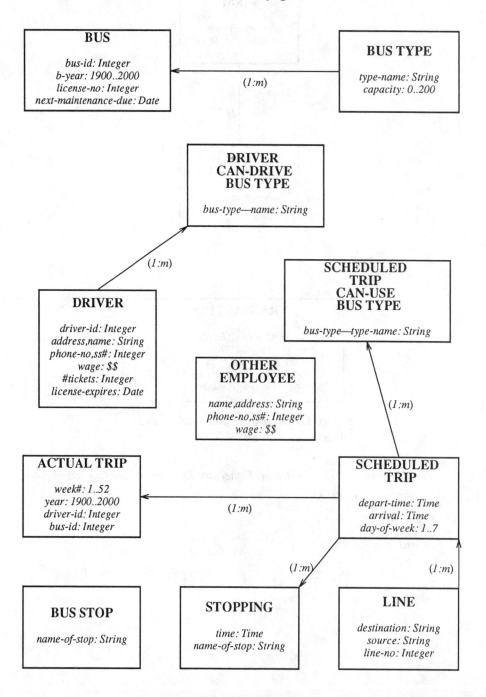

Solution for Problem 7-4 on page 289

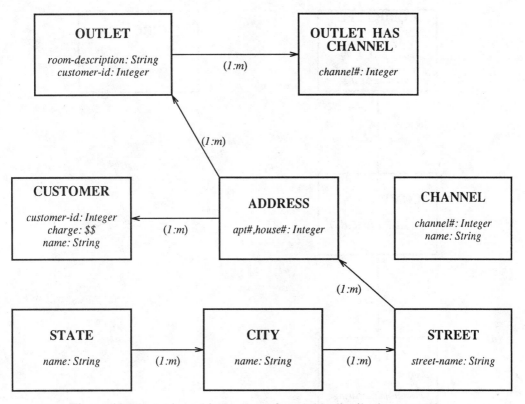

Figure 13-44. A hierarchical schema for a cable distribution network.

Some of the Integrity Constraints Generated During Schema Conversion

(**for every** x **in** *OUTLET--HAS--CHANNEL*:

    exists y **in** *CHANNEL*:   y.channel# = x.channel#) **and**

(**for every** x **in** *OUTLET*:

    for every y1 **in** *OUTLET--HAS--CHANNEL*:

        for every y2 **in** *OUTLET--HAS--CHANNEL*:

            if x --- y_1 **and** x --- y_2 **and** y_1.channel# = y_2.channel# **then** $y_1 = y_2$)

Solution for Problem 7-5 on page 289

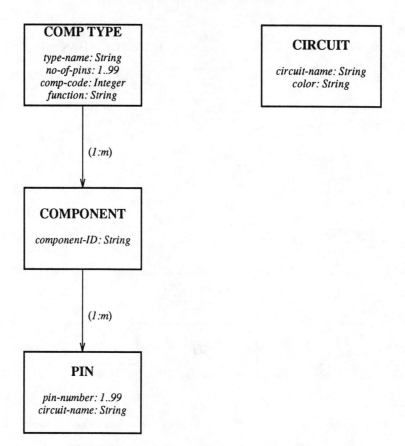

Figure 13-45. A hierarchical schema for a circuit board.

Some of the Integrity Constraints Generated During Schema Conversion

(**for every** x **in** *PIN*:

    x *circuit-name* **null or**

    exists y **in** *CIRCUIT*:   x.*circuit-name* = y.*circuit-name*)

Solution for Problem 7-6 on page 289

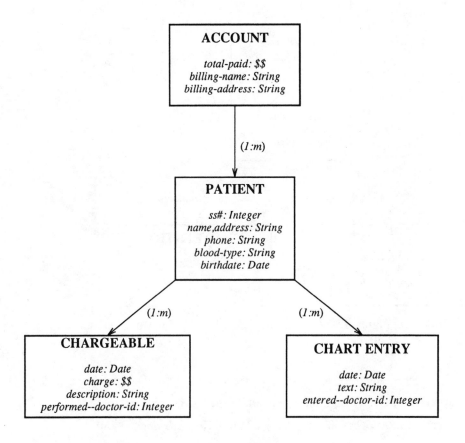

Figure 13-46. A hierarchical schema for a medical clinic. Alternative I.

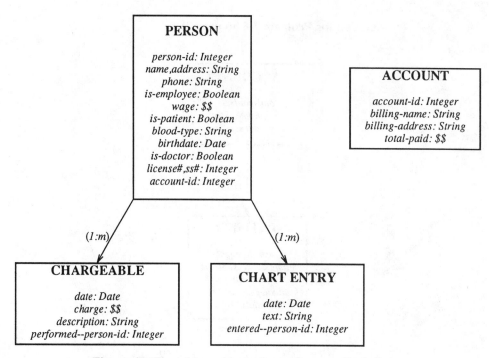

Figure 13-47. A hierarchical schema for a medical clinic. Alternative II.

Some of the Integrity Constraints Generated During Schema Conversion

(**for every** x **in** *PERSON*:   **if not** x *wage* **null   then** x.*is-employee*) **and**

(**for every** x **in** *PERSON*:   **if not** x *license#* **null   then** x.*is-doctor*) **and**

(**for every** x **in** *PERSON*:   **if not** x *blood-type* **null   then** x.*is-patient*) **and**

(**for every** x **in** *PERSON*:   **if not** x *birthdate* **null   then** x.*is-patient*) **and**

(**for every** x **in** *PERSON*:   **if not** x *account-id* **null   then** x.*is-patient*) **and**

(**for every** x **in** *PERSON*:   **for every** y **in** *CHART-ENTRY*:
       if x *the-patient-of* y **then** x.*is-patient*) **and**

(**for every** x **in** *PERSON*:   **for every** y **in** *CHARGEABLE*:
       if x *for-of* y **then** x.*is-patient*) **and**

(**for every** x **in** *CHART-ENTRY*:

   exists y **in** *PERSON*:

y.is-doctor **and**

y.person-id = x.entered--person-id)
and
(**for every** x **in** *CHARGEABLE*:

exists y **in** *PERSON*:

y.is-doctor **and**

y.person-id = x.performed--person-id)

Solution for Problem 7-7 on page 289

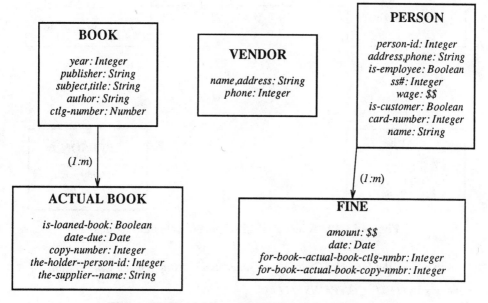

Figure 13-48. A hierarchical schema for a library.

Some of the Integrity Constraints Generated During Schema Conversion

(**for every** x **in** *PERSON*:   **if not** x *ss#* **null**   **then** x.*is-employee*) **and**

(**for every** x **in** *PERSON*:   **if not** x *wage* **null**   **then** x.*is-employee*) **and**

(**for every** x **in** *PERSON*:   **if not** x *card-number* **null**   **then** x.*is-customer*) **and**

(**for every** x **in** *PERSON*:   **for every** y **in** *FINE*:

if x *must-pay* y **then** x.*is-customer*) **and**

(**for every** x **in** *ACTUAL-BOOK*:   **if not** x *date-due* **null**   **then** x.*is-loaned-book*)

(**for every** x **in** *PERSON*:

    for every y **in** *ACTUAL-BOOK*:

        if x.person-id = y.the-holder--person-id

        then x.is-customer **and** y.is-loaned-book)

Solution for Problem 7-8 on page 289

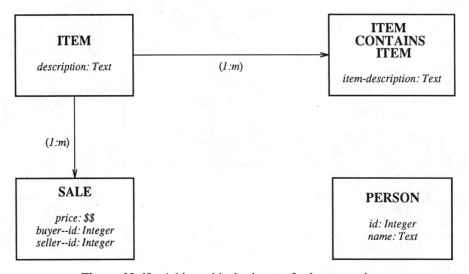

Figure 13-49. A hierarchical schema of sale transactions.

Some of the Integrity Constraints Generated During Schema Conversion

(**for every** x **in** *ITEM--CONTAINS--ITEM*:

    exists y **in** *ITEM*:   y.description = x.item-description) **and**

(**for every** x **in** *ITEM*:

    for every y1 **in** *ITEM--CONTAINS--ITEM*:

        for every y2 **in** *ITEM--CONTAINS--ITEM*:

            if x *contained-item* y_1 **and** x *contained-item* y_2 **and** y_1.item-description = y_2.item-description   **then** $y_1 = y_2$)

Solution for Problem 7-9 on page 289

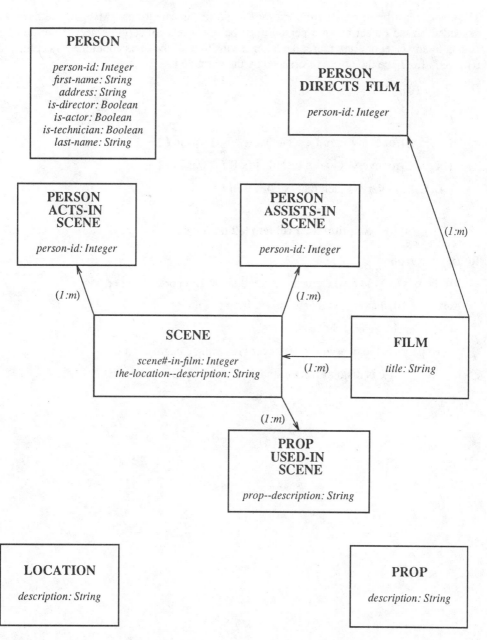

Solution for Problem 9-1 on page 318

The object must be removed from *PERSON* and its subcategories. Also, all the facts that depended on the object being a person must be removed. Since the object is not going to belong to any category any more, the latter means that all the facts about the object must be removed. Let i_0 be the object referenced by the variable i.

$$D := D \cup \{(i_0 \ast), (i_0 \ast \ast), (\ast \ast i_0)\}$$

$$I := I -$$

$\qquad \{(i_0 \ R \ x) \,|\, \text{for every R and x such that } (i_0 \ R \ x) \text{ was in } I\} -$

$\qquad \{(x \ R \ i_0) \,|\, \text{for every R and x such that } (x \ R \ i_0) \text{ was in } I\} -$

$\qquad \{(i_0 \ C) \,|\, \text{for every C such that } (x \ C) \text{ was in } I\}$

Solution for Problem 9-2 on page 320

for $(x \ c)$ **in** I **do**

$\qquad$ **if** there is $(x \ s)$ in I where c and s are disjoint categories **then** error

$\qquad$ **else if** $x < 0$, that is, x is a new object, **then** (* OK *)

$\qquad$ **else** (* check against the database *)

$\qquad\qquad$ perform the query $(x \ ?)$; for every resulting category s do

$\qquad\qquad\qquad$ **if** s is disjoint from c and $(x \ s)$ is not in D **then** error

Solution for Problem 10-1 on page 354

The following Extended Pascal program merges the two departments.

program Merge-Departments(Input,Output,UNIVERSITY-DB,UNIVERSITY-MASTER-
    VIEW);

var dept, mcs-dept, student-object, instructor-object : *ABSTRACT*;

begin

(* Create a new department and assign it a name *)

    create new mcs-dept **in** *DEPARTMENT*;

    insert-name(mcs-dept, 'Dept. of Mathematical and Computing Sciences');

for dept **in** *DEPARTMENT* **where** (dept *NAME* 'CS Dept') **or** (dept *NAME* 'Math Dept')
    do begin

    (* Assign each instructor who works either in the Mathematics or in the Computer
        Science department to the new department *)

        for instructor-object **in** *INSTRUCTOR* **where** instructor-object *WORKS-IN* dept
            do

               update-work-dept(instructor-object, mcs-dept, dept);

    (* Change the major of each student whose major is mathematics or computer
        science *)

        for student-object **in** *STUDENT* **where** student-object.*MAJOR* = dept **do**

               update-major(student-object, mcs-dept);

    (* Change the minor of each student whose minor is mathematics or computer
        science *)

        for student-object **in** *STUDENT* **where** student-object.*MINOR* = dept **do**

               update-minor(student-object, mcs-dept);

    (* Remove the department of Mathematics and that of Computer Science from the list
        of the University departments *)

        decategorize: dept **is no longer a** *DEPARTMENT*;

    end

end.

Solution for Problem 10-2 on page 354

(* show a frame *)

```
procedure show (f: FRAME )
     begin
     show(f.PICTURE)
     end
```

(* show a scene *)

```
procedure show (s: SCENE )
     begin
     show-frames-to-the-end-of-the-scene(s.FIRST-FRAME)
     end
     procedure show-frames-to-the-end-of-the-scene(f: FRAME )
     begin
     show(f);
     wait(time-delay);
     if not (f NEXT-FRAME null) then show(f.NEXT-FRAME)
     end
```

(* show the personal information and movie clips of an actor *)

```
procedure audition (a: ACTOR )
     begin
     show(a.PHOTO);
     wait(10);
     show(a.FIRST-NAME, a.LAST-NAME);
     wait(5);
     for s in SCENE where a ACTS-IN s do begin

     show("Scene", s.SCENE#-IN-FILM, "of", s.IN-FILM.TITLE);
          wait(3)
          show(s)
          end

     end
```

Index

The following is a comprehensive index to the database concepts covered in this book. The labels in brackets indicate the topic or field in which the term is used. Thus, the entry "application [databases], 2" means: the term *application* in the general field of *databases* is explained on page 2, where it appears in bold face, allowing easy locating.

c

ABOUT THE AUTHOR

Naphtali Rishe is an associate professor at the School of
Computer Science, Florida International University, Miami.
He has worked as a database consultant, software engineer,
systems analyst, and manager of application systems
development for the U.S. government, Hewlett-Packard, and
other companies. Dr. Rishe has published over 50 research
papers, primarily on database design, languages, and DBMS
implementation. He has a Ph.D. from Tel Aviv University.

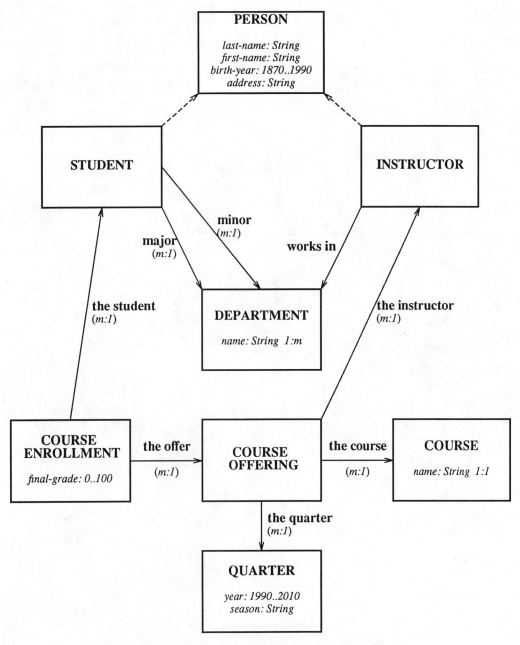

Figure Ref-1. A semantic schema for a university application.

DEPARTMENT NAMING

name-key: String
main-name: String

WORK

instructor-id-in-key: Integer
department-main-name-in-key: String

STUDENT

id-key: Integer
last-name: String
first-name: String
birth-year: 1870..1990
address: String
major-department-main-name: String
minor-department-main-name: String

INSTRUCTOR

id-key: Integer
last-name: String
first-name: String
birth-year: 1870..1990
address: String

DEPARTMENT

main-name-key: String

COURSE ENROLLMENT

instructor-id-in-key: Integer
course-name-in-key: String
year-in-key: 1990..2010
season-in-key: String
student-id-in-key: Integer
final-grade: 0..100

COURSE OFFERING

instructor-id-in-key: Integer
course-name-in-key: String
year-in-key: 1990..2010
season-in-key: String

COURSE

name-key: String

QUARTER

year-in-key: 1990..2010
season-in-key: String

Figure Ref-2. A relational schema for the university application.

SOFTWARE

If you wish to receive information about software supporting the methodology and languages described in this book, would you please fill this form.

☐ Educational use or ☐ Business use or ☐ Other: _____

A relational database design tool

☐ Top-down design of a relational schema (semantic description of the enterprise; automatic conversion into a relational schema; automatic production of documentation and project reports)

The following DBMS-dependent modules are ☐ for ORACLE databases or ☐ for other DBMS: _____

☐ Automatic conversion of a relational schema into a full application (including schema loading, data dictionary, multi-table data entry screens, integrity constraints, etc.)

☐ An automatic report generator

☐ Database restructuring with reloading of data

☐ Other tools

Semantic Binary Database Management System

☐ Physical DBMS

☐ Extended Pascal compiler

☐ Predicate Calculus compiler

☐ SQL to Predicate Calculus converter

Computer(s) used: _____

Operating system(s) used: _____

Other remarks:

Name and address (it is sufficient to attach a business card):

Please send [a copy of] this form to: Dr. Rishe's Software, School of Computer Science, Florida International University, Miami, FL 33183, USA